Dubious Facts

SUNY SERIES IN CHINESE PHILOSOPHY AND CULTURE
―――――――――――――――――
Roger T. Ames, editor

Dubious Facts

The Evidence of Early
Chinese Historiography

Garret P. S. Olberding

Published by
STATE UNIVERSITY OF NEW YORK PRESS
Albany

© 2012 State University of New York
All rights reserved

Printed in the United States of America

No part of this book may be used or reproduced in any manner whatsoever without written permission. No part of this book may be stored in a retrieval system or transmitted in any form or by any means including electronic, electrostatic, magnetic tape, mechanical, photocopying, recording, or otherwise without the prior permission in writing of the publisher.

For information, contact
State University of New York Press
www.sunypress.edu

Production, Diane Ganeles
Marketing, Anne M. Valentine

Library of Congress Cataloging-in-Publication Data

Olberding, Garret P. S.
 Dubious facts : the evidence of early Chinese historiography / Garret P. S. Olberding.
  p. cm. — (SUNY series in Chinese philosophy and culture)
 Includes bibliographical references and index.
 ISBN 978-1-4384-4389-8 (hardcover : alk. paper)
 ISBN 978-1-4384-4390-4 (paperback : alk. paper)
 1. China—History—To 221 B.C.—Historiography. I. Title.
 DS741.25.O43 2012
 931'.01—dc23   2011047447

10 9 8 7 6 5 4 3 2 1

To Joe Gordon

who ever has faith

Contents

Acknowledgments	ix
CHAPTER ONE Introduction	1
CHAPTER TWO The Subversive Power of the Historian	13
CHAPTER THREE Politicized Truth and Doubt	21
CHAPTER FOUR Interactive Constraints at Court	39
CHAPTER FIVE Salient Formal Characteristics of the Addresses	47
CHAPTER SIX Rhetoric in Opposition: Two *Zhanguoce* 戰國策 Addresses	71
CHAPTER SEVEN Commitment to the Facts	99

CHAPTER EIGHT
Moral Norms as Facts: Arguing Before the Emperor   111

CHAPTER NINE
How Did Ministers Err?   137

CHAPTER TEN
A Diversity of Evidence   155

Appendices

    A. Li Zuoche 李左車 and Chen Yu's 陳餘 Exchange   177
    B. Liu Jing's 劉敬 Address to the High Emperor
       (Liu Bang 劉邦)   178
    C. Zhufu Yan's 主父偃 Address to Emperor Wu (Liu Che 劉徹) 179
    D. Chao Cuo's 晁錯 Address to Emperor Wen (Liu Heng 劉恆)   183
    E. Zou Yang's 鄒陽 Address to the King of Wu (Liu Pi 劉濞) 188
    F. Liu An's 劉安 Address to Emperor Wu (Liu Che 劉徹)   191
    G. Zhao Chongguo's 趙充國 Exchange with Emperor Xuan
       (Liu Bingyi 劉病已)   198
    H. Wei Xiang's 魏相 Address to Emperor Xuan
       (Liu Bingyi 劉病已)   207
    I. Hou Ying's 侯應 Address to Emperor Yuan (Liu Shi 劉奭)   209
    J. Yan You's 嚴尤 Address to Wang Mang 王莽   212

Notes   215

Bibliography   267

Index   275

Acknowledgments

Many hands have stirred the pot of this work over the years it has been in the making. The members of my doctoral committee at the University of Chicago—Donald Harper, Edward Shaughnessy, and Danielle Allen—deserve profound thanks for their incisive remarks, without which the flaws of the work would have been that much greater. But there are others, earlier influences, particularly those at the University of Hawaii, especially Roger Ames and Ron Bontekoe, who helped shape and form the ideas and questions I eventually would bring into some focus here. Sincere gratitude also must be offered to a number of scholars who, in spite of their own onerous workloads, gave me rich, detailed comments on various portions, including Rachel Barney, Philip J. Ivanhoe, Rivi Handler-Spitz, Justin Tiwald, David Schaberg, Michael Loewe, and, most especially, Michael Nylan, who astounded me by reading through completely, and offering detailed comments for, the early stages of the manuscript. I further wish to acknowledge the debt I owe the scholars who attended the workshop I hosted at the University of Oklahoma in March of 2009, with the generous support of a grant from the Chiang Ching-Kuo Foundation for International Scholarly Exchange. Whatever the strength of certain added portions of this manuscript is due to their critique. I am also very grateful for the steady assistance of Nancy Ellegate and Diane Ganeles of SUNY Press in bringing this book to print.

Lastly, there are those whose presence in my life and work go beyond any acknowledgment I could ever hope to compose. Amy Olberding, my wife and most supportive critic, has touched every aspect of my work, and, indeed, my life. I could not have written a word of this without her love and support. Adelein, our daughter, daily brings a joy I never thought I could have. But there is also one whose figure has accompanied me in spirit since I began my intellectual and personal journey into this at times very dark and forbidding forest. It is to him that this work is humbly dedicated.

An abbreviated earlier version of Chapter Eight appears in Peter Lorge, ed., *Debating Warfare in Chinese History* (Leiden: Brill, 2012).

CHAPTER ONE

Introduction

THE EVIDENTIARY RELIABILITY OF MEMORIALIZED UTTERANCES AT COURT

Of the many problems surrounding the study of early Chinese historiography, one of the most troubling is the conspicuous tension between the narrator's moralizing commentary and the description of events. The earliest works of historiography—such as the *Book of Documents* (*Shangshu* 尚書), the *Spring and Autumn Annals* (*Chunqiu* 春秋), and the seminal commentary to the *Annals*, *Zuozhuan* 左傳—cannot be securely ascribed to a single author.[1] Perhaps because of this, scholars often attribute the tension to the complex accretion of commentarial intrusions and editorial changes. By contrast, with the Han histories, with the *Records of the Grand Historian* (*Shiji* 史記) and the *History of the Former Han* (*Hanshu* 漢書), there is the presumption of a dominant authorial voice, and with this authorial voice attends the assigning of a unitary authorial intent. Nevertheless, as in the earlier works, there often remain frustrating contradictions between moralizing commentaries and the specifics of the narrative. Consequently, as with the earlier works, the reader is often left to wonder what their authors' intentions actually were. Such concerns touch upon not only the ideological tensions between moral and narrative detail but also numerous tensions proceeding from various internal narrative contradictions, ironic voices, and complicated dramatic devices. Both the narrator and the historical characters at times appear to speak duplicitously, or at least disingenuously. Thus when interpreting the narratives, the discussions, the debates, and the references that comprise the material of the histories, we simply cannot take the speaker, whether narrator or character, at his word. This tendency toward vagueness and subtlety suffuses even some of the most outspokenly critical historical characters, particularly when their words are intended for submission to the court. Early Chinese historiography is a history frustratingly complicated by encoded speech.

Of course, encoded speech was vital to the monarchical circumstance. An anecdote about Emperor Yuan 元帝 misunderstanding the meaning of his own orders illustrates its ubiquity:

> At this time the emperor had just come to the throne and he did not realize that the phrase "instruct the master of guests to summon them and turn them over to the commandant of justice" meant that they were to be taken to prison, and he therefore approved the recommendation. Later, when he asked to have Chou K'an and Liu Keng-sheng called into his presence, he was told, "They are bound and in prison!" Astounded at this information, he said, "I thought they were only to be taken to the commandant of justice for questioning!" and he began to berate [the Chief of Palace Writers] Hung Kung and [his assistant] Shih Hsien. The two knocked their heads on the floor in apology, after which the emperor said, "See to it that they are released from prison and restored to their positions!" 時上初即位, 不省「謁者召致廷尉」為下獄也, 可其奏。後上召堪、更生, 曰繫獄。上大驚曰：「非但廷尉問邪?」以責恭、顯, 皆叩頭謝。上曰：「令出視事。」[2]

To interpret court speech successfully, the reader, like the monarch, is obliged to pay attention to the rhetorical undertones. Naturally, there can be unjustified and excessive interpretation of insinuation (as all too many traditional commentators of the *Annals* have engaged in), but a heightened awareness of insinuation is nevertheless important, particularly in the interpretation of the highly rhetoricized ministerial addresses. That ministers must rely upon muted insinuations is clearly reflected in the numerous recommendations by early Chinese thinkers about the need for extreme delicacy in the choice of language. Regarding the selection of illustrative examples, the *Xunzi* 荀子 proclaims: "Channel [examples] as if with canal ditches, force them as if with the press-frame, and accommodate them to the circumstances so that your audience will get hold of the idea under discussion, yet will not be given offense or be insulted."[3] In the selection of even small illustrative details, the minister must always be aware of the need to avoid risking offense.[4] When directed toward political ends, court address had to be formulated carefully, both to avoid arousing the ire of the monarch and to address certain doubts that the speaker (or writer) presumes the monarch may have.

On a general level, this study is driven by a concern with the factual reliability of memorialized utterance, but its central focus is actually somewhat narrower—to understand the logic of ministerial address through an analysis of its evidentiary conventions. The material for my investigations are the "memorials" concerning the waging of military campaigns (which, for my argumentative purposes, I hereafter label as "hortatory addresses" or "addresses," for short). Save for a few recent studies, most notably by David Schaberg and Yuri Pines, these texts are treated as contributing very little to the study of early Chinese historiography.[5] Yet as reflections of the manner in which intellectual debates were actively drawn into contemporary court discussions, discussions of matters of immediate political and social import, these addresses are invaluable. They show how, or whether, various intellectual trends were imported into court debates, and thus can potentially reveal the extent to which these debates had direct and obvious influence on the handling of court affairs. They also can offer unique insight into the everyday developments of policy: what was discussed, what were the major concerns, and what considerations were possibly effective in shaping the course of state action, of the political realities as they were taking place. Naturally, much like the remonstrances of the Eastern Zhou period, these recorded addresses certainly cannot be treated as exact transcriptions of actually presented addresses but as either loose representations or reductions of such, whether originally presented in writing or orally. The accuracy of the representation of any original content does not fatally impact the quality of their general representation of the content of a particular address or of the rhetorical conventions of their time.

As my concern is with the role of evidence, I focus on those addresses that discuss the pursuit of military campaigns, for unlike numerous other topics of court deliberation, they regularly depend on evidentiary claims with bases in something other than pure hearsay or moralizing precept. While the military addresses do not completely avoid grandiose moralizing, in the main they are very considerate of specifics significant to any military decision, including details relating to geography, population, foreign relations, and previous military enterprises, of both recent and distant vintage. Unfortunately, as will be explained later, there are no obvious linguistic or genre characteristics by which the early histories signify a ministerial memorial or address. The criteria by which I denote recorded statements as "addresses" are two:

1. The statements are relatively thorough and deliberative; that is, they are not merely brief evaluative comments or reports. They present a certain vision of the undertaking, the problems that would be faced in the undertaking, predictions for its outcome, and explicit or implicit recommendations.
2. They are, in the main, not marked as part of a larger extemporaneous conversation.[6] They employ certain rhetorical conventions common to those statements explicitly described as being presented to the monarch.

While these criteria do not delimit the number of statements to a quantity that allows for a comprehensive survey, they still permit the formation of a focused and coherent picture of the typical structures present in military address.

My ultimate concern in these analyses is to articulate how evidence was used to ground political deliberations, to determine in what way it functioned as warranting the knowledge claims and the consequent judgments and recommendations ministers submitted to influence executive action. Through these investigations, we can see how political persuasion, how rhetoricized speech appropriates externally produced information, and what role externally guided "proof" plays in the political process. In its broadest application, the study can assist in evaluating the extent to which ancient Chinese history is the handmaiden of rhetoric, how driven it is by the demands and outcomes of court politics, not just in terms of its narrative course (i.e., what policies the addresses appear to have been instrumental in effecting)[7] but also in terms of its general evidentiary bases. But there are other narrower, yet equally significant implications, for example, the detailing of the limited effect of knowledge claims on political discussions.

Because debate in the Chinese imperial court was most often conducted before a general, nonspecialist audience, the evidentiary bases had to be those that could garner the widest appeal, what Aristotle, still among the greatest analysts of political address, referred to as *endoxa*, or "reputable opinions," that is, opinions that most or all could easily accept. Of course, not all "reputable opinions" were equally believable. Thus what we must explore is the difference between those statements that appear to be treated as beyond doubt—statements I formally label "common sense"—and those that are shown, through questions raised and critical comments made, as being somewhat open to doubt, statements I categorize as "popular knowledge." Through an analysis of what was potentially available to doubt and what was not, we can begin to understand what was considered firm evidentiary ground, or "fact." The analyses I will perform are naturally contingent upon discerning evidentiary distinctions. Given the indirect and sometimes cryptic nature of communication within the monarchic environment, the analyses will require careful attention to nuance and subtlety. If performed satisfactorily, they could help to reshape our current understanding of just exactly what was at issue in the deliberations, what was considered a fundamental truth or essential matter for the discussion of these military matters, and what was considered merely a suggestion or comment worthy of some brief consideration.

Making the above knowledge-related distinctions presumes that the addresses were composed to speak to substantive debates, rather than, for example, merely serving formulaic, ritualized ends. I argue they do, that they attend to the doubts specific to the circumstances in the most cogent manner possible. But a fair evaluation of the addresses' use of evidence, I argue, will demand that we establish a more appropriate notion of the standard of truth by which they were judged. Instead of accuracy, a standard that ideally admits of no competing claims to truth, I suggest that truth in this context must be defined as a standard of relevance to the overarching concerns of the executive, a formulation I will represent as the "truth of the matter." Indeed, this formulation accords with what has been suggested to be a primary function of historical literature in classical Chinese civilization: to provide the reader with an education on the issues and details that would maximally impact his assessment of what action to take, or to reaffirm the conduct that is most becoming to a superior ruler. Such a function is most manifest in the ritual representations of historical occurrences but it is certainly not limited to such.

While my central concern is with the ministerial addresses of the early Han, I inaugurate my investigations with an analysis of two models of late Warring States military address presented by Su Qin 蘇秦 and Zhang Yi 張儀 to the King of Wei 魏, both included in the *Zhanguoce* 戰國策, a miscellaneous collection of persuasions and intrigues.[8] My examination of these serves several ends. First, it offers support for my claim that the use of evidence in political discussions was restricted to neither an individual style nor a discrete time period. If the military addresses of the *Intrigues* are representative at all of the late Warring States, it appears that the evidentiary standards of the early Han shared significant resonance with those of the late Warring States. And if standards of evidence are diachronic, it follows that they were restricted to neither an individual style nor single official norm or guideline. Indeed, upon extensive survey of the early Han addresses, it appears the norms for the use of evidence were not significantly altered across station or person. The standards used by the highest levels of early Han officials were the same, or very similar, to those used by lower-level officials.

Assessments of the factual content of ancient historical literature find ample precedent in studies of classical Greece and Rome. Classicists, most notably Paul Veyne, have struggled to understand how history was understood, in what way history could or should include what we now might consider to be fictional accounts. My work takes inspiration from these studies and hopes to offer a greater insight into how ancient societies framed themselves to themselves. In previous studies of Han intellectual history, scholars have tended to represent the debates and arguments of the time ungenerously as intellectually deficient, as leaning too heavily on propaganda, stock formulae, and specious argument.[9] Debates on military affairs, for instance, are usually characterized as being between two stereotyped positions—the dovish Confucian moralizer and the bellicose realist. This stereotype extends to debates on other issues as well, most notably the debates on economic policy recorded in *The Debates on Salt and Iron* (*Yantielun* 鹽鐵論). My analyses, I contend, will reveal that such stereotypes can often result from an incomplete understanding of what was generally accepted as legitimate evidence, augmenting past research through a careful evaluation of what theoretical notions, canonical references, and historical details were possibly accepted as general knowledge when justifying a course of action, in matters relating not only to military affairs but also perhaps to other topics.

Because the force of the endoxic claims forwarded at court in overcoming prospective knowledge-related, or epistemic, doubts cannot be fully assessed in terms of their accuracy or justifiability, I introduce two approximate evaluative concepts: "epistemic quality" and "epistemic weight." The term "epistemic quality" derives from H. P. Grice's seminal paper, "Logic and Conversation," wherein Grice defines four categories of maxims necessary for meaningful contribution to dialogue. The most important category relates to the "quality," or general truthfulness, of the contribution: "Under the category of *quality* falls a supermaxim—'Try to make your contribution one that is true.'—and two more specific maxims: 1. Do not say what you believe to be false. 2. Do not say that for which you lack adequate evidence."[10] For a conversational contribution to really be any kind of contribution at all, Grice asserts, it must be truthful. If not, the contribution is not an *inferior* kind of information, "it just is not information."[11] The primary question is what can be considered truth and under what auspices it can be considered such. I use the term both in the singular, "epistemic quality," when speaking of the overall quality, or "truth-content," of a statement, and in the plural, "epistemic qualities," when speaking of the factors that impact whether it can be seen as truthful. I describe the epistemic qualities of a statement as relating to its derived inferences, its place in the context of the argument, the appearance of its generally being undoubted by proponents and opponents, its pertinence to the argument, and so forth.

The second evaluative concept, "epistemic weight," bears close kinship with the standard notion of justification. As with the justificatory value of a statement, in its ideal expression epistemic weight depends solely upon the epistemic qualities of a statement or class of statements. The epistemic qualities of a statement are those that give a statement weight. Yet in contrast to the notion of justification, the epistemic weight of a statement is constrained by the rhetorical demands of the politicized court environment; thus it is not solely limited to the objectively testable effect the evidence bears upon the course of the argument. Simply put, the epistemic weight of rhetoricized evidence has both subjective and objective components. Its objective components derive from features that can be tested against a generally accepted standard—distances to be traveled or the comparative size of troops or provisions relative to the enemy's or what is needed for a campaign, for instance. Its subjective components are related to the "popularity" a belief has acquired, without any obvious relation to an objective standard.[12] Both would be of significance in the weighing of the credibility of the evidence presented in the politicized court environment.

In the typical scenario in which an address is presented, the monarch, faced with a problem of state, requests his ministers present their thoughts. Among the discursive challenges faced by ministers, two impinge heavily on the problem of doubt: the monarch neither takes well to challenges to his authority nor does he often have patience for lengthy instruction.[13] The former speaks to the general risk of advising the monarch, for advice naturally involves some measure of critique, and even oblique assertions of error may result in gruesome punishment. The latter, a demand for concision, bears on avoiding raising not only the monarch's ire and personal self-doubts but also his *epistemic* doubts. Such a concern is aptly exemplified in Grice's maxim relating to the "quantity" of information one should provide when one is following what he calls the "cooperative principle": "Make your conversational contribution such as is required, at the stage at which it occurs, by the accepted purpose or direction of the talk exchange in which you are engaged."[14] When cooperating in discursive interaction, according to Grice, one should limit the quantity of information to the amount that is needed and of relevance, no more, no less. Overinformativeness is as detrimental to cooperative conversation as underinformativeness because, in Grice's words, it can raise "side issues" and because the hearer "may be misled as a result of thinking that there is some particular *point* in the provision of the excess of information."[15] This caution about being overinformative bears upon my concern with raising doubts in the hearer, for not only can the hearer be led to think that there is a particular point in the excess information, he can also be led to reassess the issues involved and be more prone to objections, of his own devising or others'. I will show that the avoidance of being overinformative uniformly affects the addresses.

In terms of knowledge-based, or epistemic, claims, the task of the minister is to present, as succinctly as possible, the points he believes to be of objective relevance that would survive possible challenge. Thus if he wishes to be persuasive on grounds other than psychologically manipulative ones, he must offer bases that are held to be reliable evidence. But if a minister wishes to legitimately persuade the monarch, he must have some sense of what doubts he can usually expect. One can discover the doubts ministers attempted to assuage by analyzing either the evidence or arguments using that evidence. The focus for this study is on the former.

As with any historical study, this one is circumscribed by various limitations and ambiguities. When evaluating the quality and weight of evidence, one must ideally take into account the manifold relationships that such evidence possesses in relation to all of the particular factors, both internal and external to the address, that could bear upon evidence being accepted as such. Naturally, my analyses are constrained by several factors: one, the inevitable omission in the histories of pertinent details; two, the incomplete or inaccurate recording of the addresses; three, the conflicting commentarial interpretations upon which we often must depend to make sense of the text; and finally, our still restricted understanding of the numerous cultural and rhetorical norms under which evidence was presented.

Furthermore, because it is increasingly unclear to what extent executive power was held in the hands of the emperors of the early Han—a point I will address later—the question of to whom a court address is actually directed becomes frustratingly problematic. For instance, if an addressor merely ironically dresses up his speech with the clothes of humility, any hypotheses about a stereotypical "monarchic" application, that is, its application to situations in which executive authority more definitely lies in the hands of the monarch, must be treated, at the very least, with some suspicion. Perhaps even more unsettling for this study are the uncertainties associated with the impossibility of knowing, when executive power is not centralized, exactly to what executive party or parties the address may be directed. In other words, if the monarch is not actually in charge, is the very structure and format of an address changed to accommodate this? The answer with regard to the presentation of evidence, it appears, is negative. Within both the addresses of the *Intrigues* and those of the early Han histories, evidence appears to be presented in a similar manner and for similar effect, whether because of the presence of stable conventions, either synchronic or diachronic, or, much less probably, because of the chance imposition of artificial, yet similar, conventions by the authors of these various texts.

Because of these limitations, I do not hope to capture every nuance or implied suggestion that could bear upon how evidence would be received and its impact on the executive's deliberations. My aspiration, in fact, is not to detail all that might be shown to have an impact. Instead, what I will attempt is to show *that* there were evidentiary standards and various ways in which evidence was used to answer doubt. I also aspire to reveal various diachronic constants relating to the use of evidence, to establish that the manner of its use extended across pedagogical and ideological boundaries.

Introduction 9

CHAPTER OUTLINE

My argument proceeds along the following lines: Chapter Two examines the value of facts for the early Chinese historian. Though early Chinese historians had notions of evidence, it is not clear exactly what they were, nor is it clear to what extent they valued "hard" facts. Chapter Three addresses the book's overarching theoretical concern, that is, how to categorize the knowledge claims often used in political address. In broaching this, I seek to establish the evidentiary standards for rhetorical truth. Chapter Four investigates the court dynamics surrounding the composition of the addresses. I argue that the manner of use and selection of evidence was in part determined by the monarchic court environment in which the addresses were composed. In Chapter Five, I describe the stable rhetorical components of the Han addresses. I maintain that each rhetorical constituent expressed a distinct structural effect, the purpose of which was calculated to increase the overall effectiveness of the address, the "proof" of the argument. Chapter Six offers the above-mentioned comparative analysis of the addresses presented by Su Qin and Zhang Yi to the King of Wei, in which I meticulously examine the manner in which each address lays the epistemic groundwork for its position and then highlights epistemically weighty points while simultaneously minimizing doubts raised in the opposing address. In Chapter Seven, I argue that Warring States-styled addresses, characteristic of their time, emphasize nonmoral strategic considerations, considerations that become less dominant in the Han addresses. This shift to an emphasis on moral considerations is significant for the analysis of the Han addresses. I further maintain that their examination reveals no robust commitment to factual accuracy. Chapter Eight employs the exemplar of the early Han debate between Wang Hui 王恢 and Han Anguo 韓安國 who argue for alternate solutions to the frequent raiding of the northern border areas by the nomadic Xiongnu tribes. My aim is to explore in detail the strategic interplay of the two opposing positions, each stage of the arguments offered responsively, in contrast to the formally independent addresses submitted by Su Qin and Zhang Yi. In my analysis, I elaborate on the role of concrete particulars, or "facts," in the Han addresses and the increasing salience of moral considerations. I subsequently offer samples of moral premises that consistently appeared in various Han addresses and evaluate their justificatory role. I argue that their role is not secondary to that of concrete considerations and thus must have been considered of equal, or similar, justificatory value. Because of this, the relative weight of the rhetorical constituents of the addresses appears to have shifted, with an increasing burden supported by moral concerns. The ninth chapter focuses on the key question of how ministers could have erred in their addresses to the executive and possible reasons for the lack of accuracy in the evidence. The tenth, and final, chapter presents the conclusions and possible extensions of the analysis, collating the trends identified in the preceding chapters to derive a comprehensive account of evidence in court addresses. Referring to the representative exemplars taken from the original translations preserved in the appendices, I examine various commonly used premises that frequently appear in the addresses and discuss their relative rhetorical importance and justificatory function. I additionally offer suggestions as to which claims were of greatest consequence for the addresses and what possible doubts they would have answered. In my conclusion, I propose that if we can assess the logic of the evidence informing the imperial decision-making process, we can better evaluate the driving forces, obfuscated by the restrictions on honest and open discourse imposed by the monarchic circumstance, that underlie the actions of historical personalities and the direction and scope of the plot of the historical narrative *in toto*.

Though my specific aim for this study is the detailed analysis of the structure of political address in the Warring States and early Han periods, I expect that the implications of this study will not be limited to an evaluation of Warring States and Han political discourse alone. I would also submit that this study could influence how historians, whether specialists of early China or not, think about the narrative logic of the histories and the sympathies in narrative logic shared with historical fiction composed in later dynasties. I offer suggestions as to how my method of analysis could have applications in the study of other realms of political address. I argue that this study can contribute not only to understanding the various modes of persuasion but also to understanding possible divisions between political persuasion and relatively apolitical "technical" proof, proofs of claims about natural phenomena. Using this mode of analysis, we can begin to see the distinction Han Chinese courtiers drew in their argumentative approaches to the problems of the social realm versus those of the natural realm.

If nothing else, this study should make abundantly clear that the material included in the addresses was not unintelligently arranged, that opposing positions should not be characterized as unthinkingly adhering to standardized, formulaically conceived antipodes. A focused investigation shows that much, or even all, of what is included in the addresses is doing work, that is, is contributing in a significant way to their thrust. Meaningless or redundant ornamentation is kept to a minimum. Of course, ministers often reiterate claims, but their reiterations are rephrased in a way that tries to offer an additional rhetorically effective punch. There is a complexity in the use of tropes in political address that, I maintain, has been overlooked or de-emphasized in previous characterizations of early Chinese political discourse. I argue that the use of tropes, the reiterations of previous assertions, and so forth are meant to positively contribute not simply to the effective manipulation of the emperor but to his *conviction*—an important distinction, because they are actively, positively contributing to his change of perspective, a change of mind, not merely his emotional response to the problems and solutions with which he is presented. This study, I assert, should contribute to the reevaluation of any presumption of crude didacticism in topics relating to political matters.

CHAPTER TWO

The Subversive Power of the Historian

As stated previously, the singular commitment of premodern Chinese historians to moral didacticism, to their use of historical tales or anecdotes to recommend a particular moral (or immoral) vision, deeply influences modern scholars' estimations of early Chinese historiography.[1] In his study of *Zuozhuan*, Henri Maspéro succinctly notes that "where we look for facts, nothing but facts, [a Chinese literatus] looks for a rule of life, a moral."[2] This impression finds ample reinforcement in the various early Chinese commentaries to the *Spring and Autumn Annals* (*Chunqiu* 春秋). For most premodern Chinese commentators, all events in the *Annals* were treatable as signs or symbolic indicators addressing a religio-moral concern. But the casting of moral judgment on historical events was not an innocuous undertaking. By pronouncing judgment on events, the compiler of the *Annals* dangerously arrogated the traditional prerogative of the monarch. This arrogation of the monarch's prerogative was a usurpation of the monarch's religious and political power. In classical China, any final judgment or prognosis about the meaning of events required the monarch's imprimatur. Only the ruler could authorize the interpretation of oracular signs[3] or the final rendering of a historical record.[4] Those "scribes" or "historians" (*shi* 史) who "treasonously" offered unsolicited critique of the monarch's judgments were liable to face execution. An oft cited tale from *Zuozhuan*, Cui Zhu's 崔杼 assassination of Lord Zhuang of Qi 齊莊公, exemplifies the scribe's idealized function. After usurping his lord's position and executing him, Cui Zhu claimed the lordly prerogative of authorizing the portrayal of his act in the historical record. But a series of scribes insisted on characterizing the act in their records as an "assassination" (*shi* 弒), and thus on its iniquity. Though Cui Zhu clearly rejects this depiction, and kills several scribes for recording the event as such, the scribes are relentless in their condemnation. Their perseverance, even in the face of death, underscores their insistence on the mortal importance of their critical role. Though this tale is generally mentioned to reinforce an ideal model of the historian's mandate, it also reveals the implicit norm: scribes, in their writings, were not to contradict the ruler's judgments on affairs.[5]

As the presumed compiler of the *Annals*, Confucius in essence "ruled" through the text, subversively dispensing reward and punishment through his subtly encoded annalistic notations. In the absence of a "true" king, Confucius, appointed by high Heaven, created a "'true' history' as a way of restoring the realm to the rites and the Right."[6] The attribution of the authorship or editing of the *Annals* to Confucius is now given little credibility, but the story achieves a phenomenally transformative effect: by ascribing to the "sage king" Confucius the monarchial prerogative of passing judgment, scholars authorized themselves to do so. Through this, early Chinese literati assert the separation of executive power from juridical power, the power of physical coercion ascribed to the executive from the normative authorization of power ascribed to scholars, the power to distinguish what is from what should be. In claiming the judge's mantle, scribes were asserting an independence that would forever frustrate the executive's desire to maintain hegemony over his own legacy. It is this standard that underlies the enormous prestige conferred by the Chinese literati on those who have the courage to speak truth to power, to "directly remonstrate" (*zhijian* 直諫).[7]

THE VALUE OF FACTS

Yet the immense power of the historian had little to do with the accuracy of his account. Accuracy in recorded accounts was clearly not emphasized. Numerous modern scholars make the point even more strongly. For them, premodern Chinese historians and scholars were simply not interested in facts, or the accuracy of their accounts. Some modern scholars, such as Paul Goldin, offer an even bolder thesis, that not only did the early Chinese intellectuals not trouble themselves with carefully representing the details of events, they went so far as to actively *distort* such details. For Goldin, Chinese scholars were little concerned with representing events accurately in accordance with available evidence; indeed, he is not sure that many of the major intellectual figures of early China, including such "rationalists" as Xunzi, even "*had* a concept of evidence."[8] Referring to Xunzi's representation of the past, Goldin avers that "there is not much support for the inference that [he] would have taken care not to 'distort' history in order to buttress his ethical theories."[9] In sum, according to Goldin, "our notion of illegitimately 'distorting' the past would have been quite alien to the early Chinese intellectual world."¹⁰ It is incorrect to propose that Chinese historians "would have looked down on *deliberate* distortions of history."¹¹

Evidence, for Goldin, "necessarily involves a concept of fact." Early Chinese thinkers and writers, including the historians, "valued statements about the past that embodied what *should have been* true, regardless of whether they embodied what *was* true. History was expected to be edifying, not necessarily factual."¹² Goldin offers intriguing cases (such as the *Shi Qiang Pan* 史牆盤) in which the facts were garbled by those who must have known what had happened and wonders how this could have been possible. His conclusion, like Maspéro's, is that factual truth was often sacrificed on the altar of a grander moral truth.

Scholars such as Goldin and Maspéro rightly acknowledge the general carelessness or disinterest of historians regarding the *precise* representation of the facts, and are certainly correct that many premodern Chinese historical documents are not reliable in every particular they represent. However, it remains unclear that historians were utterly unconcerned with preserving the general outline of the facts at all, or, to put it in Goldin's even bolder formulation, that they would simply not appreciate the importance of accuracy and the problems involved in willfully distorting the facts; in other words, that they would have had no sense about the ideal of avoiding the commission of factual errors. Though early Chinese historians, like Sima Qian 司馬遷 (145 BCE–?), indeed never seemed to have developed a robust commitment to factual accuracy, this is not due, I argue, solely to a personal or cultural blindness to the salience of facts or the importance of accuracy. I hypothesize that it is also due to basic limitations on debate and discourse within a monarchic environment.¹³ It was not that early Chinese historians had no concern with preserving facts but that in the uncertain monarchic climate, all knowledge was politicized and thus ultimately unreliable.¹⁴ Because of this, I suspect, it was difficult for a historian to be certain whether his sources contained a factual error. Furthermore, for a government official much more worrisome than a simple factual error was risking the charge of slander, of an intentional, politically motivated distortion. In the intrinsically politically charged monarchic climate, a climate of intrigue and manipulation, the factual reliability of one's sources was, in all likelihood, extremely difficult to assess, or achieve.

With the *Annals*, given its laconic annalistic form, any judgmental message needed to be decoded. It is thanks to the commentaries later associated with the *Annals*, particularly *Zuozhuan*, that we begin to have a tradition of historical narration in which anecdotal accounts flesh out the events only indicated in the *Annals*. These anecdotes are romanticized, clearly, but they both align with known astronomical events and with other early records (such as the *Bamboo Annals*) to such an extent that we can rely on their general factual accuracy. Their romantic aspects are revealed in the dramatization of particular events, specifically in the included speeches and other narrative embellishments.

Yet as David Schaberg has persuasively argued, the speeches are central to the logic of the historical narrative. Schaberg remarks that, in *Zuozhuan*, "narrative imports the events of the world into the text and in the process naturalizes assumptions of all sorts. But it is speech that makes assumptions patent."[15] In previous interpretations of the agenda of the documents or speeches recorded in the early commentaries and histories, the emphasis has been on norms and symbolic gestures through which the documents or speeches indicated their underlying moral lesson.[16] My concern is to offer a renewed perspective into the basic construction of historical narrative, to ask in what way the facts were acknowledged within cited debates and addresses and, more specifically, in what ways error was perceived. To what extent was error related to the misuse of evidence, of the facts?

THE POLITICS OF FACTUAL ERROR

In a relatively obscure letter to one of his aides, the great Song-dynasty historian Sima Guang 司馬光 (1019–86 CE) offers an uncommon glimpse into his historiographical process, one in which his concerns about the evidentiary quality of his sources come to the fore. In the beginning sections of the letter, he asks specifically for numerous corrections and emendations relating to the "Veritable Records" of the Tang Dynasty. He adjures a collaborator, Fan Mengde 范夢得, to err on the side of generosity when deciding what materials to include. What is truly fascinating for my purposes is the account of the method by which Fan Mengde should decide which materials to include that Sima Guang provides in the middle of the letter. The following is Pulleyblank's translation of the passage:

> If the accounts contain discrepancies as to dating or facts, then I request that you choose one version for which the evidence is clear or which in the nature of the case seems to be closest to the truth and write it into the main text. The result should be placed below in a note and in addition you should set forth there the reasons for accepting one version and rejecting the others. 若彼此年月事迹有相違戾不同者，則請選擇一證據分明情理近於得實者修入正文。餘者注於其下，仍為敘述所以取此捨比之意。
>
> First note the rejected version thus, "Such and such a book says . . . such and such a book says . . . ." Comment, "Such and such a book has such and such evidence", or if there is no such evidence, then

reason it according to the circumstances of the case ... [Then say] "Now we follow such and such a book as established." If there is no means of deciding between true and false, then say, "Now we retain both versions." Veritable Records and Official Histories are not necessarily always to be relied upon, miscellaneous histories and anecdotes are not necessarily without foundation. Make your choice by your own scrutiny. 先注所捨者云某書云云某書云云, 今案某書證驗云云。或無證驗則以事理推之云云, 今從某書為定。若無以考其虛實是非者則云今兩存之。其實錄正史未必皆可據。雜史小說未必皆無憑在。高鑒擇之。[17]

In Pulleyblank's analysis, this passage expresses two main criteria "for distinguishing false from true, (*a*) positive evidence—chiefly in the form of contradictions with known facts such as the calendar, and (*b*) inherent probability." In the examples in the "Examining Discrepancies" (*Kaoyi* 考異) section of Sima Guang's *Comprehensive Mirror for Aid in Government* (*Zizhi tongjian* 資治通鑒), Pulleyblank maintains there was indeed "meticulous care in examining the sources for discrepancies, especially in the matter of dating but also in other particulars." "Apart from this," he continues,

> we find judgements based on what is considered inherently unlikely. Stories are rejected because they are contrary to a man's character or probable motivation, because they are considered to be the slanders of his enemies or the inflated praises of his friends or kinsmen, or simply because they are regarded as frivolous anecdotes.[18]

Both Pulleyblank's translation and assessment of Sima Guang's work reveal his admiration for what he sees as Sima Guang's "scientific" leanings, through his attempts, as Pulleyblank puts it, "to reduce the field of such subjective judgement by rigorous techniques of textual analysis and the confrontation of each question with all available evidence."[19] However, Pulleyblank takes some liberties in his rendition of the text, translating terms such as *shiji* 事迹 loosely as "facts," rather than more literally as "traces of affairs," or *shi* 實 as "truth" rather than as "substance" or "kernel." Naturally, these translations are not entirely incorrect but they evince more Pulleyblank's own concerns than perhaps Sima Guang's or, indeed, one might argue, most Chinese historians, even the "scientific" or "skeptical" ones whose major concern is the accurate representation of affairs.

Sima Guang was, for Pulleyblank and others, a forerunner of the modern historiographical consciousness, concerned with basing the composition of his work in what was reliably accurate, or at the very least, somewhat probable or consistent with other sources. However, this insistence on grounding his assertions in what is probable or reasonable does not distinguish Sima Guang substantially from his Han-era forebears. Sima Qian, as I will discuss, also declares his intention to avoid that which is improbable or without evidential basis. The difference between them, if there is any, is what would qualify as evidence. For Sima Guang, as expressed in the note above, something akin to factual accuracy is a crucial standard by which historical materials are evaluated. In Sima Qian's own brief statements relating to his historiographical process, there are no clear references to concerns with correspondence with the facts. Nor do there appear to be any references in Ban Gu's 班固 (32–92 CE) remarks.

Nevertheless, there is ample evidence that, if there is not a solid commitment to "factual accuracy" in the premodern Chinese histories, there was indeed among many historians a strident commitment to honesty and forthrightness when speaking to power. Indeed, the famous Tang-dynasty historian, Liu Zhiji 劉知幾 (661–721 CE), excoriated ministers (and historians in particular) who were *not* forthright when speaking to power, stressing that a major reason for the errors of the historical record was not just carelessness but outright deliberate twisting or concealment of the "facts"—literally "twisting the brush" (*qu bi* 曲筆). As with Sima Guang, Liu's rubric for measuring error was mostly coherence, either within the text itself, or with other more reliable sources. There was a third rubric—inherent impossibility—but it certainly could not be identified with a standard of correspondence with any fixed factual reality. As Pulleyblank once noted, Liu rejected a story about a murder using poisoned wine because, he asserted, it was inherently impossible—the poison would have dissipated after six days—revealing "inadequate conceptions of what was inherently possible."[20]

The classical Chinese term that seems to most closely correspond with our notion of evidence is *zheng* 證.[21] Its earliest appearance in a historiographical source is in the *Records* but it is not the term that the earliest historians, such as Sima Qian, employed to discuss their own historical choices. Rather, at least in Sima Qian's case, the crucial concern is not of evidence, but of doubt, *yi* 疑. A tally and examination of the appearance of these two Chinese terms in the histories indicates that the problem of doubt suffuses them, while the concern with evidence, perhaps somewhat surprisingly, does not. Indeed, it is the proper addressing of "what is doubtful" that modern historians point to when asserting that Sima Qian is committed to objectivity. Largely on the basis of such remarks, Sima Qian is deemed by some to be a "true" historian, objectively and carefully sifting through and selecting the data, the "facts" that are the grist upon which any historical narrative must depend, if it is to be seen as accurate, as "true."

Sima Qian's peers, both during the Han and thereafter, praised him for his commitment to representing the past directly and without exaggeration. Wang Su 王肅 (195–256 CE) offers a spirited defense of Sima Qian in his response to a question posed by Cao Rui 曹叡 (205–239 CE), then Emperor Ming 明 of the "empire" of Wei 魏. In his query, Cao Rui remarked that Sima Qian secretly harbored misgivings about Emperor Wu of Han and that his *Records* castigated the emperor. Wang Su responds with evaluations taken directly from Ban Gu, Liu Xiang 劉向 (77–6 BCE), and Yang Xiong 楊雄 (53 BCE–18 CE), saying that Sima Qian was a clear and honest writer. They blame Emperor Wu for concealed misgivings (and resentments), not Sima Qian:

> When Sima Qian recorded events ("affairs"), he did not vacuously eulogize, nor did he conceal wrongs. Liu Xiang and Yang Xiong lauded his excellence in giving an account of events, saying that he had the gifts of an exemplary historian. They deemed his *Records* "records of substance." Emperor Wu of Han heard that Sima Qian was compiling the *Records* and that Sima Qian was perusing [and including portions of] the basic annals of his reign, along with those of Emperor Wu's father, Emperor Jing the Filial. Emperor Wu became enraged at this, excising these annals and throwing the excised portions away. Even today there are records on these two annals but not the documents themselves. Later, Sima Qian was involved in the Li Ling affair and thereafter was sent to the Silkworm Chamber to be castrated. This is all due to the concealed misgivings on Emperor Wu's part, not on the Historian Sima Qian's part. 司馬遷記事，不虛美，不隱惡。劉向、揚雄服其善敘事，有良史之才，謂之實錄. 漢武帝聞其述史記，取孝景及己本紀覽之，於是大怒，削而投之。於今此兩紀有錄無書。後遭李陵事，遂下遷蠶室。此為隱切在孝武，而不在於史遷也。²²

The initial sentiment, that Sima Qian's work did not vacuously eulogize the exemplary nor cravenly conceal the flawed, was expressed earlier by Ban Gu in his biography of Sima Qian. For Ban Gu, who asserts that he is echoing Liu Xiang and Yang Xiong, Sima Qian's work is "subtle but not embroidered, substantive but not coarse. His language is direct, the affairs he records essential" 辨而不華, 質而不俚, 其文直, 其事核.²³

Though these appraisals are certainly noteworthy, here I wish to highlight the context in which these appraisals are repeatedly forwarded, that is, the conflict between Emperor Wu and Sima Qian. I would also emphasize their mutual dislike. Both Ban Gu and Wang Su are defending Sima Qian's work against the charge that it was created for partisan reasons, to surreptitiously castigate the Han emperors, specifically Emperor Wu. The claim that the *Records* are "of substance" (*shilu* 實錄), that is, are in some measure accurate, is thus not forwarded as a review but as a defense. Sima Qian's work is "of substance" insofar as it is not partisan.

In keeping with the traditional occupation of the "scribe" or historian to convey the details that would support the moral evaluation of state events (a battle, an accession, an assassination), Sima Qian, in the estimation of his peers, is just doing his job, morally evaluating the actions of the monarch and, using subtle language that speaks to the heart of the matter, passing judgment. Mindful of this standard, the standard of speaking honestly to the powerful executive, we can begin to question just how far evidentiary concerns informed the addresses included in the histories and, more broadly, the composition of the histories themselves. Just what doubts were being answered by the introduction of evidence?

CHAPTER THREE

Politicized Truth and Doubt

In general, for any persuasive argument, political or otherwise, the end is by definition the broaching and overcoming of certain doubts assumed on the part of the audience relating to the issues at hand.[1] To attempt to investigate the qualities of such doubts requires a careful consideration of what could be put into doubt. And before we can do this, we must attempt to answer some general considerations relating to the expression of doubt, particularly as it relates to matters of deliberative politics. A thorough analysis of expressions of doubt, enmeshed in a whole system of epistemic values, demands addressing, among other questions, what we consider worthy of doubt, how and whether we need to answer such doubts, and whether these doubts will lead us to any simulacrum, if we believe it to exist, of the truth. Complicating these matters even further is that, realistically, these doubts, like persuasive speech, do not spring from an unfettered discursive space but from the frequently constrictive, or just directive, atmospheres of culture, society, and language. Doubts are limited not only by the language that expresses them but also by the social dynamics that permits or forbids their communication. A doubt expressed among a group of sympathetic friends is clearly not the same doubt as that expressed to a suspicious or hostile audience, regardless of its import. Similarly, a doubt expressed within a discursively open environment must be evaluated completely differently when expressed within a regime that, even if its demands seem harmless, inevitably inspects and suspects the speaker's motives and underlying meanings, such as a monarchic one. It is clear that the memorial addresses were attempts not merely to manipulate the audience, but to persuade it using legitimate knowledge claims to overcome the various doubts that the audience could have been or would prospectively be entertaining over the course of deliberations about a certain issue. I thus take the addressors as attempting to "reach" another's mind, informed by cultural constants, yes, but also informed by what doubts were typically associated with a particular issue and the various means by which such doubts could be overcome.

The avenue I wish to pursue will treat the speeches of the Warring States and early Han periods, in particular the hortatory addresses (or "memorials") relating to military affairs addressed to the monarch, as politically engendered texts, in which the aims and modes of argumentation were less guided by state-independent norms of (relatively) careful argument than by state-dependent norms of persuasion, by the norms of political rhetoric. In this study, I attend to the architecture, the basic components that structure and organize the arguments, or persuasions. I attempt to determine, from the structural form of the persuasion, what might have been considered open to doubt and what was deemed a relatively fixed axiom. These divisions, by necessity, are imprecise, for we neither have, nor ever can have, an unfailing insight into the processes of another's mind, and specifically what he might doubt, nor can we have an unfailing insight into the cultural codes of a distant temporal and cultural context. Nevertheless, I insist that a thorough and careful reading of the texts does point to, if not conclusively define, certain boundaries.

THE EPISTEMIC FOUNDATIONS OF POLITICAL ADDRESS

The axiomatic foundations necessary for rhetoricized argumentation that are removed from probable or reasonable doubt are what could be called axioms of "common sense." Commonsense propositions are, by definition, transparent, self-evident, their truth perceived as immediate and obvious. They are the propositions to which members of a community would readily assent and, in general, are so pedestrian as to be almost banal. At times, however, especially when touching upon nonconcrete matters—moral or metaphysical—they can involve propositions that may appear odd or dubious to those lying outside the community.[2] But the lack of comprehension, ours or others, should not automatically render them spurious. Though they may not be firmly certain to all, they have the certainty of a life community, thus, for that community, of being certain beyond reasonable doubt. In this way, they are fundamentally acceptable to a wide audience, a crucial constituent in the effectiveness of a rhetorical address.

As rhetoric deals with subjects in a nontechnical, general way for people who are nonspecialists, or simply "untrained thinkers," the addressor must have a sufficient grasp of the topic to know which propositions are available to general understanding and are most useful at effecting persuasion. If any proposition is so common as to be almost incontrovertible, in the words of Aristotle, "there is no need to mention it; the hearer adds it himself."³ Since the aim of the rhetor is to bring about persuasion as efficiently and effectively as possible, he is best served by forwarding as few propositions as required, both to give the necessary attention to those which are problematic as well as not to make conspicuous, and thus open to doubt, those that are not. The rhetor depends on the reputable commonsense propositions, whether or not she believes they are defensible, to support those that require defense. Truth, while useful for the understanding of the problem at hand, does not necessarily serve the end of persuasion; frequently, as is so often apparent, it does not.

As stated above, the parameters of commonsense propositions are somewhat culturally defined. In Aristotle's analysis, that men desire to flourish and thus be "happy" (*eudaimonia*) falls within the bounds of common sense, but to understand exactly what constitutes flourishing requires sympathy with their needs and backgrounds. Aristotle implicitly acknowledges this by both listing what are commonly regarded as that which contributes to flourishing—prosperity, independence, secure enjoyment of maximum pleasure, the "good condition of property and body"—and assenting that such are constituents to common agreement, rather than to any universalized norm: "That happiness is one or more of these things, pretty well everybody agrees."⁴ He furthermore admits that people can differ as to the relative "goodness" and the relative "utility" of "two things which are both useful."⁵ Yet Aristotle does not question, or necessarily even seem critical of, the justifiable warrant of these commonsense propositions. Indeed, it appears that he either draws only on those of which he himself would approve or is confident that the propositions he forwards would be accepted by his learned peers. There is little to suggest that Aristotle believed that the entire realm of "reputable opinions," of *endoxa* itself is to be skeptically dismissed or investigated for any possible culturally embedded assumptions.

We can extract similarly commonsensical propositions from the comparative analysis of addresses. As I will later argue, late Warring States and early Han political addressors implicitly and explicitly forwarded propositions that never appeared to be questioned or doubted. These propositions ranged from simple military and economic assertions to more culturally bound moral or ritual propositions. For instance, in Su Qin 蘇秦 and Zhang Yi's 張儀 addresses presented to the King of Wei 魏, which, I argue, are representative of a late Warring States mind-set, they both leave unchallenged certain basic premises, premises that they could theoretically have opposed, but did not. For instance, both appear to agree, not surprisingly, that geographic, demographic, and economic considerations define one's most basic military strengths and weaknesses. Furthermore, both raise concerns that assume further agreement, such as that there are inherent manipulative possibilities of language, dangerous possibilities that should be guarded against.[6] Neither of these propositions is controversial; indeed, they are so incontestable as to be trivial. But this is exactly the major province of common sense—the incontrovertible. Though the exercise of exhaustively raising to consciousness such trivialities may seem tedious, it nevertheless is essential to a thorough analysis of political address. In the rest of the chapter I will attempt to lay out some of the qualities that distinguish commonsense propositions from other endoxic propositions, as well as to offer an initial defense of the "facticity" of propositions that on first glance may seem fictitious.

COMMON SENSE VERSUS POPULAR KNOWLEDGE

As just mentioned, commonsense propositions, by definition, must allow for universal acceptance within the community in which they are forwarded. Clifford Geertz, in a cultural anthropology study of commonsense propositions about natural causation among the Zande, suggests that there are certain qualities that define commonsense propositions. Though these propositions may seem "mystical," "they are actually employed by the Zande in a way anything but mysterious—as an elaboration and defense of the truth claims of colloquial reason."[7] The reasons given to explain a natural occurrence do not proceed from some overly complex underlying metaphysic but rather are simply a part of the "tissue of common-sense assumptions"[8] that the members of the Zande community share. This tissue cannot, as Geertz notes, be fused together into systematic coherence. As with any culture's commonsense notions, they may share some premises in common, but their relationships are scattered and tenuous.

Geertz enumerates five "somewhat unstandard" qualities that define commonsense propositions, qualities also applicable, in broad measure, to the early Chinese circumstance: naturalness, practicalness, thinness, immethodicalness, and accessibleness. The first, which Geertz considers the most fundamental, is descriptive of their "of-courseness," of their being easily acceptable. Because of this aspect, commonsense propositions are, Geertz asserts, "depicted as inherent in the situation, intrinsic aspects of reality, the way things go."[9] The second, practicalness, emphasizes the levelheadedness, the evenhandedness, the sensible moderation intrinsic to commonsense sagacity, to know what is necessary to know about one's world and not bother too much with the unfamiliar or unusual. The third, thinness, is common sense's limiting aspect: to represent things merely as they uncomplicatedly are, underscoring the mind-set that "the really important facts of life lie scattered openly along its surface, not cunningly secreted in its depths," the "obviousness or the obvious."[10] The signs of the world that anthropologists often take to be symbols of something else are, Geertz insists, taken literally by their informants. The fourth, immethodicalness, embraces the ad hoc, the diversity, and sometimes incoherence, of life experience. The final quality, accessibleness, is "simply the assumption, in fact the insistence, that any person with faculties reasonably intact can grasp common-sense conclusions, and indeed, once they are unequivocally enough stated, will not only grasp but embrace them."[11] Commonsense propositions for Geertz, like the *endoxa* of Aristotle, are "the general property of at least . . . all solid citizens."[12]

Taking a bead from Geertz's list of basic qualities of commonsense propositions, I will define commonsense propositions as those that are relatively uncomplex ("thin"), easily comprehensible ("natural"),[13] and accessible by an average contemporary audience, that is, nontechnical propositions. I forgo on attribution of a "practical" quality, that is, a disregard of things that are uncommon or unusual, for that does not appear to be a limitation common to Han discourse. Expanding upon these traits, common sense, as I define it, is expressible in ordinary, everyday language, though the commonsense propositions underlying an address are usually not explicitly stated. This, however, does not preclude an easy extraction, for even if they are not, as defined, readily accessible, they are repeatedly employed, appearing in many or all of the addresses. These propositions may or may not seem entirely sensible to us. My rule of thumb for deciding that they are believed by their Han addressors to be commonsensical is just their redundant assumption across addresses. The total epistemic weight they will carry and thus the level of doubt they are meant to buttress against will be determined by how and where and how often they are used: whether they are used as only a small part of a long argument train (suggesting a relative lack of epistemic importance) or whether they are clearly necessary for the forwarded proposals to be supportable (one need merely imagine if they were removed), whether they are elaborated upon or stressed (which could show either their importance or, alternatively, the concern that they are not familiar), and so forth. In this study, my aim is not to evaluate each of these aspects pertaining to the epistemic weight of the propositions; such would be more exhaustive than one study could allow. Instead, I will highlight only those features that appear to be central to overarching thrust of the thesis.

In many cases, the endoxic propositions abstractable from the addresses are unexceptional and indubitable—that words can be twisted or abused (especially in a monarchic environment), that one must take advantage of present opportunities or they may slip away—in other words, they are commonsensical, even to us. But in other cases, they are not clearly so immune to query, such as Zhang Yi's assertion that overwhelming military force in general demands subservience[14] or Xiao Wangzhi's

萧望之 (?–47 BCE) moralizing insistence that the army must be used only for righteous ends. In the latter cases, we would be safer to group them under the broader class of popular-knowledge claims.

As Josiah Ober explains, questionable claims of popular knowledge were also regularly treated as evidentiary bases concurrently within the public sphere of democratic Athens. In ancient Greece, Ober contends, "common reports" about the character of a litigant, something everyone "knew," was used to great effect in the law courts. Speechwriters would use this tactic, according to Aristotle, "to secure the agreement of even those who did not know it, because the latter would be ashamed at their ignorance of what was common knowledge."[15] The arguments based on common report were believed by some to be just and democratic, fully worthy of the assent of the community. A contemporary politician, Hyperides, contended that common reports were generally believable because of the overall reliability of the popular consensus. Indeed, as Aristotle perhaps wryly noted, in public debates, claims by "the wise" were acceptable only if they did not go against popular perceptions. In his *Topics*, Glenn Most observes, "The *endoxa* that may be admitted can include the 'things said' by the wise only if these do no conflict with the 'things said' by the many (1.10.104a8–12, 14.105a36–105b1)."[16] In fact, according to Most, Aristotle even seems to view, at least relating to ethical concerns, those philosophical claims that "flagrantly" contradict the *endoxa* as somewhat deficient, for the truth cannot be "radically counterintuitive": "[E]ven if individual 'things said' often go astray, the *endoxa* are likely to hit the truth."[17] I will speak to the place of unsubstantiated common reports, of "rumors" in the classical Chinese context in a later chapter.[18]

The truth of popular-knowledge claims lies not in their own indubitability, but in the truth of a larger narrative, which Plato called *eikos mythos*, a "reasonable" or "probable" myth or story relating to a broader truth. As Woodruff maintains, for the ancient Greeks appeal to that which was *eikos*, or "probable," occurred only when there were no other more reliable means to accessing the verifiable truth. Appeals to *eikos* did not imply, Woodruff explains, "that they have lost interest in the truth." *Eikos* statements do not have claim to total veracity; they lie somewhere between true and false.[19] For Plato, though true stories must be factually true, "accurate reports about matters (human affairs) concerning which factual knowledge is possible,"[20] *mythos* deals with truths about which no accurate facts can reliably be ascertained. Thus *mythos* that has truth to it deals with things about which we do not yet know the accurate truth—in other words, matters that are only "probable." These myths, or stories, are reflective of factual truth and are useful when they contribute to people's greater well-being. But in order to be epistemically valuable, they must be consistent with what we know.[21] In this way, they can be seen not only as "probable" but as "reasonable." A myth is *eikos* not simply because it offers the likeness of a factual representation but because the representation is a *reasonable* one. For the myth to be *eikos*, the likeness it forwards must be "permanent and stable and manifest to reason."[22] The reasoning here is a practical sort, a reasoning that is rarely deductively valid.

Employing "reasonable" narratives or stories to convey a grander truth was a common tactic in early Chinese political address. Indeed, one could state that such stories were the coin of political address, and, as I will argue later, for possibly very good reasons.[23] These stories might not be factually true, but they are, for all intents and purposes, taken as knowledge claims, because of the larger truths they communicate. Many of the historical examples may have to be treated in this way, as "stories" that, while containing perhaps a shred of factual truth, may not be completely reliable or accurate. As is explained in Chapter Seven, four wise men convince Liu Bang not to send his son in his place on campaign based on a "reasonable," but not indubitable, narrative about the reaction of the generals to his son's leadership. Any number of alternative narratives could have been offered, but the narrative objecting to the leadership of Liu Bang's son stuck. It was not its factual accuracy but its "reasonableness" that was persuasive.[24]

Upon these grounds, we can begin to build a case against treating the factual and the semifactual—or even fictional—as epistemologically of necessarily different categories, as having categorically different qualities and weights. We may begin to consider the possibility that the stories told about a former king or a metaphysical process could have been treated as credible and worthy of consideration as descriptions that accord with independently established documentary or archaeological evidence. The glue that holds these together is that of coherence, of the possibility of weaving the features of an address into a comprehensible whole. All that must be utterly avoided is outright contradiction regarding what a particular addressor has previously stated about the object or topic under discussion. The defining criterion of this coherence conception of truth is that the "truth-determinations ensue from inter-propositional comparisons."[25] A coherence theory of truth does not require any foundational definition of truth, only that true statements accord with the comparisons by which any statement in question is granted provisional authorization to being true. Such a theory does not present the constitutive essence of truth; rather, it should be seen in an "essentially regulative role governing the considerations" relating to the classification of propositions as true.[26] Coherence requires both that there is consistency among propositions and that these propositions are rationally connected in some way. Basic to it is the notion of a "datum," which, rather than being a fundamental and undeniable "fact," is "a proposition which, given the circumstances of the case, is a real prospect for truth in terms of the availability of reasons to warrant its truth-candidacy."[27] In accordance with the demand that inter-propositional comparisons operate as the determining factor for truth, no datum can be judged in isolation. Data need not be actual or even probable truths, they need only be "'in the running' as a genuine candidate or a live possibility for truth."[28] Evidence is just the means of adducing truths by which "the claims of a truth-candidate are to be supported."[29] Evidence, of course, is also data, but it is judged to be more secure, for the particular justification for which it is being employed, than the propositions that it is justifying. On this account of the coherence theory, data and evidence are taken from general experience, except in more technical or scientific circumstances. Some data are, however, essentially more reliable than others. Within most of our modern investigative paradigms, dreams, omens, and premonitions, commonly adduced as evidence in the premodern circumstance, while not a priori excludable as potential data, do not usually serve our explanatory or predictive purposes well, and thus are frequently not treated as valid evidence.[30]

OFFERING "FICTIONS" AS EVIDENCE

However, in the premodern circumstance dreams, fantastic or fabricated descriptions of historical or current events, and of metaphysical (or quasi-metaphysical) generalizations, regularly served as evidence of truth-bearing propositions that would be acceptable for justificatory purposes, particularly within the realm of political persuasion. The question that will face us, and that will demand a carefully detailed analysis of the Han addresses, is this: How do we determine what, if any, truth-bearing, or epistemic, weight the various types of assertions and justifications explicitly (or implicitly) employed in the early Han addresses could be given and whether the weight can be assessed categorically or not; that is, whether a particular class can hold a categorically different amount of weight than another? Should, for example, propositions of metaphysics or moral principle be judged more or less epistemically weighty or truth bearing than, for example, semifactual historical anecdotes? Can we classify these separately at all? The question comes down to the problem of what I will term "epistemic quality," of determining the demonstrative qualities distinguishing a proposition that could bear upon how it may be received as evidence and how important an evidentiary function it plays.

Ruth Morse, in her *Truth and Convention in the Middle Ages*, posits that there is a significant gulf between how Western culture pre- and pos-tempiricism sought to define truth. For preempiricist medieval historians, "the 'embellishments' of words bore a complex relationship to the 'truths' they depicted."[31] There was, in short, no clear line between truth-bearing "history" and invented "fiction": "Readers coming to medieval historians for the first time may be perplexed to find patent fictions presented as part of a true account; readers of medieval fictions may wonder why invented stories are offered as 'true'."[32] This style of historical representation (or misrepresentation, as the case may be) finds its roots in the rhetorical education of the classical world, of Greece and Rome. Medieval writers, states Morse, inherited from their Greek and Roman predecessors

> some of the [rhetorical] categories of thought and of composition which underlay, for example, the depiction or dramatization of direct speech which appeared in histories and poems. They inherited the literature which was written in those categories, and which came accompanied by commentaries which emphasized the achievement of great writers in such identifiable terms as metaphoric language, dramatic and persuasive speeches, and moving descriptions of many kinds.[33]

History was for all but those who reported on events occurring within their own lifetimes[34] a verisimilar narrative in which truth was definable as that which served the purposes of the narrator and needed merely to meet the criterion of minimal plausibility—it did not necessarily require full verification. Thus when the fifteenth-century historian John Capgrave writes that the corpse of the twelfth-century English king, Henry I, stank, he is not cynically attempting to slip a "fiction" into his narrative to provide a modicum of historical precedent for his claims. He may very well have deemed the story quite historical in its way, for neither could it be completely invalidated, being beyond the bounds of recent memory, nor did it fail to accord with the universal truths of humankind.[35] These universal truths, these fundamental principles of human activity, particularly those guided by religious sympathies or faiths, could of themselves provide the necessary sanctity, and thus undeniable truth, of a historical event.[36] Not all "fiction" was "history," but neither was it inevitably unhistorical.

Paul Veyne makes similar remarks relating to the classical Greek and Roman traditions. As with the references in Han addresses, the source of information was not at issue in this idiom. Pausanias, for example, was also content merely to remark "I learned that . . ." or "According to my informants."[37] And his representation of the "facts" could be presented with bias without, says Veyne, betraying these facts. The historian, according to Veyne, was a reporter or journalist of sorts: "The historian had neither to interpret (since facts existed) nor prove (because facts are not the stakes of a controversy). He had only to report the facts, either as a 'reporter' or a compiler... He needed only three virtues, which any good journalist possesses: diligence, competence, and impartiality."[38] Whatever the tradition from which the source originated, mythical or not, it was seen as preserving an authentic kernel of truth, which is not to say that such reports were accepted in the same way that everyday experience is. Referenced legendary worlds were accepted as true in that they were not subjected to harsh skepticism or to sneering scrutiny.[39] Like the sources in medieval histories, they were seen to possess some universal value that legitimated their citation. Mythical worlds beyond the horizon of collective memory merely asserted what Veyne terms a different "program of truth," a truth that holds within its own parameters, just as the plays of Shakespeare or *Alice in Wonderland* can be considered truthful, according to their parameters. "All we need to do is open the *Iliad* and we enter into the story, as they say, and lose our bearings... There are societies where, once the book is closed, the reader goes on believing; there are others where he does not."[40]

Instead of adhering to a strict division between truth and falsehood, ancient historians, Veyne argues, were guided by a looser distinction between being informed and being ignorant, with the overarching general concern not a correspondence with reality, but an achieved internal coherence within the information presented. In other words, the criterion by which historical representation was measured was not its precise mapping onto a verified reality but the internal logic of its causal structures. This minimal requirement of coherence, comprised of what Veyne sees as relatively arbitrary collections of minor causes, could easily allow numerous equally viable explanations for events occurring in the same period of time. The metaphors of causality, in their apparent simplicity, "[camouflage] a complexity we are unaware of, a polarity between action and passivity,"[41] the active agent "causing" or "forcing" the consequent activity of the passive agent, as a billiard ball "causes" another ball to move or fire "causes" water to boil. These causal explanations depend on a regular chain of events, with active and passive components. Yet what we consider the active and passive components is not fixed. It is quite possible to imagine numerous, workable alternatives. It is also possible to imagine a coherent explanation without reference to active or passive components, or even to causality at all. Causality, for Veyne, is merely a convenient metaphor.

My implicit suggestion here is that the understanding of historical narratives proposed by Morse and Veyne provides a useful analogue for the analysis of Han history. Their suggestions regarding how historians composed history guided by the demands of rhetoric offer an alternate hermeneutic by which the current disparaging divides between truth and falsity, between history and literature, can be obviated and suggest how we might regard the evidence, "historical" or otherwise, presented in Han addresses. The addresses, like the dramas that surrounded them, were guided by chains of causal reasoning, the logic behind both extremely similar, if not identical. Veyne's and Morse's possible, and to my mind persuasive, explanations of the guiding epistemic principles behind the composition of premodern history thus may plausibly also speak to the assessment of how the evidence of the addresses is weighted. Instead of placing the evidence within the framework of verifiable "reasons," in a harsh positivistic sense, and finding them woefully lacking, we would be better off, I propose, evaluating them as Veyne suggests we evaluate classical historians—with an eye toward internal coherence.[42]

DOUBT IN EARLY CHINESE TEXTS

This leads us to ask what was intended in the offering of such evidence—what doubts were meant to be addressed by such statements? What statements would not have answered such doubts? I have suggested that the "truth" supporting truth-bearing propositions was not an absolute, independently verifiable truth, but a truth within a context that pointed to, or was expressive of, a more generalizable truth to which those not privy to the particulars of the context could also subscribe. For early Chinese texts, the issue of truth is better described as one of pertinence or suggestiveness relating to broader aims, moral or otherwise. The statements in support of the "truth" of the address could just as accurately be described as those that were pertinent to its aim, suggestive of the general proposition(s) that the addressor was aiming to persuade the audience to consider. The aim, on this reading, is to get the audience to see the "truth of the matter" (or ironically to subvert it), not the accuracy, the truth or falsity, of any single statement. The consequence of this is that no statement in and of itself will lead to the failure of an attempt to produce persuasion or conviction in the audience. Because complete accuracy is not at issue, falsity also is not. The evidentiary doubts of the audience would thus be directed at the structural and associative relevance of the evidence as it relates to the axiomatic commonsense assumptions upon which the addressor is relying and to the proffered argumentative thesis. Doubts would not be present in relation to the "facticity" of a historical anecdote, or even in relation to its consistency with other anecdotes involving the referred figures or events, nor would doubt be present in relation to the correct interpretation or elaboration of a general principle or theoretical system, nor even would it necessarily be in relation to the overall description of various particulars involved in the address. No class of statement is intrinsically necessary to the addresses. Yet it is highly noteworthy that certain standard classes of statements were used repeatedly. These classes of statements, I contend, can be associated with distinct types of "suggestiveness," and thus of answers to certain concerns, or doubts, related to the executive's various epistemic commitments and political aspirations. What we need to ask, in their specific analysis, is what suggestions they are providing.

In the Han histories, the term translatable as "doubt" (or "suspicion"), *yi* 疑, at least occasionally denotes knowledge-related, or epistemic, concerns, referring to an uncertainty about the perceptual or logical validity of one's (or another's) impressions or about the likelihood of an event coming to pass. On other occasions, it characterizes interpersonal reservations, reservations about the credibility of statements offered by a particular speaker that are based on his personal disposition or conduct. The following instances can be classified as interpersonal:

> 1. "King Cheng of Zhou did not doubt the Duke of Zhou. Emperor Zhao the Filial of Han employed Huo Guang. Both relied on the times to achieve fame. How great!" 成王不疑周公, 孝昭委任霍光, 各因其時以成名, 大矣哉! [43]

> 2. In the third year of the Han dynasty, the King of Han and Xiang Yu were locked in a struggle in the area of Suo in Jing. The King several times sent emissaries to reward Counselor-in-Chief Xiao He for his labors. Master Bao spoke to the Counselor-in-Chief, saying, "While the King exposes himself to the elements, he frequently sends emissaries to reward Your Lordship for your labors. It seems that he harbors doubts about Your Lordship. If I were to propose a plan on Your Lordship's behalf, nothing would be better than to send all of Your Lordship's sons and brothers who are able to bear weapons to report at the army barracks. The King would then certainly have greater trust in Your Lordship." 漢三年, 漢王與項羽相距京索之間, 上數使使勞苦丞相。鮑生謂丞相曰:「王暴衣露蓋, 數使使勞苦君者, 有疑君心也。為君計, 莫若遣君子孫昆弟能勝兵者悉詣軍所, 上必益信君。」[44]

The following, in contrast, can be classified as knowledge related:

> 1. Zhang Liang said, "The Qin armies are exceedingly powerful and cannot be underestimated. I ask that we first dispatch men to add to the number of flags placed on the mountain tops in order to cause them to doubt the size of our armies." 張良曰:「秦兵尚彊, 未可輕。願先遣人益張旗幟於山上為疑兵。」[45]

> 2. "The Royal Scribe is to inspect the registers of the accounts. Where he doubts their accuracy, he is to have them examined, to ensure that truth and falsehood are not confused." 御史察計簿, 疑非實者, 按之, 使真偽毋相亂。[46]

Occasionally, definitive categorization is impossible, not because these distinctions are inapplicable to the doubts arising in Han texts but because establishing the precise cause of doubt is impossible. For instance, on some occasions, as with the final epistemic example, it was documentary accuracy that was at issue. Were the recorded information or judgments themselves in doubt, such would be an instance of an epistemic doubt; if the issue was one at the level of recording, such would be an instance of interpersonal doubt.[47]

It is important not only to note that there are indeed (as we would expect) both interpersonal and epistemic doubts but to note in just what manner these doubts are phrased; in other words, to pay attention to exactly what was at issue. We can see that, for example, both classes of doubt range over numerous issues. Under interpersonal doubt are subsumed concerns about another's responsibility to holding himself true to a certain course of action or a particular relationship. Under epistemic doubt are subsumed concerns about judgments regarding the accuracy of figures and the reliability of general impressions or observations. Furthermore, although epistemic doubts certainly may involve doubts about the source of information, they cannot be identified with such. The categories are distinct.

The central questions relating to an examination of the place and consequences of knowledge-related doubt are the following: What would it be like to make a mistake? By what type of error would a doubt about the address be raised? Answers to these questions require an investigation into the inherited background, the background of *endoxa*, of commonly held reputable beliefs, for it is within the realm of popular knowledge, in general, that court debates were held. Indeed, only rarely did addresses discuss issues requiring technical understanding. And yet we must not presume that the evidence, though general, was considered less "factual," less epistemically weighty than evidence that had the appearance of arising out of the inquiries of specialists. What may appear to be coarse moralizing or general impressions about the ethnic characteristics of a people or vague and imprecise description of landscape or military resources might have well been seen as very "hard" evidence.

"TRUTH OF THE MATTER"

The epistemic norm for rhetorical truth is what I conveniently term "the truth of the matter," in order to distinguish it clearly from any necessary association with verifiable truth. I argue that the "truth of the matter" is a form of truth insofar as it offers a vision that is in some way justifiable, both because one can marshal credible evidence and arguments for it and because the points of emphasis that are forwarded can reasonably be asserted to impact its realization. That the good of the state allows for different interpretations does not thereby inevitably impugn it as a credible norm of truth. That this form of truth is rooted in an ethical or pragmatic vision (or perhaps, if the intention is the failure of the state, a murderous one, an intention that would have to be masked with certain measure of duplicity) need not compromise its use in determining how the value of justificatory statements should be assessed or in deciding what course of action should be pursued. Of course, unlike more phenomenal truths, its indubitability is more open to question simply because of there being believable and justifiable alternatives. Such alternatives cannot easily be imagined regarding a city's location or how many troops one has. Nevertheless, numerous well-founded arguments can be, and have been, made for why such second-order truths, truths embedded in human interactions rather than external conditions, are still justifiable as truth.[48]

Characterized in this way, the "truth of the matter" shares kinship with certain uses of a commonly employed term in classical China—*zhi* 志, usually translated as either "intention" or "aim." Numerous other alternate translations exist, exposing its variant use (at least in the translations) as adjective, verb, and noun—"inner mind," "thoughts," "goals," "will," "mental factors," "mind," "setting one's sights," "resolute," "ambition," "hope," "unity," and so forth.[49] Common to many of these is a mentalistic or conativistic essence, a recurring reference to the mind or will. I do not deny that *zhi* involves elements that share sympathies with those of the mind and the will. But I would like to suggest that there may be a nuance of an individualized commitment to an inner vision believed to reflect something true about the world that is lacking in some of these translations, a commitment that involves both intellectual and conative components but also expresses a conviction about how things should be or actually are in relation to what actions one should take or direction one should follow. An illustrative example of this nuance is found in the *Analects of Confucius*, where Confucius cites an apparently familiar precept: "'[d]welling in seclusion in order to pursue one's aspirations, practicing rightness in order to realize the Way'" 隱居以求其志, 行義以達其道.[50] Here, *zhi* is translated as "aspirations," which apparently pertains to an activity pursued alone, in solitude. But, if the parallelism with *dao* ("way") is meant to be elucidatory, the activity pursued in solitude is, like *dao*, normative. The employment of *yi* 義, commonly translated as "appropriateness" or "rightness" or "righteousness," further informs the parallel. Acting in an appropriate manner assists one in realizing the "way," the ultimate moral demands that guide one's conduct. Because of this parallel, I argue, the reader must presume a normative ethical stance akin to *yi* in the calculation of *zhi*. This need not involve a moral estimation, but a broader conviction of the "the truth of the matter." With *zhi* interpreted as "the truth of the matter," Confucius's remarks could be translated thus: "[d]welling in seclusion to pursue the truth of the matter, practicing what is right to realize the way." Under this interpretation, the adherent of this precept lives in a hermitic fashion to ponder the truths relating to how he should live.

While there are no explicit connections between the notion of *zhi* and the purpose or aim of the addresses regarding military affairs, there are any number of passages in the classical literature that insist that part of what is essential to knowing a person, or a text, is to know her or its *zhi*, the most famous being the introductory remark to the *Book of Odes* (*Shijing*): "The Odes express *zhi*" 詩言志.[51] Steven van Zoeren, in his *Poetry and Personality*, presents an extensive and elaborate analysis of the use of the term in classical Chinese texts, beginning with what he believes to be its earliest surviving appearance, in the "Pan Geng" 盤庚 chapter of the *Book of Documents* (*Shangshu* 尚書). There, he avers, the term means "aim": "I tell you about the difficulties [to be overcome], just as an archer aims [at the target]" 予告汝于難, 若射之有志.[52] He takes other examples from the Confucian classics, the *Analects*, the *Mencius*, and the *Xunzi*, arguing that, on his reading, *zhi* "was thus an organizing and guiding preoccupation, either moral or frankly secular . . . The *zhi* symbolized or rather exemplified the whole thrust of a person's being, for it was connected to and represented personality in a particularly direct and important way. If you knew an individual's *zhi*, you knew who that person was."[53]

In its basic thrust, I agree with Van Zoeren's explanation of *zhi*. I concur that the *zhi* exemplified something fundamental about a person. Yet I would add that there is an objectifying element of *zhi* that relates not only to the person but also to that toward which he aims. The archer himself is the one aiming, but he is aiming at a discrete, objective target. The Confucian is committed to the "way," to use another of Van Zoeren's examples,[54] but his commitment strives to capture something about the world that he believes to be there, to be true. Thus, I would like to propose, *zhi* is not only the reflection of the person but a reflection of what is essential to him in his judgments about that reality. Extending such to the "aim" of the political address, the *zhi* of the address is not merely a reflection of the personal predilections, interests, and values of the person who is composing it but also a reflection of what he perceives as the essential features of his reality.[55] His perceptions, naturally, are guided by his commitments but they are not therefore merely subjective. They must, in an essential way, be informed by an estimation of the features of external reality. Accordingly, a more apt translation of *zhi* may perhaps be something like "one's vision about the truth of the matter" or, to abbreviate, "one's vision."[56] One's "vision" involves what one perceives as essential to a particular matter (or the world in general) and is directive; that is, it makes demands on how one should act or dispose oneself. It demands commitment toward a certain course of action; thus its common translation as "intention" or "will" or "aim." But translating *zhi* as "vision" can more easily accommodate passages in which *zhi* does not appear to demand any immediate action or movement toward a goal, as suggested by such translations as "aim," "intent," or "purpose," such as the following from the *Annals of Lü Buwei*, in which Knoblock and Riegel translate *zhi* as "inner mind": "In musical tones as well there are balances that should be kept. If they are too grand and large, the inner mind (*zhi*) is unsettled" 夫音亦有適, 太鉅則志蕩.[57] It also can accommodate those passages in which it is "distorted," as in *Analects* 14.36, in which Ji Sun's "vision" is "distorted" by Gongbo Liao.[58]

Several other classical texts provide additional substantiation for this interpretation of *zhi*. In the Mencius, as Robert Eno maintains, *zhi* is sometimes used to indicate "a notion that the actions of an exemplary person must be understood as expressions of a unified ethical perspective that embodies the character of the person in a basic and holistic way."[59] Further compelling evidence is offered in Michael Nylan's interpretation of the aims of the *Records of the Grand Historian*. According to Nylan, in the *Records zhi* appears to take less of a strictly moralizing cast than it did in the *Mencius*. Nylan interprets it to be indicative of a personal ethical "commitment," a "vision" that one is obliged to follow. Sima Qian, according to Nylan, feels sympathy for those who are committed to their personal ethical vision, just as he is committed to his own vision of history, a vision he hopes his readers will share.[60] Nylan points to several passages in the *Records* that substantiate her interpretation, one of which I believe is particularly interesting. In an oddly self-depreciating assessment of the historical enterprise, Sima Qian appears to apologize for the failure of history to mirror present circumstances and thus its limitations as a guide for resolving current problems: "He who lives in the present age but takes as truthful (*zhi*) the ways of the past uses the ways of the past as a means by which he reflects his own age. Yet, they are not necessarily completely alike" 居今之世, 志古之道, 所以自境也, 未必盡同.[61] Here Sima Qian is not describing simply those who are personally committed to an ethical vision expressed in the histories but the ability of historical records themselves to capture something truthful about the present.[62]

There are many other instances in the Han histories in which *zhi* is employed in a way that suggests a commitment to a vision about the way things are or should be, a commitment to a vision about what is essential to an assessment of the truth about a certain state of affairs. In many, they are most easily translated as "intention" or "state of mind," but these are not merely dispassionate and uncommitted means-ends calculations or conativist dispositions relating to an objective. They also intrinsically involve a vision about what is important, as embodying something essential and true about the state of affairs one is attempting to realize. For instance, in the first chapter of the *Records*, Sima Qian writes that only after the mythical Xuanyuan 軒轅 fought three battles with the Flaming Emperor was he able to "put his vision into practice" 得其志.[63] Executives and other officials striving to put their vision into practice is an oft repeated refrain but it frequently is not an ethical one.[64]

Zhi thus speaks to more than simply an intended objective but less than a strictly moral point of view. It refers to an objective to which one is personally committed and in which the actor believes there is something essential about the world that is either captured in it or realized through it. The *Odes* "bespeak" something essential about the world, just as Confucius's vision captures something essential about the world and thus is worthy of undying personal commitment. The essential feature of *zhi* is not that it is ethical but that it is stable, true, and thus merits undertaking.

Of course, I am not arguing that *zhi* is an exact correlate to my notion of the "truth of the matter." It extends beyond this notion to involve an active pursuit of the personal commitment to such a vision. But it is apt for my purposes in that it is applied to the directionality of times and narratives (as was expressed in Sima Qian's remark above) and is a performative notion; that is, it is not one that is stable regardless of its context, as other notions commonly interpreted as relating to a Western notion of truth are, as I will discuss briefly below. Interpreting *zhi* as involving some notion of truth offers a possible culturally embedded guiding norm undergirding the composition of early Chinese historical narrative. In keeping with this more flexible norm of truth, the "vision" of the addresses, like the "vision" of the Odes or the "vision" of historical narrative, could be treated as not merely conveying a subjective appraisal of things or a crass individual appraisal but actually involving some measure of an objective assessment.

Some might object that there are other classical Chinese terms that would be more apt analogues to my notion of "a vision of the truth of the matter," notions that have a long and entrenched history of being used in ways that suggest an axiomatic standard by which one judges the accuracy of descriptive statements about phenomena or the general applicability of ethical or metaphysical statements. Of those that are employed as standards for statements regarding the phenomena, some of the most commonly used to translate "truth" or one of its synonyms are *shi* 實, *qing* 情, *zhen* 真, and *li* 理. For ethical and metaphysical statements, the usual classical Chinese analogue is *dao* 道 ("way" or "principle"). Since, however, the notion of truth I wish to capture is a performative notion, one that bespeaks a certain vision regarding what is essential for deciding why to pursue a certain course of action, that does not necessarily connect with ethical concerns, and is relatively individualized and thus somewhat prone to distortion,[65] the above terms are unsuitable. As they are used in most literature, they are employed to express a relatively constant, reliable, and generally unrevisable standard by which perceptions or actions are judged. A vision of the truth of the matter is neither necessarily constant nor closed to revision. It is thus a notion that can be amended or improved upon during the course of a debate or discussion.

CHAPTER FOUR

Interactive Constraints at Court

Between parties as uneasy and often mutually distrustful as the monarch and his advisors, political persuasion is always complicated by competing and at times contradictory interests and personal idiosyncrasies. In the classical Chinese corpus, monarchs are repeatedly and severely warned against the seductions of a glib tongue, of ministers too ambitious or "talented" to provide the unswervingly loyal service necessary to defend the throne against the clutch of plots hatched by conniving relatives or powerful gentry.[1] Advisors, in turn, are admonished not to touch upon the monarch's hidden motives for fear of upsetting his composure or unveiling a tightly guarded vulnerability or preference that others could manipulate and thereby use to gain some advantage.[2] Instead, advisors are directed to investigate and ascertain the manner in which a monarch, given his preferences and character, would wish to be addressed, instruction that would seem to promote nuanced, unformulizable, individualized persuasions. Nevertheless, there are numerous rhetorical formats and turns of phrase repeatedly employed to structure the persuasions presented to the monarch. Furthermore, many of these formats, whether intentionally or not, whether by the direct instruction of a master or simple convention, survived over centuries. Traces of these forms appear from the early Zhou literature[3] on into the imperial period beginning with the Qin and Han dynasties.

From every indication in the early Chinese corpus, the executive power of the monarch was extensive.[4] Though his influence was never fully secure—indeed it was constantly challenged and manipulated—the consequences of raising his ire or just provoking his disagreement were often swift and disastrous, punitive of both the body politic and, quite relatedly, the addressor's own body. Hanfeizi, in his "Difficulties in Speaking to the Monarch," an essay about the problems with adapting one's speech to conform to the monarch's personal predilections, warns,

> Although one's calculations [about how to present one's case to the monarch] might be correct, it is still uncertain whether it will be heard. Although the rightness and reasonableness of one's speech might be irreproachable, it is still uncertain whether it will be employed. If the Great Monarch takes one's statements to be untrustworthy, then one's minor statements will be taken as slander and calumny and because of one's more significant statements misery, catastrophe, and even death will be dealt to one. So, Zixu was adroit at plotting and yet the King of Wu executed him, Confucius was adroit at persuasion and yet the men of Kuang took him prisoner. Guan Yiwu was truly worthy and Duke Huan of Lu imprisoned him. Were any of these three Grand Masters not worthy? Instead, it was their three lords who were unenlightened. 故度量雖正，未必聽也；義理雖全，未必用也。大王若以此不信，則小者以為毀訾誹謗，大者患禍災害死亡及其身。故子胥善謀而吳戮之，仲尼善說而匡圍之，管夷吾實賢而魯囚之。故此三大夫，豈不賢哉！而三君不明也。⁵

The perils ministers faced in their dealings with executives were often horrific: not only could they be subject to gruesome torture and a slow painful death, their extended families could also be, simply on the basis of unsubstantiated slander, summarily wiped out. But it was not only the ministers who were in jeopardy; executives were as well, thus the constant warnings by their officials to beware of possible intrigues and conflicted allegiances among their advisors. This had an effect on both the manner in which advice was presented and the frequency of well-meaning and loyal officials withdrawing their services.⁶

The interaction between ministers and monarchs was, in theory, extremely formal. The *Yili* 儀禮, the *Book of Etiquette and Ceremonial*, for instance, prescribes the following codes when speaking to a lord or government official:

> (a) Whenever one speaks with the Lord—but not when one is responding to his questions—one settles himself properly and thereafter conveys what one wishes to speak about. 凡言，非對也，妥而後傳言。⁷

> (b) In speaking with the Lord, one talks of one's official business; with a person of high-rank, of one's service to the Lord ... with those working in the government offices, about conscientiousness and trustworthiness. 與君言，言使臣。與大人言，言事君 ... 與居官者言，言忠信。⁸

(c) In speaking to a person of high-rank, one begins by looking him in the face; towards the middle of the interview one looks at his breast; and at the end of the interview, one again looks at his face. The order is never changed and is used in all cases. 凡與大人言始視面, 中視抱, 卒視面, 毋改。眾皆若是。[9]

This formality quite rationally accorded with the possibility of an extremely punitive response to ill-mannered or simply misunderstood gestures or expressions. In the Han, physical demeanor was certainly both ritually and legally circumscribed, though not perhaps actually to the degree prescribed in this passage from the *Yili*. Physical expressions of deference, for instance kowtowing (*dunshou* 頓首 or *qishou* 稽首) or bowing (*bai* 拜), are ubiquitous in the Han histories.

But in practice exchanges were sometimes relatively unrestrained by formal etiquette prescriptions. In the Former Han, ministers at least occasionally acted or spoke in ways that demonstrated an informal relationship with the imperial household.[10] Nevertheless, as David Schaberg has recently discussed, jocular indirection, with the critic behaving as court jester, was more of an ideal than an actual modus operandi for Han addressors. Tales of jocular indirection, Schaberg argues, "were the fictional invention of the *shi* 士 (men of service) and reflect the development within that group of a self-conscious conception of its identity and its relation to imperial power."[11] This idealization of a feigned jesting posture, naturally, was conceived in response to the typical harshly punitive response of the displeased executive. Whether jocular or not, indirection was a natural response in the punitive monarchic setting: if the minister could ironically distance himself from his criticism by the suggestion that the monarch had misinterpreted him or had taken his comedic gestures too seriously, he could potentially save himself from the executioner's axe.

In early Han historiography, many, if not most, of the speech acts made by ministerial officials can be construed as hortatory addresses, even if they are not explicitly stated to be so. They serve to assess and make recommendations on multifarious issues of governance: the waging of a military campaign, the collection of revenues, punishment or compensation, marriage, ritual, posthumous honors, oracles, and so forth.[12] It is unclear what level of influence, if any, the addresses have on the course of events, for the interplay of the various forces influencing such a course is only occasionally laid bare. Sometimes the addressee makes no comment and the issue is not pursued, at least not immediately in the narrative;[13] sometimes there is a brief note that the "the presentation is acknowledged" (*zou ke* 奏可);[14] sometimes, the addressee demands that the relevant officials discuss the address further among themselves;[15] and sometimes the addressee provides an extensive response. Nevertheless, there is no necessary, indubitable connection—nor, of course, could there be—between the statements made and the actions pursued. Often there is no explicit articulation of the superior's future intentions and the reasons for them. Such follows naturally from the reality of the monarchic situation, for to state explicitly what advice one would follow and why would be to render oneself vulnerable to the future machinations of various parties.

HAN BUREAU OF MEMORIALS

In name, if not in discrete function, the Han central government created an office to oversee the collection, review, and censoring of addresses made for submission to the emperor called the Bureau for Hortatory Addresses (*zou cao* 奏曹). This office operated under the supervision of the Supreme Commander (*tai wei* 太尉) and possibly also the Chancellor (*cheng xiang* 丞相),[16] and was headed by an administrator of relatively low rank, about four hundred bushels.[17] This bureau was formed upon the creation of the Imperial Secretariat (*Shangshu tai* 尚書臺), during the reign of Emperor Wu (140–87 BCE). Its existence, however, did not signal a consistent or rigorous censorial oversight, nor did its creation indicate an absence of official oversight prior to its creation. Indeed, the bureau's functions are not amply in evidence in the historical records of the Former Han: it is explicitly mentioned only twice.[18] And while there are officials described as handling and, if remiss, reprimanded for not properly handling court documents (or for improperly intervening in their preparation), their activities are not precisely described nor are they frequently shown to intervene when submissions are deemed inappropriate, unfavorable to a powerful official, or not in order.[19] Moreover, officials associated with one bureau are not infrequently given duties formally associated with another bureau.[20] An example of the manner in which addresses were submitted to the throne can be found in the biography of Wei Xiang 魏相, which reveals that around 68 BCE, when Wei Xiang was Imperial Counselor (*yushi dafu* 御史大夫), it was the custom, "when presenting a document to the throne to always present two sealed copies, marking one as 'duplicate.' The supervisor of the Imperial Secretariat would first open the duplicate copy and if the contents were not of merit, he would discard them and not present them to the emperor" 諸上書者皆為二封, 署其一曰副, 領尚書者先發副封, 所言不善, 屏去不奏.[21] It is of interest to note that the text thereafter reports that Wei Xiang, wary of giving petty bureaucrats the responsibility to decide which addresses would be submitted to the throne, asked that this system of duplicate copies be abolished. Clearly, if this example is any indication, the process of submission and censorship was not immutable or closed to abuse.[22]

Whether it was by petty bureaucrats or more elevated officials, addresses were routinely vetted for review, with only a fraction of the total submissions being selected for formal presentation to the monarch. In the biography of Xiao Wangzhi 蕭望之, it is stated that Emperor Xuan turned over the received addresses proposing various measures of benefit for the Han government to Xiao Wangzhi, at the time an Imperial Messenger (*yezhe* 謁者), to examine and vet them:

> Those that were superior, Xiao Wangzhi would request the Chancellor or Secretary to the Imperial Counselor to act on them; with those that were of the second rank, officials at grade of two thousand bushels tested the matter, and, after a year, a report was made public. Those that were of the lowest rank were returned, merely reported to have been heard. Sometimes their authors would be dismissed [without a response from the court], sent home to their fields and hamlets. 高者請丞相御史, 次者中二千石試事, 滿歲以狀聞, 下者報聞, 或罷歸田里。[23]

There are also numerous examples of officials complaining about not being heard. In the biography of Mei Fu 梅福, for instance, Mei Fu alludes to such difficulties, emphasizing the frustrations of the supplicants:

> The *shi* 士 are important tools for the nation. Obtaining *shi* makes the nation stronger; losing them makes it weaker. The *Book of Odes* says, "In throngs are the many *shi*, King Wen depends upon them to bring tranquility to the empire."[24] The discussions of the court are not where people from the wilds are allowed to speak. I, Your servant, truly fear that my body will be smeared on wild grass, my corpse lying with those of the infantry brigades. The documents I frequently submitted asking for an interview have been immediately dismissed upon being reported. I, Your servant, have heard that in the time of Duke Huan of Qi, there were men who used the nine times nine strategy to have an interview, and Duke Huan did not turn back any of them, because he wanted their assistance to become great. Now, what I speak of is not merely a nine times nine strategy,[25] and yet Your Majesty has refused Your servant three (i.e., several) times. This is the reason the *shi* of All-Under-Heaven do not come to court. 士者, 國之重器; 得士則重, 失士則輕。詩云:「濟濟多士, 文王以寧。」廟堂之議, 非草茅所當言也。臣誠恐身塗野草, 尸并卒伍, 故數上書求見, 輒報罷。臣聞齊桓之時有以九九見者, 桓公不逆, 欲以致大也。今臣所言非特九九也, 陛下距臣者三矣, 此天下士所以不至也。[26]

Though Mei Fu clearly upbraids the emperor for not paying attention to his previous submissions, later in the address he also castigates those remorseless officials within the court who, on various pretenses, lawful or not, have prevented myriad remonstrances from being heard or read by the emperor.[27] Blaming the scheming intervention of others who might have been involved in court deliberations for the emperor's disinterest was a common rhetorical device. It was also quite common for responsibility to be attributed even to those who were probably not involved at all.

FORM OF THE ADDRESSES

In form, the addresses are quite diverse and without consistent use of preceding verbs that later came to mark the differing genre forms. The term in later studies denoting a formal address, *zou* 奏 ("to present"), does not always precede those speech acts that are clearly meant to be addresses. Addresses are alternately preceded with numerous other verbs: frequently *yan* 言 or *yue* 曰 ("to state"), *dui* 對 ("to respond"), *shang shu* 上書 ("to submit a document to the throne"); sometimes *gao* 告 ("to report"), *ying* 應 ("to retort"), or *jian* 諫 ("to remonstrate"). In either the *History of the Former Han* or the *Records of the Grand Historian*, there does not seem, on investigation, to be much that wholly prevents the use of one verb over another, no rhetorical, topical, or linguistic markers that are particular to one verbal marker, nor are there any status distinctions embedded in the use of one particular verbal marker over another. Regardless of which verb form precedes it, an address may be directed at any higher-level official to whom a lower-level official is offering a policy recommendation. As far as current research has shown, only *jian* 諫, "to remonstrate," seems relatively stable in its rhetorical application, usually employed to introduce a direct critique of the emperor's current conduct or general principles of government.[28] However, even when *jian* is employed, as with other verbal markers, once the speech act has been made, the conventional expression used to describe its receipt is *zou ke* 奏可, "The presentation is acknowledged."

If we attempt to find our literary bearings in an investigation of the rhetorical features of the hortatory address by referring to the earliest extant study of Chinese genres, *The Literary Mind and the Carving of Dragons* (*Wenxin diaolong* 文心雕龍), authored in the Northern Wei dynasty (386–534 CE) by Liu Xie 劉勰, we quickly discover that the features presented under the category of *zou* offer little assistance.[29] A translator of Liu Xie's work, Vincent Shih, frequently rued Liu Xie's many inconsistencies in his classificatory terminology, his criticism sharpest in his discussion of two other of Liu's genre classifications, "Edicts (*zhao* 詔) and Script (*ce* 策)":

> From the text of this chapter, it seems obvious that no one of the terms used to stand for different types of writing has a specific sense

in which it is used consistently in different contexts; and it is also obvious that our author made no attempt to clarify this confusion. As a matter of fact, this tendency to treat a term, which has many senses, as if it had only one sense, and to raise it to the status of a genre, while using it as inconsistently as it originally was used in different settings, is one of the major faults of Liu Hsieh, against which we have a legitimate complaint.[30]

Shih then gives numerous examples demonstrating Liu's imprecise classifications—that *zhao* 詔 ("edicts") is used both to specify a royal pronouncement and as a general term for all royal edicts; *ce* 策 ("script") is simultaneously a term for a "script of enfeoffment" and "writings in general"; and *lun* 論 ("treatise"), specifically discussed in chapter 18 of Liu's study, "Treatise and Discussion," groups works together in ways that, in the previous chapter, "Speculative Writings," Liu explicitly distinguishes.[31] This carelessness, Shih states, forces the student of Liu's work to try to look past Liu's terminological definitions and analyze his cited exemplars, a task fraught with complications, for to analyze the exemplars is, first and foremost, to accept that they indeed are exemplars of particular styles of writing, a premise that is far from certain.[32]

Since the features of hortatory addresses are, on investigation, not distinguishable by the rank of the presenter and do not appear to have clearly distinguishable genre characteristics, analysis of such submissions is best served by grouping them topically. In this way the salient features of addresses can be thoroughly and rigorously compared without concern for the already dubious genre distinctions. As mentioned previously in the first chapter, the focus of this investigation is addresses that speak to the merit of military campaigns, for it is within these addresses, addresses that often present a hard-nosed assessment of the concrete demands of the campaign, that questions of facticity—the epistemic value of various types of "facts" and the weighted selection and presentation of "facts" within an address—can be most carefully adjudicated.[33] By cross-referencing these "facts" with historical evidence gleaned from various other nonhistoriographical sources, one would expect it to be possible, ideally speaking, to evaluate whether details presented as factual were verifiable, and thereby assess how and whether the arguments presented in the address cohere. Were such a comparison of the factual content of historiographical and nonhistoriographical materials workable, we could then conceivably estimate how many speech acts have historical value and how many may merely be serving a dramatic purpose, that is, the purpose of driving the historical narrative, whatever its truth content, forward. More generally, and more importantly for my own particular line of research, it would also be possible, with such an analysis, to penetrate the general manner in which arguments were presented, regardless of their historical merits. By contrast, statements relating to punishment of official behavior or the request to alter or reevaluate the general attitude of the emperor or another official toward governance usually have less on the basis of which one could possibly judge the truth content of the facts presented, or even their coherence.

As with other topics, statements regarding military campaigns are of wildly varying lengths, from the very brief, no more than a short quip, to the very long, sometimes hundreds of characters long. They are also presented by various types of officials, from generals to kings to lower-level officials. Whether or not these officials are of potential import for Ban Gu's putative ideological (i.e., Ruist) purposes (or Sima Qian's, however his may be characterized) is of little relevance, for the aspects of note for this study are probably not ideologically driven. Though the evidence employed in the addresses is not at all strictly limited to concrete observations, for example, the description of the natural obstacles facing an army, the provisions necessary to feed and clothe the army, and so forth, it nevertheless does not inevitably stray into issues or opine about characters or events that could be taken to reveal grosser ideological leanings. Much has been written about the motives informing Ban Gu's representations of historical events and his perceived Ruist agenda.[34] While it is important to keep in mind the possibility that these speeches are composed or edited for some ultimately ideologically driven portrayal of a reign period or the dynasty in general, the military addresses, taken as a group, do not seem to support consistently such an aim.

CHAPTER FIVE

Salient Formal Characteristics of the Addresses

MAJOR FEATURES

Addresses regarding military campaigns usually touch on many, if not all, of the following considerations: obstacles of climate or of terrain; the military preparedness of the enemy's forces; the openness of the enemy to negotiation and the likelihood that they will take advantage of negotiations to gather their forces; the preparedness of the Han forces and the economic and social demands that a campaign would incur; portentous cosmological signs; historical or prehistorical analogues; general strategic, philosophical, or political statements; the moral force of the leaders of the campaign; and the possible benefits—economic, social, military, or moral—of such a campaign. These considerations are not unusual in early Chinese texts.[1] What is of greater interest, as has been discussed earlier, is exactly *what* is chosen for presentation and *how* it is presented. In consideration of the monarchic context in which these addresses were presented and the sociopolitical constraints that impinged upon the freedom of composition, one cannot overlook even the smallest detail. The inclusion, or omission, of evidence, a train of argument, an aphorism (and its source), stock phrases, the arrangement of the address and its emphases and elaborations—all of this must be examined to obtain secure conclusions about the direction and aim of the address.

Prior to the quotation of an address, there is an introduction of historical particulars, frequently quite short, that bears on its content.[2] For example, in the "Biography of Chao Cuo 晁錯," before his celebrated military address we have merely this: "At this time, the Xiongnu were powerful, frequently marauding the border regions. The emperor sent off an army to control them. Chao Cuo submitted a statement to the emperor on military affairs, which stated . . ."³ Another, less succinct, example is the following:

> In the third year of *shen-jue* (59 BCE), Xiao Wangzhi replaced Bing Ji as Imperial Counselor. During the *wufeng* era (57–54 BCE), the Xiongnu tribes experienced great internal strife, and many of the council members said, "The Xiongnu have harmed us for many a day. It is thus permissible to take advantage of their current weakness and disorder, raise an army, and destroy them!" The imperial edict dispatched the Chariot and Horse General Serving as Marshal of State Han Zeng, and Inspector of Officials, the Marquis of Fu Ping, Zhang Yanshou, the Superintendent of the Palace Yang Yun, and the Superintendent of Transport Dai Changle to inquire of Xiao Wangzhi what strategy he thought best. Wangzhi responded. 三年，代丙吉為御史大夫。五鳳中匈奴大亂，議者多曰匈奴為害日久，可因其壞亂舉兵滅之。詔遣中朝大司馬車騎將軍韓增、諸吏富平侯張延壽、光祿勳楊惲、太僕戴長樂問望之計策，望之對曰。⁴

These relatively brief historical, or "dramatic," introductions are only the barest outlines required to give the necessary details to inform the reader of the issue at hand and the characters involved. Of significant interest is how similar they are in form to certain of the dramatic introductions given in the *Intrigues*. The *Records of the Grand Historian*, and therefore also the *History of the Former Han*, clearly followed narrative conventions similar to those used in the *Intrigues*. Following is a narratively complex introduction taken from the *Intrigues* that prefaces a debate on a military matter:

> Yen attacked Ch'i and took seventy cities; only Chü and Chi-mo held out. From Chi-mo T'ien Tan of Ch'i struck back at Yen and killed her general Ch'i-chieh. Earlier, the general who had taken Liao was accused by someone at the Yen court and, fearing execution, he settled down to hold Liao, for he dared not return to Yen. T'ien Tan assaulted Liao for over a year and suffered heavy losses, but the town still stood. Then Lu-lien wrote a letter, lashed it to an arrow shaft and had it shot into the city that it might be delivered to the Yen commander. 燕攻齊，取七十餘城，唯莒、即墨不下。齊田單以即墨破燕，殺騎劫。初，燕將攻下聊城，人或讒之。燕將懼誅，遂保守聊城，不敢歸。田單攻之歲餘，士卒多死，而聊城不下。魯連乃書，約之矢，以射城中，遺燕將。⁵

Accepting James Crump's thesis that the anecdotes in the *Intrigues* were composed as rhetorical set pieces, akin to Latin *suasoriae*, their similarity with Han compositions might suggest that the Han addresses may also have been composed, whether by a historian or the addressors themselves, in the style of rhetorical set pieces. Regardless of their ultimate function, although these narrative compositions might be in some measure historically accurate (as some of the pieces in the *Intrigues* are), they cannot be taken as utterly factual.[6] Their historical value, that is, their factual reliability, may not have been of central concern for their composition. I shall return to this point later.

At the end of the addresses, the monarch's reaction is often not explicitly described but merely noted with conventional formulations indicating that the emperor was "pleased" (*yue* 說,[7] *jia zhi* 嘉之[8]), acknowledged or accepted the address (*ke* 可 or *cong* 從[9]), sent it off to counselors and advisors for discussion,[10] or did not "accept" (*nei/na* 納) or "listen to" (*ting* 聽) the address.[11] Similar statements regarding the reactions of the monarch are common to the *Intrigues* as well, and are found in various other classical Chinese texts, although earlier texts, such as *Zuozhuan* and *Lüshichunqiu*, frequently represent the contact between minister and monarch in a dialogue form, a form only occasionally found in the *Intrigues* or the Han histories.[12] In the *Intrigues*, by comparison, the verbal response of the monarch, when a response is recorded, is almost invariably positive, sometimes expressed in exclamatory language that reveals the monarch greatly impressed by the force and the eloquence of the persuasion.[13] Frequently the monarch begins with an affirmative, usually "Good" or "Excellent" (*shan* 善).[14] Sometimes, however, the response is merely narrated[15] that the monarch was "pleased" (*yue* 說)[16] or employed the persuader's advice (*yong* X *yan* 用 X 言),[17] acted in accordance (*yi wei ran* 以為然),[18] or, when not pleased, that he did not listen (*bu ting* 不聽).[19] Though the exact wording used in the Han histories and the *Intrigues* may be different, the laconic decisiveness is very similar. Never, unless the persuasion is represented in a dialogue format, does the monarch express any concluding doubts or questions about the contents of the persuasion. Either the monarch accepts the advice or he does not.

Generally speaking, each address begins and ends with polite, decorous formulations meant to acknowledge and accentuate the sociopolitical distance between the presenter and the audience and thereby to assert the tentativeness of the address, to highlight that the address is, at least on the surface, meant to be considered only insofar as it is of some use to the audience. They are also meant to defer responsibility for any flaws in the analysis and the possible consequences arising from accepting the recommendations proceeding from the argument. Thus the obsequiousness of the presenter is a clever means by which the presenter attempted to avoid punishment for his inadequacies. Such self-denigrating formulations include "I brave death to present these stupid suggestions," "I face the axe," and "[if I fail the throne,] Your servant's error deserves ten thousand deaths."[20] Enno Giele points to a statement by a commentator to the *History of the Former Han*, Zhang Yan 張晏, that suggests that at least some of these humilifics could have first arisen in the Qin and were formulaically employed in the Han: "The Qin considered that whenever common people or officials presented letters to the throne, they should say, 'I risk committing a capital offense' (昧犯死罪) before speaking. The Han subsequently upheld this protocol" 秦以為人臣上書當言昧犯死罪而言, 漢遂遵之.[21]

Another related ubiquitous rhetorical commonplace answering the demands of decorum is the use of expressions of hesitancy or fear to promote an especially judgmental remark. These sites of hedging self-retraction, which in their hesitancy acknowledge the force of the remark, are marked by certain, in themselves unobtrusive, and yet psychologically effective, terms or turns of phrase: "in Your servant's humble opinion" (*chen yu yiwei* 臣愚以為, *chen qie* 臣竊, *qie* 竊), "Your servant has humbly overheard" (*chen qie wen* 臣竊聞), "I fear that" (*kong* 恐). These types of remarks are to be distinguished from remarks preceded merely by "in Your servant's opinion" (*chen yiwei* 臣以為) or "Your servant has heard" (*chen wen* 臣聞), a subtle, yet important, distinction. For instance, in Chao Cuo's address regarding the constant raids by the Xiongnu along the border regions, the distinction is visible at the very beginning, where Chao states:

> I, Your servant, have heard that since the rise of the Han, the Xiongnu vermin frequently have penetrated the border lands, smaller incursions bringing them smaller profits, larger incursions bringing them larger profits. At the time of the High Empress Lü, they invaded the area of the Longxi Commandery (the commandery west of Dragon Mountain) twice, attacking the walled cities and slaughtering the people in the townships, taking their animals and robbing them of their crops. Later they again invaded Longxi, killing clerks and infantry soldiers. It was an egregious act of banditry. I *humbly* have heard that "With the fearlessness that comes from victory in battle, the energy of the common people increases a hundred-fold. However, the infantry soldiers of a defeated army will never return." 臣聞漢興以來, 胡虜數入邊地, 小入則小利, 大入則大利; 高后時再入隴西, 攻城屠邑, 毆略畜產; 其後復入隴西, 殺吏卒, 大寇盜. 竊聞戰勝之威, 民氣百倍; 敗兵之卒, 沒世不復.[22]

The last two lines are what Chao seems to present as a culminating, and critical, judgment, for he prefaces them with a humilific, *qie*, "furtively," or more figuratively, "humbly." These concluding statements are pointedly judgmental in that they are openly and stridently urging the emperor

Salient Formal Characteristics of the Addresses 51

to take military action against the Xiongnu. If he does not, the passage suggests, the empire will be faced with destruction similar to, or worse than, that encountered during the reign of Empress Lü.

Criticism of any kind, but particularly criticism of executives, is the most natural and frequent site of indirection. The criticisms may be extremely subtle but also quite unflattering. Consider the following passage:

> From time to time, the Xiongnu have had a beneficent attitude and have returned the Han commoners that they had taken hostage and have not invaded the border regions. Even though they have had disputes[23] with the garrison and the agricultural settlements in the state of Cheshi, such is not sufficient to take it as[24] representing their essential attitude toward us.
>
> Now, I have heard that there are many generals who desire to initiate campaigns to penetrate the Xiongnu's lands. I, Your *benighted servant*, do not know what name to give to this type of campaign. Now the border commanderies are beset by hardship and deprivation. Fathers and sons share the pelts of dogs and goats, consume the seeds of wild grasses and grains, and constantly worry about not being able to keep themselves alive. In this scenario it would be difficult to begin a campaign. 間者匈奴嘗有善意, 所得漢民輒奉歸之, 未有犯於邊境, 雖爭屯田車師, 不足致意中。今聞諸將軍欲興兵入其地, 臣愚不知此兵何名者也。今邊郡困乏, 父子共犬羊之裘, 食草萊之實, 常恐不能自存, 難於動兵。[25]

This passage is the culmination of a categorical analysis of the manner in which and the purpose for which military campaigns are executed, an analysis, according to the dramatic introduction, in response to the emperor's desire to "take advantage of the weakness of the Xiongnu and send out armies to attack their right (i.e., western) territories, to cause them not to dare to again disturb the western regions of the Han empire."[26] Wei Xiang's criticism is harsh and unflattering, as evidenced by his "inability" to name the current campaign. Despite his categorization of previous campaigns, of which he is notably also critical, here Wei Xiang's inability to assign a name, almost certainly a refusal, is a forceful marker of disgust and disapprobation. The campaign is criticized for its wastefulness, its wanton, superfluous aggression, and the socioeconomic (and thereby moral) strain it involves, criticisms, coincidentally, that could have been applied to any of the former categories of campaigns of which Wei Xiang was critical. Most pertinent is that the ostensible object of the critique is the generals of the campaigns, when it is clearly suggested, given the narrative introduction, that Wei Xiang's ultimate target is the emperor himself.

This particular form of indirect critique, including some of its rhetorical markers, is a natural, and often necessary, feature of monarchic intercourse, one that is not limited to the Han situation, for we see it frequently in the *Intrigues* as well. A clear example appears in Su Qin's persuasion of the king of Wei for the alliance. After enumerating the (curiously inaccurate) geographic features of Wei that serve as defenses, its economic strength and military resources (human population and number of chariots and horses), Su Qin lambasts those who advise the king of Wei to align Wei with Qin, saying, "In my humble view (*chen qie* 臣竊) your state is no less powerful than [Chu]. But evil men (or, alternately, those who speak for the Horizontal Alliance) make plans for your majesty to seek relations with mighty and savage Qin to share in taking over the empire."[27] This might appear to be a direct criticism of the advocates for the (likely only legendary) group of states called the Horizontal Alliance that had agreed to fight for the militarily powerful state of Qin, were it not for a later critical remark, identifying the root of the problem as both "the craven persuasions from the king's ministers and the king's wish to be Qin's vassal." Clearly, the primary source of Wei's problem, and the true object of Su Qin's critique, are not the "craven" ministers. It is the monarch himself.

Cloaking partisan summary critiques, this decorous indirection of the addresses immediately affects, on a more general level, the overall epistemic quality of the evidence offered. Even the manner in which evidential premises expressly forwarded by the addressor to introduce a new phase in the argument of the address is circumspect, ubiquitously marked by the qualifying "I have heard that" (*chen wen* 臣聞). This qualifier is meant not merely to express a hesitancy by the speaker but also to condition the very source and validity of the evidence itself. It also disengages the speaker from any responsibility for guaranteeing the evidence's reliability, though to a lesser extent than those statements preceded by variations on "I have humbly heard that" (*chen qie* 臣竊聞 et al.). While it conditions the epistemic quality of the evidence, this disengagement does not of itself, however, automatically invalidate or lessen its epistemic weight.

The decorous indirection of "I have heard that" stands out when one notices that addresses from the emperor, even those that show stark similarities to ministerial addresses, completely omit any similar marks of indirection when offering evidence. Consider the following reply Emperor Wen offers to Li Guang 李廣, a Han military commander, when Li Guang apologizes for executing a drunken watchman who had forbidden him passage:

> The emperor replied: "Generals are the claws and teeth of the nation. The *Rules of the Marshal* says that when a general rides in

his carriage, he does not bow in greeting from the carriage bar, and when a death occurs, he does not don mourning. He calls out his brigades and deploys his troops in order to bring the unsubmissive to their knees, to unite the hearts of all the soldiers of the three armies, and to pool the strength of his fighting men. Therefore, when his anger blazes forth, there is terror for a thousand miles, and when his power is made manifest, ten thousand creatures bow low. In this way his fame may become known even to the Yi and Mo barbarians, and his awe and majesty strike fear into neighboring lands. To requite anger and wipe out injury, to cast off, to destroy, to do away with, to kill—this is what I expect from my generals! If you come with doffed hat and bare feet, knocking your forehead on the ground and begging for punishment, you will be fulfilling no wish of mine! Now, General, you will be good enough to lead your troops and turn the shafts of your wagons to the east, slowing your pace at Po-t'an so as to keep an eye on Yu-pei-p'ing while autumn is at its height." 上報曰:「將軍者, 國之爪牙也。司馬法曰:『登車不式, 遭喪不服, 振旅撫師, 以征不服; 率三軍之心, 同戰士之力, 故怒形則千里竦, 威振則萬物伏; 是以名聲暴於夷貊, 威稜憯乎鄰國。』夫報忿除害, 捐殘去殺, 朕之所圖於將軍也; 若乃免冠徒跣, 稽顙請罪, 豈朕之指哉! 將軍其率師東轅, 彌節白檀, 以臨右北平盛秋。」[28]

In terms of its content and general format, the emperor's remarks could well have been made by a minister. He begins with a textual reference with which he grounds his claims regarding the responsibilities of a general. He then briefly elaborates on the reference employing broad generalizations in his account of what the ideal general should try to accomplish: bringing the unsubmissive to their knees, uniting the hearts of soldiers and armies, and carefully deploying his forces for the maximum effect. He adds striking literary flourishes in his description of the general's countenance. The general's anger "blazes" forth, there is "terror for a thousand miles," and he causes the ten thousand creatures to "bow low." He then ends with a concise summation of the general's duties. All of these features are common to ministerial address: commencing with a textual reference, the use of broad generalizations, literary flourishes, and a concise summation. Yet in contrast to a minister, the emperor naturally does not employ the humilifics common to ministerial address. Where the emperor directly and brusquely declares, the ministerial would merely indirectly suggest, repeatedly inserting humilifics, such as "I have heard that," that would render the presentation of the evidence and the argument of the address less likely to bring about offense or an unfavorable reaction.

Indicative of a rhetorically submissive stance, the phrase "I have heard that" (*chen wen* 臣聞) precedes all manner of evidence,[29] from the legendary or that of imprecise generalization to that built on hearsay or third-party accounts to that which could be easily verified by the emperor and his courtiers. Following are three corresponding examples:

> I, Your servant, have heard that when the high ancient kings dispatched generals, they kneeled and pushed the axle [to the generals' carts], saying, "Within the city gates, I, the solitary person, make regulations, outside the city gates the generals make regulations. The degrees of merit, orders of honor, and material rewards to be awarded to members of the army are all determined abroad. Only when you return do you present them." This is not an empty saying. 臣聞上古王者遣將也, 跪而推轂, 曰:『闑以內寡人制之, 闑以外將軍制之; 軍功爵賞, 皆決於外, 歸而奏之.』此非空言也。[30]

> I, Your servant, have heard that the First Emperor of Qin, relying on the power of the Qutai Temple, placed All-Under-Heaven in the balance, delineated the boundaries [of law] and thus people did not commit crimes.[31] He applied military force to the Xiongnu and Yue. In the Qin dynasty's final days, Zhang Er and Chen Sheng, with the support of the united Vertical Armies, knocked at the gates of the Hangu Pass, and Xianyang (i.e., the Qin capital) was soon in danger of being conquered. 臣聞秦倚曲臺之宮, 懸衡天下, 畫地而不犯, 兵加胡越; 至其晚節末路, 張耳、陳勝連從兵之據, 以叩函谷, 咸陽遂危。[32]

> I, Your servant, have heard that the northern frontier barriers reach all the way to Liaodong. On the other side of the barrier lies Mount Yin. From east to west, the distance between the frontier barrier and Mount Yin is over a thousand leagues. [In this area between the frontier barrier and Mount Yin,] the grasses and trees grow luxuriantly and there are many wild beasts. 臣聞北邊塞至遼東, 外有陰山, 東西千餘里, 草木茂盛, 多禽獸。[33]

The primary function, it seems, of the evidence posited by such introductory phrases is to commence a new phase in the argument forwarded by the address.[34] However, the varying quality of evidence presented in this fashion raises questions regarding the weight assigned each type of evidence, that is, whether the addressor meant for each piece of evidence to carry the same quantity of epistemic weight, or to have the same rhetorical force for driving the address forward. It is important to note that although all three serve as some manner of evidentiary ground for the proceeding phase of the argument, their epistemic weight, from our perspective, is not identical. From our standpoint, the epistemic weight of the first, a representation of a practice drawn from the mythic past, the time of the "high ancient kings," and culminating in a proverb is compromised by the inherent (and almost certainly purposefully calculated) impossibility of verification. The second, an extremely common, almost hackneyed rhetorical device—the historical comparison—is phrased so as to be verifiable in some respects, for example, the Qin emperor's "applying military force" to the Hu and Yue tribes, but is mixed with statements that detrimentally impact our perception of its overall (justifiable) epistemic weight, such as the Qin emperor's supposed reliance—symbolic, religious, or otherwise—on the Qutai Temple. The third limits itself to observations that make no attempt at greater generalization. It directly, without much elaboration or literary ornament, presents what one could most easily deem "fact," something that lends itself to quick and easy verification.

CATEGORIES OF PROPOSITIONS IN THE HAN ADDRESSES

An extraction of commonsense propositions in the early Han addresses and an introduction to their rhetorical and argumentative interplay will follow in Chapter Eight. Here, I will simply expand upon what I defined broadly as the components of the addresses. As stated earlier, each address is composed of propositions falling under three categories: the propositions of general principle; the historic (or prehistoric) analogues; and the details that ostensibly inform (sometimes only obliquely) the issue under discussion. All three categories of propositions are usually present in the addresses, though occasionally one (rarely, two) might be missing. Their order is also not fixed. Addresses may open with a general proposition, but they might also open with a discussion of pertinent details or a historic analogue, offering general propositions for their organization only later in the address. Behind the inclusion of the three categories is a clear and forceful logic, principles providing the argumentative thrust; historic analogues, the memorialized precedent; and the details, the realm of the signified. All three are intended to serve an epistemic function, to delimit the aporetical space, the space of doubt.[35]

Propositions of general principle are most frequently attributed to an anonymous source (or even unattributed), short and to the point, though that point is not always made explicit.[36] In the addresses regarding military affairs, the counsel they proffer ranges from norms of political rulership, either practical or metaphysical, to the tactical principles of battle and warfare, to the socioeconomic consequences of war, to the relationship between ministers and monarch. Primarily, the aim of the advice is organizational, to direct the audience's (the executive's) attention to those facets of the matter that the addresser considers important and that will be (or have already been) enumerated or expanded upon in the course of the address. Secondarily, however, its aim is exhortative, a call to the audience either to ignore what the addressor deems petty or self-defeating notions or emotional responses, to focus on a de-emphasized or misperceived aspect of the matter, or, if the address attempts to offer an idealization of political or military rulership, to rise above the mean, uncompassionate, or defensive calculations that so frequently drive political decisions. These three secondary aims may be captured in the following categorical examples. The two selections below offer illustrations of the first type of secondary aim, the dismissal of petty or self-defeating notions or emotional responses:

> I, Your servant, have heard that the armies of the five thearchs and the kings of the Xia, Shang and Zhou dynasties achieved victory through completed preparations. In view of this, we should privilege strategy and disparage battle. To do battle and overcome one hundred times is not the most superior way. Better to first act as that which cannot be overcome and await the appearance of that which can be overcome in the enemy. 臣聞帝王之兵，以全取勝，是以貴謀而賤戰。戰而百勝，非善之善者也，故先為不可勝以待敵之可勝。[37]

> I, Your servant, have heard that those campaigns that are meant to rescue the nation from chaos and punish violence are called righteous campaigns. When one's campaigns are righteous, one is acting as a true king. If one's enemies exert military force against oneself and there is no other choice but to rise up against them, this is called a "responding campaign." Campaigns that are "responding" will succeed. In those situations where a dispute arises with another[38] over a trifling matter and the leader cannot contain his anger, such campaigns are called "campaigns of rage." Campaigns of rage will fail. In those situations where the campaign is taking advantage of people's lands and treasures, such a campaign is called an "avaricious campaign." Avaricious campaigns will be crushed. In those situations where the campaign relies on the great size of the nation, and is boastful about the multitude of their commoners and people, wishing to appear fearsome to the enemy, such campaigns are called "arrogant campaigns." Arrogant campaigns will be destroyed. These five categories are not simply abstracted from the affairs of men, they are also abstracted from the ways of Heaven. 臣聞之，救亂誅暴，謂之義兵，兵義者王；敵加於己，不得已而起者，謂之應兵，兵應者勝；爭恨小故，不忍憤怒者，謂之忿兵，兵忿者敗；利人土地貨寶者，謂之貪兵，兵貪者破；恃國家之大，矜民人之眾，欲見威於敵者，謂之驕兵，兵驕者滅：此五者，非但人事，乃天道也。[39]

Salient Formal Characteristics of the Addresses 57

In both of these instances, the principles advance a vision of warfare that reduces or eliminates costly campaigns, whether calculated in terms of human casualties, strain on the economy, or political unrest. They are, for good reason, introduced as hearsay, for they are meant to be critical of the manner in which the respective campaign is currently being administered. Yet while these principles are applicable to the current circumstances, their potential for application, as general principles, easily extends beyond them. Their presentation as principles insists on a change in the manner in which their audiences are ostensibly inclined to practice warfare, suggesting that the misguided behaviors confronted by such principles are long-standing. Neither professes an outlook that is particularly surprising or perceptive about the nature of warfare, which suggests that their inclusion is not to unveil a misunderstood or infrequently appreciated aspect of warfare, but to reemphasize an already well-understood but too often ignored commonplace: that wars well fought are not those in which masses are indiscriminately led to the slaughter but those that are a careful, well-placed direction of resources.[40]

By contrast, those propositions that focus on a de-emphasized or misperceived aspect of the matter are meant to reveal, or merely rediscover, something the audience is not considered to understand fully or to which he has apparently not given his full attention:

> There was a constant stream of people fleeing. Gangs of commoners began to thieve and rob and thereupon the difficulties in the region east of the Mountains (i.e., the central Yellow River plain, near Chang'an, the Han capital) began to arise. This is the situation which the *Laozi* describes: "Where troops have encamped, there will brambles and thistles grow." Military campaigns are inauspicious enterprises. If on one border there is an emergency, all four sides of the four border regions will be incited [to rescue it].[41] I, Your servant, am afraid that the emergence of upheaval and the creation of criminal behavior begins with this state of affairs. 亡逃相從，群為盜賊，於是山東之難始興。此老子所謂「師 之所處，荊棘生之」者也。兵者凶事，一方有急，四面皆從。臣恐變故之生，姦邪之作，由此始也。[42]

In this instance, the addressor employs the rhetorical technique of *epicrisis*, or the quoting of and commenting on a passage, a technique that is common in classical Chinese argumentative prose. Though its lesson—that warfare is a troubled and dangerous enterprise, with far-reaching, sometimes cataclysmic consequences—is not difficult to grasp, it is one that is frequently underappreciated until the costs incurred have caused irreparable damage to the political and social fabric. Other instances of this kind of proposition, for instance the one, quoted in a passage above, made by ancient kings upon dispatching generals to the front,[43] are less immediately accessible. In the passage, the addressing minister, Feng Tang 馮唐, cites an unattributed, apparently ritualized, declaration the ancient kings made to their generals just before their departure on a military campaign.[44] Simultaneous with his declaration, the king humbles himself before them, playing the part of a common foot soldier, or perhaps even an indentured laborer, symbolically announcing himself to be a lowly servant to his commanders. Yet he also, by using a traditional monarchical self-designation, "the solitary person," solitary in his rank and power, makes it clear that he is not a lowly servant, that he is merely acknowledging that he is dependent on the commanders to achieve his military objectives. What Feng Tang wishes to direct his audience's attention to is just the unavoidability of a division of labor that nevertheless preserves the status quo, and that without this division of labor, the king would not be able to reign. However, Feng Tang also wishes to emphasize, a point upon which he will elaborate at length later in the address, that this particular division of labor requires a potentially unsettling physical, and political, distance. The king, in setting his shoulder to the wheel of the generals' carts, initiates an action over which, as he will not be physically present, he will have a lesser degree of control. He will neither be able to control the movement of forces, nor, more alarmingly, be able altogether to prevent mutinous rebellion. The monarch sets his shoulder, in a way, to the possibility of the demise of his own political order.[45]

The distinction between these two secondary categories dividing propositions of general principle is subtle but important, the first category expressing what is probably accepted as generally true, already known or personally internalized, the second what may be understandable, but not—as it is centered on the realm of the possible, the uncertain, the future, those consequences that can be surmised only, that can be contradicted and rejected—within general understanding. Of the examples illustrating the first category, both set forth general claims that are easily accessible and of general experience: One, privileging strategic use of resources is infinitely better than, however strident and courageous, ceaseless and thoughtless onslaught. Two, the use of an army must not be for egotistical, vengeful, or self-aggrandizing ends; rather, it should be either for defense (the "responding" campaign) or for just cause (the "righteous" campaign). Of those examples illustrating the latter category, both set forth claims that are deniable, not immediately obvious: that military campaigns are inauspicious and lead to upheaval and criminal behavior and, second, that the military campaign can easily set into motion dangerous forces, forces that can lead to political demise. Only a monarch who is thoughtful or wise will be cognizant of propositions of this latter sort.

Salient Formal Characteristics of the Addresses 59

The final subdivision of principled propositions, those openly moralizing propositions that exhort the executive to rise above crass calculation and to aim for the ideal of leadership, are abundant in early Chinese literature. These frequently draw in mythic, or prehistoric, analogues as precedents that serve to demonstrate that high ideals have been not only reached before but reached by the esteemed originators of civilization. Interestingly, few of these idealized symbols of virtue are to be found in addresses on military affairs. When Ruist texts, often employed in the histories in the service of a moralizing agenda, are cited in the addresses on military affairs, their use is to reinforce the import and seriousness of war and the need for courage and determination in its pursuit. For example:

> The *Zhouyi* states, "The High Ancestor did battle with the Ghostly Border Region. After three years, he overcame them." The Ghostly Border Region denotes the lesser Manyi tribes (i.e., southern tribes, like the Yue). The High Ancestor is the magnificent Son of Heaven of the Shang. The statement about the magnificent Son of Heaven doing battle with the lesser Manyi tribes and defeating them after three years says that the use of the military cannot *not* be given weight. 周易曰:「高宗伐鬼方，三年而克之。」鬼方，小 蠻夷; 高宗，殷之盛天子也。以盛天子伐小蠻夷，三年而後克，言用兵之不可不重也。[46]

The citation above from the famously abstruse *Zhouyi* speaks nothing of specific moral or political virtues, nor does the interpretation that follows it. In the proffered interpretation, the citation appears merely to proclaim the gravity of warfare. If even the mighty High Ancestor needed three years to defeat minor barbarian tribes, then it is clear that a military campaign is not a matter to be treated lightly.[47] Another ancient classic frequently employed by Ruists for moralizing purposes, the *Book of Odes* (*Shijing*), is cited later in the same address, but, again, the message of the citation is not obviously moralizing:

> The *Book of Odes* says, "The King's way has been faithfully effected. The people from the regions of Xu (i.e., the Yi tribe that resided in the Huai River Valley area)[48] have already come [to submit]." This means that the way of the king is very great, so much that distant regions embrace it. 詩云「王猶允塞，徐方既來」，言王道甚大，而遠方懷之也。[49]

The addressor, Liu An 劉安, King of Huainan 淮南, questions whether the use of imperial military resources to attack the Yi and Di tribes is worthwhile. "How can the land of the foreign tribes be worth a single day of intervention?"[50] Like the citation from the *Zhouyi*, the *Book of Odes* quotation is by itself rather opaque. When read in the context of the entire poem, the quote would appear to have little immediate logical relevance with Liu An's query. In its received version, the poem eulogizes the terrifying martial might of King Xuan of Zhou 周宣王, his ability to overcome the then powerful Xu tribes. It would seem paradoxical that this quote, as embedded in the received poem (and we need not doubt that the poem, even allowing for adulterations and variations, would have been anything other than a eulogy), would be used as support of an argument *not* to send troops out to fight.[51] Only with a creative extension of its meaning—that the "virtue" or reputation of the emperor can, of itself, still hold sway over distant tribes—could one imagine that it has anything to do with the previous statements, or with moral (meaning nonviolent) conduct.[52]

This apparent lack of moralizing principled propositions does not mean that there is no moralizing in the addresses focusing on military affairs or that there are not a host of other addresses in the Han histories that mix statements about the pursuit of a military venture with a discussion of political leadership that frequently do refer to moralizing principle. In the addresses focusing on military affairs, moralizing is usually reserved for the sections discussing historical analogues or, less commonly, those miscellaneous details that inform the address. Those addresses in the histories in which there is a combination of discussion of political leadership and the pursuit of a military venture often wax eloquent and at length about the virtues of the ideal leader.[53] They almost inevitably are the products of those ministers typically classified as Ruists, deploying moral terms cultivated by Ruist thinkers—terms such as "benevolence" (*ren* 仁), "righteousness" or "social propriety" (*yi* 義), "ritual propriety" (*li* 禮), and so forth—terms that are not much in evidence in the addresses focusing on military affairs. In the addresses focusing on military affairs, by contrast, there are only a handful of places in which any moral terms appear. Usually, it is the relatively ambiguous terms of "social propriety" (*yi* 義) or "virtue" (*de* 德) that are emphasized.

There is a final, less forthright method of moralizing, but this moralizing is less informative about how the emperor should actively proceed in his affairs than how he should dispose himself. It appears in the idealized portrayals of the monarch, which usually present to the monarch a flattering image of himself (though sometimes very poignantly not),[54] portrayals that sometimes are neither elaborated upon nor seem to have much to do with later developments. In a way, these idealized representations can be seen as merely decorous phrases, phrases that are superficially meant to aggrandize the monarch, but are really stylized prefaces to advice or criticism:

> Your Majesty's virtue joins with Heaven and Earth, Your enlightenment as radiant as the sun and moon, Your charity extended even

to the birds and beasts, Your bounty proffered even the grasses and trees. If a single person were to die before reaching the end of his natural life due to cold and hunger (as could happen on a long campaign), Your Majesty would grieve. 陛下德配天地, 明象日月, 恩至禽獸, 澤及草木, 一人有飢寒不終其天年而死者, 為之悽愴於心。[55]

The addresser, Liu An, lauds the emperor to the point of hyperbole, declaring the emperor so beneficent that even the flora and fauna are favored. The emperor is so compassionate that if only one person were to die from other than natural causes, the emperor would grieve. Yet Liu An continues:

Now within the four borders no dogs are barking in alarm and yet Your Majesty's armed conscripts are being sent to their deaths. They are exposed to the elements in the Central Plains, their blood stains the mountains and valleys. Because of this, the commoners of the border regions shut their city's gates early and open them late [for fear that] morning will not last until night. I, Your servant, Liu An, humbly feel a deep concern for Your Majesty about this. 今方內無狗吠之警, 而使陛下甲卒死亡, 暴露中原, 霑漬山谷, 邊境之民為之早閉晏開, 朝不及夕, 臣安竊為陛下重之。[56]

The stark contrast is entirely calculated, an example of *insultatio*.[57] Through this contrast, Liu An is declaring the emperor to be very much the opposite to his idealized portrait. He is neither enlightened, nor charitable, nor munificent. He does not seem at all to grieve that men are dying long before their natural end. Instead, his unceasing military adventures result not only in premature death but in rampant violence and terror, violence "staining" the mountains and valleys like the blood of their troops, terrified commoners desperately, but fruitlessly, attempting to defend themselves. Morning, under Emperor Wu's rule, does not extend into night.

The above idealization ends in a particularly biting critique; other idealized portrayals, however, are not nearly so derisive. Often, their purpose is simply to coax the monarch to act in ways that will reduce the strain on his people. In his address, Hou Ying advises Emperor Yuan to guard himself against trusting the Xiongnu to defend the borders:

Now Your sageliness and virtue blanket vast areas, Heaven lays the Xiongnu low, and the Xiongnu receive Your life-preserving charity, bowing their heads and coming to court as Your servants. As for the psychological disposition of the barbarians, when they meet with trouble then they are lowly and submissive, when they are strong, then they are arrogant and rebellious. This is their Heaven-sent nature. 今聖德廣被, 天覆匈奴, 匈奴得蒙全活之恩, 稽首來臣。夫夷狄之情, 困則卑順, 彊則驕逆, 天性然也。[58]

Here Hou Ying criticizes the emperor, if anything, for excessive moral rectitude, not its lack, and cautions him not to deal too softly with the Xiongnu. He implies in his final comment that the Xiongnu will, if not monitored carefully, inevitably take advantage of the emperor's charity. Whether or not the emperor truly is sagely or virtuous is actually beside the point. It is against the prospect of the emperor's not reflecting on their possible ulterior motives that Hou Ying advances an idealized portrait. In this instance, being virtuous is determined to be to the emperor's disadvantage, a paradox that suggests that these terms are not meant to be taken as holding much actual moral content. Moral virtues, if propounded genuinely, should not contradict a recommended moral course of action.

It is to provide memorializing support for (or, when they are presented ironically, to contradict) proposed principles or the analysis of various particulars that historic analogues, the second of the three broad categories of propositions, are offered. The analogues can be taken either from the distant, that is, the mythic or prehistoric, past or from the more recent past. Those taken from the prehistoric past are superficially meant to be taken as relatively positive, while those retrieved from recent history, usually the Qin dynasty, most often negative. It is of some significance to note that only a very small minority of precedents are taken from the prehistoric past. In the following example, Mei Sheng 枚乘 cites stories regarding the ancient sage kings, Shun 舜 and Yu 禹, and the founders of the Shang and Zhou dynasties, Tang 湯 and Wu 武, in his attempt to dissuade the King of Wu 吳, Liu Pi 劉濞, from inciting a rebellion against the Han:

> I, Your servant, have heard that when wholeness is obtained, such results in complete prosperity. When wholeness is lost, such results in utter privation. Without having land enough to stick an awl in, Shun acquired All-Under-Heaven. Without even a group of ten households, Yu became the monarch of the feudal lords. The lands of Tang and Wu did not exceed one hundred leagues. Above not blocking the brightness of the three shining heavenly bodies (i.e., the moon, the sun, and the stars), below not injuring the heart-minds of the commoners, this is what is involved in possessing the technique of kingship. 臣聞得全者全昌, 失全者全亡。舜無立錐之地, 以有天下; 禹無十戶之聚, 以王諸侯。湯、武之土不過百里, 上不絕三光之明, 下不傷百姓之心者, 有王術也。[59]

Salient Formal Characteristics of the Addresses 63

One should first notice that the length and detail provided in the prehistoric precedent is not extensive. Because of its chronological distance and the lack of record, the prehistoric analogue, though perhaps meant to be treated as legitimate as more recent historic analogues, can offer only limited detail about the described situation or event. The prehistoric analogue merely provides an idealized standard by which the actions of the executive can be measured, although that standard, imprecisely defined, can serve as little more than a broad-brush critique. In Mei Sheng's address, the examples of the ancient kings are to emphasize the importance of moral and sagely rulership, and, by extension, to de-emphasize rulership supported by military and political might. He suggests that the King of Wu, like the ancient sage kings, would rise in stature just by being in tune with the natural order of things ("not blocking the brightness of the heavenly bodies") and showing compassion toward his people ("not injuring their heart-minds"). What such an *ethos* would entail is either expected to be understood or not important. The effect is simply meant to be rhetorical, an instance of *antisagoge*.[60]

By comparison, the numerous recent historical analogues are often full of informative, elaborate details, and frequently negative. Consider the following lengthy reference to the military actions of Qin:

> No one who has devoted himself to success in warfare and spent all his efforts on military endeavors has ever failed to regret it.
>
> In earlier times the First Emperor of the Qin, relying upon his overwhelming might in battle, nibbled at All-Under-Heaven until he had gobbled up the other warring states, and all areas within the four seas became one. His accomplishments rank with those of the rulers of the Three Dynasties (the Xia, Shang and Zhou). He devoted himself to overcoming his enemies without rest and wanted to go on and attack the Xiongnu. His minister Li Si remonstrated with him, saying, "This is not permissible. The Xiongnu have no cities or forts and no stores of provisions. They move from place to place like flocks of birds, and thus are difficult to catch and control. If parties of lightly equipped soldiers penetrate deeply into their territory, their food supplies will certainly become exhausted, and if we try to send provisions after them in order that they may continue on, the baggage trains will be too encumbered to make it in time. Even if we were to seize control of the Xiongnu lands, it would not be enough to profit us any, and even if we were to treat their common people properly, we could never subjugate or control them. And if, after we had won victory, we were to decide to massacre them, such would not be in accord with the way of being a father and mother to the common people. To weaken the Central States and lead to their

collapse, and thereby bring satisfaction to the Xiongnu is not a long-range policy." But the First Emperor would not listen to his advice and sent his general Meng Tian with troops to attack the barbarians. He extended the borders of the empire 1,000 leagues, making the Yellow River the frontier, but the land he won over was nothing but swamps and salty flatlands, in which the five grains would not grow.

After this the First Emperor sent forth the young men of All-Under-Heaven to control the frontier area at the north of the Yellow River. The troops and divisions were exposed to the elements for over ten years, and the number of dead was immeasurable. In the end they were not able to extend the empire north beyond the Yellow River. Surely this was not because there were not enough men, or because their weapons and equipment were insufficient? Rather it was because the circumstances did not allow it. The First Emperor ordered All-Under-Heaven to rush fodder and grain to the soldiers. Shipments were sent from [as far away as] the provinces of Huang, Chui and Langya by way of the seacoast commanderies and were transported to the frontier area at the north of the Yellow River, but no more than one picul out of an original thirty bushels arrived. Though men labored over their fields, there was not enough grain for the army. Though women wove and spun, there were not enough tents and hangings for the army. The commoners were weakened and exhausted. The orphans and widows, the old and the weak could not be fed, so that dead bodies were seen lying all along the roads. This was why All-Under-Heaven began to revolt against the Qin. 夫務戰勝窮武事者，未有不悔者也。昔秦皇帝任戰勝之威，蠶食天下，并吞戰國，海內為一，功齊三代。務勝不休，欲攻匈奴，李斯諫曰：「不可。夫匈奴無城郭之居，委積之守，遷徙鳥舉，難得而制也。輕兵深入，糧食必絕；踵糧以行，重不及事。得其地不足以為利也，遇其民不可役而守也。勝必殺之，非民父母也。靡獘中國，快心匈奴，非長策也。」秦皇帝不聽，遂使蒙恬將兵攻胡，辟地千里，以河為境。地固澤鹵，不生五穀。然後發天下丁男以守北河。暴兵露師十有餘年，死者不可勝數，終不能踰河而北。是豈人眾不足，兵革不備哉？其勢不可也。又使天下蜚芻輓粟，起於黃、腄、琅邪負海之郡，轉輸北河，率三十鍾而致一石。男子疾耕不足於糧饟，女子紡績不足於帷幕。百姓靡敝，孤寡老弱不能相養，道路死者相望，蓋天下始畔秦也。[61]

The Qin, the stereotype of the cruel, overly ambitious, bellicose regime, is not merely represented, as with prehistoric examples, by short selections from classic literature or terse literary sketches probably taken from common folklore, but instead is described in elaborate detail, as if to render it present. Indeed, immediately following this passage, Zhufu Yan tells a similar tale about the founder of the Han. This elaborate style, characterizing what I am calling "recent" historical analogues, is typical of anecdotes depicting events of the current Han era and of several earlier eras, up into the Spring and Autumn period. And the level of detail is of surprisingly similar character. Compare the above to the following passage in Liu An's address referring to recent Han-era events:

> Previously when the King of Nanhai rebelled, Your Majesty's former servant, King Li of Huainan, sent General Jianji to lead troops to attack him. Once his troops surrendered, the King of Nanhai was made to reside at Shanggan. Afterwards, he rebelled again. Just at that time the weather was hot and there was much rain. Soldiers on board the storied warships lived on the water and pulled the oars. Without having ever done battle, over half died of illness. Their family elders wept and cried, their orphaned children wailed, their households were destroyed, their enterprises were dissolved, and their families had to retrieve their corpses from over a thousand miles away, wrap up the remains and return home. The atmosphere of melancholy and woe did not dissipate for many years. Mature adults and the elderly take these circumstances as a warning,[62] even to this day. So without having invaded their territory, the disaster already reaches to this extent. 前時南海王反, 陛下先臣使將軍間忌將兵擊之, 以其軍降, 處之上淦。後復反, 會天暑多雨, 樓船卒水居 擊櫂, 未戰而疾死者過半。親老涕泣, 孤子諻號, 破家散業, 迎尸千里之外, 裹骸骨而歸。悲哀之氣數年不息, 長老至今以為記。曾未入其地而禍 已至此矣。[63]

In spite of the difference in their length, there are several points of similarity. First, the introductory background is depicted in gross outlines, with only a few names or places added to lend it concreteness. Second, in the description of the central event, both follow a familiar pattern: Troops are forced to undergo extremes of climate and terrain, which leads to exhaustion and illness and renders little or no military advantage. Inevitably, there is misery among the general population, whether because of the loss of the men or the demand for more supplies. Such leads to catastrophic consequences—the dead littering the streets, clouds of melancholy and woe hanging over all. In fact, the details of value to the modern historian are few: the names of the peoples involved and the places at which military action was taken or over which troops or supplies were moved, the types of defensive or logistical (e.g., wayhouses (*ting* 亭)) structures built, and so forth. Much of the analogue is devoted to what would be judged stock literary artifices: the foul and intemperate foreign climate; the exhaustion of overextended troops; the impatient, diligent, and frequently unrealistic commander.

Nevertheless, these literary tropes are not so indiscriminately deployed that the depiction of the historical event they describe is utterly inaccurate.

Certainly they are not used to describe prehistoric events. They highlight, in passionate, perhaps histrionic language, the real dangers of waging a campaign at the outer regions of the empire. Disease, exhaustion, depletion of supplies, social revolt—all of these are valid concerns, deserving of the attention and consideration of the executive. Their communication, rhetorically colored, does not lessen their import.[64] In fact, the risks they portray are almost identical, in type and manner portrayed, to those laid out in those details informing the current military campaign regarding which Liu An submitted his address. The lessons derived, the way in which concreteness and "reality" is bestowed, and the manner in which the risks are portrayed—there is a marked affinity, a similarity in evaluation and description between the recent past and the present. There is, in a sense, no functional gap between them. Their only salient dissimilarity is their level of detail.

Under the third category of propositions regularly found in the addresses are the miscellaneous concrete particulars deemed relevant for the addressor's recommendations regarding current actions. They are, like the recent historical analogues, often expressed with a literary flair: troops are massed in the tens of thousands or hundreds of thousands, commoners weep unrestrainedly at the loss of their loved ones, soldiers go to sleep hungry, generals fight with terrifying ferocity, the dead are pulled away by the cartload, and bandits are forced cold and deprived into uncivilized and uncultivated lands. At times, the details are presented in a methodical, matter-of-fact manner, seemingly complete in their scope; at others, they are merely hinted at by way of literary depiction or metaphor. In either, names and chronological periodizations, at the very minimum, seem to be accurately represented with regard to their overall contexts. In any case, details are rather sparing, limited to a couple of sentences regarding any one particular. Each topic of concrete import is only briefly mentioned, which, whether enforced or not, suggests a degree of literary or argumentative restraint. The order of the presentation of each topic is surprisingly logical, with points supportive of a certain train of argument carefully organized, though their relevance for the argument is only occasionally made explicit (this explicitness possibly operating as a rhetorical accentuation of their importance). And the matters touched upon are consistent and entirely relevant to military endeavors: the amounts of available or procurable provisions, the numbers of allied or enemy troops, the strength of the army and its military implements, geographical or climatological difficulties, likelihood of illness or physical hardship, the logistical support network (wayhouses, fortresses, etc.), the probability of friendly support from the general populace, and the psychological or ethical dispositions of those involved. Only the most comprehensive of the addresses discuss the majority of these matters, but even among those that do not there appears to be an understanding of what is at issue.

In terms of detailing concrete matters, one of the most methodical and comprehensive addresses is that presented by Zhao Chongguo, a general under Emperor Xuan. Over the course of his address, he touches on many of the issues listed above. Toward the end of his address, he enumerates twelve considerations supportive of his argument. The considerations are carefully arranged, the first six relating to positive actions that add to the overall military and economic strength of the border region, the seventh through tenth arguing the merits of avoiding conflict, and the last two arguing for preparatory measures, conserving resources, and making their delivery more efficient. His address is uncommon in its general lack of literary embellishments and complete absence of historical analogues. Zhao matter-of-factly lays out what he considers important to address, apparently little concerned with approbation or sympathy. His is the attitude of the technician, to speak about only what is necessary, and with utmost precision (though he is not invulnerable to some exaggeration). He lists exact quantities of provisions needed for his troops and their animals, the borders and size of the territory under contention, concrete plans for rehabilitating the infrastructure and encouraging agricultural production (thereby increasing tax revenues), the military strength of the enemy, and so forth. He moves quickly from topic to topic, laconically presenting his case.

We might believe that this would be the paradigmatic case of an address unbesmirched by rhetorical flourishes. Yet the details he presents, even in their very precision, are rhetorically drawn. For example, at the beginning of the address, Zhao offers two estimations of the provisions his troops will need, the first of which is as follows:

> For Your servant to feed the generals, the clerks, the *shi*-officials, horses, and oxen, Your servant each month will need 199,630 *hu* of rice and millet, 1,693 *hu* of salt, and 250,286 *shi* of hay. 臣所將吏士馬牛食, 月用糧穀十九萬九千六百三十斛, 鹽千六百九十三斛, 茭藁二十五萬二百八十六石。[65]

Surprisingly, these tallies do not accurately correlate with the second, which follows shortly thereafter:

> I wish to disband the cavalry and to retain the amnestied convicts, volunteers, and also the foot soldiers from Huaiyang and Runan, together with private attendants of the clerks and *shi*-officials, amounting in all to 10,281 men. Each month they will require 27,363 *hu* of grain and 308 *hu* of salt, to be distributed to the

strategically significant places in the settlements. 願罷騎兵, 留弛刑應募, 及淮陽、汝南步兵與吏士私從者, 合凡萬二百八十一人, 用穀月二萬七千三百六十三斛, 鹽三百八斛, 分屯要害處。⁶⁶

The above two calculations are the only ones that use exact figures; all of the other numerical estimations in Zhao's address are only approximate, rounded up to the nearest thousand or ten thousand. The precision of the above tallies is uncommon in the addresses on military affairs, and yet their precision is not strictly correlated, an arresting discrepancy, given how proximate these estimations are in the addresses and how simple the calculations to affirm their correlation are. Chen Zhi, in his commentary to the *History of the Former Han*, explains that the estimation of needed grain in the first passage is approximately 117 (actually closer to 118) times as much as the estimation of required salt. In the second passage, Zhao estimates that 10,281 men will need 27,363 *hu* of millet and 308 *hu* of salt, the ratio of grain to salt now around a multiple of 89.⁶⁷ Unless these figures are meant to denote a difference in status or rank, with the soldiers, clerks, and their attendants for some reason receiving more grain than salt, that these dispensations are inaccurate is odd.⁶⁸ Any inaccuracy, even if quite minor, indicates either an error in the transcription of the historical documents, whether by Ban Gu himself or a later copyist, or that the calculations were inaccurate to begin with. If the latter, we may wonder whether the precision of the estimations was for a rhetorical effect, to impress the monarch with an attitude of serious purpose and careful diligence. Whether Zhao Chongguo himself truly had such an attitude or merely affected such is not as important as whether the use of measurements and concrete language is meant to have a rhetorical effect. I contend that it is, that it is a relatively common rhetorical device, that the pretense of rigor is more important than the accuracy of the information. I will detail its place and function in subsequent chapters.

In contrast, there are addresses that are not restrained in their use of literary devices—metaphor, allusions, hyperbole, epicrisis, cataplexis, historical anecdote, and so forth—and appear, even in their discussion of salient details, more impassioned than an address such as Zhao Chongguo's. Their tone, when their aim is to provoke attack or, antithetically, to dissuade from engagement, is a sound of alarm and a call to immediate action. Their estimations of various particulars are composed to navigate between excessive worry and naive optimism. The enemy is close, an imminent threat, but he is manageable, if proper action is taken swiftly. The forces are exhausted and malnourished, but there is an alternate course that will revive the campaign as well as masterfully manage vulnerabilities in the defenses. Details, especially those pertaining to an argument for or against a campaign, are almost universally colored to contribute to the persuasion, their phrasing accentuating the emotional force of the risks involved or the recommendations for salvation. In the following, Li Zuoche 李左車, the Lord of Guangwu, offers an (unsuccessful) recommendation to Chen Yu 陳餘, the Lord of Cheng'an, about how to rebuff the campaign being waged against the state of Zhao by Han Xin. Portraying Han Xin as a murderous warmonger whose thirst for conquest will not be slaked, Li Zuoche obliquely hints that Han Xin's forces, having traveled so far, must be thoroughly enervated. The soldiers have a "malnourished look" and the troops "do not go to sleep with a full stomach." On a forced march and needing to travel quickly, Han Xin's carts of provisions are "sure to be" at the rear. He then presents his plan: to take a little-traveled road around Han Xin's army and, when they travel through a tight pass, cut off the troops from their supply wagons and simultaneously block their escape and their ability to search for new provisions. Meanwhile, the Lord of Cheng'an is to fortify his defenses and prepare for a siege, forcing the enemy troops to use up the remainder of their supplies:

> Now, the road through the Jing Gorge is such that two carts cannot drive side by side, nor two horsemen ride in formation. On a march of several hundred leagues in such a disposition their provisions are sure to be in the rear.
>
> I beg Your Majesty to lend me a force of 30,000 surprise troops which I can lead by an obscure route to cut off their supply wagons. If Your Majesty deepens his moats, heightens his ramparts, strengthens his camp, and forbids [his generals] to engage in battle, they will be unable either to advance and fight, or to retreat and return home. With my surprise force I will cut off their rear and cause these men from the wilds to have no way to plunder. Before ten days are out, the heads of their two commanders will be brought and laid beneath Your banners.
>
> I beg my Lord to give heed to Your servant's plan. If You do not, You will most certainly find Yourself the captive of these two men (i.e., Han Xin and Zhang Er). 今井陘之道，車不得方軌，騎不得成列，行數百里，其勢糧食必在其後。願足下假臣奇兵三萬人，從閒道絕其輜重；足下深溝高壘，堅營勿與戰。彼前不得鬭，退不得還，吾奇兵絕其後，使野無所掠，不至十日，而兩將之頭可致於戲下。願君留意臣之計。否，必為二子所禽矣。[69]

This very effective trap, whether it is historically accurate or not, is a commonly recommended strategy, one also found in the persuasions of the *Intrigues*.[70] Li Zuoche is neither insouciant nor irrationally exuberant. He is presenting a plan that, if the situation is as he describes, could indeed be quite effective in hamstringing the enemy. Naturally, there are any number of contingencies that could lead to its failure: a defending force protecting the train of provisions, the discovery of his troops by enemy scouts, the defensive measures not being adequate to rebuff the enemy's attacks, and so on. But the plan, nevertheless, is a good one and one that deserves consideration. For all of its bias and alarmist urgings, Li's portrayal of the situation is not ill-conceived.

Such impassioned characterizations do not, I argue, necessarily compromise these miscellanea. In fact, as with Pausanias or the medieval and Renaissance historians, details could be presented in a colored light without thereby wholly undercutting their epistemic weight. The representation of fact, whether in history or in the present, may merely have needed to meet the criterion of minimal plausibility. Thus for an addressor to assert that the road is not wide enough for two carts to travel side by side or that the enemy's lands are writhing with vipers and rank with pestilences, or that the foreign tribes, not being members of the human race, cannot be reasoned with, does not equate with prevarication or worthless distortion. The employment of literary devices is probably an attempt to highlight difficulties—the climate, the terrain, the enemy's habits—that are real and undeniable. Whether they are exactly "as represented" is not important for the addressor, or, I maintain, even for the addressee. The address is exhortative, a crafted composition that must, if it is to succeed, gain the attention and interest of the executive. For literary devices to be used to this end is not deceptive, it is efficient and wise, in spite of any Aristotelian hopes that the ungarnished "truth" will prevail.

CHAPTER SIX

Rhetoric in Opposition
Two *Zhanguoce* 戰國策 Addresses

HISTORICAL SITUATION OF THE ADDRESSES

Though the *Zhanguoce* 戰國策 (*The Intrigues of the Warring States*) represents events taking place in the Warring States period, it is by no means a genuinely historical document. Much of the material was clearly invented, not only its addresses but its representation of historical events. Nevertheless, Sima Qian clearly saw some of the stories it contains as sufficiently illustrative of a Warring States *ethos* that he included several in his *Records*, one of them being the political struggle between alliances advanced by two professional persuader-diplomats, Su Qin 蘇秦 and Zhang Yi 張儀. Their contest is symbolic of the larger confrontation between the mighty western state of Qin and its rivals. As an illustration of political address in the Warring States, I have chosen two addresses Su Qin and Zhang Yi presented to the king of Wei. At the time Su Qin and Zhang Yi appeared before the king of Wei 魏, Qin's major opponent was the southern kingdom of Chu 楚. As depicted in the stories of the *Intrigues*, Chu wished to stay, or at least defer, Qin's drive toward conquest by forging a "vertical" alliance with a group of states directly to Qin's east. Qin naturally wished to erode the ties of this alliance, by convincing the more geographically vulnerable central states of Han 韓 and Wei, vulnerable by dint of their being surrounded by essentially untrustworthy competitors, to switch sides and ally with Qin, forming a "horizontal" alliance. Whereas successful alliances with Qin contributed to Qin's ultimate hegemony, successful "vertical" alliances against it were fragile because, as Mark Lewis remarks, they "strengthened the preeminent ally and led the others to turn against it."[1] In the *Records*,

Su Qin was the official spokesperson for the "vertical" alliance, Zhang Yi for the "horizontal" one.

According to Sima Qian, the two addresses were presented to two separate kings of Wei: Su Qin's to King Xiang of Wei 魏襄王 (r. 334–319 BCE) and Zhang Yi's to his putative successor, King Ai 魏哀王 (r. 318–296 BCE). These reign dates are taken from the "Tables" (*biao* 表) in the *Records*,[2] yet some sources suggest that King Ai actually did not exist and that the reign dates ascribed to King Ai should be ascribed to King Xiang and those of King Xiang to King Huicheng 惠成, who, according to these sources, had an incredibly lengthy reign of over fifty years, from 370 BCE to 319 BCE.[3] There are several other possible chronological markers that could substantiate this alternate dating. One is Su Qin's reference to a "king of Zhao" dispatching him to Wei. Unless Su Qin was merely rhetorically "promoting" him to the same status as the king of Wei, that would have to have been King Wuling of Zhao 趙武靈王, who, according to the *Records*, reigned from 325 BCE to 299 BCE, for Zhao took the royal title only after ascending to the throne.[4] Second, Zhang Yi, according to the "Tables," had resigned his chancellorship in Qin, becoming chancellor of Wei in 322 BCE. But according to his biography, this was merely a political maneuver aimed at convincing the current king of Wei, apparently King Huicheng, to submit to Qin.[5] Dispatched by the king of Wei apparently in the following year, in 321 BCE, to Qin to beg an alliance, Zhang Yi returned to his Qin chancellorship.[6] Wei, however, surreptitiously preserved its alliance with the other states, mounting a joint attack in 318 BCE, the corrected first year of King Xiang's reign. The attack failed and Qin then in 314 BCE forcibly took Wei territory. Both of these markers would point to the possibility that both Su Qin and Zhang Yi are appealing to King Huicheng sometime before the attack in 318 BCE, with Zhang Yi addressing the king between 322 and 321 BCE and Su Qin between 322 and 319 BCE.

Regardless of whether this timeline is supported by the corrections to Sima Qian's chronology—and, indeed, Su Qin's very existence is in serious doubt—an analysis of both addresses seems to show that there is an awareness of the arguments of the other. The addresses are really merely representative of the major positions articulated to the king of Wei, whether they were ever presented by the two opposing figures of Su Qin and Zhang Yi. Indeed, from my analysis, the persuasions reveal an uncanny, improbable anticipation of the opposition's arguments, strongly suggesting that they were the work of a single author and were meant to be taken as representatives of the larger debate. The manifold difficulties with Sima Qian's chronology of this time period, and thus the historical background of these two addresses, I maintain, are in the end basically irrelevant for their analysis.

THE ROLE OF THE EVIDENCE

As I argued in both Chapters Two and Three, because full objectivity does not provide the most appropriate standard, in our analysis of the epistemic quality and weight of a proposition, or a class of propositions, the emphasis then must be solely on how the proposition(s) functioned *within* the addresses. The proposition's objective content, certainly, should not be completely ignored, but, as the discussion of the truth-content of fictional objects in Chapter Three showed,[7] it does not conclusively govern whether a proposition (or class of such) should be treated as epistemically weighty. We should instead seek to discover whether the proposition is exposed to some measure of doubt and how these doubts are expressed: what about the proposition(s) was defending against, or seems to have been defending against, possible skepticism? Skepticism directed toward the role propositions play in the argument speaks to their justificatory function, their epistemic weight. Skepticism directed toward the propositions themselves speaks to their epistemic quality. One way to expose doubts relating to the epistemic quality of the propositions, and thus to the extent that their quality directly bears upon the course of the argument, their epistemic weight, is to analyze, as I will shortly, adversarial addresses represented as being directed toward the same monarch on the same question. By closely observing how the addressors structured their responses, how they addressed each other through their responses, we become immediately aware of what they targeted for debate, what was contentious, and how they responded to unstated objections. We can also see what they held as worthy of epistemic weight. For instance, it seems, as often as not, that what was considered of note, of weight when characterizing the enemy were vague generalizations about the tactical strengths of the enemy or the size of their army or their fleetness of foot.

By assessing how propositions were cast as evidence, how particulars, principles, and historical precedents were meant to serve the addressor in his ultimate aim of convincing his audience, we can begin to describe their epistemic quality. We can assay what features of the proposition(s) prospectively influenced its role in defending the addressor's claims to the best understanding of the situation at hand and, by extension, the most useful suggestion for what actions the executive should take in response to the problems he faced. The propositions' epistemic quality must be linked to a standard of truth, a stable standard by which their epistemic weight, their justificatory claims can be assessed. Because truth cannot be equated with certain accuracy, we must turn to a more flexible notion of truth, one I have termed the "truth of the matter." As I define it, such a notion of truth must be determined by the gauge of pertinence to a broad aim, an ultimate end. For early Chinese addresses, indeed for all deliberative addresses presented to a decision-making body, the ultimate end, broadly conceived, is the good of the state. Naturally, assessments of the good of the state vary, as is what is emphasized as being central to its realization. Some examples of points of emphasis in the addresses are the following: the justifiable general use of the military, the role of moral or religious virtue in decision making regarding state action, the need and importance of peaceful coexistence with foreign tribes, and the value of exhausting the Han economy in pursuit of the domination, eradication, or civilizing reformation of foreign tribes. All of these points of emphasis impinge upon the need for, and the extent to which, military engagement is demanded by the situation under discussion. Indeed, the discussion of the military may ultimately be considered extraneous to the more fundamental problem at hand.

DEBATE'S ULTIMATE AIM: THE LEAVING OF AN IMPRESSION

Upon analysis, we will discover that, much like debates between our current politicians, the consequence was probably not genuine persuasion or thorough engagement with the issues but the leaving of the impression that the addressor had the best grasp of what was important for the good of the state and, as they contributed to such, about the issues under contention. True, the impressions left by the addresses were grounded in their asserted propositions, and these assertions did indeed respond to doubts and questions, but perhaps, one might object, it was just as much their manner and phrasing, their ornamental eloquence that contributed to their impact as their detail or pertinence, features relating to their epistemic quality. An address that argued against waging a military campaign, as did Zhao Chongguo's,[8] might elaborate on numerous specifics, but it might as well, and perhaps just as persuasively, have reiterated hackneyed stereotypes about one's foes and the difficulties of traveling to and through their lands. There is no one point at which the argument appears to be unavailable to all objection and the arguments of one's opponents thoroughly overcome. The arguments, it seems, could easily have continued on (again, much like our contemporary political debates), introducing additional points, whether to add new arguments or simply to distract from the weaknesses of previous arguments.

Nevertheless, as we will see, epistemic factors did play a role. Addressors did speak to one another's objections and did attempt to reduce or eliminate the objections' impression. Indeed, their engagements were not merely displays of eloquence. Addressors *argued* with one another, contested the validity of opposing assertions and propositions, however much they depended upon rhetorical devices in their replies. In addition, they also, often tacitly, acceded to certain common premises. Not everything was argued about or, presumably, even believed to be open to argument. So, for example, whereas two opponents might dispute about the probability of a small, centrally located state suffering repeated onslaughts by its neighbors, they do not dispute the basic premise that a state's geographic size and location, the size of its population, and the robustness of its economy are central factors in determining how strong the state is. It is not as if any of their arguments ever questioned fundamental premises, such as whether a white horse is a horse, as the infamous Warring States rhetorician Gongsun Long did, or, as the Greek rhetorician Gorgias even more provocatively queried, whether being is or is not nonbeing. Their arguments do not become embroiled in logic chopping or recondite questions of definition, however effective at distracting the audience from the issues at hand these strategies might have been. Clearly, there were some limits to what was permissible in political argument.

In addition, addresses attempted to remain coherent and consistent in their use of arguments. Thus concerns about internal contradiction were certainly present. Had the arguments merely rested upon displays of eloquence, these standards would not have been adhered to. That they contested the validity of opposing assertions and propositions, that they were concerned about internal contradiction demonstrates that addressors were concerned with epistemic issues—how they used evidence, what evidence they used, and what its effect would be, what impression it might leave. Even if opposing addresses spoke past each other, even if they did not always attempt to contest, and sometimes simply ignored, certain arguments, they nevertheless aspired to the relating of coherent and effective arguments for a certain "purpose" or, in my term, "vision." Of course, whether the addressors themselves were committed to the arguments they forwarded is moot and can never be known. But their own personal commitment, or lack thereof, is not essential to their addresses possessing a "vision." Personal conviction is obviously not necessary to obtain the conviction of one's audience.

Because they had to be prepared to defend their arguments, the addressors would have had to have been careful that the premises they used, whether they could be described as common sense or popular knowledge, were consistent with the vision they were forwarding. Commonsense premises do not necessarily accord, whether in assertion or consequence, with one another, but it would be damaging for his argument for an addressor to assert reputable premises that would diminish those he had asserted previously. For the argument to be coherent, the vision, whatever its acceptability to the audience, would have had to have been taken as a truth that had to be adhered to, and it's fair to assume, because arguments and conclusions were being forwarded, that it was. In my analysis of the addresses, I wish to determine not only how the commonsense propositions provided support for the address's vision, but to determine what epistemic relationship, if any, can be drawn between the commonsense propositions and the three basic structural categories[9]—general principles, historical precedents, and concrete particulars—in which they are embedded. Through such, I hope to discover what the epistemic function of the three categories was, whether these categories had any epistemic import, how they contributed to the thrust of the argument. In other words, how did these categories lend epistemic weight to the argument? Through an analysis of the address's other rhetorical features, that is, repeated emphases, eloquent elaboration, context within the argument, derived inferences, and so forth, can we determine the epistemic qualities each category had and the justificatory force, that is, the epistemic weight that the asserted propositions within each category expressed?

INTERPRETATIVE GOALS

If we wish to suggest that not just individual propositions but the defined categories of propositions are epistemically efficacious, or weighty, in our analysis of the addresses we must ask in what way does each class of propositions contribute to the establishment of the vision about the truth of the matter, that is, the evaluation of what is important in achieving the good of the state? In what way is it important for the "proof" that certain propositions are highlighted? Such is very difficult to assess, for although their apparent epistemic effect may be clear, without a phenomenological standard by which to judge their accuracy or the aim of genuine persuasion, in which rhetorical deviousness is not tolerated, their intended epistemic effect is less so. For instance, though concrete particulars cannot be treated as the objective factual ground, they appear to offer a general picture of certain elements conceived as essential for the representation of the problem under discussion. They may also, however, conceivably be data that serve to draw attention away from other more relevant particulars. Principled propositions appear to draw together or give meaning to particulars or historical anecdotes, abstracting for the audience what is being implicitly suggested by the particulars and historical precedents. But they may additionally just be devised to forcibly insert a didactic moral that has no unique independent claim to believability.[10] Similarly, the third category of propositions, historical precedents, may have been fabricated or altered to lend credibility to the moral expressed through the principled propositions.[11] Indeed, with all three categories, there appears to be no concern for their corroborability. As with any process by which abstract relations are woven together with the particulars that give them specificity and warrant, the true question, especially for political or ethical concerns, is not "Is this workable?" but "Is this the most workable alternative?" What is open is how many alternatives can be devised (and thus what responses might be available for one's political opponents). My estimations of their epistemic weight will be founded upon the substrate of the forwarded commonsense propositions.

A thorough analysis involves at least four levels of interpretation: one, at the most superficial level, the language of the statements of the addresses, how the statements can be translated; two, what propositions, whether premises or not, the statements of the addresses are asserting; three, what basic human needs seem to be at issue, seem to be informing what is being expressed and, thus, what commonsense propositions may be in play; and four, what the combined effect of the propositions suggests in regard to the overall vision of the address, what is considered central and essential to what it is suggesting to be the truth of the matter. The ultimate aim of these interpretations is to be able to discern the standard, the truth of the matter, with which we can turn back and assess what was placed in doubt, how the three classes of propositions were able to serve as evidence in answer to these doubts, and then, finally, to able to suggest some of the kinds of doubts that could have led to the failure, at the level of the epistemic, of the address. At every level of interpretation, of course, there is a hermeneutic openness and, consequently, the possibility for alternate, dissenting interpretations. Thus as I have previously mentioned, my analysis is necessarily provisional. My examinations are founded merely on the principle of charity, which asserts that, when interpreting texts, it is imperative that we give them the most reasonable, the least ludicrous interpretation possible. Hypothetically, there may be propositions that were actually asserting something I would have to deem nonsense. However, to assert such without attempting to find more sensible readings does a disservice to the text and our appreciation of it.

Comparative analysis allows deeper penetration into the workings of an address. Through such analysis, we can more rapidly and incisively analyze the strengths and weaknesses of the addressors' reasoning. An opponent's address, if directed to the same question, will attempt to expose propositions that were open to doubt. It can also, consequently, call into question his opponent's vision about the truth of the matter and can affect whether the address ultimately succeeds or not. For these two reasons, in this chapter I will lean heavily on insights afforded by two opposing addresses. My aims for this chapter will be the following: (1) extricating the premises that seem to be indubitable; (2) proposing what human need(s) seem to be informing these premises; and (3) with this complex of human needs and an analysis of the logic of the specific address, determining which of the indubitable propositions were candidates for common sense. (4) Once I have determined what appear to be commonsense propositions, I will attempt to determine their epistemic weight, that is, how they contributed to the establishment of what appears to be the truth of the matter. (5) Finally, I will offer tentative suggestions as to how the categories of propositions are themselves epistemically efficacious and what relationship their epistemic role has to the epistemic weight of the propositions they forward. The method and process of this analysis will serve as a model for the analysis of the Han addresses.

PREMISES OF THE DEBATE

Though the results of this analysis rely on only two exemplars, the addresses presented by Su Qin and Zhang Yi to the King of Wei, many of their epistemic features, as with their rhetorical features, are shared by the Han addresses. As mentioned previously, these two addresses, whose authors are portrayed as representing the opposing Vertical and Horizontal Alliances, were composed as if their authors were addressing not simply the same monarch but also each other. Indeed, the similarities in their structure and content are such as to give the impression that the addresses were offered in sequence, though it is unclear which took precedence. The addresses forward various commensurable premises, attack weaknesses in the other address's argument and structure, and offer rhetorical flourishes that seem to be meant to undermine their opponent's thrust. Such features display a remarkable creativity on the part of their author(s) in representing two distinctly structured and styled addresses, yet they consistently employ certain rhetorical and argumentative conventions. The structure of these conventions used in the text, not the individual persona of the narrator, is what I hope to highlight—that there are conventions and that these conventions are not associated with any particular personal style of addressing the monarch. What is of import for us is not whether the addresses could actually represent personal styles but how they speak to each other, how each address attempts to weaken the opposing position.

The addresses argue the question of whether a smaller state should join with other states and resist being overpowered by a large, aggressive state or accept probable invasion and domination by a larger state and thus a position of subservience. The first, arguing the former position, begins only with the introduction of the celebrated diplomat, Su Qin, his audience, the King of Wei, and his objective, to make an alliance between Wei and Zhao. I have broken the address into what I see as its natural structural, or rhetorical, breaks.[12]

When Suzi (Su Qin) was attempting to create an alliance on behalf of the state of Zhao, he persuaded the king of Wei, saying 蘇子為趙合從, 說魏王曰:

(1) "Within the lands of the Great King (i.e., the King of Wei), to the south there are the Honggou tributary, Chen, and the lands south of the Ru river. There are the city of Xu, the city of Yan, Kunyang, the city of Shaoling, Wuyang, and Xinqi. To the east are the Huai river,[13] the Ying river, the Yi village,[14] Huang lake, the cities of Zhuzao, Haiyan, and Wushu. To the west is the border of the Great Wall. To the north is the Area South of the Yellow River, Juan, Yan, Yan, and Suanzao (the latter four were all south of the Yellow River). The area of Your lands traverses a thousand leagues square. Though it is considered small, nevertheless all over there are peasants' huts and farm buildings, between which there is no space given for pasture for grazing cows and horses. Your population is so large, the number of horses and carriages is so many that it would take a whole day and night of constant parading for You to see all of them. They are indistinguishable from an army. 「大王之地, 南有鴻溝、陳、汝南, 有許、鄢、昆陽、邵陵、舞陽、新郪; 東有淮、潁、沂、黃、煮棗、海鹽、無疏; 西有長城之界; 北有河外、卷、衍、燕、酸棗, 地方千里。地名雖小, 然而廬廁田舍, 曾無所芻牧牛馬之地。人民之眾, 車馬之多, 日夜行不休已, 無以異於三軍之眾。

(2) "Your servant humbly estimates that the Great King's state is not a lesser state than the state of Chu. Yet the men of the Horizontal Coalition (alternatively, 'wicked men') plot for the King to establish diplomatic relations with the mighty tiger-wolf, Qin, to assist it in taking over All-Under-Heaven. Such would be to the eventual harm of the King's state, but these men will suffer no misfortune. Relying on the strength of mighty Qin, these men will steal from their lords. No crime is greater than this! 「臣竊料之, 大王之國, 不下於楚。然橫人謀王, 外交強虎狼之秦, 以侵天下, 卒有國患, 不被其禍。夫挾強秦之勢, 以內劫其主, 罪無過此者。

(3) "Furthermore, Wei is a powerful state within All-Under-Heaven. The Great King is a worthy ruler within All-Under-Heaven. Now for You to have a mind to face west and serve Qin, to call Your state its eastern buffer zone, to build imperial palaces for Qin, to receive its titled cap and sash, to present offerings to Qin for the annual sacrifices—this would lead Your servant to humbly feel shame on behalf of the Great King. 「且魏, 天下之強國也; 大王, 天下之賢主也。今乃有意西面而事秦, 稱東藩, 築帝宮, 受冠帶, 祠春秋, 臣竊為大王媿之。

(4) "I, Your servant, have heard that Goujian, the King of Yue, with three thousand soldiers from a routed army, captured Fuchai, the King of Wu, at Gansui.[15] With three thousand foot soldiers and

three hundred war chariots, King Wu of Zhou cut down King Zhou of Shang in the Shepherds' Wilds. What did it have to do with the number of their troops? Such was accomplished in all truth because they were able to project their fearlessness. 「臣聞越王勾踐以散卒三千,禽夫差於干遂; 武王卒三千人, 革車三百乘, 斬紂於牧之野。豈其士卒眾哉? 誠能振其威也。

(5) "Now, I, Your servant, have humbly heard that of the soldiers under the Great King, over two hundred thousand are infantry, two hundred thousand are blue-turbaned crack troops, two hundred thousand are strike forces, and one hundred thousand are support staff. You have six hundred chariots and five thousand cavalry. These greatly exceed those of Goujian, King of Yue and those of King Wu of Zhou. 「今竊聞大王之卒, 武力二十餘萬, 蒼頭二[十]¹⁶萬, 奮擊二十萬, 廝徒十萬, 車六百乘, 騎五千疋。此其過越王勾踐、武王遠矣!」

(6) "Now then You have been held captive by the persuasions of criminal courtiers and wish to serve Qin as its vassal. In order to serve Qin it would be necessary to apportion off land to pledge Your troth. Thus, without even having put Your armies into action, Your state would already be at a loss. 「今乃劫於群臣之說, 而欲臣事秦。夫事秦必割地效質, 故兵未用而國已虧矣。

(7) "All of those among the many courtiers who speak of service to Qin are wicked courtiers, not loyal courtiers. Any courtier who would apportion off his lord's lands in order to pursue diplomatic relations, snatching a day's success without giving thought to the consequences, destroying the communal household (i.e., the state) in order to build his own gate, outwardly relying on the strength of powerful Qin to steal from his lord, to urge him to apportion off land, I, Your servant, would wish that the Great King would carefully investigate him. 「凡群臣之言事秦者, 皆姦臣也, 非忠臣也。夫為人臣, 割其主之地以求外交, 偷取一旦之功而不顧其後, 破公家而成私門, 外挾彊秦之勢以內劫其主以求割地, 願大王之熟察之也。

(8) "The *Book of Zhou* states, 'If very short threads are not cut, how with the long do we make out? If delicate tendrils are not pulled, from these are then the battle-axe hafts culled.' If previous deliberations are not settled, later there will accrue great harm and then what can be done? If the Great King is truly able to heed Your servant, the six states will join in fraternal alliance with concerted purpose and united strength and there will certainly be no harm done by mighty Qin. 「《周書》曰:『綿綿不絕, 縵縵柰何; 毫毛不拔, 將成斧柯。』前慮不定, 後有大患, 將柰之何? 大王誠能聽臣, 六國從親, 專心并力, 則必無彊秦之患。

(9) "From his rude village, the King of Zhao has sent me as emissary to offer my foolish plans and present a covenant. I, Your servant, await the Great King's summons." 「故敝邑趙王使使臣獻愚計, 奉明約, 在大王詔之。」

(10) The King of Wei stated: "I, the Solitary One, am not worthy. I have never before listened to such enlightened teachings. Today, honorable lord, you come with a summons from the King of Zhao to summon [my state]. I respectfully join my state [with his in alliance]." 魏王曰:「寡人不肖, 未嘗得聞明教。今主君以趙王之詔詔之, 敬以國從。」[17]

Su Qin founds his address on various general premises, some of the more prominent being the following, listed in the order of their most prominent appearance in the text, with their corresponding sections noted in parentheses:

(a) Geographic, demographic, and economic considerations inform one's most basic military strengths and weaknesses. (#1)
(b) Small geographic size does not always imply military weakness. It can be compensated by a large population. A large population translates into a powerful army. (#1)
(c) A state with such a large population does not need to be subservient to a larger state. (#2)
(d) Being subservient to a larger state when it is unnecessary is not in one's best interests. In fact, it will lead to one's state's (and one's own) demise. (#2)
(e) It is shameful for a great, sage-like king who rules over such a large state to submit unnecessarily. (#3)
(f) One doesn't need enormous, overwhelming force to overcome a militarily stronger enemy. One only needs to convey an impression of fearlessness. (#4)
(g) It is shameful to capitulate when one's forces are more than adequate. (#5)
(h) Words/language can mislead. (#6)
(i) It is better to be clear than confused. (#6)
(j) Larger states will, once a smaller state submits, inevitably take advantage of the smaller state. (#6)
(k) Those who speak in defense of a larger state that wishes to take advantage of a smaller state are wicked and destructive of the public interest. (#2, 6, 7)
(l) One must think carefully to get clear on the issues that could inform one's decision. (#7)

(m) One should not trust those who have something to gain through their persuasion. (#2, 6, 7)
(n) One must act in a timely fashion to prevent future problems. (#8)
(o) When strong states join an enterprise, other (weaker) states will join as well. (#9)

With a comparative analysis of Zhang Yi's opposing address we can pinpoint those premises that were not called into question, suggesting that these were premises that were acceptable to either the addressor and/or believed to be held indubitable by his denoted audience, the King of Wei. Again, I do not aver that my proposed list of premises is exhaustive or could not be augmented or altered to reveal additional nuances. I am simply attempting to show that there indeed are premises that certainly seem to be held beyond doubt, by either the addressor or the audience, and that others are put into doubt within the opposing address. For those few that do not appear to be addressed in the opposing address, we must suspend judgment, although we can, I believe, based on the analysis, offer reasonable hypotheses about whether they could have been held as open to doubt.

Following is Zhang Yi's opposing address. Again, I have broken the address into what I see as the natural structural, or rhetorical, breaks:

Zhang Yi, forming Qin's Horizontal Coalition, persuaded the King of Wei thus 張儀為秦連橫, 說魏王曰:

(1) "The lands of Wei do not constitute a square of a thousand leagues nor do Your troops number more than three hundred thousand. Furthermore, in all directions Your land is level and open to the other feudal lords. Straight roads converge on it as do the spokes of a wheel upon its hub. Not a single notable mountain nor great river lies athwart them. From Zheng, the capital of Han, to Liang, the capital of Wei, is but a hundred leagues; from Chen, the capital of Chu, to Liang, slightly more than two hundred. A horse might gallop or a man run the distance and not feel weary on arrival in Liang. To the south of Liang are the borders of Chu; to the west are the borders of Han; to the north are the borders of Zhao; and to the east are the borders of Qi. On all four sides Wei soldiers stand guard and those defending the wayhouses and border fortresses are on alert. Grains are stored and transported along the waterways for not less than a hundred thousand troops. Wei is an ancient battleground because of its geographic position. 「魏地方不至千里, 卒不過三十萬人。地四平, 諸侯四通, 條達輻湊, 無有名山大川之阻。從鄭至梁, 不過百里; 從陳至梁, 二百餘里。馬馳人趨, 不待倦而至梁。南與楚境, 西與韓境,

北與趙境，東與齊境，卒戍四方，守亭障者參列。粟糧漕庾，不下十萬。魏之地勢，故戰場也。

(2) "If Wei joins with Chu in the south but not in the east with Qi, she will be attacked on her eastern front by Qi. If it joins with Qi in the east but not with Zhao in the north, Zhao will attack it on its northern front. If relations with Han are not harmonious, Han will attack from the west. Should Wei be at odds with Chu, then Chu will attack Wei from the south. These would be the way to 'four cuts and five rifts.' 「魏南與楚而不與齊，則齊攻其東；東與齊而不與趙，則趙攻其北；不合於韓，則韓攻其西；不親於楚，則楚攻其南。此所謂四分五裂之道也。

(3) "Now the lords who form the Vertical Alliance would have society safe, leadership respected, the military strong, and reputations widely known. They would unify the empire, make a covenant to be as brothers, sacrifice an unblemished white horse, and swear an oath on the altar at Yuanshui to support each other. 「且夫諸侯之為從者，[將]以安社稷、尊主、強兵、顯名也。合從者，一天下、約為兄弟、刑白馬以盟於洹水之上以相堅也。

(4) "But even brothers with the same father and mother quarrel over property. It is perfectly clear that nothing will be accomplished by depending on the many schemes devised by the false and deceitful Su Qin, who often changes his allegiances. 「夫親昆弟，同父母，尚有爭錢財。而欲恃詐偽反覆蘇秦之餘謀，其不可以成亦明矣。

(5) "If the Great King should refuse to serve Qin and Qin sent down its troops to the Area Beyond the Yellow River to take Juan, Yan, Yan, and Suanzao, to plunder the district of Wei and seize [Yangjin],[18] Zhao would not come south to rescue You, and Wei would be able to go north no more. If Wei cannot go north, then the road to members of the Vertical Alliance is cut off. With the road to the Vertical Alliance cut off, even if the Great King's nation would want to seek assistance [from the others in the Alliance] to eliminate the danger, it could not get it. 「大王不事秦，秦下兵攻河外，拔卷、衍、燕、酸棗，劫衛取晉陽，則趙不南；趙不南，則魏不北；魏不北，則從道絕；從道絕，則大王之國欲求無危不可得也。

(6) "Qin would carry Han with her in an attack on You; Han has been threatened by Qin and dares not disobey. When Qin and Han join together as a single state, Wei's destruction is definite. For these reasons I am alarmed for the Great King. Were I to make plans for the Great King, [I would suggest that] nothing would be better than to serve Qin. If You serve Qin, then Chu and Han would certainly not dare take any actions [against You]. With no concerns over Chu

or Han, the Great King might then rest back against His pillow, because His state would certainly have no troubles. 「秦挾韓而攻魏, 韓劫於秦, 不敢不聽。秦、韓為一國, 魏之亡可立而須也, 此臣之所以為大王患也。為大王計, 莫如事秦, 事秦則楚、韓必不敢動; 無楚、韓之患, 則大王高枕而臥, 國必無憂矣。」

(7) "Qin would like nothing better than a weakened Chu, and none is in better position to weaken her than Wei. Although Chu has a grand reputation, the reality is hollow. Though her troops are legion, they are quick to flee and easy to force into retreat. They do not have the mettle to put up a strong fight. Were You to muster all Wei's forces and attack southward, You would certainly overcome Chu. 「且夫秦之所欲弱[者]莫如楚, 而能弱楚者莫若魏。楚雖有富大之名, 其實空虛; 其卒雖眾多, 言[19]而輕走, 易北, 不敢[20]堅戰。[悉]魏之兵南面而伐, 勝楚必矣。」

(8) "Now to diminish Chu and augment Wei, to attack Chu and please Qin, to marry off Your troubles while keeping Your state at peace—this would be an excellent state of affairs. But, if the Great King does not heed his servant now, once Qin's armored soldiers have moved eastward, even were You to desire to serve Qin, You could not. 「夫虧楚而益魏, 攻楚而適秦, 內[21]嫁禍安國, 此善事也。大王不聽臣, 秦甲出而東, 雖欲事秦而不可得也。」

(9) "The men of the Alliance often wrangle with words but are seldom trustworthy. If one of them can persuade a king from among the feudal lords, he may ride off in one of the king's chariots; if he can commit a state to turn against Qin, he may acquire a fief in that state as his base. This is why every roving *shi* (i.e., every persuader) in All-Under-Heaven spends all day and every night grabbing his wrists,[22] bulging his eyes, and grinding his teeth to speak in favor of the Vertical Alliance and persuade leaders [of its benefits]. The ruler who is taken in by their words or led around by their persuasions— has he not been [merely] dazzled? 「且夫從人多奮辭而寡可信, 說一諸侯之王, 出而乘其車; 約一國而反, 成而封侯之基。是故天下之遊士, 莫不日夜搤腕瞋目切齒以言從之便, 以說人主。人主覽其辭, 牽其說, 惡得無眩哉?」

(10) "Your servant has heard, 'Many feathers will sink a craft, a pile of what is light will break a shaft ("axle," *zhou*).' Many mouths can melt metal. I would wish that the Great King would deliberate carefully about this." 「臣聞積羽沉舟, 群輕折軸, 眾口鑠金, 故願大王之熟計之也。」

(11) The King of Wei said, "I, the solitary one, have been stupid. My previous plans have all been wanting. I now beg to become Qin's hedge in the east, to build it palaces, to receive its cap and sash, to make annual sacrifices on its behalf, and to cede it my lands in the

Area Beyond the Yellow River."[23] 魏王曰：「寡人惷愚, 前計失之。請稱東藩, 築帝宮, 受冠帶, 祠春秋, 效河外。」[24]

Throughout his address, Zhang Yi's overall tone and direction is distinct from Su Qin's. In contrast to Su Qin, Zhang Yi does not speak to religio-moral or psychological dimensions of the problem (meaning to those aspects that call on the monarch's sense of self-respect), only to "hard" strategic considerations. In his address, one can abstract the following conspicuous general premises, again listed in the order of their most prominent appearance in the text, with their corresponding section(s) in parentheses:

(i) Geographic, demographic, and economic considerations define one's most basic military strengths and weaknesses. (#1)
(ii) Being centrally located and surrounded by a number of states means repeated military onslaughts. (#1, 2)
(iii) A centrally located, smaller state will need to bribe surrounding states in order to prevent military onslaughts. (#2)
(iv) Bribing one state will incur requests from other states. (#2)
(v) Affectionate relationships, however strong or morally/religiously binding, will not last under mortal pressure. (#4)
(vi) If one governs a weaker state, one needs allies to repel pressure exerted by a stronger state. (#5)
(vii) Initial actions that foretell greater, more detrimental military action will deter interference or resistance, if such seems to be unnecessary or pointless (e.g., Zhao not responding, Wei capitulating to Qin). (#5, 6)
(viii) If one cannot transact with one's allies, one will be vulnerable to devastating attack. (#5)
(ix) Large size (i.e., Chu's) doesn't imply great power. Power is defined by the force that one can apply to counter another force. (#7)
(x) Assisting another to defeat an enemy will result in profit to oneself. (#8)
(xi) If one does not take advantage of present opportunities, they may slip away. (#8)
(xii) One should (be more easily able to) trust those who have no self-interest motivating their persuasions. One should not trust those who have something to gain through their persuasion. (#9)
(xiii) Emotional displays do not mean genuine dispositions/beliefs. (#9)
(xiv) Words/language can mislead. (#10)
(xv) It is better to be clear than confused. (Thus one should be careful about those who try to confuse.) (#10)
(xvi) One must think carefully to get clear on the issues that could inform one's decision. (#10)

POINTS EXPOSED TO DOUBT

The premises that seem to be clearly accepted, placed beyond a certain level of doubt, by both addressors are the following:

1. Geographic, demographic, and economic considerations define one's most basic military strengths and weaknesses.
2. Words, and/or language itself, can mislead.
3. It is better to be clear than confused.
4. One must think carefully to get clear on the issues that could inform one's decision.
5. If one does not take advantage of present opportunities, they may slip away.
6. One should not trust those who have something to gain from their persuasion.

It is noteworthy to add that the majority of these premises are found at similar stages in both addresses, suggesting that there is an accepted rhetorical format or logic to their organization. These accepted premises are also those to which we ourselves could concede a level of acceptability, whether or not at a level similar to theirs. Of these, the only shared premise that is really relevant for the central argument of each address is the first. It is not explicitly stated, but only tacitly assumed by both addressors. However, whereas one, Su Qin, attempts either to distract the King of Wei from these concrete, strategically realistic considerations or to augment them with the addition of an ethical dimension, Zhang Yi, for either argumentative or stylistic reasons, does not draw upon—indeed he even speaks against (in #4)—such a dimension. Su Qin asserts the ethical or psychological demand (i.e., in defense of the king's public or the king himself) that the king not submit unnecessarily to the threat of invasion by a larger state. Zhang Yi directs the king's attention to the very real threat of invasion, defeat, and death.

Of the remaining listed premises, the majority are responded to in the opposing address. Some, such as Su Qin's premise (d) that a state with such a sizeable population does not need to be subservient to a larger state, are opposed openly and explicitly. Others, such as Zhang Yi's premise (ii) that being centrally located and surrounded by a number of states means repeated military onslaughts, are opposed more indirectly. Zhang Yi's premise appears to be contradicted implicitly by Su Qin's premises (b and c) that small geographic size does not always imply military weakness, being compensated by a large population, and a large population translates into a powerful army. Su Qin's premises indicate that while Wei is small and thus prone to attack, its population is so enormous that conquering it might require overwhelming force and sustained application of resources, commitments that the monarchs of threatening larger states might consider better spent elsewhere. Su Qin thus disengages the asserted connection between geographic size and the probability of military onslaught. While Zhang Yi's premise is usually correct, all else being equal, Su Qin emphasizes the points at which all else is not equal, thereby defusing Zhang Yi's unilateral claim. If we look over what I have suggested are some of the more conspicuous premises of each address, we see that many are explicitly or implicitly propositions in opposition to those made within the other address. Some premises, however, do not recommend the abstraction of a proposition strong enough to stand up to the opposing statement, nor do the inferences or conclusions that proceed from them. In Su Qin's suggestion, for instance, that Wei's joining the Vertical Alliance will prompt other states to join, we have no interpretable ground on which to demonstrate a clear defense against Zhang Yi's opposing claim, in (iii), that these alliances, built on nothing more than hopes of defense in unity and mutual regard, will not last under sustained mortal pressure from larger states. None of Su Qin's other assertions offer any defense against Zhang Yi's cynicism, nor really could they. Military alliances, particularly when they are among numerous smaller states that occupy a central and strategically important region, as was the case with the smaller states in the late Warring States period, are extremely fragile. If one member betrays the alliance, it upsets the entire fraternity and can lead to strategically disastrous consequences. All that Su Qin can rely on is the hope that the king of Wei's strategic calculations, based on the many particulars relating to political relationships between the kingdoms, to the probability of betrayal by the various adjacent kingdoms, to the benefits accruing from an alliance outweighing the potential consequences arising from openly opposing a larger state, to the shame and possible danger of being a subservient, and so forth, will lead him to join with the others. Nothing he could say could stand absolutely against Zhang Yi's cynicism. Su Qin, in some ways, has the harder case to make.

There are, of course, other premises that have no corresponding opposition, whether because the opposing addressor had nothing to offer against them or because they would have assented to them. In such a case, we cannot know, from an analysis of these two addresses alone, whether these premises would have been considered beyond reasonable doubt. Any hypotheses regarding such a question will have to await the analysis of other addresses from the *Intrigues*, for it will be upon the analysis of a larger domain of addresses that we can see which of the above uncontested propositions might have been considered, in general, to be beyond a reasonable doubt. Two examples of premises that do not appear to have opposing premises are Su Qin's tenth premise (j), which proposes, on my interpretation, that larger states will, once a smaller submits, inevitably take advantage of the smaller state, and Zhang Yi's seventh premise (vii), which avers that initial actions that foretell greater, more detrimental military action will deter interference or resistance, if such seems to be unnecessary or pointless (e.g., Zhao not responding to Wei's pleas for assistance and Wei's capitulating to Qin). It might seem reasonable to assume, based on common military principles, that these were premises that are so obvious that they could not have been contradicted, but such perhaps underestimates the addressors' creative powers. We certainly could imagine, for example, a response to Su Qin's premise suggesting an exception to his rule. Zhang Yi could simply have responded that Qin would not have done so, for whatever reason. Similarly with Zhang Yi's unopposed premise, we could imagine Su Qin posing an exception. Whether such unopposed premises should be construed as so beyond doubt as to be common sense or principles of popular knowledge that merely are left unopposed cannot be determined from this single comparative analysis.

My assertion has been that the premises that are laid open to doubt are certainly not those that could be treated as common sense, though they could be treated as popular knowledge. It could be asserted that it is popular knowledge that, as Zhang Yi asserts, overwhelming military might, in general, demands subservience, but as Su Qin's opposing claims demonstrate, it can be qualified and thus is open to doubt. This is not to say that any of the claims could not, on some interpretation, be qualifiable and thus open to some doubt, only that they are not presented as being open to doubt in these addresses, suggesting a level of axiomaticity that, in view of the rhetorical principle that proof need never engage with what is beyond doubt,[25] raises them to a level of acceptance that makes them candidates for categorization as premises of common sense. The struggle that will face us in the selection of commonsense premises from among those that appear beyond reasonable doubt is the determination of whether they accord with what Nicholas Rescher has justifiably asserted as a further criterion for commonsense premises, that is, that they speak to fundamental human needs. Our assertion of just what such human needs are will have to depend on what we can abstract to be the needs of the situation, as the situation is depicted in the address.

Unfortunately, this assertion of a fundamental human need grounding common sense risks raising the specter of circularity, of begging the question. In order to determine which of the undoubted propositions are serious candidates for categorization as common sense, we must assert the presence of a human need to which they are responding. But one could easily argue that we are simply manufacturing a dubious or highly generalized human need, such as, for instance, the need for conviviality or social contact, to justify the proposition's selection as a proposition of common sense. The universe of human needs is prospectively so vast that any number of them could be informing the direction of the address.[26] This is certainly true. Yet to say that a human need informs the direction of an address is not to say that it is central to it. If we are to doubt whether we can judge that a human need is central, such would merely call into question whether we can truly understand the addresses at all. Furthermore, my assertions have been governed by what appear to be human needs across a series of texts discussing basically the same problem—whether or not to go to war. While it is possible that there may be the rare exception of a need that is both completely beyond our ken and of import for only a single address, the majority, certainly, will be neither. And clearly, if a need is common, it should not be emphasized in only one address. If it is uncommon, then its assumption probably could not have been central for the persuasiveness of the address.

QUALITY AND WEIGHT OF THE EVIDENCE IN THE DEBATE

A more elaborate discussion of how and whether the members of this set of indubitable propositions function in the two above addresses as common sense is pursued in succeeding chapters, where I group and analyze candidates for common sense extracted from the Han addresses relating to military affairs. However, I here offer a sample, provisional analysis, based on the structure of these two opposing addresses alone, of the pertinent epistemic aspects of these two addresses, beginning with the evaluation of the epistemic quality and weight of the candidates for common sense. I suggest that, given certain shared rhetorical and argumentative features in the *Intrigues* and the Han addresses, there are commonsense propositions that the addresses of the *Intrigues* and the Han addresses relating to military affairs might share in common, propositions employed in similarly epistemic ways. Because of these similarities, the analysis of these two *Intrigues* addresses will serve as the model for my analysis of the Han addresses. Future analyses will presume and be based upon, but not explicitly conduct, examinations at the level of detail as I have so far conducted.

Above I observed six propositions clearly accepted by both addressors, only one of which, however, spoke to military concerns. The remainder aims at the appraisal of the arguments and decision making itself—with what attitude the executive should approach the opposing arguments and the time one should take to decide. On the surface, none appear to be terribly controversial—they are, in Geertz's formulation, "thin," representative of things as they uncomplicatedly are. Because they are unquestioned, one might expect their epistemic weight to be correspondingly great. But, despite this, the scope of the doubts they could possibly answer (e.g., what defines the state's basic military strengths and weakness?) and the answers themselves are too broad to provide much traction for the arguments. Their contribution toward the establishment of the truth of the matter is somewhat important, but general; their function as evidence is fundamental but limited. The first proposition establishes the basic parameters for assessing military strength; the rest establish just how (and how long) the arguments themselves should be assessed and what attitude the executive should maintain (an attitude of distance and skepticism) toward the arguments. Could they be considered as common sense? What needs might they satisfy that would sufficiently distinguish them from other propositions? For the majority, I suggest, the answered need is akin to Rescher's suggested general human need for relevant and reliable information: it is the need for reliable criteria and methods for the analysis of a concrete problem or a confusing set of factors, particularly when their presentation is prejudiced. They are also all substantially reinforced by general experience. The first, the most particularly and obviously salient for a discussion of military affairs, is reinforced by the general experience that these are the considerations that most pragmatically define how militarily strong a state is. The rest are sustained by the general experience of human persuasion and decision making and the consequences of thinking unclearly or delaying action when attempting to make decisions about complex matters. Though such general experience is not sufficient in itself to justify their selection as common sense, it is quite germane to their being considered as such. Finally, unlike the majority of the remaining propositions, none are worthy of any serious contestation.

Their categorization as common sense alone, however, is not sufficient to establish them as serving the most important evidentiary function for the addresses, as being the most epistemically weighty. This is, however, not surprising, for it is not uncommon for the commonsense premises to be those that merely lay the groundwork. As Aristotle noted, that of which it is important to persuade the audience are not the *endoxa*, the "reputable opinions," which are already recognized as authoritative, but those that are "proven" from them.[27] It is those premises that are open to objection that do more work for the addresses. Although the commonsense premises are epistemically fundamental and provide a basic justificatory function for the addresses, because they do less to move the argument forward, they are less epistemically weighty. Though they are primary, they are not the premises on which the argument is judged as standing or falling. In this sense, they are trivial. For example, in itself, the commonsense assertion that geographic, demographic, and economic considerations define one's most basic military strengths and weaknesses is an unopposed, basic premise, but it does not, of itself, lead to or substantiate the arguments and conclusions that follow.

And yet, when this commonsense assertion is evaluated with respect to what seems to be the truth of the matter for the two addresses, its inferential significance, and thus its epistemic quality, is altered. Its pragmatism is a necessary consideration but, for Su Qin, it is insufficient. While in Zhang Yi's address the first premise is held as preeminent, in Su Qin's, its epistemic quality is augmented by the assertion of an ethical dimension. For both Su Qin and Zhang Yi, I argue, their vision of the truth of the matter, their *zhi*, centers upon the definition of how a sovereign should dispose himself in a moment of extreme military risk. Should the king, as Zhang Yi recommends, bow to the concrete, the fact that, in terms of geography, demography, and economy, Qin is vastly superior to Wei and compromise whatever dignity he possesses (if not shortly his own life)? Or should he, as Su Qin recommends, maintain such dignity, press on against overwhelming odds, retain faith and courage in his ability to overcome, to rally his population, and, by joining the Vertical Alliance, persuade other (presumably weaker) nations, to embark upon the incredibly dangerous and portentous task of waging war against Qin? Su Qin's vision—that the sovereign, in order to be a sovereign, must remain independent and thus contest Qin's domination—compromises the epistemic quality of the first premise, that is, that geographic, demographic, and economic considerations define one's most basic military strengths and weaknesses. It is uncontested and yet, his recommendation suggests, it must be augmented by how one conceives of oneself as a sovereign. A strong military in the hands of a weak sovereign is substantially weakened. Similarly, a weak military in the hands of a strong sovereign is strengthened. The question for the king of Wei is—can he be confident enough in himself to maintain his dignity, and his life? Or must he relinquish his sovereignty, bow to the power of Qin in the hopes of saving himself? Clearly, once he submits to Qin, his options are considerably limited. Qin will be able to remove him, to place spies in his court, to send courtiers to govern, to take hostages. On the other hand, if he defies Qin, given the instability of the political alliances supporting the Vertical Alliance, he may soon find himself militarily overcome. Not an easy choice, indeed.

HUMILIFICS INDICATING THE TRUTH OF THE MATTER

It is perhaps not a coincidence that what I propose as Su Qin's and Zhang Yi's visions of the truth of the matter are indicated by those statements that are qualified by humilifics or an expression of internal disturbance.

In Su Qin's address, there are three, which are the following (here marked with italics):

1. "Your servant *humbly* estimates that the Great King's state is not a lesser state than the state of Chu. (#2)
2. "Now for You to have a mind to face west and serve Qin, to call Your state its eastern buffer zone, to build imperial palaces for Qin, to receive its titled cap and sash, to present offerings to Qin for the annual sacrifices—this would lead Your servant to *humbly feel shame* on behalf of the Great King." (#3)
3. "Now, I, Your servant, have *humbly* heard that of the soldiers under the Great King, over two hundred thousand are infantry, two hundred thousand are blue-turbaned crack troops, two hundred thousand are strike forces, and one hundred thousand are support staff." (#5)

In Zhang Yi's address, there is one (again, the humilific is marked with italics):

> If the Great King should refuse to serve Qin and Qin sent down its troops to the Area Beyond the Yellow River to take Juan, Yan, Yan, and Suanzao, to plunder the district of Wei and seize [Yangjin], Zhao would not come south to rescue You, and Wei would be able to go north no more. If Wei cannot go north, then the road to members of the Vertical Alliance is cut off. With the road to the Vertical Alliance cut off, even if the Great King's nation would want to seek assistance [from the others in the Alliance] to eliminate the danger, it could not get it.
>
> Qin would carry Han with her in an attack on You; Han has been threatened by Qin and dares not disobey. When Qin and Han join together as a single state, Wei's destruction is definite. For these reasons I am *alarmed* for the Great King. (#5,6)

The three remarks made by Su Qin all cajole the king not to sell himself short too quickly and become Qin's vassal. In two, the first and third, he calculates that Wei's power and stature are considerable, equal or greater than that of Qin's most formidable enemy, Chu. Su Qin substantiates both, however hyperbolically. Wei is as mighty as Chu because of the enormity of its population and its armies. Because Wei's power is so substantial, it is shameful for Wei to hastily submit to Qin's demands. But Su Qin is careful to anticipate doubts about his estimation of Wei's power by asserting that even if Wei were not as powerful as Qin, were the king of Wei to behave as Goujian, King of Yue, or King Wu of Zhou, Wei would still be strong enough to overcome a mighty enemy. Whether or not Wei has sufficient resources or manpower to overcome Qin is entirely dependent, Su Qin insinuates, on whether, like King Wu of Zhou or Goujian, King of Yue, the King of Wei has the strength of character and wit to outmaneuver Qin. The crux of Su Qin's address is to forward a vision of a sovereign who does not flinch at facing his opponents, regardless of their size. This vision is emphasized in his statements preceded by humilifics.

What Zhang Yi "humbly" recommends is for the King of Wei to accede that his situation is extremely precarious, that his state is endangered not only by Qin but by all other surrounding states as well. Throughout his address, Zhang Yi accentuates the willingness of the other states to betray and invade Wei, or simply demand that Wei parcel itself off to avoid invasion. His main point is that he is "alarmed" that the King of Wei might be foolhardy enough to believe that Wei could defend against Qin's incursions by forming alliances with the other states. All Qin needs, Zhang Yi states, is the assistance, however begrudging, of a neighboring state such as Han, the right to pass through this neighbor's lands and move swiftly against Wei. Even if Wei were to join an alliance with the other states, and the other states were to honor that commitment, Qin could, with well-placed attacks, destroy the Vertical Alliance's infrastructure and physically, or psychologically, deter the other states, for example, the great state of Zhao, from intervening. Zhang Yi aims to ensure that the King of Wei will see his situation as hopeless, his destruction definite, unless he joins with Qin. But Zhang Yi does not wish the King of Wei to believe himself or his state impotent. He mollifies any sense of shame by suggesting that Wei would be essential in Qin's quest to overcome Chu. The essence of Zhang Yi's argument is a vision of sovereignty in which extraordinary courage is a defect. For Zhang Yi, the best sovereign is one who acknowledges his weaknesses and accepts a short-term humiliation in order to survive, to retain his sovereign status.

SUCCESSFULLY MANAGING DOUBT

Neither address, of course, is indisputable, even if we ignore their possible inaccuracies. Often those places at which the argument appears to be its most vulnerable carry the most epistemic weight for the argument. Doubts relating to the asserted propositions that could lead to the argument's failure could be directed at just such places. In the case of Zhang Yi's address, there are numerous places at which Su Qin could, and occasionally did, raise questions. Contrary to what Zhang Yi proposes, centrally located small states may not be forced to endure repeated military onslaughts (ii).[28] It is also not inevitable that neighboring states will, upon noticing Wei's weakness and willingness to negotiate with them for its security, immediately make their own demands (iii, iv); nor is it impossible that affectionate relationships, or political relationships, could last under severe external pressure (v). Preliminary military actions may not deter interference or resistance (vii); nor is it definite that one will be vulnerable to devastating attack if one cannot transact with one's allies (vii). There are numerous additional doubts relating to issues not discussed explicitly in Zhang Yi's address: the ability of Qin to overcome the Vertical Alliance, the attenuation of Wei's status in its service to Qin, how Qin would prevent the allies it has among the smaller states from defecting, and so forth. All of these doubts could be damaging for Zhang Yi.

With Su Qin's address, there are just as many opposing propositions that could lead to his argument's failure, some of which Zhang Yi raised in the course of his address. Following are those he either tacitly raised or could have potentially raised:

1. While small geographic size does not necessarily imply military weakness, it is an indicator of it (b).[29]
2. Being subservient to a larger state, even when one's state has a large population, may still be in one's best interests (c).
3. It is not shameful for a king to submit to a larger state, particularly when it may be to his ultimate benefit (e).
4. Fearlessness is not sufficient to overcome a superior military force (f).
5. Even when strong states join a risky alliance, smaller states may still not join (o).
6. Qin is so overwhelmingly powerful that it will crush Wei's forces.
7. Even if Wei were to join the Vertical Alliance, Qin would easily be able to isolate Wei from its allies.

The objections and doubts that these opposing propositions raise would be substantial enough to give even the most doughty and independent-minded of leaders pause.

But the success of either address does not depend on their propositions' indubitability, their immunity to query. As will be discussed in more detail in Chapter Seven, the evidence presented in a rhetorical address is, at best, merely probable rather than definitive.[30] Neither addressor needs to prove that his propositions are immune from critique to prevent the failure of his address. He needs only to direct the king's attention to those that appear to be probable and reasonable, such as the assertion, which Zhang Yi forwards repeatedly, that Qin's military strength is immense, capable of not only forcing the subservience of Wei's smaller neighbors, such as Han, but also dissuading larger and more powerful states, such as Zhao, from intervening. Both Zhang Yi's and Su Qin's necessary objective is to leave the impression that they possess a comprehensive understanding of the situation and that their assessments are sufficient to move the king to action.

What then would cause Zhang Yi's or Su Qin's address to fail ultimately? How could their addresses go wrong? With evidence being merely probable, with the end goal being an impression, with the debate being fundamentally open-ended, what would a mistake look like? For either address to fail, the king of Wei would have to doubt not only the reasonableness and relevance of their assertions but also that they capture what is essential to the evaluation of Wei's situation. In addition, the king of Wei could doubt the wisdom of their advice regarding what action to take. He could question the merits of pursuing the proposed course of action and the probability that Wei's situation would be improved by it. These doubts are not directed primarily toward the statements themselves but toward the main concern involved in the arguments, which, I argue, centered on the assertion that Wei's compromising its sovereignty is the only way to ensure its survival. In Zhang Yi's case, the king would have to doubt that the survival of his state depended on the assistance of Qin and, furthermore, that his self-conception as sovereign would not be compromised. For Su Qin's address, ruinous doubts would be those that questioned the ability of Wei to profit from an unstable alliance with the other states and that this alliance would be sufficient to guarantee protection from Qin's onslaughts, or, if Wei were unallied, that it could defend itself alone. Su Qin's address also has the additional pressure of overcoming any doubts that the king of Wei has about himself and his abilities as a statesman and military commander. For either Zhang Yi or Su Qin, failure would be for the king not to correctly conceive himself and what is necessary for the survival of his state.

For these doubts to be epistemically efficacious, for them to lead to the improvement of the argument, they must be answerable; they must lead to either clarification, explanation, or correction. Indeed, Su Qin's address makes clear that doubts were answered, if only prospectively. As discussed earlier, Su Qin anticipated that the king of Wei might disagree with his estimation of Wei's military power and explained that, even if Wei were not as powerful as Chu, it need not be so powerful to defend against Qin.[31] This explanation, this elaboration and extension of Su Qin's argument that Wei does not need to capitulate, alters the epistemic quality of the proposition that Wei already has sufficient force to overcome a militarily stronger enemy (in my list, propositions (b) and (c)) by allowing for a possible exception, that perhaps, in Wei's current situation, overwhelming military force is not required. The place of the primary claim, that is, that Wei's forces are adequate, is thus compromised relating to the security of the conclusions that can be drawn from it, that is, that they can overcome Qin, but its justificatory force is not negated. Su Qin's general claim is that

Wei's forces may be sufficient to overcome Qin, regardless of how large they are. The difference is only Su Qin's suggestion that Wei's king would contribute to the success of his forces by being a strong leader.

If we see the statements forwarded by Su Qin and Zhang Yi as attempts to reinforce their arguments against doubts, then we become quickly cognizant of the explanations and clarifications they use to defend against doubts. Su Qin defends his flattering estimation of Wei's forces by allowing that, even if they were not a multitude, in the hands of a strong leader, they would still be sufficient. Zhang Yi defends his argument for the inevitability of Qin conquering Wei in numerous ways: by insisting that Wei will be weakened by the demands of its neighbors; that the members of the Alliance will not be faithful to the Alliance; that when Qin invades, even the larger members of the Alliance won't intervene; and that small, neighboring states will be cowed into assisting Qin.

Explanation or clarification are the means, most generally, by which addressors responded to doubt. Self-correction was rare, perhaps because the evidence presented was vague and general enough not to require it and because it would entail the admission of a flaw, rather than of a simple "misunderstanding." Such admissions could, one may imagine, entail the rejection of the addressor's case and a refusal to hear him again. Explanation and clarification also allowed for the addressor to "save" his argument by reconstructing it in the face of damaging objections or doubts. Instead of retracting his argument, he would merely need to offer another aspect of it that would either lead the argument on another tack or revise, subtly or not, what had already been presented.

In our assessment of the epistemic function of statements and propositions, we should not forget to note that their reinforcement of the monarch's self-perception; their contribution to a flattering but also possibly self-improving impression is important. For an addressor to offer a proposition that is flattering or emotionally supportive, as Su Qin and Zhang Yi both do, is to give it more emotional weight and thus, in some measure, more epistemic weight, a weight that is grounded in what the king perceives to be true about himself and will contribute toward his being convinced. This is not, however, to say that the most sugary, sycophantic addresses are those that are most likely to win approval. Most sovereigns were too aware of the willingness of ministers to fawn over them to be persuaded by openly manipulative statements. But were the appraisal to be perceived as honest, complimentary, and relevant to the argument, its value would not only be emotional, it would be epistemic. Deluded or not, sovereigns placed an epistemic value on their own standing and self-impression. Their belief in themselves as power holders, as executives, as moral leaders is an assertion of knowledge, even if their associates and servants would disagree. Again, in a culture where accuracy was not central, its claim to knowledge was rooted in providing some weight in offering arguments for how a situation should be described and what action should be taken.

EPISTEMIC FUNCTIONS OF THE THREE CATEGORIES OF STATEMENTS

Are there then any important epistemic functions associable with the categories of statements appearing in these two addresses? In Su Qin's address, for example, is there any particularly salient and relevant epistemic function that accompanies the historical anecdotes about the King of Wu and Goujian, King of Yue? Certainly. They offer psychologically reinforcing exemplars of strong men who, we must assume, fought against overwhelming odds. The classical sources that mention Goujian's campaign—the *Intrigues*, the *Records of the Grand Historian*, and *Zuozhuan*—cite details that reinforce Su Qin's message. With Wu of Zhou, as an almost prehistorical mythical figure, classical sources cite fewer details regarding his campaign and the odds he faced. But the absolute accuracy of these stories is obviously not the point. It is to *suggest*, to point to possible exemplars, whether or not their actions were actually as represented. With this historical anecdote, Su Qin wishes to encourage the King of Wei to act heroically, with self-confidence and courage. Thus the epistemic function of the anecdote is to recommend a course of action that, in itself, does not appear particularly appealing or profitable.

In terms of statements of general principle, unlike those in many of the Han addresses, those employed in Zhang Yi's and Su Qin's addresses are not important for the thrust of the argument. In Su Qin's address we have the statement from the *Book of Zhou* in section 8, which states, "If very short threads are not cut, how with the long do we make out? If delicate tendrils are not pulled, from these are then the battle-axe hafts culled." In Zhang Yi's address, we have the unattributed statement, "Many feathers will sink a craft, a pile of what is light will break a shaft." Furthermore, while it is not a "principled" statement per se, because it is not asserted as a statement of principle as the others are (and as most in the Han addresses are), Zhang Yi also forwards a general statement, in the fourth section of his address, about the tendency for families to quarrel over their possessions (as the members of the Vertical Alliance would quarrel over their borders). Among these three examples, only the last is central to either's argument. The first two are expressed at the end of the addresses, serving to emphasize the difficulty of the decision-making process, of arbitrating between conflicting advice and finally deciding what to do. Because they are not essential to the arguments being forwarded, they do not provide an important argumentative thrust. They do, however, attempt to limit the king's tendency to doubt himself and his advisors, to procrastinate. They reemphasize what the king almost certainly already understands: that not all advice is good and that a decision, to be effective, must be made in a timely fashion.

Finally, as in Zhao Chongguo's address, the third category of propositions, those regarding the concrete particulars, while they are frequently presented in a matter-of-fact manner, with little literary embellishment, their effect is almost purely rhetorical, to represent the case as either addressor believes it is necessary to justify his argument.[32] Both Su Qin and Zhang Yi offer geographic details that substantiate their case. Su Qin enumerates at length the territories and waterways that are within Wei's borders. Zhang Yi emphasizes the short distances that lay between Wei's capital and the capital of adjacent countries. Both addressors' accounts may or may not be accurate, but what is more important is the salience of the details for the substantiation of their argument. Similarly, the sample battle plan for a Qin invasion that Zhang Yi forwards may or may not be accurate. Yet its presentation is enough to preclude its realization (for the king of Wei would surely be careful to prepare later for such a line of attack). They are merely meant to reinforce the impression that successful battle plans are easily imaginable. We may presume Zhang Yi's example is only one of many.

For Su Qin, it appears, it is the historical precedents and the emphasis of a hoped for courage that are the greatest driving forces of his argument. Thus they carry the most epistemic weight. The details he offers regarding the impressive size of Wei, the size of its population, and the size of its military forces are necessary but do not serve as the axes of his argument. They are offered merely to convey the impression that what he recommends is not completely ungrounded in Wei's concrete circumstance. For Zhang Yi, on the other hand, the details regarding Wei's circumstance—its proximity to other kingdoms, its unstable relations with them, the ease with which Qin could level an attack against Wei, and the possibility that Wei could act in an important way in an attack against Chu—are the focus and the crux of his argument, providing the most epistemic weight. Without these details, Zhang Yi's argument is a succession of perhaps only empty threats. Without the historic precedents and an insinuation of the possibility of success with the show of courage and fortitude, Su Qin's argument is composed only of flattery and warnings of the dangers of domination.

CHAPTER SEVEN

Commitment to the Facts

THE CONVICTION OF THE EMPEROR: FOUR WISE MEN CONVINCE LIU BANG

As mentioned earlier, because the executive's response recorded in the *Intrigues* is usually laconic, it is almost impossible to be sure of the influence of the epistemic aspects of the addresses presented to him. In other words, it is not clear that his beliefs about the truth of the matter were, or could have been, altered. By contrast, the Han histories have examples of more extensive executive responses. One thus has the opportunity to verify that, at least in some cases, the persuasions and rhetoricized addresses presented to the executive were meant to achieve conviction, that is, the firm establishment of an affirmative belief or disposition (as opposed to the audience's mere entertainment of the proposal or being cursorily swayed). Furthermore, one can be almost certain that conviction was at times achieved. One particularly notable instance is found in the biography of a highly influential senior advisor to Liu Bang, Zhang Liang. The relevant anecdote reveals the High Emperor, Liu Bang, being forced to arbitrate between conflicting pressures and his primary inclinations and purposes being overcome by more compelling concerns because of the advice offered by a minister.

Around the time of the Han general Ying Bu's 英布 revolt in 196 BCE, Sima Qian reports that the High Emperor decided to get rid of the heir apparent, Liu Ying 劉盈, and replace him with Liu Ruyi 劉如意, his son by the Qi 戚 consort. Before embarking on the campaign to put down the rebellion, the emperor is reported to have fallen ill.[1] He thus made plans to send Liu Ying to lead the attack against Ying Bu, hoping, we can presume, that Liu Ying would be killed in the fighting. A group of four elderly advisors, who had been recommended to Empress Lü by

Zhang Liang, advise Lü Ze 呂澤, the empress's eldest brother, to suggest to the empress that she find an opportunity to tearfully plead with the emperor not to send out the heir. Though the emperor may be unwell, they argue, he should be told that he would be better off taking command himself. If he sends out the heir, the generals will not support him, and once Ying Bu becomes aware of this, he will take advantage of their dissent and move his troops westward to attack. Were the emperor himself to command the troops, the generals would not dare not to follow orders. "To put the heir apparent in command of a group of men such as this," they assert, "is like sending a lamb to lead a pack of wolves. None of them will be willing to do his best for such a leader, and the failure of the expedition will be assured."[2]

Lü Ze takes their advice and speaks to the empress, who pleads with the emperor exactly as the four advisors had suggested. The emperor's quoted response, which follows immediately in the text, and the record of his succeeding actions demonstrate that the reader is meant to believe that he paid attention to, and was in some way convinced by, the empress's attempt: "The emperor said, 'I have thought it over. My incompetent son is not fit to be sent out, so I, your lord, will go myself.' Thereupon the emperor put himself in command and went eastward with his troops" 上曰:「吾惟之, 豎子固不足遣, 乃公自行耳.」於是上自將而東.[3] The emperor's denigrating reference to his son reveals his irritation at having his plot defused but he seems to understand and agree with the four advisors' estimations of the consequences. They very shrewdly raise epistemic doubts regarding whether Liu Ying was up to the job and force Liu Bang to weigh whether it was more important to successfully put down Ying Bu's rebellion or to do away with Liu Ying. The aim of these advisors was not merely to manipulate the executive, but to convince him, by employing propositions that carry epistemic weight, that their presentation of the matter and their recommendations for how to proceed were correct. We can see that their arguments did not rest on the raising of interpersonal doubts, or irrelevant slanderous remarks, but on very relevant epistemic doubts. Their ability to convince the emperor was not simply through eloquent artifice or unfounded assertions but by arguments and claims of significant consequence.[4]

EPISTEMIC QUALITY AND WEIGHT OF THE EVIDENCE IN THE PERSUASION OF LIU BANG

Using this short example, I can briefly articulate the epistemic quality of the evidence offered by the four advisors and of the doubts that could be raised against them. The four wise men forwarded their premises and arguments in response to or to guard against epistemic doubts, doubts that bear upon whether their understanding of the situation was correct. At least in part, the epistemic qualities of their claims, arguments, and implicit assumptions won the emperor over. The epistemic quality of the evidence is rooted in their plausible connection—each a distinct connection—to described events or general psychological or political constants that could be sufficiently justifiable for them to be accepted as worthy of consideration in the emperor's calculations.[5] The following are a sample list of evidentiary premises and possible reasons for their positive epistemic quality, that is, that they are treated as evidence, in themselves, as claims that both can be known and are probable:

1. The aim of the emperor is both to defeat the enemy and to get rid of the heir apparent.
   Basis: This is a reasonable psychological estimation of the aims of the emperor, based on his previous actions and his described negative relationship to Liu Ying and positive relationship to his Qi consort and her son, Ruyi.[6]
2. Ying Bu is a serious military threat.
   Basis: As described in the histories, Ying Bu is a powerful Han general with a sizeable army. The Han empire is not stable enough for it to allow for such a concentration of military might and rebellious intentions.[7]
3. The generals probably will not respond to the heir apparent's commands.
   Basis: Seasoned generals, in the majority, do not treat novice commanders seriously and would be insulted by the emperor's sending one to lead them.[8]
4. Many, if not all, of the generals would more likely respond to the emperor's commands than to those given by the heir apparent.
   Basis: Perhaps this is flattery, but it is flattery grounded in the probable political configurations of Han military power.

Upon the ground of these premises, the four wise men argue that, when faced with the choice of either defeating Ying Bu or getting rid of the heir apparent, because of the seriousness of the consequences of Ying Bu's rebellion, the political future of the emperor and the nascent Han state would be more secure were the emperor to choose to concentrate on putting down the rebellion and relinquish his aim of getting rid of Liu Ying, at least for now. None of the above premises, and thus the argument itself, rests upon anything more than vague appraisals of general situational particulars: psychological dispositions, military threats, the probability of defeat or success. Were the emperor to insist upon their careful, detailed justification, many would be difficult to justify precisely, for they are based on broad generalities or personal estimations. They are not in the category of slander or mere hearsay, but neither are they easily verifiable. Yet they all relate to the vision of truth of the matter expressed in their arguments, of what is of real and unavoidable consequence for the security of the state and the emperor himself. As I argued in the previous chapter, for early Chinese addresses, the ultimate end, broadly conceived, is the good of the state. The central issue, in this instance, is the state's military security. If the emperor wishes to preserve the state's, and his own, security, he commonsensically should not—to use a cliché—send a boy to do a man's job. In plainer terms, the commonsense basis that the four wise men are emphasizing is simply that military ventures are risky and benefit from an experienced hand.

The epistemic weight of the forwarded propositions must be evaluated somewhat differently from their epistemic quality. With epistemic quality, as explained previously, I refer to the features that make the proposition a knowledge claim in itself (which of course include the consequential implications that can be drawn from it in itself). Epistemic weight, by contrast, is the manifestation of how the qualities of various propositions interact for the specific aim of conviction. Though these claims and arguments of the four wise men are all of definite, positive epistemic quality, their epistemic weight is varied, having to do with their place in the argument, their applicability to this specific circumstance, and their emotional or psychological effect. The weight of a proposition is the justificatory function it has in comparison or conjunct with other propositions employed in the argument. For instance, one might plausibly claim that, in general, major premises, for example, the emperor's aims, have greater weight than those minor premises to which they are applied, because of their wider applicability and relevance. Or that situational estimations are not as convincing as those drawn from extensive experience.

But can these distinctions of epistemic weight be *regularly* applied to the three stable rhetorical categories—statements of principle, historical precedents, and concrete particulars? Do they themselves carry distinct and discrete epistemic weight? In other words, is it possible to determine, from the epistemic vantage point, the point of conviction (and not simply manipulation), why one rhetorical category was used instead of another, for example, whether more or less weight was accorded to a historical precedent than, say, a statement of principle? How does one determine, if we wish to evaluate the three classes of rhetorical propositions in play in the addresses, whether a strictly "factual" proposition has more weight than a historical analogy or a statement of principle? I argue such a determination is not by any quality of the propositions themselves but by how they are related to other propositions, how and what place they hold in the argument. This still can be a categorical judgment—that is, one that applies to a category of propositions as a whole—but it need not be. For example, to place a proposition at the head of an argument chain and then to elaborate on its consequences would appear to give that proposition more weight. In addition, to suggest a proposition as supportive of a flattering or an emotionally positive proposition is to give it more emotional weight and thus, in some measure, more epistemic weight, a weight that produces greater probability of conviction. That emotionally weighted propositions are relied upon is not to say that monarchs who are persuaded by them are misguided in their acceptance of them as justifications, that they are "deluded" by their own personal interests (although, from our postempiricist viewpoint, they are), but that they place an *epistemic* value on their own standing and self-impression. The executive's belief in himself as power holder, as executive, as moral leader is an assertion of knowledge, even if his associates and servants (and the populace at large, whose opinions counted for virtually nothing) would disagree. Thus the above claims all have some amount of epistemic, or justificatory, weight. Where we will see this as becoming most salient is in the place and function of moral considerations—what types of justificatory role they play and whether such are legitimate epistemic functions or manipulative ploys.

Of course, a monarch such as Liu Bang could pose reasonable objections to either the epistemic quality or weight of the claims, raising doubts about their relevance or import as they relate to the truth of the matter, namely, the need for the state to be militarily secure and thus for Ying Bu's revolt to be put down. The more devastating doubts, I would maintain, would be related to the epistemic quality of the claims, to their acceptability as knowledge claims in themselves, apart from their justificatory role in the address.[9] And because each claim would require a different manner of defense—to defend the supposition about Liu Bang's aims would require a different strategy than any defense of the generals' reaction to the heir apparent taking charge—we can say that the manner of the doubts to which these claims can be exposed and the method of inquiry and critique by which these doubts could be answered are different. Any method by which one could assess the generals loyalty to the mission, regardless of who leads it, would not be the same method—not in the means of questioning, not in the manner of the gathering of any salient evidence, not in the mode of analysis—as the method required to assess Ying Bu's military might and the threat of defeat by his armies. As the epistemic qualities of their propositions are thus varied, so too are the ways an error can have been made. Perhaps the generals would not have been unwilling to follow Liu Ying; perhaps Liu Ying might have surprised them with his leadership skills. Perhaps Ying Bu's armies were in turmoil and could easily have been overcome, in spite of Liu Ying's lack of experience. None of these doubts about the epistemic quality of the propositions were raised in the text, but such does not mean that they were not felt or considered.[10]

COMMITMENT TO FACTUAL ACCURACY IN THE HAN ADDRESSES

Even though some of the statements within the Han addresses are founded upon propositions of certain epistemic quality and carrying an amount of epistemic weight (as opposed to, say, those statements merely casting unfounded aspersions against another's character or impugning the credibility of another's statements), as I have claimed earlier, we should not assume that their presentations or recommendations were founded upon any solid commitment to factual accuracy or that adherence to accurate accounts was held as important in addressing the executive, whatever the subject matter being related. In the case of metaphysical principles or prehistoric exemplars, because of their generality and lack of specifying detail, that is, their lack of anything that would give them certain purchase in the present circumstances, clearly we cannot presume a commitment to their accurate representation or apposite application. Yet with historical exemplars of more recent vintage and concrete particulars—geographic, ethnographic, logistic, or otherwise—we might expect there to be more care given to their representation, for the simple reason that their very inherent specificity delimits the freedom a speaker could have, however broad, to present them with no consideration for the possibility of their verification. Accuracy may not play a role in representations of statements from texts for which absolute fidelity or incorruptibility was materially difficult (copyists could always have transcribed in error), yet accuracy should, one would think, play some role for the concrete particulars and recent memory. As mentioned in Chapter Five, even in Zhao Chongguo's remarkably detailed address accuracy does not appear to be the fundamental standard by which propositions were judged. Too often, the details were put forward only to buttress the overarching concern, what I have called the "truth of the matter." The psychological dispositions of the enemy's or one's own troops or leaders, the economic and logistical requirements for their movement and support, even the geographic spaces that must be traversed to meet with the enemy—all of this is flexible in its representation depending on what is required to express the truth of the matter. If, for example, the Xiongnu need to be seen as fierce and disloyal partisans who cannot be trusted and thus must be attacked, they will be represented that way. If the geographic space to be traversed must be represented as too far or too beset by natural boundaries to prove the point, then it will be represented that way. But this flexibility in the representation of various "facts" should not lead us immediately to criticize the historian for a lack of commitment to truth, for distorting psychological, geographic, or economic configurations.[11] Though we cannot completely rely upon the represented configurations, we can rely upon their justificatory function. They serve the purpose of proving the point of the address and driving the course of action forward. The address to Liu Bang, whatever its inaccuracies, did apparently, according to the historical records, convince the executive to act in a certain way.

Nevertheless, it is difficult to believe that there is no detail, no concrete particular whose accuracy would not be an inflexible constant. One possible exception that would not permit distortion is the representations of geographic space. To be sure, in its gross outlines, geographic space was not inaccurately portrayed. The area of the kingdom of Qi, for instance, was never depicted as being located to the west of Chu. But in the smaller details, there was much that was either exaggerated or represented without concern for its total accuracy, or even its plausibility, within the framework of the narrative. Often, just as with other spatio-temporal representations (such as distances), a location was not fixed, open to distension or contraction. There was no overweening concern for precision.[12] Within the narrative, troops were often moved across vast areas in impossibly short periods of time. The essential point was the determination and drive of the troops, and the efficient leadership of their commander. For instance, in Sima Qian's famously detailed account of the battle of Jingxing 井陘, though we have a time frame and a specific place for the battle, we cannot precisely locate in the current landscape where the battle actually took place, at least according to Kierman's assessment of available maps.[13] Even if it were to be precisely located, it would not be because of the reliability of the historical record. On the contrary, Kierman asserts, "the written tradition is for the most part rather counterproductive."[14] According to Kierman, many of the maps dependent on Sima Qian's account either are useful only to obtain a "relatively broad idea" or they do not cohere with descriptions of the movements of troops or they "enshrine" local traditions that are "incredible."[15] It is thus imprudent to expect that the analyses of the Han histories provided by Qing-dynasty or twentieth-century scholars could reliably ascertain the location of various localized geographic areas, given how they are employed, both relationally with each other and as loci for human action. While it is not impossible for maps dependent on the record to be somewhat accurate, we must take all historical representations as not necessarily striving for utter precision. Kierman himself acknowledges this, averring that what Sima Qian offers, while perhaps "fictional," is consistent with and reinforces other data, which certainly is not enough as basis for establishing precise locations.[16] In the addresses themselves, representations of geographic space was just as imprecise, if not more so, than in the narrative.

STRATEGIC CONSIDERATIONS IN THE ADDRESSES

Within those Warring States addresses or exchanges regarding military affairs that were recorded in the Han histories, the focus frequently is couched purely in strategic terms, with few references to general metaphysical or ethical principles and only occasional references to historical or prehistorical examples.[17] Across many of the addresses included in the *Intrigues*, much like Su Qin's and Zhang Yi's addresses to the King of Wei, there is a distinct rhetorical style of argumentation in which the addressor raises pragmatic concerns: the balance of allegiances, the psychological reactions of the parties involved, and the situational particulars that could inform whether or not a military endeavor should be pursued.[18]

This emphasis on strategic considerations did not, of course, end with the beginning of the Han. Indeed, many of the addresses from the early Han that spoke to military matters also focused quite determinedly on the concrete particulars relating to the assessment of military strength or weakness. While concrete particulars surely must have been believed to be of considerable persuasive value, as they dominated large sections of the addresses, they were not treated in themselves as independent and objective information. Liu (*né* Lou 婁) Jing, a professional counselor, attempted to persuade the first Han emperor, Liu Bang, that he should not locate the capital in Luoyang but instead should locate it in the lands of the former kingdom of Qin. Openly dismissing the emperor's self-comparisons with the kings of Zhou, whose capital had been located at Luoyang, he judges the emperor not to have sufficient moral probity to locate his capital in such a militarily vulnerable area. The Zhou house, once it declined, Liu averred, was unable to maintain its hegemony: "It was not that its virtue was too slight, but that by its geopolitical conditions it was too weak" 非其德薄也, 而形勢弱也.[19] The Han emperor, by contrast, has none of the moral force of the Zhou house, having caused much unwanted bloodshed and trauma, which he describes in emotionally charged terms:

> [Your Majesty has countless times caused] the people of the world's livers and brains to be smeared on the ground, and father and son to expose their bones in the fields; the sound of weeping has not yet stopped, the wounded have not yet risen again, and yet You want to make [the capital] as splendorous as the times of [Kings] Ch'eng and K'ang. I, Your servant, humbly consider there is no comparison [between these times and the time of Kings Ch'eng and K'ang]. 使天下之民肝腦塗地, 父子暴骨中野, 不可勝數, 哭泣之聲未絕, 傷痍者未起, 而欲比隆於成康之時, 臣竊以為不侔也。[20]

Liu Jing then goes on to list the geographic and agricultural advantages of the old Qin kingdom, its "vast and fertile" fields, the natural borders of the mountains and the Yellow River, and its large population, capable, in sudden need, of supplying a force of one million soldiers.[21] The emperor, not entirely convinced, consulted his various officials, who countered that, even with its many natural advantages, the Qin dynasty did not last much longer than the reign of the First Emperor, while the Zhou dynasty lasted for hundreds of years.[22] The emperor is then described as still unresolved when Zhang Liang "made clear to him the advantages of locating the capital within the Pass."[23] The emperor then immediately set off to the old Qin lands beyond the Hangu Pass, newly determined to establish the capital there. Thus, at the last, the doubts of the emperor shifted from epistemic to interpersonal, from the reliability of the information to the reliability of the source. It was only when Liu Jing's recommendation was supported by Zhang Liang's that the emperor made up his mind.

What is exceptional about this passage is not the presence of the interpersonal element in the resolution of the emperor's doubts but the fact that relevant concrete factors were not in themselves sufficiently convincing to the emperor, even though the objections to Liu Jing's proposals posed by the emperor's various officials were insubstantial and could easily have been responded to by Liu Jing himself. It thus seems that their epistemic aspect was, in itself, compromised by political circumstance. The conviction of the emperor about his course of action did not proceed from the overcoming of his objective epistemic doubts. Neither did the discussion lead to merely a reconfirmation of what he already believed. Instead the address reveals that his epistemic doubts had to be assuaged by a personally trustworthy source. To the weight of politically compromised concrete particulars there had to be added the force of a perceived personal loyalty, of an allied and trustworthy source. In this and many of the other early Han political discursive interactions, it is painfully clear that there often is no actual objective, genuine discourse about the course of action the executive wishes to take, no careful weighing and consideration of what is important for reasonable deliberation of the issues. No class of proposition, no persuasion in itself, necessarily could bring conviction with it. At times, the epistemic value of the evidence is acceded to only when the source is considered reliable. The evidence is not therefore itself impugned; it is merely dependent upon trustworthy confirmation.

However, we cannot therefore simply dismiss all discursive interaction as molded simply by personal prejudice or allegiance. As in the example above, we see that the issues raised are germane and to the point. The topographical details of the landscapes of the old Zhou and Qin lands are being thoughtfully compared and presented to the emperor. Surely, their presentation should mean that the emperor was believed to have been interested in such. It is only that the information itself, as I will argue in a later chapter, was not expected by the emperor to have been unadulterated, unsullied by political allegiances or hopes for personal advantage.[24] By their being presented to a figure of prominence, concrete particulars were, in all probability, automatically suspect, for the emperor's very position of influence made distortions and manipulations common. It is no wonder then that there was no secure concern for accuracy in political discourse. For there to have been a concern with accuracy, there would have to have been a faith in the value of accuracy and that there were sources that would have been trustworthy in themselves, that would have been trusted *as* accurate. Whatever the emperor was looking at, whatever information he received, could not have but been treated as coming from its particular source, one who, in the protean monarchic environment, was never fully trustworthy. Perhaps even the historian did not consider them trustworthy. Indeed, many of the addresses recorded in the Han histories are driven by "information" classifiable only as hearsay or slander. It is thus no surprise that emperors refused, or were just reluctant, to heed the reasonable advice of their courtiers, even though the actions they took directly or indirectly impacted the permanence of the contours of the empire and, ultimately, their hold on power and their lives.[25]

THE INCREASED PROMINENCE OF MORAL CONCERNS IN THE HAN ADDRESSES

In military matters, the goal is to overcome or destabilize enemy forces, aborting their plans for further military confrontation. To the furtherance of this end, basic operational and strategic matters would seem to be the only matters of any importance. For the persuasions of the *Intrigues*, this was largely the case. Yet commencing around the beginning of the Han era, the histories reveal a discernible and consistent interjection of moral concerns into military matters. Such moral concerns were present, as mentioned previously, not only in the addresses of moral didacts but also by matter-of-fact generals and statesmen. An insistence on the awareness of moral issues, it seems, pervaded even the most unsentimental of governmental affairs, revealing the moral aspects of military affairs to be quite important, almost as central, if not *as* central, as the nonmoral aspects. I will later propose that certain moral propositions were treated as reputable popular knowledge.[26] Though not all addressors discussed moral matters, in none of the addresses from the early Han were they dismissed out of hand. One might even argue that the general necessity of the projection and consideration of moral demands was widely accepted as to be practically beyond doubt, that is, common sense. Abundant research has been conducted on the insinuation of moral demands, especially Ruist (i.e., "Confucian") moral demands, in the early Han. Michael Loewe, in his *Faith, Myth and Reason in Han China*, remarks that

> The major change that was accomplished in Han is sometimes described as the victory of Confucianism . . . [H]ad any statesman

needed to define the objectives of government in, say, the first century [BCE], he might well have professed the aim of serving humanity, by providing for human welfare and improving living conditions. Such an ideology corresponded with the ideals believed to have informed the administration of the kings of Chou . . . These ideas included the principle that human quality and potentiality may be improved by noble leadership; that moral precept and example are more effective than coercion; and that government is not justified in imposing force on individuals save in the last resort, or so as to protect them from evil.[27]

In itself, the rising prominence of the moral is no unprecedented development. Moral concerns are frequently introduced in the anecdotes of *Zuozhuan*. What is of import for this study is not the presence of moral matters but their inclusion in the official Han-era addresses preserved in the early Han histories. Compared to the more conversational exchanges of *Zuozhuan*, many of the Han addresses are more formal in their rhetoric. If we can take this formality as pointing to the addresses being representative of how actual early Han state business was discussed, an analysis of these addresses allows insight into how exactly moral matters affected, and were used as evidence for, discussions of state business as brutal and unfeeling as military campaigning. For moral lessons to have been included so frequently must have meant that they were deemed of some effect. My concern is whether that effect was merely ornamental or more substantive, as claims holding similar, if not equal, epistemic weight to those that were more strictly strategic; thus my analysis in the following chapter will consider the place and function of these moral elements in relation to those that are more strictly strategic. In more analytic terms, through this comparison I aim to assess the relative epistemic quality and weight of moral and nonmoral premises. In this way, we can see exactly how entrenched such moral ideas (or, perhaps, ideologies) were in the early Han mind-set, even in areas, such as formal court discussions of military strategy, in which one wouldn't automatically think they ought to belong.

Liu Jing's address to Liu Bang is an example of the role of moral claims in the addresses of the Former Han. On an initial reading of his petition, the moral element does not seem to act so much as an epistemic justification of Liu Jing's claims as an upbraiding of the Han emperor for attempting to assume the moral superiority of the Zhou kings. His references to the moral power or symbolic power of moral kingship are expressive of his disgust with the Han emperor's desire to appear morally elevated. He does not consider the Han emperor able, or even willing, to assume the responsibilities associated with that type of leadership. Yet because Liu Jing's objections are meant to contest the emperor's self-conception, they perform a legitimate epistemic function in speaking to the monarch's self-impression. In Liu Jing's assessment, the Han emperor does not have the moral authority or presence to be able to bolster his claim to power with a geographic association to the Zhou kings. He does not attempt to persuade the emperor to act morally. He merely presumes the emperor will not act morally and that, given such, it would be best to locate the capital based on purely strategic considerations. These strategic considerations, as elaborated above, do not immediately persuade the emperor. Neither do the remarks of the other "various officials," remarks that do not adequately respond to Liu Jing's objections but merely seem to assist the emperor in his rationalizations, saying nothing about whether the emperor is justified in assuming the mantle of the Zhou, just that the Zhou dynasty lasted much longer than the Qin. That Liu Bang ultimately accedes to the need to be concerned about Luoyang's natural vulnerabilities leads one to believe that the emperor really did fear being militarily weak and accepted that his claims to a moral standing akin to the early Zhou kings were not enough to overcome his worries about the geographic vulnerabilities of Luoyang.

CHAPTER EIGHT

Moral Norms as Facts
Arguing before the Emperor

RHETORICAL INTERPLAY IN A HAN DEBATE

Though the moral voice becomes more prominent in Han addresses, the format of the use of nonmoral strategic concerns is still quite similar to their use in the persuasions of the *Intrigues*. Relating to nonmoral strategic concerns we thus can naturally draw sympathetic comparisons in our analysis of the early Han addresses and exchanges to the opposed addresses presented by Su Qin and Zhang Yi to the king of Wei discussed in Chapter Six. An early Han example that shows certain similarities to the exchange between Su Qin and Zhang Yi is the exchange between Grand Messenger Wang Hui and Imperial Counselor Han Anguo (an exchange that is notably absent in Sima Qian's account)[1] in response to a query put by Emperor Wu. The exchange is also published in a collection of anecdotes and tales entitled *Xinxu* 新序, or *New Arrangements*, which Liu Xiang, the reputed editor of the *Intrigues*, also allegedly either collected or edited. Numerous disparities exist between the *History of the Former Han* and *Xinxu* renditions of the exchange, but, in most cases, they do not alter the overarching thrust of each discussant's remark. Often they seem merely to be extending or curtailing the elaboration of a particular point. Indeed, there appears to be so much overlap that Yang Shuda, in his commentary to the *History of the Former Han*, asserts without comment that Ban Gu probably took the exchange from the *Xinxu*.[2] Whether or not this is the case, because of their overwhelming similarity, and thus their common ancestry, I have altered or amended the text appearing in the *History of the Former Han* only when its sibling offers a somewhat illuminating alternative or addition.[3] I do not, as Yang seems to, presume that the *Xinxu* version is primary.

First, some historical context for the issues involved and positions forwarded in the debate: One of the central problems almost every early Chinese ruler was forced to handle was the constant incursions by foreign non-Chinese tribes on the borders of the empire, particularly the northern and western borders. Being nomadic, these tribes were difficult to contain and subjugate militarily; indeed, in spite of the actions Chinese rulers took to control them, the northern steppe tribes grew in size and influence. In 209 BCE, around the very end of the Qin dynasty, the most powerful of the tribes, the Xiongnu, conquered or made alliances with numerous other foreign tribes and established a formal empire. The Xiongnu empire, emerging under the leadership of Maodun 冒頓, forced the nascent Han Chinese empire to accept the northern steppe peoples as a vigorous military presence.

The debate between Wang Hui and Han Anguo was conducted before the preeminent military emperor of the early Han period, Emperor Wu. His campaigns into the steppes not only destroyed the unity of the steppe tribes but also extended Han influence deep into Central Asia, a feat that was not to be repeated until centuries later at the beginning of the Tang dynasty under Emperor Taizong. In his dealings with Maodun, Emperor Wu initially pursued a policy of peaceful negotiations (*heqin* 和親), in which the Han court was obliged to submit annual tribute to the Xiongnu and, when the Xiongnu leader (the *Chanyu* 單于) came of age, to send a Chinese princess in marriage. But because the Xiongnu were perceived as routinely breaking agreements and terrorizing the frontier areas, Emperor Wu was soon predisposed to discontinue such an arrangement.

In line with the common manner in the Han histories and the *Intrigues* of introducing addresses or debates about state affairs, the text begins with the introduction of the narrative particulars that will inform the discussion. As with the prefatory remarks preceding Xiao Wangzhi's address regarding the necessary response to the recent incursions of the Xiongnu that was discussed in Chapter Five,[4] we find the simple format of the year of the discussion, the problematic, and the executive's request for counsel, with the slight distinction here being the emperor asking a specific question and expressing a predilection for military engagement rather than merely asking for counsel. In the remainder of the discussion, he offers no further remarks or queries. The two participants, Wang Hui 王恢 and Han Anguo 韓安國, like Su Qin and Zhang Yi, adopt starkly opposed stances regarding military engagement, with Wang Hui speaking for and Han Anguo speaking against engagement. Their initial responses characterize the overall tone of their positions throughout the debate. Wang Hui, as a supporter of the emperor's ostensible predilection, begins the exchange, openly (and perhaps sycophantically) agreeing with the emperor's apparent intentions. He then follows with a brief psychological analysis of the Xiongnu, insinuating that, unlike in the Xiongnu's interactions with the Dai peoples, when the Xiongnu were awed by obvious military or economic (or moral) strength, they now do not seem to be aware of or impressed by the Han preparations and make repeated incursions into the border areas. Given their unrestrained belligerence, Wang concludes, they must be subdued militarily. Han Anguo's response advocates restraint, raising the examples of the first and third emperors of Han, Gaozu and Wen, as models of how military expeditions are neither necessary nor, as in the case of Emperor Wen's, even considered advantageous. Both of these emperors are given a moralizing cast, framed as "sages" who took the sufferings, potential or actual, of the common people ("All-Under-Heaven") into consideration when deciding not to pursue, or not to pursue further, military resolutions.

These two responses—one advocating for military engagement, the other advocating for diplomacy—could be characterized as representative of the stereotypically contrasted voices of the relatively amoral hawkish Realpolitiker and the dovish Confucian moralist.[5] That, however, would be a mistake, for moralizing language is employed in both addresses, demonstrating the import of moral facets. Yet such moral facets do not seem to be the foundational edifice upon which Han Anguo or Wang Hui are building their arguments. Even in the responses of the "dovish" Han Anguo, moralizing language appears to be most often used as a secondary support to aggrandize the actions of select exemplars while denigrating the desire to engage militarily. Han Anguo urges restraint and diplomacy, but it is not only because military engagements cause unnecessary suffering (as one would suspect they always do) but also because they do not always result in a conclusive resolution of the initial difficulty. He repeatedly emphasizes both the moral and the calculating angle in each repartee, and reiterates them in the same order, moralization followed by calculation, spending the most time elaborating on the frequent futility and ensuing exhaustion of military campaigns. Wang Hui, for his part, parries with his own moralizations and references to sagely precedents, showing a willingness to fight Han Anguo on his own ground, even to the point of taking Han Anguo's examples and turning them back on him. Regardless of this moralizing aspect, his message remains constant: that military action is the only way to resolve the conflict. But though the basic thrust of their positions remains stable, an analysis of the particulars of their interplay, of their repeated attempts to unsettle and dislodge the arguments or rhetorical position of the other, reveals that the tactics they used to pursue their objectives was fully responsive to their opponent's previous remarks. Wang Hui and Han Anguo's stances may remain unchanged, but the strategies deployed most certainly do not. An examination of the particular strategies they employ, and the motivations for their employment, provides certain insight into how other of the Han addresses were composed, in both what was emphasized and why it was emphasized. These emphases may assist us in determining what may have been taken to be reputable propositions of popular knowledge, or even of common sense. It thus is of benefit to probe in detail the particulars of their exchange. Because of its dialogic format, with Wang Hui's and Han Anguo's responses being informed by what was said previously, their exchange does not permit the easy systematic comparison allowed by the two persuasions of the *Intrigues* analyzed in Chapter Six. Instead of examining each statement separately as it contributes to an uninterrupted, seamless monologue, I will analyze their responses holistically informed by their opponent's previous replies. My analysis will succeed each response:[6]

> The following year (the second year of the Yuanguang 元光 era, 133 BCE), a prominent man from the District of Mayi in Yanmen Commandery, Nie Yi, brought word to the emperor via the Grand Messenger Wang Hui, saying, "As the Xiongnu have initiated peaceful relations and act in good faith and friendship toward our people on the borders, it is possible to tempt them with certain advantages to bring them to us. With hidden soldiers we can then attack them. This is a sure method to their destruction." The emperor thereupon sent for the noble lords and asked them, "I have bequeathed My daughter to the Chanyu, given him silk fabrics and silk brocades. I have showered him with gifts. Yet the Chanyu has been very lax in responding to My commands and has marauded our lands without cease. The border territories have suffered surprise attacks numerous times. I am deeply grieved by this. Now I wish to raise an army to do battle with him. What do you think?" 明年, 雁門馬邑豪聶壹因大行王恢言:「匈奴初和親, 親信邊, 可誘以利致之, 伏兵襲擊, 必破之道也。」上乃召問公卿曰:「朕飾子女以配單于, 幣帛文錦, 賂之甚厚。單于待命加嫚, 侵盜無已, 邊竟數驚, 朕甚閔之。今欲舉兵攻之, 何如?」

a) The Grand Messenger Wang Hui responded,

"Even though Your Majesty has yet to voice his plans, I, Your servant, absolutely wish to represent them. I, Your servant, have heard that during the time when the lands of Dai were unified, to their north lay their enemies, the Xiongnu. Within the lands of Dai were lined the armies of the Central States.[7] And yet the [Dai people] also cared for their young and aged and planted their crops in line with the seasons. Their granaries were consistently full {and they had made defensive preparations}. The Xiongnu did not treat invasion of their lands lightly. Now because of Your Majesty's fearlessness, all within the four seas is unified and All-Under-Heaven work together. You have also sent your sons and younger brothers to guard the frontiers at the borders and have shipped grain down the waterways [to the border areas] as a preparatory measure. And yet the Xiongnu invade and maraud our lands without cease. Our not using other means is the reason that they are unafraid. I, Your servant, humbly consider that attacking them would be to our benefit." 大行恢對曰:「陛下雖未言, 臣固願效之。臣聞全代之時, 北有彊胡之敵, 內連中國之兵, 然尚得養老長幼, 種樹以時, 倉廩常實, 守禦之備具>, 匈奴不輕侵[8]也。今以陛下之威, 海內為一, 天下同任, 又遣子弟乘邊守塞, 轉粟輓輸, 以為之備, 然匈奴侵盜不已者, 無它, 以不恐之故耳[9]。臣竊以為擊之便。」

After an expression of sympathy, a rhetorical defensive tactic frequently utilized when the speaker is about to raise uncomfortable criticisms, Wang Hui continues his response with a historical reference to the confrontation between the Xiongnu and the kingdom of Dai, a kingdom that, as far as the Han histories tell us, has been in existence since early in the Warring States period, located on the northwest border of Han China. The tale he relates depicting the people of Dai as both militarily and economically well organized is not found anywhere else in the histories. Repeatedly mentioned in the Han histories in reference to this period of Dai's history is its conquest and occupation by the powerful kingdom of Zhao, which ended with the Qin onslaught. But this mention of Dai in particular is somewhat curious, for it is offered without elaboration as to why its history with the Xiongnu is of relevance for Emperor Wu's own deliberations, save that the kingdom is located on the border of the realm of the Central States and has previously also experienced difficulties with the Xiongnu, over whom it reputedly triumphed. Though these details are certainly pertinent, they are not sufficient to explain why this *particular* period in Dai's history is emphasized. I thus would argue that Wang Hui is actually obliquely making reference to other more recent periods of trouble in the Dai area. Assuming that this historicized anecdote is meant to be relevant, we might posit that that to which Wang Hui is probably making a deliberate indirect reference (if we are to see Han Anguo's immediately following direct reference to the event as not wholly arbitrary) is Liu Bang's troubles with the Xiongnu in the Dai area.[10] Following is an excerpt about the beginning of Liu Bang's troubles with them in "The Account of the Xiongnu":

At this time Gaozu, the founder of the Han, had just succeeded in winning control of the empire and had transferred Xin, the former king of Han, to the rulership of Dai, with his capital at Mayi. The Xiongnu surrounded Mayi and attacked the city in great force, whereupon Hann Xin surrendered to them. With Hann Xin on their side, they then proceeded to lead their troops south across Mt. Juzhu and attack Taiyuan, marching as far as the city of Jinyang. Emperor Gaozu led an army in person to attack them, but it was winter and he encountered such cold and heavy snow that two or three out of every ten of his men lost their fingers from frostbite. Maodun feigned a retreat to lure the Han soldiers on to an attack. When they came after him in pursuit he concealed all of his best troops and left only his weakest and puniest men to be observed by the Han scouts. With this the entire Han force, supplemented by 320,000 infantry, rushed north to pursue him; Gaozu led the way, advancing as far as the city of Pingcheng.[11] Before the infantry had had a chance to arrive, however, Maodun swooped down with 400,000 of his best cavalry, surrounded Gaozu on White Peak, and held him there for seven days.[12]

Surrounded, without a way to receive provisions or assistance, Liu Bang and his men are forced to starve. A minor discrepancy of note between this account and the account to be given by Han Anguo below is the description following this anecdote of the Han troops being surrounded by horses of different colors, each group having the color symbolically associated, according to Chinese tradition, with the cardinal direction in which it is located, white on the west, blue-green on the east, black on the north, and red on the south.[13] According to this anecdote, Liu Bang extricates himself from this unbearable situation with a secret envoy who persuades Maodun's consort to speak to Maodun. The ploy is successful and Maodun withdraws his troops "from one corner of the encirclement," allowing Liu Bang to escape.[14]

This anecdote is the starting point and a driving force for the entire exchange between Wang Hui and Han Anguo. If I am correct in my assertion that Wang Hui was deliberately making reference to it by his selection of a historical anecdote about the land of Dai, it appears that Wang Hui is drawing an unflattering contrast between the Warring States occupants of the Dai lands and the Han experience within the Dai area.[15] Not only were the Dai leaders of yore able to fend off attacks by the Xiongnu (or simply cow the Xiongnu into not attempting an attack), they were able, it seems, to deter a full-scale onslaught by the southern Central States, as well as remain economically and politically strong and prosperous enough to allow the common people to care for their dependents and attend to their agricultural affairs (i.e., they did not need to conscript them). By contrast, the Han emperors not only were unable to keep hold of the kingdom but also were constantly facing attacks from the Xiongnu, in spite of the numerous preparations and the achieved military and political unity of "All-Under-Heaven." What Wang Hui seems to be suggesting is that it is only a lack of will (or moral probity)—certainly not a lack of economic resources or manpower—that prevents the Han empire from overcoming its Xiongnu adversaries. If the relatively small kingdom of Dai can intimidate the Xiongnu, why cannot the Han empire?

Han Anguo replies:

b) The Imperial Counselor Han Anguo said,

"That is incorrect. I, Your servant, have heard that when the High Emperor was previously surrounded at Pingcheng, the Xiongnu who had come threw their saddles into numerous piles as high as city walls.[16] There was starvation at Pingcheng. For seven days there was nothing to eat. All-Under-Heaven have composed songs about it.[17] After the siege was broken and the Emperor returned to his throne, he nevertheless was not angry. {It was not because he didn't have the manpower that he, though he possessed All-Under-Heaven, did not avenge the disgrace he experienced at Pingcheng.} A sage takes All-Under-Heaven into consideration. He does not allow his private anger to injure the good of All-Under-Heaven. Thus the Emperor subsequently sent Liu Jing[18] to the Xiongnu with 1,000 *jin* of gold in order to form peaceful relations with them. Because of this, down to this day there have been five generations of profitable relations. The Filial Emperor Wen also previously unified and controlled the elite armies of All-Under-Heaven. He gathered them at the Chang Stream in the Guangwu District. Yet in the end not an inch of accomplishment (i.e., territory) was gained and among the black-kerchiefed {beleaguered common people} of All-Under-Heaven there were none who were not worried. The Filial Emperor Wen became aware that the armies were not able to remain in any one place for long and thus reauthorized the covenant establishing peaceful relations with the Xiongnu. Both of these are the signatures of the sage, sufficiently indicative for us to be able to mirror [sagely action]. I, Your servant, humbly believe that not attacking is to our benefit." 御史大夫安國曰:「不然。臣聞高皇帝嘗圍於平城,匈奴至者投鞍高如城者數所。平城之飢,七日不食,天下歌之,及解圍反位,而無忿怒之心。{雖得天下而不報平城之怨者,非以力不能也。}夫聖人以天下為度者也,不以己私怒傷天下之功,故乃遣劉敬奉金千斤,以結和親,至今為五世利。孝文皇帝又嘗壹擁[19]天下之精兵聚之廣武常谿,然終無尺寸之功,而天下黔首{約要之民}無不憂者。孝文寤於兵之不可宿,故復合和親之約。此二聖之跡,足以為效矣.臣竊以為勿擊便。」

The account Han Anguo gives of Gaozu's travails at Pingcheng does not accord with the account in the *Records*, "Account of the Xiongnu," in that it appears it was not (only) the horses that were blocking the escape of the Han troops but also obstructing piles of saddles. Yet the discrepancy is minor, only more vividly illustrating the number of Xiongnu and their military savvy. The main point of the anecdote is Liu Bang's later restraint and magnanimity toward the Xiongnu.[20] Not only does he not avenge his disgrace, he sends Liu Jing on a diplomatic mission bearing gold. Because of this, Han Anguo concludes, there have been five generations—meaning until the current crisis—of profitable relations, a conclusion that is curiously belied by the succeeding historical anecdote. In it, Emperor Wen is described as having used his best troops to pursue the Xiongnu. But once he realized the futility of the campaign, the impossibility of capturing the Xiongnu, and the enormous economic and personal burden that the campaign had been placing on the empire, he reestablished an accord. Because of their restraint, their willingness to forgo military conquest for the prosperity and well-being of the common people whose sacrifices fund the state, Han Anguo asserts, these two previous Han emperors behaved as sages, as morally exemplary leaders, and these two short anecdotes are sufficient to demonstrate how properly, in a sagely way, to manage the current crisis. In contrast to Wang Hui's confrontational response, Han Anguo offers flattering and sanctimonious appraisals of the current emperor's forebears, no doubt in part to win the emperor's sympathies. Turning Wang Hui's historical precedent against him, Han Anguo accentuates the moral dimension, one that might appear to be added justification for peaceful accord but that also seems to be an attempt to gain the higher ground. Han Anguo is asserting that not only is a military expedition economically unwise, it is morally reprehensible.[21]

Wang Hui immediately adjusts his rhetorical strategy, parrying with a generalizing mytho-historical precedent to forward the general principle of adapting to the needs of the time. Its reference to the earliest sage kings, like all references to the sage kings, is meant to rhetorically sanctify its applicability:

c) Wang Hui said:

"That is not correct. I, Your servant, have heard that the five thearchs did not adhere to the same rituals, the three kings did not emphasize the same musical tradition. This was not because they were in opposition to each other's [preferences] but because each was attuned to what was appropriate to his time. Now, the High Thearch's body had borne hardness and grasped sharpness, been drenched by mist and dew, bathed in frost and snow. He was abroad for close to ten years. The reason he did not respond to the episode at Pingcheng with resentment is not because his strength was not sufficient but because he wished to put at ease the heart-mind of All-Under-Heaven. At present, the borders have repeatedly been surprised [by attacks]. Officers and infantrymen have been injured or killed. Carts with temporary coffins going to the Central States are constantly in view of each other on the road. Both of these are points that cause humane people to feel pity. I, Your servant, thus speak for the benefit of attacking them." 恢曰:「不然。臣聞五帝不相襲禮, 三王不相復樂, 非故相反也, 各因世宜也。且高帝身被堅執銳, 蒙霧露, 沐霜雪, 行幾十年, 所以不報平城之怨者, 非力不能, 所以休天下之心也。²² 今邊竟數驚, 士卒傷死, 中國槥車相望, 此仁人之所隱也。臣故曰擊之便。」²³

A version of the generalizing historical precedent Wang Hui uses is quoted in the first chapter of the *Book of Lord Shang*.²⁴ Its assertion, one could plausibly suppose, is meant to remove Han Anguo from the moral high ground, offering an alternative model of "sagely" conduct. The sages, Wang asserts, were able to adjust their principles to fit with current circumstances. Applying ancient moral codes to current problems without modification is not only unwise, it is unnecessary to be morally righteous. Wang then deviously makes a remark that renders Han Anguo's depiction of Liu Bang extremely unflattering. He "objects" that, contrary to what Han Anguo's initial depiction of the reasons for Liu Bang's recommencement of diplomatic relations with the Xiongnu seemed to suggest, it was not Liu Bang's sense of his military weakness that motivated his magnanimity toward the Xiongnu but, again, his moral probity.²⁵ Wang Hui adopts Han Anguo's moralizing language—indeed, he goes so far as to use one of the most central of Confucian moral terms, *ren* ("humanity")—but he uses it for different purposes. He suggests that Liu Bang had every reason to avenge his defeat, but restrained himself because of his concern for the welfare of his people and, just as important, because the Xiongnu and he formed an accord that was, it is implied, respected by both sides. At present, by contrast, the Xiongnu are not respecting the Han attempts to form a peaceful accord. It is thus highly immoral *not* to respond, to allow the wanton waste of human life to continue.

Wang Hui's generalizing statement marks a decided rhetorical shift to the inclusion of abstract generalizations, for Han Anguo then commences with his own statement of principle:

d) Han Anguo said:

"That is not correct. I, Your servant, have heard that if profit has not increased tenfold, then do not alter the enterprise; if accomplishments have not increased a hundredfold, do not change what is constant. For this reason when the lords of old laid plans, they were certain to turn to the ancestral temples for guidance. When they acted on political matters, they divined in accord with the ancient sayings (alternately: inquired about the ancient sayings) and took care when proceeding with their affairs. Since the Three Dynasties (Xia, Shang, and Zhou) were at their height, the Yi and Di barbarians did not agree to recognize the first lunar month [as established by the newly appointed emperors] or the imperial colors. If we do not display fearlessness, we cannot keep them under control. If we do not display might, we cannot bring them under submission. I believe they are distant, far-off peoples who cannot be acculturated. They are not worth causing the Central States aggravation. The Xiongnu have an army that is light and quick, brave and fast. They will arrive like gale winds and will depart like retracting lightning. Their occupation is raising animals. They use wooden longbows to shoot and hunt. They pursue their prey following the pastures. They do not stay anywhere for long. It is difficult to keep them under control. Now we have caused the border commanderies to let off planting and weaving for some time in order to provide support for this ongoing situation with the Xiongnu. The disposition of each does not balance out with the other's. I, Your servant, thus state that not attacking is of benefit." 安國曰:「不然。臣聞利不十者不易業, 功不百者不變常, 是以古之人君謀事必就祖, 發政占古語, ²⁶ 重作事也。且自三代之盛, 夷狄不與正朔服色, 非威不能制, 彊弗能服也, 以為遠方絕地不牧之民, 不足煩中國也。且匈奴, 輕疾悍亟之兵也, 至如猋風, 去如收電, 畜牧為業, 弧弓射獵, 逐獸隨草, 居處無常, 難得而制。²⁷ 今使邊郡久廢耕織, 以支胡之常事, 其勢不相權也。臣故曰勿擊便。」

Here, Han Anguo's initial statement of principle reframes his position, shifting from moralizing language to the language of profit.[28] Wang Hui, in his second response (c), makes direct reference to moral concerns, apparently playing off of Han Anguo's moralizing language in (b). Here in (d), in a rhetorical shift, Han Anguo speaks directly against the possible resolution of the problem by military subjugation, the option that Wang Hui has been emphasizing throughout, stating that the Xiongnu are difficult to control and that they respond only to displays of strength. They are unresponsive to attempts to civilize and normalize their lifestyle. Furthermore, they are both quick in the saddle and nomadic by nature, never remaining in one place for long.[29] Though in this response Han Anguo does not elaborate on the suffering of the people, his substantive conclusion is the same: to pursue them would be an unending and exhausting enterprise, causing significant economic hardship. What is striking about this response is his shift to a defensive stance, one in which he no longer positively asserts the benefits or morality of diplomacy, as he did before, but merely cautions that pursuing military action would be unprofitable.

Wang Hui's response begins with a literary reformulation of his principle that the sage leader needs to adapt to changing circumstances:

e) Wang Hui said,

"That is not correct. I, Your servant, have heard that the phoenix bird rides on the wind, the sage relies on the times. In the past, Duke Mu of Qin had his capital at Yong, the area of which was three hundred leagues. He knew the changes in current practices and attacked and overcame the Western Rong. The lands he took over were a thousand leagues, the states he united were fourteen, including the lands within the Longxi and Beidi Commanderies. Later Meng Tian invaded the Xiongnu lands for the state of Qin, taking over many thousands of leagues of land, with the Yellow River as a border. He piled stones to make a wall and staked elm logs to create a barrier. The Xiongnu did not dare to water their horses at the Yellow River. Once the daytime and nighttime defensive signal fires were in place, the Xiongnu dared to shepherd their horses (because they realized that they would not be perceived as a threat, as the Chinese army was prepared to defend themselves). Only with fearlessness can the Xiongnu be forced to submit. It is not possible to train them in the ways of humanity. Now to send off one one-hundredth of the wealth of the Central States, of its ten-thousand-fold reserves, to fight the Xiongnu is akin to shooting an arrow from a powerful crossbow to lance an ulcerating abscess.[30] The army's advance will certainly not be halted. This being the case, then the Beifa and the Yuezhi tribes can be won over and be made your subjects (and therefore be recruited to fight against the Xiongnu).[31] I, your subject, thus say that attacking is of benefit." 恢曰:「不然。臣聞[32]鳳鳥乘於風, 聖人因於時。昔秦繆公都雍, 地方三百里, 知時宜之變, 攻取西戎, 辟地千里, 并國十四, 隴西、北地是也。及後蒙恬為秦侵胡, 辟數千里, 以河為竟, 累石為城, 樹榆[33]為塞, 匈奴不敢飲馬於河, 置烽燧然後敢牧馬。夫匈奴獨可以威服, 不可以仁畜也。 今以中國之盛, 萬倍之資, 遣百分之一以攻匈奴, 譬猶以彊弩射且潰之癰也, 必不留行矣。若是, 則北發月氏,可得而臣也。臣故曰擊之便。」

The sage leader, like the phoenix, knows when and how to adapt. The phoenix, a mystically empowered bird, is able to ride through turbulent winds; correspondingly, the sage, well-nigh mystically enlightened, knows when to act. Wang Hui ties this point to a fierce and mighty historical exemplar. Duke Mu, like the sage, knew the "changes in the proper time," as, it appears, did his general, Meng Tian. Wang Hui, as Han Anguo did just previously in (d), emphasizes that the Xiongnu respond only to force, again asserting by implication that Emperor Wu could overcome them if he, too, would seize the moment and attack. Once they are overcome, the Xiongnu, as during Duke Mu's time, would understand that, were there defensive signal fires in place, the army could return at a moment's notice, and thus would not invade again.

But although in these two responses Han Anguo and Wang Hui both start from the same premise—that the Xiongnu react only to displays of force—their conclusions are quite divergent. Han Anguo concludes that because they are nomadic and difficult to pin down, a military engagement with them would be long and costly, demanding that the Chinese army go deep into enemy territory. Wang Hui counters that any campaign against the Xiongnu would not need even a one-hundredth of the wealth of the empire. He thus tacitly accedes to Han Anguo's reiterated concern that a military campaign would be costly but suggests that large expenditures can be avoided by, for example, supplementing a smaller Chinese force with a group of Yuezhi barbarians.

Han Anguo responds:

f) Han Anguo said,

"That is not correct. I, Your servant, have heard that when using armies one should offer satiety in response to hunger, upright governance in response to the border troubles, pacification in response to their travails. Because engaging an army brings defeat to many and waging battle against a state razes city walls, the sage's army stays put and the sage conscripts men from enemy states.[34] Now, I, Your servant, have also heard that once the force of the rushing wind wanes, the wind cannot even lift up a small hair or feather; at the end of its flight, the arrow from a powerful crossbow does not even have the power to enter the soft white silk of Lu[35]; the waning of prosperity is as inevitable as morning becoming dusk. Nowadays, generals unroll their armor and gingerly put it on, deeply invade enemy territory and press their horses to travel great distances. It is difficult to bring such to a successful conclusion. If they travel in single file, then there is the threat of pressure from the sides. If they travel in group formations, then there is the threat of being driven apart in the middle. If they are too quick, then provisions will run out; if they are too slow, then the advantage will be lost. Before they have gone 1,000 leagues, the men and horses will lack food. The *Art of War* states, 'Give them men and capture them.' If the sense [behind these schemes, as with this statement from the *Art of War*,] is that there are alternative crafty stratagems by which one can trap them, then I, Your servant, do not know them. If all this is not correct, then I have just not yet seen the profit in invading deeply into enemy territory. I, Your servant, thus state that not attacking is of benefit."

安國曰：「不然。臣聞用兵者以飽待饑，正治[36]以待其亂，定舍以待其勞。故接兵覆眾，伐國墮城，常坐而役敵國，此聖人之兵也。且臣聞之，衝風之衰，不能起毛羽；彊弩之末，力不能入魯縞。夫盛之有衰，猶朝之必莫也。今將卷甲輕舉，深入長歐，難以為功；從行則迫脅，衡行則中絕，疾則糧乏，徐則後利，不至千里，人馬乏食。³⁷ 兵法曰:『遺人獲也。』³⁸ 意者有它繆巧可以禽之，則臣不知也; 不然，則未見深入之利也。臣故曰勿擊便。」

At the beginning of his response, Han Anguo briefly returns to the theme of peaceful diplomacy and educative discourse, reemphasizing that a military commander should always be compassionate and morally upright when handling border difficulties. He then speaks to Wang Hui's suggestion of using foreign tribes to attack the Xiongnu. Redeploying the analogy of a powerful crossbow, he raises the question of whether the distance from which an arrow is shot will affect its piercing its target. With this analogy, Han Anguo seems to suggest that, if it travels too far, the army will inevitably be weakened. Just as the wind loses its force, an arrow can fall from flight, and the wealth of a nation can be exhausted. He warns that the army will be prone to attacks, no matter what its formations, and that either it will not be able to move fast enough to catch the Xiongnu or it will move too quickly and use up its supplies in the process. He thus raises doubts as to the possibility of any military force, regardless of its configuration or size, not encountering obstacles or harassments that would lead to its defeat. No longer calling historical precedents into question or challenging the principle of having to change with the times, he focuses now simply on strategic concerns. Using the analogy of the arrow, he seems to be arguing that the army would have to travel great distances in its campaign and would exhaust itself before reaching its target. Thus it would be better, Han Anguo appears to suggest, to pacify the Xiongnu using peaceful means, rather than to fight with potentially little or no gain. At the end of his address, he asserts that there are no stratagems of which he knows that could bring about the capture of the Xiongnu, insinuating that if others insist the Xiongnu could be defeated, it would be using ruses that are both crafty and flawed, ones that would not account for the basic difficulties of the venture.

Wang Hui, in the final repartee, responds immediately to Han Anguo's thinly veiled *argumentum ad hominem*, to the insinuated charge that he means to mesmerize the emperor with sophisticated but empty stratagems. He suggests that it is Han Anguo who wishes to confuse the emperor with his "cultured phrases." Yet, like clear water or frost-encrusted grass and trees, the enlightened emperor will not be deceived by fleeting images or gusts of refined phrasing:

g) Wang Hui said,

"That is not correct. The grasses and trees that are covered in frost will not permit the wind to pass; the clear mirror of pure water will not permit a formation to escape notice. The official who understands secret recipes cannot be made confused by cultured phrases.

Now I, Your servant, have said that we should attack them, but this absolutely does not mean that we should send our forces out to invade deeply into enemy territory. If our generals act in accord with what the Chanyu wants, we can tempt him to come into the border areas. I will then select elite cavalrymen and strongmen to hide in the shadows and will place them all about in preparation for the Chanyu. I will scout out hidden crags for their bases. Once my position is secured, some of my men will surround his left, some will surround his right, some will block him in front, others will cut off his retreat. If the Chanyu can be captured, hundreds of his followers will certainly be completely overcome." 恢曰:「不然。夫草木遭霜者不可以風過,清水明鏡不可以形逃,通方之士,不可以文亂。今臣言擊之者,固非發而深入也,將順因單于之欲,誘而致之邊,吾選梟騎壯士陰伏而處[39] 以為之備,審遮險阻以為其戒。吾勢已定,或營其左,或營其右,或當其前,或絕其後,單于可禽,百全必取。」

Wang Hui insists that no deep penetration into enemy territory is required. Instead, the generals need only (somehow) entice the Chanyu to come to the border areas, where elite troops will be placed in strategically advantageous positions, awaiting the order to ambush and entrap the Chanyu, attacking him from all sides. Were the leader of the Xiongnu captured, the rest of the Xiongnu army would then be easily overcome. Wang Hui thus ends the debate with the suggestion of a stratagem that would make deep penetration into enemy lands superfluous, saving time, men, and resources, and that would lead to the defeat and capture of the Xiongnu army. His tone is definitive, but, in keeping with the lack of emphasis on precisely detailed accounts in the Han histories, the details of his proposal are unclear. Certainly, having elite troops placed in hidden crags that surround an area in which the Xiongnu will ride increases the chances of their capture, but how the Xiongnu are enticed to come, how the "generals act in accord with what the Chanyu wants," is left open. Wang Hui gives the impression that victory will be swift and convincing, but we cannot tell how this is achieved. The emperor, however, is convinced, and dispatches troops according to Wang Hui's recommendations. Unfortunately, upon his approaching the border areas, the Chanyu becomes aware of an eerie stillness and, sensing a trap, flees, evading capture and defeat. Because the ruse fails, the Xiongnu are further antagonized, willing to continue their invasion and harassment of the border areas. To resolve their difficulties with the Xiongnu, the Han will have to expect the need for either extensive diplomacy or a drawn-out military campaign.[40]

In reviewing the details and elaborations of the advice of the two counselors, it appears that the manner of their argument counts more than the actual content of their argument, that the arguments rest not only on the content of the arguments but on the repeated rhetorical reframing of the debate, of borrowings and redirections that aim to unsettle and destabilize what the other had stated previously. These reframings and redirections occur throughout the debate. In Han Anguo's very first repartee (b),[41] for instance, instead of directly speaking to the merits of Wang Hui's answer (a) by questioning the accuracy of the historical example of the Dai people or the point Wang is trying to make in using it, he reports on the example of the High Emperor. On my interpretation, this was indeed a cogent and salient response to Wang Hui's remarks, but it was not a direct one. It reframed the debate, demanding that the auditor sympathize with and appreciate Liu Bang's humanity, with his unwillingness to continue attacking the Xiongnu and causing unnecessary suffering among his people, rather than criticizing Liu Bang for his military strategy. These redirections are not formulated to truly answer the opponent's objections or anticipate further objections, but instead are attempts to distract the emperor from noticing the weaknesses in one's own argument that were brought out by one's opponent's previous response. These rhetorical reframings are common to early Chinese argument, appearing in the *Intrigues* debates as well, such as those between Su Qin and Zhang Yi. In the debate between Su Qin and Zhang Yi analyzed in Chapter Six, though its format was not dialogic, one can see that, in their responses to the doubts raised in their opponent's response,[42] they often attempt to assuage unspoken doubts (or parry those raised by the opponent) by redirecting attention away from a weakness in their argument. For instance, Su Qin in (d)[43] asserts that a state with a sizeable population does not need to be subservient to a larger state, a premise I claim was opposed openly and explicitly by Zhang Yi in segments 1–6 of his address. Su Qin seems to anticipate this objection or doubt by reframing his argument in terms of honor or duty in segment 3.[44] In segments 4 and 5, Su Qin takes another tack, one that does not attempt to speak to the monarch's sense of honor but instead his sense of shame. If Goujian of Yue and Wu of Zhou could overcome their enemies with small armies, why couldn't the king of Wei with his much larger army? Finally, as a last resort, he asserts in segments 6 and 7 to the motives of his opponents and the detrimental consequences of capitulation. He dashes any hopes of saving the nation through peaceable means. Yet he never weighs the merits of this possibility against the disastrous consequences of military defeat. As with Zhang Yi, he does not consider it his mission to consider all angles and deliberate carefully but to distract from the weaknesses and highlight the strengths of his claims and arguments.

HAN ADDRESSES STRESSING MORAL REGARD

One of my central aims, as I have repeatedly mentioned, is to evaluate the function of the commonsense premises that are regularly in play across the wide array of Han addresses regarding military affairs. The commonsense premises used in this debate, I maintain, are in large measure reflective of the type of commonsense premises used in other Han addresses. But to discern such commonsense premises, we need first discuss the basic human needs that are fundamentally driving Wang Hui's and Han Anguo's addresses. I will here only offer an analysis of what appears to be the basic human needs that are fundamentally driving Wang Hui's and Han Anguo's addresses. Certainly, the most central need assumed by both addresses—indeed by almost any address regarding military affairs—is the need for security. Both Wang Hui's and Han Anguo's addresses are informed by such. A second requirement is reliable information. When Wang Hui emphasizes the habits of the Xiongnu or when Su Qin cautions the king of Wei against being taken in by harebrained schemes, both assume its centrality. Of Rescher's list of basic human needs—food, shelter, clothing, information, sociability, safety, and health—which Rescher proposes are behind commonsense claims, only safety and information inform Wang Hui's and Han Anguo's addresses. But this list does not seem comprehensive enough to cover all of the needs that seem to be in play in Wang Hui's or Han Anguo's addresses. If the increased appearance of moral language in the Han addresses is any indication, there also appears to be a fundamental need for moral esteem, for the esteem of All-Under-Heaven.

The desire, indeed, the *need* for esteem, for moral praiseworthiness is, according to many pre-Han texts, both beneficial and natural, and, if such is representative, an entrenched aspect of early Chinese intellectual culture. Mencius states this categorically, declaring that "[a]ll men share the same desire to be exalted" 欲貴者, 人之同心也.[45] This declaration, by itself, is of little real consequence, yet one can see numerous episodes in which emperors were persuaded to act in ethical ways by appealing to their desire to be worthy of esteem. For instance, Zhang Liang persuades the newly victorious Liu Bang not to occupy the palaces of the former emperor, the First Emperor of Qin, by emphasizing Liu Bang's duty to show "sympathy for the sufferings of the people."[46] Similarly, Dongfang Shuo 東方朔 attempts to persuade Emperor Wu not to permit the love affair between a Han princess and a commoner, Dong Yan 董偃, to continue by expressing the moral significance of such an affair. Though the emperor acts only when Dongfang Shuo restates the significance of the affair in more political terms, I argue that, if we can take the mention of his "lengthy silence" after Dongfang Shuo's moral assessment to be indicative of serious concern, both the moral and the political phrasing of the problem had an impact on his response.[47] Dongfang Shuo's renderings of the problem, first moral, then political, neither compromise nor negate either aspect.

Yet even though, according to Mencius, all men wish to be exalted, not every generation of persuader sincerely considered such moral concerns essential for persuasions regarding political or military leadership. The era (or, perhaps, authors) that produced the *Intrigues* was clearly often insincere and cynical in their usage of moral terminology. In addition, there are certain morally colored terms that would have been in common use at the time of the *Intrigues*, terms such as "Heaven's mandate" (*tianming* 天命) that, though applicable to discussions of leadership, were never employed. Although comparative evaluations of the authentic application of moral terminology in political debates are tricky because of the ubiquity of the duplicity in their usage, it is significant that, in the case of *tianming*, while there are more than thirty appearances of the term in the *Records* and over fifty in the *History of the Former Han*, the term appears only once in all of the over five hundred persuasions regarding political affairs in the *Intrigues*, in a persuasion offered by Su Li (Su Qin's younger brother) to the ruler of Zhou. But even this one instance does not obviously possess a moral inflection. Su Li 蘇厲 is explaining the extraordinary success of a military commander, Bo Qi 白起, saying that he is adept at using his armies and, in addition, "has Heaven's mandate."[48] Su Li goes on to discuss Bo Qi's current military engagements and does not elaborate on any particular moral qualities that Bo Qi has that might explain his having obtained "Heaven's mandate." Thus even in this instance, it appears that "Heaven's mandate" is a sign of his great fortune, rather than any mark of his moral probity.[49]

Perhaps the absence of *tianming* in the *Intrigues* merely is the result of its persuasions not questioning the Zhou king's right to the mandate to rule All-Under-Heaven. Assuming that the *Intrigues* were meant to capture the Warring States' political environment, it would be understood that the Zhou king, though weakened, was nevertheless still the titular ruler of the Central States until the death of the last Zhou king in 256 BCE. While this is true, I consider that the absence of the term is indicative of a larger absence, the absence of any interest in moral leadership, whether of its support, as should have been offered to the Zhou king, or of its assumption.[50] The leaders addressed in the *Intrigues* were neither concerned with preserving the Zhou king's mandate nor obtaining any morally inflected version of Heaven's mandate for themselves. Were they to do so, they might have been exposed to instruction or criticism about inflicting unnecessary suffering and would have been advised to resist the urge to act in purely instrumental and self-serving ways—hardly a commonplace among the anecdotes of the *Intrigues*.

If all of this is so, if the premises of the Han addresses were grounded not only in basic, nonmoral considerations—in, for example, the need for security and information—but also in a demand for moral standards and moral praiseworthiness, what relevant commonsense premises might we argue are in Wang Hui's or Han Anguo's addresses? Because their addresses do not allow, as Su Qin's and Zhang Yi's did, quick and easy comparison, we cannot be terribly certain which of the forwarded premises would have been acceptable to either party. Nevertheless, there appear to be premises, some of which are implicit, that both answer the need for security and information and would seem to be acceptable to both Wang Hui and Han Anguo. Here are some examples:

1. Military concerns require stratagems and proper strategic deploying of resources.
2. Each time has its own needs, yet one must live by certain principles.
3. War is an uncertain business and can lead to political and financial ruin.

I do not aver that each of these is explicitly accepted or forwarded by each addressor. Certainly none are explicitly forwarded in these formulations and, in fact, had they been, some would probably have been left unacknowledged or even ignored. For example, Wang Hui, though he did not (and, I would argue, could not) deny the third premise, neither did he actively engage with it. Though this premise suffuses many of Han Anguo's addresses, Wang Hui never responds to it or raises it as a valid point, yet neither does he deny it. Again, as I have argued, the weaknesses in one's argument frequently were left unaddressed. Rather than openly engaging with one's opponent's valid criticisms, addressors would attempt to distract from them by beginning another line of argument or reiterating past points.

In addition to these above premises that speak to the basic nonmoral needs for security and information, there also seems to be a salient moral facet underlying many of Wang Hui's and Han Anguo's responses. Even though Wang Hui appears to be more of a "realist" than Han Anguo, his responses are nevertheless permeated by a consciousness of the importance of moral considerations. Indeed, in my interpretation, such a consciousness is revealed even in his first response, when he speaks to the considerateness of the Dai people toward their young and aged. For both Wang Hui and Han Anguo, I argue, the articulation of such a moral consciousness is not merely for pedantic upbraiding or for purely aggrandizing or denigrating ornamentation but a central feature of the discussion of how to proceed. Unlike the purely calculating and amoral persuasions offered by earlier Warring States addresses such as Zhang Yi's, both sides mention in their arguments not only strategic considerations, but moral ones. So, in keeping with this, we may assert a fourth commonsense premise:

4. Showing compassion toward those who will suffer from the campaign will ultimately result in greater dividends.

Han Anguo's addresses rely upon this premise most heavily, but Wang Hui's also make reference to the sufferings caused by unmitigated violence (e.g., in c).[51] I will argue that this shift is indicative of a larger, more holistic shift in former Han era addresses and can be seen in the majority of the addresses presented to the Han emperor.

Thus to reiterate my general argument, the style and shape of the rhetoric involved in addresses speaking to military affairs apparently began slowly to shift between the end of the Warring States period, the period of the *Intrigues*, and the beginning or middle of the Han period, the point at which the historical records of the *Hanshu* begin to fill out and complete the history of the former Han. As discussed above, in the previous Warring States-era addresses, though the language of moral standards was not altogether absent, it was not nearly as conspicuous as it became in the later addresses. Yet I do not believe we can automatically attribute this to the perspective of the historian, as being representative of his (or their) ideological preference, for the influence of the moral is hardly ideologically overbearing. Most often, as stated earlier, it appears to serve as a secondary buttressing edifice. Moral language can be, and has been, applied both in addresses speaking for military engagement and in those speaking against it. In those addresses in which it does occupy a prominent role, the rest of the argument is usually relatively weak on nonmoral grounds and the rhetorical embellishments of nonmoral statements or propositions insubstantial. The introduction of the moral seems to reflect either a de-emphasis of nonmoral considerations or a weakness in the parts of the argument regarding nonmoral considerations. To rephrase these observations regarding the structure of the arguments forwarded in the early Han addresses in terms of epistemic quality and weight, more epistemic weight is carried by moral propositions in those addresses or arguments in which the nonmoral aspects of the argument are relatively weak.

THE ACCEPTANCE OF MORAL NORMS

Though it appears that moral concerns were not conspicuously mentioned in every address, their absence, whether in the addresses of the *Intrigues* or in those of the Han histories, should not equate with the lack of a general acknowledgment of, respect for, and presumption of the validity and worth of moral standards.[52] Moral standards, though they may not be accentuated in certain addresses, are never impugned in the addresses. They are treated with a level of respect, regardless of the position taken, that prevents their outright disavowal or dismissal. And this is in accord with almost every (perhaps we could say every) era of early Chinese intellectual history. The moral life, while it may not be granted primacy, is hardly ever nihilistically negated or ridiculed. Even the most flinty, matter-of-fact of generals, such as Zhao Chongguo, occasionally bring in moral language to buttress, however ornamentally, their claims.[53] And, from the executive's perspective, including from those as seemingly amoral as Liu Bang (who reportedly pushed his own children out of his cart when once in flight), moral considerations are not to be ignored. In the persuasion constructed by the four wise men discussed at the beginning of Chapter Seven, though Liu Bang eventually shows himself most concerned with military vulnerability, we cannot avoid noting his moral considerations. On the other hand, the increasing emphasis on moral considerations also does not translate into a denial or dismissal of the centrality of more concrete logistical ones. Indeed, it often seemed that the moral-symbolic considerations were easily, and frequently, interpretable as meant to be informing deliberations about the more concrete logistical ones. In other words, moral-symbolic considerations were often only of as much import as they could reinforce other more strategic assertions. They were not intended to dismiss strategic considerations altogether.

An excellent example of this is Xiao Wangzhi's address to Emperor Xuan in 59 BCE regarding the suggestions (made by "many people") that the emperor take advantage of the Xiongnu's internecine conflicts, call out the troops, and destroy them once and for all. Xiao Wangzhi's response commences with a long historic anecdote taken from the *Spring and Autumn Annals*, applauding the kindness (*en* 恩) and righteousness (*yi* 義) of Shi Gai of Jin 晉士匄:

> According to the *Spring and Autumn Annals*, Shi Gai of Jin led his troops in an invasion of the state of Qi, but upon hearing that the Marquis of Qi had died, withdrew his troops and returned to Jin. The Gentleman[54] praised him for not attacking someone in mourning, believing his kindness sufficient to obtain the submission of the mourning filial son of the deceased marquis and his righteousness sufficient to impress the other feudal lords. Previously the Chanyu, envious of the refinement of the Chinese, turned toward goodness and called himself "younger brother," sending emissaries to plead for peaceful relations. All within the four seas were delighted. Among the Yi and Di barbarians there were none who did not hear of it. But before the treaty was concluded, the Chanyu unfortunately was killed by a criminally minded subject. To attack him now would be to take advantage of the chaos and benefit from the calamity. They would certainly flee and hide in a distant region. If you were to activate the army without righteousness, I'm afraid it would be an effort that would accomplish nothing. It would be better to send an emissary to offer condolences, to assist him in his weakened state and rescue him from calamity. When the four

Yi tribes (i.e., all other barbarian tribes) hear of this, they all will honor the benevolence and righteousness of the Central States. And if the Chanyu's son because of our kindness regains his throne, he will certainly call himself "subject" and obediently submit. This is the fullness of virtue. 春秋晉士匄帥師侵齊, 聞齊侯卒, 引師而還, 君子大其不伐喪, 以為恩足以服孝子, 誼足以動諸侯。前單于慕化鄉善稱弟, 遣使請求和親, 海內欣然, 夷狄莫不聞。未終奉約, 不幸為賊臣所殺, 今而伐之, 是乘亂而幸災也, 彼必奔走遠遁。不以義動兵, 恐勞而無功。宜遣使者弔問, 輔其微弱, 救其災患, 四夷聞之, 咸貴中國之仁義。如遂蒙恩得復其位, 必稱臣服從, 此德之盛也。[55]

In his response, Xiao Wangzhi obviously wishes to emphasize the moral dimension of the problem. Separate from any question of the proper moral response, Xiao Wangzhi makes it immediately clear that there will be significant political repercussions were the emperor to capitalize on the Chanyu's son's current personal, and probable political, turmoil. Shi Gai is an exemplar of how one can act generously toward those who are suffering from a loss. He does not simply delay his attack, he aborts it, withdrawing his troops back to Jin, wasting both time and resources out of deference to, and maybe sympathy for, the troubles within the Qi leadership. Xiao Wangzhi is asking the Chinese emperor for much less than Shi Gai required of himself, that is, not to undertake a military enterprise rather than simply to call one off, as Shi Gai did. At the end of the anecdote, Xiao Wangzhi could have lingered upon the moral dimension of Shi Gai's generosity, but he does not. Instead, he refocuses his attention on the present circumstance, offering a brief characterization of the peaceful and friendly relations between the Chinese and the Xiongnu. But he frames it in such a way as to highlight the generosity of the former Chanyu, not of the emperor. Indeed, it is the Chanyu's generous, even moral, intentions that, Xiao Wangzhi implies, has preserved peace between them. Though Wangzhi describes the Chanyu as "envious of refinement," a statement that, on the surface, aggrandizes Chinese civilization and denigrates the Chanyu's generosity of spirit, such a description, even if it were accurate, does not diminish the effects and praiseworthiness of the Chanyu's willingness to submit. Because of the actions and self-designations of the previous Chanyu, peaceful relations were cemented between the Xiongnu and the Han Chinese. Wangzhi also suggests that, because of the deceased Chanyu's actions, the other foreign tribes were more positively disposed toward, or simply more cowed into, working toward peace with the Han Chinese. Why else mention that there were none among the Yi and Di tribes who did not hear of the Chanyu's extension of goodwill?

To take advantage of the Chanyu's untimely murder, then, would be to eliminate what goodwill has already been established, to destroy the progress that has been potentially made in obtaining a future ally, one that would definitely affect how other foreign tribes would respond to Chinese diplomacy. But not only would this be very short-sighted in terms of diplomatic considerations, it would also not achieve anything militarily, causing the Xiongnu, as Han Anguo (and others) have suggested, to flee to distant regions, regions beyond the easy reach of the Chinese army. Xiao Wangzhi avers that the army should be mobilized against the Xiongnu only if the campaign is "righteous," a moral condition that demands there to have been an act of aggression to which the army is responding.[56] Only if the emperor were acting in self-defense, in response to a recent invasion or other infraction of the accord that was about to be formed between the Chinese and the Xiongnu, that is, only if the army was used for "righteous" ends, would a military campaign be worthwhile because the Chinese would be justified and energized in their pursuit of them. The campaign would have the impetus of an ethical justification. Thus in the end analysis, Xiao Wangzhi appears to give the moral aspect not only rhetorical but also epistemic weight, for the moral claim incorporates an understanding of what motivates men to fight for their leaders. In the present circumstances, the emperor would achieve more just by respecting the potential of an alliance and the kindness demanded toward one in mourning, especially when the one mourned has been murdered (or assassinated). Were the Chinese emperor to do this, this, again, would affect not only relations with the Xiongnu but also those with the other tribes. And if the Chanyu's son regained control, his allegiance toward the Chinese because of their forbearance, or even because of their active assistance, would be fixed. "This," Xiao Wangzhi concludes, "is the fullness of virtue."

But how indeed would such be a manifestation of the "fullness of virtue"? Could not the moral aspects of the argument be simply reduced to political considerations? How is acting for possibly politically motivated reasons an expression of virtue? Is not Xiao Wangzhi really arguing for a calculated and politically savvy response to the trouble with the Xiongnu, rather than a morally upright response? Not necessarily. Any sheer distinction between a moral response and a political response would presume that there was an unbreachable divide between them, that to act in a politically calculating way was automatically to compromise the moral efficacy of one's actions. This however is not only an unforgiving distinction, it is also an unrealistic one. To expect, particularly when one's political, and personal, survival depended upon careful calculation of matters of state, that the monarch could be anything less than calculating would be to potentially demand political suicide. Xiao Wangzhi is not asking for the emperor to divorce moral considerations from political ones. He is merely hoping that the moral inform the emperor's thinking, and self-portrayal. Were the emperor not to attack the Xiongnu when their former leader's son is in mourning, not only would he be a more effective politician, he would be able to perceive himself (and have others perceive him) as a more morally upright one. I thus would argue that Xiao Wangzhi gives legitimate epistemic weight to the moral aspect of his response and expects this aspect to be treated with serious consideration in itself, apart from any positive political or military consequences. To describe the epistemic qualities that inform the epistemic weight apparently given to these moral premises would be to investigate the ways in which moral problems were commonly articulated and resolved, an investigation that lies beyond the boundaries of this study. Suffice to say that I would argue that early Chinese ministers held certain moral propositions as being reputable and legitimate in themselves, and that these propositions were treated as popular knowledge, if not common sense. They were thus a part of the fabric of the world, as factual, or nearly as factual, as the nonmoral considerations. Whether or not single moral propositions were treated sufficiently beyond doubt and in accord with general experience to be held as common sense, I would argue that, as frequently as moral considerations were emphasized, the relevance of moral considerations in regard to political matters was not placed in serious doubt.[57]

This moral dimension is one that, in many of the Han addresses regarding military affairs, affects, to some degree, how a military enterprise or political calculation is characterized. In some, as in Xiao Wangzhi's, cited above, or Liu An's or Wei Xiang's addresses,[58] the moral dimension is particularly salient, asserting itself repeatedly. In others, such as Zhao Chongguo's, Chao Cuo's, or Yan You's, moral considerations are not emphasized as heavily, if much at all. Nevertheless, as I have argued, in none is the moral dimension explicitly disregarded or dismissed. Even in the deliberations as prospectively free of moral considerations as Yan You's, we see an evaluative element that takes into account the burden imposed on the common people when preparing for or continuing with military action.[59] This is an ethical judgment, if it is one, that has political consequences, of course, but it is not thereby an amoral one. Though explicit use of a moralizing terminology or moral exemplars can accentuate a moral dimension, their absence does not fully preclude one. The mention of the suffering of commoners, the burden of heavy taxation, the exhaustion experienced by infantry soldiers—because these emphasize human suffering and the need for compassion, they all are sufficient to merit denotation as moral concerns.

My contention is that, in addition to the number of previously mentioned premises relating to the nonmoral aspects of pursuing a military campaign, there appears to be an undivided (or at least unquestioned) acceptance of the moral realm that informs how addresses in the former

Han were composed. As noted above, determination of the exact meaning and use of accepted moral norms (and thus their epistemic qualities) in the histories is not my aim, for such would require the precise understanding of the moral content underlying those phrases or terms that reveal moral considerations, and without a nuanced study of the norms in play in all recorded addresses found in the histories (as opposed to how they were employed in more recondite scholarly fora), their precise determination is impossible. Nevertheless, based on the evidence of the addresses regarding military affairs that inform this study, it is not irresponsible to propose a sample of moral premises taken from many of the early Han addresses regarding military affairs that appeared to be reputable, and thus perhaps treated as some form of popular knowledge:

1. There are standards of right conduct, often manifested in the ritual or religious norms of the past (generally describable as the "way of Heaven"), that must govern how a leader should pursue affairs of state.[60] If these standards are followed by the emperor, the overall moral quality of official transactions will be improved.
2. In his pursuit of victory over his adversaries, the ruler must not ignore the plight of his subjects. If they are suffering, he must alter his plans so that their situation is ameliorated.[61]
3. War is a dangerous and unpredictable affair, the consequences of which can be disastrous, not only in terms of political capital but also in terms of the suffering it causes and the negative effect on the balance of forces that affect the natural and social worlds.[62] It should not be pursued without great caution and examination of the costs and probability of success.
4. The expression of compassion and concern is the manifestation of the virtue of kindness or charity (*hui* 惠 or *en* 恩), the pursuit of which is important in a ruler's duty to treat his subjects as his children. It solidifies their bond and causes harmony to permeate the social world.[63]
5. The greatest and most effective (and really only legitimate) use of an army is to rescue the nation from chaos and punish those who are unjustifiably violent.[64]
6. The unjust pursuit of a military campaign is a criminal act and will inevitably lead to other immoral responses, leading to a state of chaos.[65]

My insistence on effective moral premises being treated as a class (or classes) of evidence that bear upon the addresses regarding military affairs directly contradicts the reduction of these by a number of scholars as superficial veneers for more opportunistic political calculations.[66] Nicola Di Cosmo, for instance, argues such explicitly in his discussion of the conflict, occurring in the sixth century BCE, between the state of Jin and the

Xianyu 鮮虞, a Di tribe. The war waged by Jin against the Xianyu "is another example of how little propriety and virtue mattered in wars fought against foreigners."[67] The moral issues "allegedly" involved in conflicts between foreign tribes and the Han Chinese "were, at their best, mere pretexts":

> Instead, the Chou states found it relatively easy to conduct military campaigns against foreign peoples, sometimes leading to their extermination, because there was no clear moral [proscription] against conquering them. There was, however, a political context that militated against the use of brute force. Less blunt instruments, therefore, such as alliances and peace treaties, were also adopted by the Chou states, though their final aim remained the pursuit of power.[68]

Di Cosmo's perception of amorality in military affairs is by no means limited to the pre-Warring States era. He repeatedly makes ironic reference to the employment of moral norms in his discussions of the Han dynasty conflicts and diplomatic negotiations. He argues that "legalist"—meaning amoral—thought "inspired many of the political ideas of the early imperial period."[69] "Religious" (the scare quotes are his) sanction influenced the workings of the empire only insofar as it was tied to a source of authority that had a firm hold on military and political power. Ministers cynically manipulated religious norms and ideologies, employing their knowledge regarding the management of state affairs (astronomy is mentioned) in order to "appropriate the right to the correct interpretation of the 'will' of Heaven."[70]

And yet, throughout Di Cosmo's interpretations and analyses of the passages he selects, he must sometimes entertain the possibility that moral considerations come into play in a way that is not reducible to the cynically political. In his analysis of the debate discussed above between Wang Hui and Han Anguo, he consistently, and sometimes forcibly, translates moralizing phrases into political terms.[71] Furthermore, as is clear from his excerpted passages, he omits much of the text that uses moral language or speaks to moral concerns. When he does include it, as in Wang Hui's remarks about soldiers being killed in high numbers and there being frequent attacks along the borders that cause "humane people" pain,[72] he passes over it without comment, implicitly suggesting that it was merely an empty flourish rather than a legitimate concern. However, several of the passages he cites, taken from both Wang Hui's and Han Anguo's responses, clearly raise and linger on the moral in more than a perfunctory way. Indeed, almost all of the responses make remarks that are somewhat moral in nature.

Were this moral aspect relatively small and inconsequential or cast into doubt by statements that make their efficacy or relevance problematic, or were this moral aspect not indeed a significant feature of several Han addresses regarding military affairs, Di Cosmo's assertions as to their reducibility would be almost incontestable. Indeed, it is irrefutable that the ministers did at times engage in disingenuous moralizing to make political decisions more palatable. But this does not, in itself, negate the presence or the indubitability of the presence and efficacy of a moral realm, a realm that, whether its roots (and thus the determination of the epistemic qualities of moral evidence) be found in a respect for religious traditions or the honor and duty one must show toward the ancestors or a more abstract (or superstitious) sensibility about the disastrous consequences, natural or social, proceeding from ignoring moral considerations, seems to have been accepted as a kind of "fact." That its elements, its terminology, its logic, was not completely fleshed out or even made complete sense was not germane to its proponents. It was there, and whatever terms like "benevolent" or "righteous" or even "heart-mind" were meant to denote, the moral was respected and valued.

CHAPTER NINE

How Did Ministers Err?

THE EMPEROR'S DESIRE FOR ACCURATE INFORMATION

Facing the onerous task of judging the merits of each address, the monarch was at a supreme disadvantage, for the information he received was almost inevitably adulterated. Officials habitually supervised, and, if they thought it prudent, censored the information the emperor received. If the emperor wished to obtain unfiltered reports from the various regions of the empire, he was often forced to depend on local officials and clerks to act as his eyes and ears.[1] However, even information requested directly from local officials was never perfectly secure, nor thus strictly reliable. There was always the danger, no matter what the source, of information being corrupted or altered before the emperor received it.[2] In spite of the difficulties, Former Han emperors are repeatedly described in the histories as actively endeavoring to obtain reliable information about the actual state of the empire and the prosecution of governmental affairs. They frequently sent emissaries to "travel to the various commanderies and kingdoms" 行郡國, to "conduct a general review" 行視, or "to travel to the various parts of All-Under-Heaven [to observe general trends]" 巡行天下. The reviews had two broadly general aims. One was to root out corruption, to determine, for example, if the people were being ill-treated, if they were unable to make a living, or if local officials were taking bribes or were overly punitive. A second was to determine whether there were extraordinary situations or projects to which the emperor needed to devote particular attention. No matter what particular problem motivated a review, the emperor presumably hoped for the delivery of relevant, generally accurate information he could use to make an informed, appropriate decision. The less accurate the information, the less effective his executive responses.

During interviews with their advisors, monarchs were clearly interested in handling state affairs efficiently and quickly. They wanted to know, presumably as succinctly as possible, just what was at issue and what was most salient in addressing it. Monarchs repeatedly complained of being "wearied" by eloquent men; consequently ministers were quite aware of the dangers of wasting the monarch's time. A Warring States persuader-diplomat, Fan Sui 范雎, phrases his hesitance even to address his monarch in this way: "Now since my neck can't stand up to a chopping block and ax and my waist can't fend off a battle-ax or war-ax, how would I dare to offer dubious matters before Your Majesty?" 今臣之胸不足以當椹質, 而要不足以待斧鉞, 豈敢以疑事嘗試於王哉!³ Here, Fan Sui worries openly that his remarks will exhaust his monarch's patience. Just as significantly, he asserts that the affairs are troubling, "dubious," matters on which a decision cannot easily be made, whether because of their complexity, or because the information on which any decision had to depend was unreliable, incomplete, or simply suspicious. The term, *yishi* 疑事, translatable as "dubious matters" or, better yet, "troubling matters," although not seen terribly frequently in the early Han histories, almost uniformly refers to those matters that result in indecision and insecurity.⁴ "Troubling" matters were those that were difficult to sort out and monarchs were loath to have to resolve them. Zhao Gao 趙高, for instance, in his plot to take control of governmental affairs, advises the Second Emperor of Qin not to handle matters himself and risk looking foolish but to entrust the administration to his ministers. Zhao Gao asserts that the emperor's removing himself from daily affairs will make officials reluctant to bring forward "troubling matters." While it is not entirely clear why Zhao Gao believes the emperor's withdrawal will suppress the number of ministers requesting an audience, I argue that it almost certainly reveals a concern on those ministers' part of wasting the emperor's time.⁵

While at court, the emperor's principal task was to listen to various reports and addresses and decide how to respond. Zhao Gao, in the same passage mentioned above, explains how, with a competent leader such as the Second Emperor's father, none of the officials would dare present false or misleading reports, for fear of punishment:

Zhao Gao persuaded the Second Emperor, saying:

The First Emperor personally administered All-Under-Heaven for a long time. The many ministers did not dare to act falsely or forward slanderous statements. Now, Your Majesty is rich in the number of years left to You and has just recently ascended to his position. For what reason would You convene with high ministers in court to decide matters? If the matters were to be mistakenly handled, this would expose to the many ministers Your shortcomings. The Son of Heaven refers to himself as *zhen* (which symbolizes his superior status). One definitely should not hear His voice. 趙高說二世曰:「先帝臨制天下久, 故群臣不敢為非, 進邪說。今陛下富於春秋, 初即位, 柰何與公卿廷決事? 事即有誤, 示群臣短也。天子稱朕, 固不聞聲。」[6]

Though Zhao Gao's most salient concern is with the emperor's committing an error, the root of the error lies with the emperor being misled by false actions (*wei fei* 為非) or malicious statements (*xie shuo* 邪說). It thus appears that the essence of the emperor's error is grounded in his misperception of the matter at hand, and it is unclear whether the emperor could ever have had access to the unbiased, unfiltered materials necessary to correct any error. Here the term that can be translated as "mistake" or "mistakenly" is *wu* 誤. Its appearance in this instance does not explain what is meant by a "mistake," nor does its appearance at any other point in the *Records*. Indeed, upon examination, any number of terms plausibly translated as "mistake," "error," or "falsehoods" either do not appear in the *Shiji* or *Hanshu* at all (as in the case of *huang* 謊[7]), or appear in contexts that suggest excesses in conduct or judgment, not inaccuracies in sources or materials. One might suspect that scarcity of references to inaccurate information indicates a general lack of interest in considering facts when discussing state business in the early Chinese court, that facts were either not deemed of much use or were not important for the historical representations of state affairs. This suspicion, however, is challenged by much in the records.

In many of the multifarious addresses submitted to the emperor, particulars relating to concrete circumstances, whether they were of the quantifiable sort or not, were judged of utmost relevance and were regularly cited in discussions of state affairs. More to the point, in those instances where his questions or responses elaborate upon the submitted addresses, the monarch's responses reveal his interest in the particulars relating to concrete circumstances.[8] His responses also acknowledge the import of concrete particulars and his judgment of their applicability to the matter at hand. However, the type of response that would definitively confirm the emperor's interest not only in concrete particulars in general but also in their *accuracy*, in a reliability commensurate with our own, is notably absent. We nowhere find an announcement by the monarch that information presented to him is actually just demonstrably *wrong* succeeded by his forwarding other concrete particulars that justify his contradiction of the erroneous materials. Nowhere in early Chinese historical documents (at least none I have read) does a monarch assert that such and such description of a concrete matter is directly contradicted by reliable information. The closest approximation we have to an outright contradiction is the monarch's calling into question the relevance of the proffered information. For instance, in Zhao Chongguo's acclaimed address to Emperor Xuan, the young emperor, exasperated by Zhao Chongguo's refusal to aggressively attack the Qiang, overtly confronts him. At one point in their exchange, after Zhao Chongguo had again insisted on pursuing a war of attrition through the encroaching on Qiang lands using military colonies, Emperor Xuan insinuates that Zhao Chongguo's detailed plan will never lead to the defeat of the Qiang:

> His Highness responded:
>
> The August Thearch questions the General of the Rear Zhao Chongguo about his remarks regarding his wish to disband the cavalry of ten-thousand men and retain the farmlands. Even if we act according to the General's plans, when will the Qiang vermin submit to punishment (i.e., military defeat)? When will the army achieve decisive action? After you consider carefully the expediency of your plan, present another address. 上報曰:「皇帝問後將軍, 言欲罷騎兵萬人留田, 即如將軍之計, 虜當何時伏誅, 兵當何時得決? 孰計其便, 復奏。」[9]

Emperor Xuan is plainly not convinced by Zhao's proposals, in spite of the extraordinary level of detail and Zhao's meticulous exposition about how his plan will work. The emperor either does not believe military colonies will be at all effective or believes they must be used in tandem with more aggressive measures.

There are, in sum, clear indications in the exchanges between monarch and ministers that securing the accuracy of relevant concrete particulars is among the monarch's interests in his deliberative process. He confesses this interest in his queries to ministers. The ministers acknowledge it in their presentations and sometimes the emperor even seeks to secure it rather directly. In no way do we see monarchs ignorant of the essential function of accurate concrete particulars and their need of such to develop effective policy.

PERCEPTION OF "REALITY"

With these select exchanges between monarchs and their ministers we can begin to prove general interest in accurate representation, but more broad-ranging signs of interest in the accurate representation of concrete reality are also found in the use of various terms pertaining to the perception of a state of affairs. Positive expressions include *ran* 然 "it is so," *shi* 是 "corresponds to this state of affairs," and *shishi* 事實 "the substance (or reality) of affairs," often translated simply as the "facts."[10] There are also, of course, negative expressions that imply a contradiction of an actual state of affairs, such as *fei* 非 "to contradict," as well as terms that seem to imply the use of incorrect or mistaken information (and not simply an incorrect or mistaken viewpoint): terms such as *wu* 誤, of course, but also *bu shi* 不實 ("not in accord with the substance [of the affair]"), *bu dang* 不當 ("not fitting"), and *yao yan* 妖言 ("deceptive statements").

As already mentioned, in most instances there is little that precisely defines just what the source of an error was. A typical example of an unexplained attribution of error is the above quoted excerpt from Zhao Gao's conversation with the Second Emperor of Qin, Huhai 胡亥.[11] In that passage, the term translated as "error" is *wu* 誤, and the error involved how a matter or affair (*shi* 事) could be handled.[12] Other instances of the use of *wu* reveal nuances of deception or being misled, instances such as King Hui of Yan's 燕惠王: "I, King Hui of Yan, was new in my position and those around me at court led me into error" 寡人新即位，左右誤寡人.[13] Fortunately, a few exchanges in the *Records of the Grand Historian* reveal more about the kinds of errors that led to distortions of perception and judgment. In the following exchange between Zhang Ao 張敖 and his supporters, Zhang Ao castigates them for their "erroneous" characterization, and thus their perception, of Liu Bang:

> In the seventh year of Han, Gaozu on his way from Pingcheng passed through Zhao. The king of Zhao, Zhang Ao, morning and evening bared his shoulders, donned sleeve guards and apron, and personally offered food to the emperor, behaving extremely deferential in his ritual conduct, acting in accord with the rites for a son-in-law. Gaozu sat with his legs sprawled and cursed Zhang Ao, showing extreme disrespect toward him. Guan Gao, the Chancellor of Zhao, Zhao Wu and others, men over sixty years of age who had long ago been Zhang Er's retainers and who always gave vent to their tempers, were furious, saying, "Our king is a weak king!" They then argued with the King of Zhao, saying, "When the strongmen of All-Under-Heaven rose up together [against Qin], it was those who were capable who were first established as rulers. Now the King serves Gaozu with extreme deference and yet Gaozu has no manners. We beg to kill him for the King!" Zhang Ao bit his finger so hard that he drew blood, saying, "You all speak erroneously! When my father lost his state, he depended on Gaozu to reclaim it. Gaozu's virtue flows to the sons and grandsons of my father. Even the smallest hair on my body is owed to Gaozu's power. I wish you all do not again open your mouths about this." Guan Gao, Zhao Wu, and the other ten or so men all responded saying, "Then we all have spoken incorrectly. Our king is an exemplary man who will not betray Gaozu's virtuous conduct." 漢七年，高祖從平城過趙，趙王朝夕袒韝蔽，自上食，禮甚卑，有

子婿禮. 高祖箕踞詈, 甚慢易之. 趙相貫高、趙午等年六十餘, 故張耳客也. 生平為氣, 乃怒曰:「吾王孱王也!」說王曰:「夫天下豪桀並起, 能者先立. 今王事高祖甚恭, 而高祖無禮, 請為王殺之!」張敖齧其指出血, 曰:「君何言之誤! 且先人亡國, 賴高祖得復國, 德流子孫, 秋豪皆高祖力也. 願君無復出口.」貫高、趙午等十餘人皆相謂曰:「乃吾等非也. 吾王長者, 不倍德.」[14]

By contradicting their perceptions, Zhang Ao wishes to dissuade his men from murdering Gaozu. His men have spoken "erroneously" (*yan zhi wu* 言之誤), their judgment about Gaozu "incorrectly" ignoring the protection Gaozu offered Zhang Ao's father in the past, an arrangement that may not be completely accurate, but that Zhang Ao offers as established fact and that none dare to contradict. Because of Gaozu's past favor, Zhang Ao insists that he has a duty to be deferential, in spite of Gaozu's poor behavior.

Such appraisals of character and what characters deserve are a common area of erroneous perception. Though these errors often involved judgments about action, they significantly center on the perceptions that inform judgment. Two additional instances further substantiate this: first, the dispute about the ranking of Xiao He 蕭何 over Cao San 曹參[15] and, second, the dispute about whether Han Xin 韓信 should trust Gaozu.[16] In both instances, the speakers make a case in which they explicitly assert that others have been mistaken in their perceptions. But as with the above instance, the insistent identification of error does not contradict what has been perceived. Returning to the example discussed above, Zhang Ao does not contest that Gaozu has been rude or disrespectful; rather the source of his men's error about Gaozu's character is their lack of cognizance of or emphasis on Gaozu's early support of Zhang's father. In the case of the ranking of Xiao He over Cao San, the many courtiers who advocated ranking Cao San over Xiao He had overlooked or undervalued Xiao He's many contributions. Regarding whether Han Xin should trust Gaozu, Kuai Tong 蒯通 insists that Han Xin is wrong (*wu* 誤) to put any faith in his relationship with Gaozu, saying that even the most secure relationships are prone to betrayal when political interests are involved. In all three of these instances, the basis of the error is less inaccuracy in perception than lacking (*que* 缺) the proper information. Indeed, their error is akin to the error of a document that "lacks" complete information: a document is "lacking" and thus flawed or mistaken.

Notably, in the above-cited instances in which people's perceptions are deemed erroneous, as lacking in some respect, there is tacit sympathy between the speaker and his audience. Zhang Ao shares his men's irritation with Gaozu; Gentleman E 鄂, in contrast to other courtiers, shares the emperor's stated preference for Xiao He over Cao San. Thus "error" in both circumstances—and, I would suggest, in most circumstances—is not an objectively incontestable error. It is instead an error of emphasis or of ignorance, a deficiency that allows the original perception of the interlocutor to remain basically unaltered. The loose boundaries of the sources of error—that it commonly appears to be treated as stemming from the manner in which information is communicated or received rather than any objective discrepancy between what is perceived and what is the case—permits an expanded boundary on what could have been treated as reliable and useful.

RUMOR AND NATURAL SIGNS AS INFORMATION

If error is not commonly characterized as a stark error in perception, the issue is less perception than what is deemed most salient in its representation.[17] Such a hypothesis would seem to be supported by various applications of not only *wu* 誤 to discussions of court affairs but also other terms such as *e* 訛, generally translatable as "rumor." In the Han histories, at first glance the term appears to denote a kind of false representation. In the following example, a young girl comes to the capital to report that a great flood was approaching the capital, terrifying the government clerks. The emperor blames this reputedly "false rumor" on the mistreatment of the common people by the local government officials:

> In the fall, there was a great flood in the capital area, the Area Within the Pass. In the seventh month, a young girl from Tishang named Chen Chigong heard that a great flood was coming and ran into the Hengcheng Gate, and without proper documentation entered a side gate into the Weiyang Palace gardener's office [and announced the news]. The clerks and commoners climbed the city walls in fright. In the ninth month, the emperor issued an edict: "Recently, certain commanderies and kingdoms suffered flooding, which led to the drowning of many people, as many as several thousand. Members of the court without basis spread the rumor that a great flood was coming. The clerks and the commoners were frightened and fled to climb the city walls. This occurred probably because the cruel, violent, and harshly punitive [local] clerks have not yet desisted [in their acts of cruelty] and a multitude of commoners have unfairly been deprived of their livelihoods. I hereby dispatch Grand Master of Remonstrance Lin, among others, to make a tour of All-Under-Heaven." 秋, 關內大水. 七月, 庛上小女陳持弓聞大水至, 走入橫城門, 闌入尚方掖門, 至未央宮鉤盾中. 吏民驚上城. 九月, 詔曰:「乃者郡國被水災, 流殺人民, 多至千數. 京師無故訛言大水至, 吏民驚恐, 奔走乘城. 殆苛暴深刻之吏未息, 元元冤失職者眾. 遣諫大夫林等循行天下.」[18]

Though it does not appear very often in the Han historical records, the employment of *e* 訛 is significant in several respects. It almost invariably describes the reaction of the common people to extraordinary natural phenomena, such as an eclipse, an earthquake, or, as in the example above, a flood, reactions that were communicated using folk songs and rhymed chants, the common vehicles of rumor. The promulgation of such rumors is often mentioned in conjunction with attempts to divine with lots, commonly phrased as, "The commoners spread rumors and cast lots" 民訛言行籌.[19] These rumors were perceived by members of the court, and by the emperor himself, to indicate the state of the common people. Thus although they are denigrated by officials as false representations of events, they nevertheless are important sources of information for the court, for they reveal the underlying discomfiture or unease among the populace, a sign that the governance of the empire is flawed, corrupt, or somehow inadequate.

While peasants could theoretically communicate their grievances through the presentation of an official petition at court,[20] in practice, most presumably did not, whether because of the difficulty of verifying its transmission to the proper authorities (venal local authorities could interfere) or because the personal risks were too great. Instead, most of the information gathered from the populace was gathered informally or through the emperor's own emissaries. Indeed, there are a host of references in early Chinese literature to the need for the monarch to listen to the grievances of the common people. Martin Kern notes that, starting with *Zuozhuan*, anonymous folk songs "frequently announce major calamities like the untimely death of a ruler, a major military defeat, or even the fall of a state. Such prophecies are couched in simple rhymes and gain much of their authority from the ideal of innocent and undistorted truth embodied in the minds and voices of the common people or, quite often, children."[21] Clearly, the major purpose of these folks songs or chants was the communication of bad news. Early employments of *e* 訛 in the *Shijing* emphasize the critical nature of folk songs, as illustrated in this passage: "Layers of frost in the first month, / My heart suffers with worry. / [Accusatory] chants among the common people / are already very prevalent" 正月繁霜, 我心憂傷。民之訛言, 亦孔之將.[22]

Although these rumors came to be treated, perhaps intentionally, by the authorities as false representations of the actual state of affairs, they were not therefore to be dismissed out of hand. Faced with the pervasive corruption of official channels, the monarch was obliged to marshal every possible resource. Indeed, monarchs were repeatedly adjured by their (presumably well-meaning) advisors to pay close attention to what the common people were saying, or risk social unrest.[23] As Liu Tao 劉陶 advocated in the Latter Han to Emperor Huan 桓 (劉志),

> Listen to the folk tunes of the commoners, inquire about that which the old man on the road worries about, scrutinize the patterned

brilliance of the sun, moon, and stars, observe the convolutions and curves of the mountains and rivers. Then will you immediately understand the mind of All-Under-Heaven, the great affairs of the states and households, and there will be no confusion born of oversight and omission. 聽民庶之謠吟, 問路叟之所憂, 瞰三光之文耀, 視山河之分流. 天下之心, 國家大事, 粲然皆見, 無有遺惑者矣。[24]

Since they apparently arose from the general populace, these "chanted rumors" avoided the corruptions that frequently plagued official information. Indeed, the repeated attention given to rumor in the early histories, I argue, highlights the general problem of informational reliability, whether official or unofficial, and the serious, entrenched problem of active misinformation, of intrigue and deception. It is highly significant that doubts or questions are rarely raised in early Han court discussions relating to the reliability of the information received from the commoners. Since all channels were somewhat unreliable, it appears that unattributed and unverified information, even rumor, was to be taken seriously, at least until there was some reason to reject it.

The catholic examination of various sources of information, both social and natural, is exactly what Li Xun 李尋, a member of the staffs of Chancellor Zhai Fangjin 翟方進 and Marshal of State Wang Gen 王根, advocates in his address to Wang Gen.[25] A student of natural signs, Li Xun was concerned about the inauspicious signs for the Han imperial house. He counsels extreme care in the choice of assistants, for "when worries and responsibilities are extremely heavy, the crux is obtaining the [right] people" 憂責甚重, 要在得人.[26] He then elaborates:

> Success or failure is a consequence of whom you hire. You must take the utmost care with this. In the past, Duke Mu of Qin took pleasure in silver-tongued orations and employed incautious Braves. He personally experienced great disgrace and his state was almost lost. He regretted his excesses and blamed himself. He thought about the yellow-haired [Jian Shu 蹇叔, who had advised him not to wage the disastrous attack on Zheng].[27] He took into his employ Bailixi, who eventually became the Earl of the Western Reaches. His virtue was in keeping with the Way of the Kings. The misfortune and fortune of these two being like this—how could one not take heed [of their experiences]? 得人之效, 成敗之機, 不可不勉也. 昔秦穆公說諓諓之言, 任仡仡之勇, 身受大辱, 社稷幾亡. 悔過自責, 思惟黃髮, 任用百里奚, 卒伯西域, 德列王道. 二者禍福如此, 可不慎哉![28]

Duke Mu of Qin was heedlessly uncritical of the various advice he received from people such as Qizi 杞子, Fengsun 逢孫, and Yangsun 楊孫 and therefore met with disaster in his attack against Zheng 鄭. With this example, Li Xun expands on his argument that not just the number but the *quality* of one's advisors, and thus the information and advice one receives from them, is crucial to the survival of the state and the preservation of one's reputation: "I pray you have worthy friends and stalwart assistants. These subjects can protect your life, extend your family line, and bring peace to the nation" 唯有賢友彊輔, 庶幾可以保身命, 全子孫, 安國家.[29]

For Li Xun, the signs of the natural world should be treated as sources of information that are as reliable as that received from one's officials. He avers that these signs must be thoroughly scrutinized in order to know better what administrative measures to take and for advance warnings about future opportunities or disasters.[30] For instance, were one to foment a rebellious insurrection—which he is almost certainly insinuating that Wang Gen should not do—"if calamitous defeat will be the result, signs and omens will reveal this beforehand" 咎敗將至, 徵兆為之先見.[31] All available signs of future changes of fortune must be surveyed: one must regard the heavenly patterns, investigate the principles of the earth, observe the waxing and waning of the sun and moon, study the movements of the stars, look into the alterations in the mountains and rivers, and pay close attention to developments in the songs and customs of the people (人民謠俗). Yet since these signs are "dark" and "hidden," they require expert readers of the natural patterns to discover them. In spite of their need to be interpreted, he asserts their truth is nonpartisan, for there is an undisputable relation between the patterns of the natural and those of the social world. Since government is necessarily affected by the changes in the natural world, one must attempt to follow these changes. The signs revealing these changes are the means by which one can know in what ways government must be adjusted. Just as iron arises out of the conjoining of iron ore with the coal fires in the extraction process, so government arises out of the conjoining of the natural forces of *yin* and *yang*. In each process, the effect is "trustworthy," believable.[32]

RELIABILITY AND INFORMATION

Li Xun's phrasing his assessment on the "correctness" of the influence of natural processes on the political world in terms of "trustworthiness" (*ke xin* 可信) is indicative of the tendency to evaluate the worth of information or arguments in these terms.[33] The "trustworthiness" of the information was judged not only in relation to its purveyor but also in relation to the quality of the information itself. Wu Zixu 伍子胥, for instance, remonstrated against the King of Wu 吳王 for employing the plan formulated by an official, Great Steward Bo Pi 伯嚭, who had been repeatedly bribed by King Goujian of Yue 越王勾踐, saying that the King of Wu "trusted," or better, "believed," "the airy phrases and deceptive falsehoods" (*fuci zhawei* 浮辭詐偽) forwarded by Bo Pi on Yue's behalf.³⁴ In the evaluation of arguments, all information and all analyses were judged for "believability," for "reliability," whether because their specific origins or purveyors were unreliable, or because, more broadly, no source was absolutely reliable. Because concern regarding the "believability" or "trustworthiness" of a source is so pervasive in court addresses and debates, because this concern seems not to be particularly directed at any one type of source or individual, it would appear that the problem is a holistic one, a concern about the unbelievability, the untrustworthiness of almost *any* source. And if all sources were potentially untrustworthy, then the primary concern in deciding to rely on them would not, at least initially, be the accuracy but rather the *plausibility* of a source's representation of a general state of affairs. In such a circumstance, it is not surprising that natural signs, such as the phases of the moon or sun, were accepted as indicators of underlying regular processes and of the correct course of action. Indeed, they might very reasonably have been deemed by some to be more believable than reports received through the usual political channels. Compared with these reports, the impersonal symbols of the natural world might have appeared well-nigh objective, as close to the undistorted factual truth as one could get.

Whatever the case, the problem of error was thus reduced to the reliability of one's informant, of whether he, and thus his information, could be trusted or believed. Those who could not be believed were deemed "slanderers." "Believing slanderous remarks" (*xin chan* 信讒) is repeatedly raised as a concern in the Han histories.³⁵ Executives were highly susceptible to the influence of false or misleading reports or remarks. Having no basis to judge, they could be utterly deceived merely by the repeated assertion of a false statement, as King Anli of Wei 魏安釐王 was by the false insinuations repeatedly forwarded by spies from Qin.³⁶ Most terms for "lying"—*chan* 讒, *chan* 諂, *yu* 諛, *hui* 毀, *huo* 惑, *feibang* 誹謗—are more properly translated as "slander," "flattery," or "distortion," not as the outright contradiction of a verifiable report. Lying at court, as with other forms of erroneous speech acts, was not defined by a discrete act involving the clear negation of discrete information or the substitution of a false piece of information for a correct one. Lying was the act of misdirecting and confusing the audience's perceptions, and thus, his judgments. If my reading is correct, if the monarch did not have ready access to reliable materials, he would have few means by which to rectify any confusion or misdirection and thus was extremely vulnerable to being manipulated. But should then the monarch strive to verify the information he receives? Wouldn't he then be less prone to manipulation? Actually, as *Hanfeizi* insightfully recommends, it would be better if he didn't bother; his aim should only be to determine the agenda of his addressors. Knowing that they will attempt to structure their remarks based on his reactions, he can assess their motives by analyzing their attempts at manipulation. It is only natural, *Hanfeizi* asserts, to assume that the monarch's addressors will attempt to play upon and take advantage of his moods. In a calmer hour, the self-conscious monarch, through careful analysis of their responses to his reactions, can "obtain the signs of their vilification and aggrandizement, of their public and private [faces]" 以得毀譽公私之徵.[37]

Surrounded by self-interested persuaders aiming to manipulate him toward their favored course of action, monarchs would naturally have been distrustful, even paranoid, about the advice they received. Monarchs would regularly voice their concern regarding corruption at court and the threat of manipulation by nefarious advisors. Concomitantly, certain monarchs also repeatedly expressed a desire for forthright, honest advice, advice that was untainted by personal agendas. Not surprisingly, in this climate of unrelenting suspicion, even straightforward, forthright advisors were vulnerable to charges of slander and manipulation. Emblematic of this problem, ministers themselves sometimes sardonically refer to honest critics as "slanderers" (*feibang de ren* 誹謗的人), as in Jia Shan's address to Emperor Wen about the First Emperor of Qin. Jia Shan's argument is that when the empire is weak, as in the final years of the Qin dynasty, there is no commitment to its strengthening, and thus to offering direct, critical advice. Why did the Second Emperor not know of the problems of the empire? Because there were none who dared report honestly what was going on. And why was that? Because government officials, and the emperor in particular, gave little concern to the problems of the empire, to taking care of those who needed help. Instead of having their advice considered seriously, those who attempted to speak honestly to the court were either "retired" or murdered:

> Why did the First Emperor of Qin live among ruins and not himself know about [the empire's decline]? Because among All-Under-Heaven, there were none who dared make a report [about the poor state of the empire]. For what reason were there none who dared to make a report? There was no righteous commitment to take care of the elderly, there were no ministers willing to assist, there were no *shi* who would come forward to remonstrate.[38] The Emperor unrestrainedly executed punishments, forcing those who "slandered" it into retirement, killing those *shi* who directly remonstrated. For this reason, the ministers speak flatteringly to curry favor and ingratiate themselves. When they assess the Emperor's virtue, he is more worthy than Yao and Shun; when they evaluate his accomplishments, then he is more worthy than Tang or Wu. All-Under-Heaven has

already crumbled and none report it. The *Book of Odes* states, "It is not that words are inadequate. Why would you refrain out of fear or worry? If he listens, then respond. If he slanders you, then retire."[39] This is the point. It also states, "Marvelous are the many *shi* with whom King Wen brought tranquility to the empire."[40] All-Under-Heaven by no means had lost its *shi*. So why did the ode about King Wen only mention those who brought tranquility? When King Wen gave preference to benevolence, then benevolence flourished. When he acquired *shi* and treated them respectfully, then the *shi* were employed. He employed them with an eye to the rites and propriety. 秦皇帝居滅絕之中而不自知者何也? 天下莫敢告也. 其所以莫敢告者何也? 亡養老之義, 亡輔弱之臣, 亡進諫之士, 縱恣行誅, 退誹謗之人, 殺直諫之士, 是以道諛諂合苟容, 比其德則賢於堯舜, 課其功則賢於湯武, 天下已潰而莫之告也. 詩曰:「匪言不能, 胡此畏忌, 聽言則對, 譖言則退.」此之謂也. 又曰:「濟濟多士, 文王以寧.」天下未嘗亡士也, 然而文王獨言以寧者何也? 文王好仁則仁興, 得士而敬之則士用, 用之有禮義。[41]

Jia Shan's ironic application of "slanderer" to those who offer forthright, genuine advice is indicative of the trend to label "false" speech, whether truly false or only politically unacceptable, as slanderous. To forward an honest appraisal of a state of affairs that could contradict what the monarch wished to hear was often highly dangerous, and self-conscious emperors knew that.[42] For the monarch and thus the court in general, "liars" are not simply those who intentionally contradict true reports, they are those who contradict the political aims and preferences of the court.[43] As Emperor Wen himself forthrightly acknowledges, when a leader who wishes to be honestly apprised of the conditions of the empire holds these aims and preferences, then the criticisms of his advisors will be more effective. Emperor Wen admits that if he is not virtuous and perceptive, the benefit of intelligent ministers will be for naught: "Were I not yet virtuous or perceptive, [even if] I were enlightened, I would not be able to bring [problems] to light, and [even if] I were knowledgeable, I would not be able to govern [properly]" 朕既不德, 又不敏, 明弗能燭, 而智不能治.[44] With an open-minded, sensitive monarch, "truth" perhaps would more closely correlate with the facts and "slander" with falsehood. But whether or not this is the case, "slander" is consistently the operative term by which false, distorted speech is described. Indeed, it is not so much falsehood as distortion and confusion that are specifically at issue.

Because of this association between slander and political aim within the operations of the government, Chinese literati repeatedly engaged with the problem of distortion and confusion. Although they could not guarantee the monarch's own interest in discovering the actual state of affairs, they were well aware that many in the court wished, through eloquent artifice, to contribute to its obscuration. In the early Chinese texts, direct, "truthful" speech is almost always represented as being antithetical to eloquent and thereby misleading speech. In *Laozi* 81 this is stated explicitly: "Trustworthy words are not beautiful, beautiful words are not trustworthy" 信言不美, 美言不信. Eloquent speakers are incessantly denigrated, as when Sima Jizhu 司馬季主 states that "rhetors" were obligated to use extended displays of verbal trickery to catch their rulers' attention.[45] The danger of manipulative remarks was extreme, for they could corrode even the strongest bonds of affection and loyalty. The Former Han official Du Qin 杜欽 speaks specifically to this problem in his remarks to Emperor Cheng's maternal uncle, Wang Feng 王鳳, about slanderous statements promulgated by King Wu of Zhou's older brothers, Guanshu Xian 管叔鮮 and Cai Shudu 蔡叔度, about the Duke of Zhou. These slanderous statements, Du Qin cautioned, could have influenced King Cheng of Zhou, were it not for King Cheng's own resolute sense of the Duke of Zhou's overwhelming virtue. Du Qin then adds a more contemporary example: before the Warring States persuader-diplomat Fan Sui 范雎 spoke with the King of Qin, the King and the Marquis of Rang 穰侯 had been inseparable. In the monarchic environment, no relationship, no commitment, whether to a person or to a view of the world, even to those views grounded in fact, was invulnerable to manipulation and distortion.[46]

MISINFORMATION AND MINISTERIAL ERROR

In the discussion above, I have highlighted the apparent consensus that all sources required circumspect treatment. Yet the veracity or accuracy of documents submitted to the central court is almost never explicitly discussed in the historical texts. There is never in the Former Han histories (or, it appears, even in the pre-Han historical documents) any extended discussion of whether the information in a report or missive—from either an official, an office, or a region—is false, forged, or distorted. The most we have are bare, unsupported assertions that a claim or document is false, such as in the following exchange, when Emperor Zhao 昭 insists to Huo Guang 霍光 that a document composed at the behest of the King of Yan charging Huo Guang with wishing to arrogate power is false:

> "The General may put his cap back on. I know this document is a swindle. The General has committed no offence." Huo Guang said, "How does Your Majesty know this?" The Emperor said, "The General went to Guangming to conduct a review of the Gentlemen [and the Feathered Forest Corps] and it has not even been ten days since the transfer and promotion of Colonels [to your command]. How

did the King of Yan become cognizant of [both of these events]? Furthermore, even if the General were acting falsely, you would not need these Colonels [to carry out any plot]." 上曰: 「將軍冠. 朕知是書詐也. 將軍亡罪.」 光曰: 「陛下何以知之?」上曰: 「將軍之廣明, 都郎屬耳. 調校尉以來未能十日, 燕王何以得知之? 且將軍為非, 不須校尉.」[47]

Though the basis of the emperor's assertion is a personal faith, however genuine, in Huo Guang, this instance reveals that the possible "falsity" or, better, "deceptiveness" of the document was recognized, that, just as with oral address, written documents could not simply be taken at face value.

In the classical corpus, extended discussions of how a monarch should evaluate the presentations made by his officials, discussions that occupy significant portions of *Hanfeizi*, appear to be meant to apply to all data received by the emperor. In these discussions, concern with the veracity of received documentation is identical with the concern with veracity in general. In the following excerpt, *Hanfeizi* offers an illuminating passage about how the emperor should dispose himself toward what he receives:

> If you do not critically attend to what you hear then you will have no means by which to interrogate your inferiors. If their speech is not evaluated with regard to its applications then you'll be faced with duplicitous persuasions. If their speech is directed at [relevant] concrete particulars, then it can be treated as thoroughly trustworthy. When the concrete particulars are not apposite, if a few people assert them, then you should doubt them; if many people assert them, then it is the case; if a multitude of people asserts them, your conviction should not be shaken. 聽不參則無以責下, 言不督乎用則邪說當上。言之為物也以多信。不然之物, 十人云疑, 百人然乎, 千人不可解也。[48]

Even though in *Hanfeizi* there is the recognition that a speech that attends to relevant concrete particulars (*wu* 物) is that which deserves the most secure assent, *Hanfeizi* discussed it only perfunctorily, which suggests that this type of speech was relatively rare. For the rest of the essay, attention is directed at what was probably a much more common occurrence, namely, when the asserted relevant concrete particulars were not reliable or were not the central piece of the forwarded argument. Because there are so many ways to confuse and distract the monarch, to play to his sympathies or even to blame him for a policy failure, *Hanfeizi* urges repeatedly that the monarch wrestle out of his advisors that which they must stand behind, to force them to assert a strong position on a focused question and not equivocate. Yet the emperor must not defer his judgment awaiting further information or intensive scrutiny of the proposals: "If the ruler of men does not vent his anger [at extended, ornate, complicated arguments] but waits to see if they accord with investigation, his power will be afforded to his inferiors" 人主不懸忿而待合參, 其勢資下也. Instead, the emperor must attend to the applied consequences and constructive uses of forwarded policy proposals: "The wise ruler listens to speeches, assesses their applied consequences, and evaluates their constructive uses. From his evaluations of their constructive uses, rewards and punishments arise" 有道之主, 聽言, 督其用, 課其功, 功課而賞罰生焉.

Consequently, the penultimate task of the monarch, as really with any executive, is to be cognizant of the prejudicial selection of information, of the personal interests that his advisors may have in the success or failure of a policy, and to extricate that interest from the mass of information and argument provided. Given that the monarch must decide swiftly how to respond, he cannot himself spend the requisite time evaluating the veracity of the facts themselves, and ministers were certainly aware of this. If the success or failure of a proposal was not dependent on the correctness of its information but rather the applied consequences or the constructive use of such a proposal, it is not surprising that proposals often lacked such concrete information or were not careful about its accuracy. Accordingly, the standard by which ministers are to be evaluated is not the factual correctness of their proposals but their ability to carry out their duties, to speak carefully about the problems at hand and follow through successfully with what they propose. Whether or not the information they use to formulate their argument is correct is actually irrelevant. This is not to say that their proposals do not need to be buttressed by relevant and accurate information—indeed, *Hanfeizi* states explicitly that they do[49]—but it is not the duty of the executive to verify this, nor is it politically wise for him to do so. If the majority of that with which the monarch is presented does not contradict what a minister proposes and the proposal itself appears to be worthy on its own merits, then the monarch has sufficient basis to consider it seriously, regardless of what figures are used. This standard, of course, falls well short of what we might ourselves believe rigorous investigation and complex government should demand. But it is one that is frequently applied, in both the ancient and modern world, to political spheres in which time is of the essence and information is often not terribly trustworthy. The greatest error that the monarch can commit in his own deliberations is to let his personal feelings about the matter get in the way (or even to be divulged), for it benefits only those who wish to manipulate him.

In conclusion, I offer a provisional answer to the question inspiring this analysis: how could a minister err in the early Chinese court? First, he could err by not thoroughly knowing what his duties are and those matters pertaining to his duties. Second, he could err on the side of vagueness that would encourage indecision, of asserting something with too many qualifications or equivocations to serve as effective advice or recommendation. Third, most egregiously and most dangerously, he could attempt to use his knowledge of the emperor's predilections to manipulate him for personal or professional advantage. This would be not only a personal error (for which he could be severely punished) but a professional error, for his policies, no matter how good or reasonable, might not be accepted and his word would be less valued.

CHAPTER TEN

A Diversity of Evidence

CATEGORIES OF "FACTS"

So where do these analyses lead us? How do these investigations into the rhetorical quality of the evidence employed in the addresses help us to better understand the nature and quality of the early Han historical project? I insist that they assist us, at the very minimum, to assess in what manner the evidence in the addresses might have been treated *as* evidence, as the support structure for the justification of an argument. This allows us to discern not only the epistemic bases upon which the executive decided to take action but also the applicability of the divide between fact and fiction, so often used in modern appraisals of the Han histories. What it also abets is our understanding of to what extent Han historians were committed to giving their readers the "facts." Indeed, a significant portion of modern scholarship on the early Han historical consciousness emphasizes its rationality and commitment to factual objectivity, with Weber's notion of rationalization through bureaucratization fundamentally informing these generalizations. The rise of the bureaucracy, according to Weber, allowed for the increasingly impartial organization of information and delegation of governmental tasks,[1] a governmental structure that permitted figures of such monumental importance as Sima Qian and Ban Gu to carefully pursue their arrangement and composition of the ancient Chinese historical narrative in a more objective and impersonal fashion, one less hampered by the limitations of incomplete information or dubious hearsay and fictionalization of events.[2] Michael Nylan summarizes what she calls this "social scientific" line of appraisal and the reasons for it:

> Supporters of the social scientific appraisal refer to Sima Qian's frequent visits to historical sites, where he gathered written materials,

surveyed the local topography, and canvassed local authorities on their knowledge of past events. They note also that in key passages, the *Shiji* reproduces several variant traditions, where the traditions cannot be easily reconciled, which suggests to them that Sima Qian is committed to the objective principle that "in doubtful cases, one transmits the doubt." They hail Sima Qian's even-handed and unsentimental treatment of historical figures. Basing themselves on this sort of evidence, adherents of the social scientific reading commend Sima Qian as a "true" historian because of his scrupulous care and apparent objectivity in handling the source materials that he had at his disposal to transmit.[3]

This "social scientific" characterization extends even into appraisals of the quality of the court documents or policy discussions themselves and, by extension, to the hortatory addresses. E. A. Kracke, for instance, writes:

> Conceptually, policy [in pre-modern China] was determined not by a preponderance of opinion but by *a rational consensus achieved through objective discussion*. Both policy suggestions and factual reports often originated with local officials, who were best informed on public needs, and passed through administrative channels to the Imperial Court. Since the Confucian ethos made each official personally responsible for popular welfare and criticism of government, officials at all levels ardently advocated one policy or another. Once policy was decided, each official had the duty of carrying it out in complete and meticulous conformity with the ruler's intention.[4]

Kracke's sentiments are not exceptional in recent scholarship. Michael Loewe praises the careful logic underlying the more concretely grounded of the addresses. For instance, in reference to Chao Cuo's address, he judges that Chao Cuo "showed a clear understanding of the relative merits and use of cavalry, infantry, bowmen and men armed with other types of weapon, and the advantages of different types of terrain."[5] He proclaims that Zhao Chongguo's argument was "systematic and forceful"[6] and that Yan You's 嚴尤 advice was "sound."[7] But on what grounds does he assert such positive appraisals? Though Loewe himself doesn't justify them, regarding those addresses that concretely and systematically detail and analyze the problems relating to the Xiongnu, he presumably somewhat shares Kracke's sentiment, namely, that these addresses were rational and objective because of their emphasis on concrete data and judgments grounded in pragmatic assessments of military realities.[8]

Yet we must ask: How much did the concreteness of these reports lend strength to their ultimate conclusions, and to the possible overcoming of the executive's doubts? Is their concreteness of the evidence fundamental for their potentially appearing persuasive to the emperor? In Chapter Five, I discussed Chen Zhi's comment that Zhao Chongguo's sequence of calculations relating to a recommendation for the amount of provisions needed for the campaign oddly did not tally with each other, even though the calculations were not complex.[9] There is no reason to suppose that this was necessarily due to Zhao Chongguo's own miscalculation.[10] Of course, it may have resulted from a scribal error, but, as I have argued, a greater tendency that is demonstrated across all of the addresses is that absolute accuracy is not the most important standard by which the "truth" of the addresses, and thus its epistemic persuasiveness, was probably judged. Rather, I have suggested, the standard is more one of the suggestibility of the address relating to what the addressor's "vision of the truth of the matter" (*zhi* 志), which, in its broadest formulation, necessarily pertains to the good, and continued health, of the state. The more particularized formulations of the "truth of the matter," naturally, depend upon exactly what the matter under deliberation is in the specific address or debate and thus the concrete specifics informing such. My analysis, I believe, calls into question our inherited, deeply embedded norms of assessing the "factual" content through the accuracy of its concrete representations. I have attempted to reveal what exactly was relied upon as fact, whether it was a concrete particular or a "reputable opinion." From my analysis, the employed "reputable opinions" are divided, in their simplest categorization, between the nonmoral and moral. This distinction, to reiterate, should not be equated with a distinction between the pragmatic/realistic and the unpragmatic/idealistic. Nonmoral and moral "facts," as was indicated in the lengthy debate between Han Anguo and Wang Hui, are offered by both perceived realists and the idealists. Indeed, I question the usefulness of these rubrics and wonder if their application does not actually blind us to the subtle nuances of the arguments relating to the broader issues at hand.

TYPES OF CONCRETE PARTICULARS OFFERED IN THE ADDRESSES

Since concrete, and assumedly nonmoral, considerations are a frequent focus for most of the early Han addresses regarding military affairs, it would be well to address the general epistemic quality and weight of these nonmoral considerations first. We can assess the general epistemic quality of concrete particulars by selecting out the most common and evaluating how they were elaborated upon in various addresses. Several concrete features of note are the psychological, cultural, and topographical generalities that are used when describing the obstacles and dangers of entering into enemy territory or fighting with the enemy. These generalities are also often found in the *Intrigues*. For example, in his address to the King of Wei, the Warring States persuader, Zhu Ji 朱己, compares the psychology of the Qin rulers to that of the Rong 戎 and Di 狄:

> Ch'in shares customs with the Jung and the Ti barbarians; she has the mentality of a tiger or a wolf; she delights in cruelty, is covetous of gain and knows nothing of good faith, protocol, righteousness or virtuous action. If she spies advantage in anything she will have it with no regard for what happens to her kin, in the manner of a wild beast. All the empire is aware of this. 秦與戎、翟同俗, 有虎狼之心, 貪戾好利而無信, 不識禮義德行。苟有利焉, 不顧親戚兄弟, 若禽獸耳。此天下之所同知也。[11]

Such an unflattering description of the psychology of barbarian tribes is present in many of the addresses and debates recorded in the Han histories.[12] The following description offered by Hou Ying 侯應 is a typical example:

> As for the psychological disposition of the barbarians, when they meet with trouble then they are lowly and submissive, when they are strong, then they are arrogant and rebellious. This is their Heaven-sent nature. 夫夷狄之情, 困則卑順, 彊則驕逆, 天性然也。[13]

Liu An offers another much harsher generalized depiction:

> The Yue people are stupid and bull-headed, simple and vapid, and fickle in upholding covenants. It wouldn't even be the length of one day before they stopped applying the laws and measures of the Son of Heaven. 越人愚戇輕薄, 負約反覆, 其不用天子之法度, 非一日之積也。[14]

Uncivilized, belligerent, and simple-minded, foreign tribes nevertheless were sources of continual frustration. Behind the arrogant and self-aggrandizing posturing, these disparaging, simplifying portrayals reveal the Han Chinese to be relatively unsure of the motives and aims of the foreign tribes. In spite of the declared simplicity of the foreign tribesmen and their motives, they were still able to pose repeated, serious threats to the borders of the empire. In fact, what is emphasized in the address is not their predictability but their *unpredictability*, how unlike the Chinese they were—how uncivilized, how unbound by any code or regulation, creatures who were historically perceived as not belonging to the human race.[15] The Chinese officials constantly had to defend against surprise attacks. If anything, the foreign tribes were shrewd and cunning, able to continuously frustrate their Chinese opponents' expectations. As Wang

Mang's general, Yan You, declared, even after hundreds of years of strife, the Xiongnu were still a menace.[16]

Another ubiquitous concrete point of emphasis is the geographic or environmental obstacles that the army will face when pursuing the enemy, particularly when the enemy is nomadic and willing to settle, or hide, in inhospitable areas. Zhu Fuyan puts this very common objection in the mouth of Li Si as Li Si remonstrates with the First Emperor of Qin against pursuing a campaign against the Xiongnu:

> His minister Li Si remonstrated with him, saying, "This is not permissible. The Xiongnu have no cities or forts and no stores of provisions. They move from place to place like flocks of birds, and thus are difficult to catch and control. If parties of lightly equipped soldiers penetrate deeply into their territory, their food supplies will certainly become exhausted, and if we try to send provisions after them in order that they may continue on, the baggage trains will be too encumbered to make it in time. Even if we were to seize control of the Xiongnu lands, it would not be enough to profit us any, and even if we were to treat their common people properly, we could never subjugate or control them." 李斯諫曰:『不可。夫匈奴無城郭之居, 委積之守, 遷徙鳥舉, 難得而制也。輕兵深入, 糧食必絕; 踵糧以行, 重不及事。得其地不足以為利也, 遇其民不可役而守也。』[17]

Yan You offers detailed calculations for the provisions needed to survive in the forbidding Xiongnu lands:

> Using the calculation that each person needs 300 days of provisions, the dry rations that will be used will be 18 *hu*. Without the power of oxen, You will not be able to overcome [the difficulties of transporting these provisions]. The oxen must also be fed, which will require an additional 20 *hu*. Such will be a heavy load. The Xiongnu lands are sandy and salty and largely devoid of fresh water and grains. If one were to make an estimate based on previous enterprises, the troops won't last 100 days out there and the oxen will certainly die, every last one of them ... The Xiongnu lands in autumn and winter are terribly cold and in the spring and summer there are great windstorms ... Eating dry provisions, drinking water throughout the entire year, with the troops worrying about plague and infections— for these reasons when previous generations fought the Xiongnu, the campaigns didn't last more than 100 days. 計一人三百日食, 用糒十八斛, 非牛力不能勝; 牛又當自齎食, 加二十斛, 重矣。胡地沙鹵, 多乏水草, 以往事揆之, 軍出未滿百日, 牛必物故且盡 ... 胡地秋冬甚寒, 春夏甚風 ... 食糒飲水, 以歷四時, 師有疾疫之憂, 是故前世伐胡, 不過百日。[18]

Liu An offers a similarly bleak description of the southern lands of the Yue tribes:

> Now You are sending troops over several thousand miles, provided with clothes and provisions, to invade the Yue lands, carrying light chariots across the mountain cliffs and dragging boats up along the rivers for hundreds or thousands of leagues. They will be hemmed in by thick forests and groves of bamboo. All along the waterways their boats will smash against rocks. In the forests there will be many poisonous snakes and wild beasts. In the hot summer months, consumptive and deranging ailments will spread among the soldiers, so that in the end, without a single blade having been raised, many will be mortally wounded. 今發兵行數千里, 資衣糧, 入越 地, 輿轎而隃領, 拕舟而入水, 行數百千里, 夾以深林叢竹, 水道上下擊石, 林中多蝮蛇猛獸, 夏月暑時, 歐泄霍亂之病相隨屬也, 曾未施兵接刃, 死傷者必眾矣。[19]

In all three excerpts, the physical hardship of entering into foreign territories is stressed, a physical hardship that is often connected, either explicitly or implicitly, to the potential strain on the political stability of the empire, which military campaigns inevitably cause. Wei Xiang provides a brief, but pathetic, estimation of the state of affairs among the common people:

> Now the border commanderies are beset by hardship and deprivation. Fathers and sons share the pelts of dogs and goats, consume the seeds of wild grasses and grains, and constantly worry about not being able to keep themselves alive. In this scenario it would be difficult to begin a campaign. 今邊郡困乏, 父子共犬羊之裘, 食草萊之實, 常恐不能自存, 難於動兵。[20]

This sympathetic detailing of the impoverishment and starvation of the common people is highlighted in several other addresses—and touched upon in most. Yan You speaks of the dangers of a poor harvest in the northwest border area and the need to draw upon numerous other geographic areas just to be able to provide the troops with the needed foodstuffs. He warns that placing too heavy a burden on the common people—to provide the necessary supplies presumably—will probably lead to either rebellion or resistance. Success demands the support and preparation both of the army *and* the common people.[21] Liu An, in his address, speaks poignantly and at length about the sufferings of the common people, reporting that, because of a poor harvest, the common people have been forced to indenture their own children for food. They desperately hope for the emperor's compassion and consideration, for his bounty to rescue them, so that they will not "roll dead into a watery ditch." The past years' crops have been poor and there has been a serious infestation of ravaging locusts. Then, in a massive understatement, Liu An reports that "the livelihood of the commoners has yet to be recovered."[22] These assessments, however impassioned, are not thereby purely subjective. Warfare certainly often did put extreme strain on the agricultural engine and leaders who did not give such due consideration in their deliberations, who, as Zhu Fuyan puts it, "empty the treasury coffers and military arsenals and exhaust the common people just to disport themselves in foreign countries have not thought through the matter completely."[23] He bluntly relates the consequences of such blithe ignorance of the sufferings of the commoners a little later in the address, when he sternly upbraids Emperor Wu for repeating the mistakes of "recent generations," that is, those of the infamous First Emperor of Qin and the founder of the Han dynasty, the High Emperor, Liu Bang:

> Your Majesty does not observe the standards by which Emperor Shun, the Xia, Shang, or the Zhou dynasties ruled, but goes about imitating the mistakes of recent generations. This causes Your servant great consternation and the common people pain and suffering. Now, prolonged warfare leads to upheaval and policies ("matters") that cause suffering lead to a pondering of changes (of rulership). A consequence [of prolonged warfare and policies that cause suffering] will be that the common people in the border regions will be dispirited and miserable and will wish to emigrate from the empire; and the generals and officers will grow suspicious of each other and will negotiate with the enemy. 夫上不觀虞夏殷周之統, 而下循近世之失, 此臣之所大憂, 百姓之所疾苦也。且夫兵久則變生, 事苦則慮易。乃使邊境之民樊摩愁苦而有離心, 將吏相疑而外市。[24]

These, indeed, are the consequences of ignorant and unfeeling leadership: The overtaxed commoners will become "dispirited," unable to see the end to the war and their continued suffering, and will wish to take the extreme measure of moving themselves and their families to regions unknown. Exhausted and sensing that the campaign will lead to upheaval within the empire, military commanders and their officers will surreptitiously bargain with the enemy commanders for their own advantage, in case the Han military campaign ends badly. Thus the emperor will potentially face disaster on two fronts. His agricultural base will vanish, and with it, the foodstuffs necessary to supply his troops and pay the wages of his staff (wages often being calculated, and dispensed, in bushels of grain), and his military commanders, sensing the weakening of the campaign—and perhaps of the empire itself—will plot with the enemy for their own advantage in the hopes perhaps of securing future power and wealth.

THE GENERAL ROLE OF CONCRETE DETAILS EMBEDDED IN A POLITICAL ARGUMENT

In truth, the exact content of the particular concrete details regarding the condition of the commoners or the uncertain loyalties of the military commanders and officers seems often to be of little significance for the aim of persuading the executive to adopt a certain course of action. The epistemic qualities of the evidence, as I've mentioned previously, are the demonstrative qualities that distinguish each proposition that could bear upon how it may be received as evidence and how important an evidentiary function it plays. The epistemic qualities of the propositions, as I have also discussed, are the basis upon which one can assess the overall epistemic quality of the propositions, just as one correspondingly could, in an ideally open, nonrhetoricized discourse (e.g., the "scientific" discourse), assess the truth-value of propositions based on their factual content and rationally justifiable relationship to other propositions. Because of the politicized environment of court discussions, because thorough objectivity does not provide the most appropriate standard, in our analysis of the epistemic quality and weight of a proposition, or a class of propositions, as I have argued previously in earlier chapters, the emphasis then must be solely on how the proposition(s) functioned within the addresses, both individually and collectively. In the early Han addresses, the executive may have doubted the general epistemic quality of the propositions but his doubts were likely not directed to their accuracy so much as to their overall relevance. Even when the accuracy of a quantity is explicitly involved, for example, with the estimated number of Han Xin's troops as it figured in the exchange between Li Zuoche and Chen Yu, the accuracy of the figure is not so much the point of contention (indeed, Li Zuoche did not offer any estimate in his address to Chen Yu) as the strategy that the executive should pursue in view of an estimate. Certainly, Chen Yu's doubts about the validity, and thus the epistemic quality, of the estimate of Han Xin's forces plays a role, but Chen Yu's general objections to their claims to relevance or "truth" is more directed toward their magnitude and the effort necessary to defeat them, than to the precise disposition and number of troops. The epistemic quality of the estimate of Han Xin's forces is defined by the comparison to the force Chen Yu has at his command and believes necessary to defeat them. Interestingly, Chen Yu's major worry is not how to defeat them but how to preserve his reputation for courage among his other foes to fend off any other schemes to attack him: his ultimate concern is for their esteem.[25] Indeed, the obtaining of their esteem, and the ability to deter their attacks and secure his state, is Chen Yu's vision of the truth of the matter articulated in response to this particular exchange with Li Zuoche.[26]

Instead of the concrete details being the main justificatory edifice, the main repository of epistemic weight, for the early Han addresses, the evidence that is more truly central for *justifying* what the address is pointing to as the "truth of the matter" are those premises of popular knowledge that provide the thrust for the addresses. As we saw in the exchange between Su Qin and Zhang Yi, their arguments hinged not so much on the claims that were unexposed to doubt[27] as on those that were. To use a Han-era example, in the exchange between Li Zuoche and Chen Yu, their disagreement lies not so much in concrete particulars as how to overcome an expert foe with a minimal expenditure of force. Both of their responses are based largely on claims whose knowledge basis is reasonable, popular knowledge. Both claims make sense to the average, nonexpert discussant and both are, unlike commonsense claims, open to objection and doubts as to their relevance and certainty. Li Zuoche's claim is that Han Xin's troops, strong in battle but weak in provisions, can be defeated with a simple maneuver to cut them off from their food train and from any means to gathering provisions from elsewhere. Were Chen Yu to be prepared for a siege, to wait for Han Xin's battle-hardened troops to become weakened enough to overcome, victory would be assured.

The epistemic weight of Li Zuoche's address rests on claims of general reputability:

1. A succession of victories indicates strength in battle.
2. Han Xin's troops are far from ready sources of provisions and thus are probably hungry.
3. Their provisions are sure to be at the rear of their train.
4. Were one to prevent them from gathering additional provisions, they would be weakened beyond any hope for success in battle.

None of these are certain, nor does Li Zuoche offer any evidence for them—no reports from spies, no experience with Han Xin's method of arranging his armies, nothing. Any of them are quite easily vulnerable to reasonable doubt but they nevertheless lie at the core of his justification. These types of propositions, based on popular-knowledge claims, are reputable yet naturally open to challenge. But they are what drive the early Han addresses forward and provide their justificatory force. Obviously, Li Zuoche's argument has no effect on Chen Yu, neither the logic nor the recommendations. Chen Yu's concerns lie with esteem, not with easy victory, and the report he has received of the size of Han Xin's army is what drives his thinking. He believes that there is no need for deceptive schemes, that an army so small deserves to be met head on. Though the estimate of Han Xin's army is the ground for Chen Yu's argument, the justificatory force of the argument, once again, lies with a common saying, which, though reasonable, is certainly open to doubt.

If popular knowledge is the type of knowledge carrying the most epistemic weight for the addresses, what then is its epistemic quality? How do we assess, for instance, the epistemic quality of a common saying or story? Of a statement of principle or historical precedent? What demonstrative qualities distinguish such propositions that lead them to be taken as claims to knowledge, as evidence? The qualities of the evidence, whether they are concrete particulars, statements of principle, or historical precedent, are ultimately grounded in the probabilities that inform all reputable evidence. But with the latter two, that is, statements of principle or historical precedents, there is the added force of a common intellectual culture, one in which such general or historical statements are part of the intellectual currency of the day. This is not peculiar to the early Han circumstance, or even the Chinese circumstance. Whatever the time period or culture, general popular discourse proceeds largely based on shared intellectual and cultural norms, norms that have no actual independent basis, save for the general, vague probabilities informing human interaction. Nevertheless, time and culture could, and do, delimit what is acceptable, normal, and what is available for quotation or reference. The cultural resources available to early Han figures were not those available to previous generations. They were bound by their particular "world picture."

Commonsense claims, by contrast, provide the general ground, however trivial, for the argument of the addresses but are not the justificatory force behind the addresses. For instance, Li Si's admonition preserved in Zhufu Yan's address holds for any of the addresses; its commonsense basis is such that it applies to any campaign.[28] Executives who refuse to acknowledge that there are limits to what their territories can provide and of the loyalties of their military staff and soldiers, who refuse to acknowledge the commonsense notion, stated previously in Chapter Eight, that showing compassion toward those who will suffer from the campaign will ultimately result in greater dividends, will prospectively face defeat in their endeavors and the heightened instability of their regime.[29] Certainly, concrete details are pertinent for buttressing even such commonsense claims. For instance, it is indeed relevant, in the selection of Yan You's address cited above,[30] that the northwestern areas are afflicted with poor harvest. But the relevance of these concrete particulars has more to do with the recommendations these particulars buttress regarding how to resolve the specific difficulties of continuing the campaign or preventing incursions or defending against invasion than with how they pertain to any overarching argument about whether or not to wage a campaign. Though not every addressor to a militarily aggressive executive will explicitly mention

A Diversity of Evidence 165

these considerations, considerations of economic and militaristic exhaustion, no addressor did, or probably would, contradict them. Most would, we can presume, acknowledge them as legitimate concerns.

THE CONTRASTS IN THE USE OF CONCRETE DETAIL IN ARGUMENTS ABOUT DOMESTIC AND FOREIGN WAR

Though they are not essential for establishing the basic points forwarded by the addresses, concrete details naturally can serve to buttress their justification, offering additional epistemic weight to the argument. In certain addresses, they are used to great effect to explain or defend the reasons for a course of action, depicting what the Chinese military forces would be up against or the enemy in relation to defending against an attack, or the risk of their waging their own. When speaking to a campaign against a domestic opponent, one of the other Central States, the use of concrete particulars shares much with those addresses recorded in the *Intrigues*, offering elaborate predictions about how the course of the campaign will proceed and what the reaction of the opposing forces will be. The salient aspect of the rhetoric of these predictions is, as noted at the end of Chapter Five,[31] their presumption and expression of the certainty of the outcome, of the ease by which the enemy can be overcome. This can be seen in the fourth and fifth sections of Su Qin's address and the fifth and sixth sections of Zhang Yi's.[32] A notable instance of the presumption and expression of the certainty of an outcome taken from among the early Han addresses can be found in Li Zuoche and Chen Yu's exchange. As discussed previously, in Li Zuoche's address to Chen Yu regarding how to handle the Han Xin's incursion into Zhao, he offers a simple yet hackneyed strategy in which the enemy troops would be bottled up in a narrow area, the Jing Gorge, and the hungry soldiers cut off from their supply train situated at the rear. Once the soldiers are physically unable to fight, Li Zuoche very reasonably argues, Han Xin's armies would certainly be overcome.[33] A similar degree of certainty is evident in Liu Jing's calculations offer to the High Emperor, Liu Bang, regarding how resettling the various powerful clans to the capital area, the Area-Within-the-Pass (Guanzhong), would provide an adequate defense both against any possible invasion of the Xiongnu as well as against the machinations of the members of these powerful clans to rebel against the nascent empire.[34]

When speaking to a campaign against a foreign tribe, because of the inevitable possibility of the foreign tribes fleeing to distant parts and the consequent open-endedness of the campaign, the use of concrete particulars does not usually speak to the prediction of the outcome of the battles. This almost surely has to do with the exotic and unfamiliar culture of foreign tribes as well as the expansive terrain open to them, distant and hostile terrain that required massive influx of resources, lengthy occupations, and long marches. The probability of a besieged foreign tribe fleeing to distant regions is the reason why certain addressers, such as Hou Ying 侯應 and Zhao Chongguo 趙充國, emphasized defensive measures. Arguing against handing over the responsibility for defending a border region to the Xiongnu king, Huhanxie Chanyu 呼韓邪單于, Hou Ying, for instance, explains to Emperor Yuan how precarious the condition of the defenses is and how necessary they are to prevent the untrustworthy Xiongnu from attempting to return to the bountiful lands they had previously occupied. Not only are they necessary to prevent the Xiongnu from seizing the advantage, they are also necessary to prevent the officials manning the offices in the border areas from abusing their authority among the foreign tribes, slaves from running off, and groups of criminally minded commoners from forming bands of thieves. Without oversight, the entire border region will erupt into chaos.[35] Zhao Chongguo enumerates several defensive measures that will obviate the need for waging yet another exhausting military campaign against the Qiang tribe. Attacking the Qiang, he argues, "is not expedient."[36] Instead, after disbanding the majority of the army stationed at the border, Zhao Chongguo proposes that he will rely on a smaller defensive force and an assortment of defensive arrangements: repairing courier stations, amassing ample provisions for any possible siege, and maintaining the interior networks of roads. Since the Qiang have been driven out of their "resplendent lands and pastures," they will inevitably, Zhao Chongguo predicts, fight among themselves, with the result that their forces will be disorganized and easy to defeat. By expelling and cutting off the Qiang "vermin," "commanding that they not be allowed to return to their fecund lands, we will impoverish and break their multitudes and thereby gradually bring about discord among the Qiang."[37] By not sending forces out against the Qiang (or simply allowing the massive forces already in place to remain), the Central States will both minimize economic and military stress as well as avoid instigating counterattacks or collaboration among the various foreign tribes who would view a military expedition against the Qiang as possible evidence of an expansionist policy.

THE PERIPHERALITY OF CONCRETE DETAILS FOR THE RESOLUTION OF THE EMPEROR'S DOUBT

What makes the episode that includes Zhao Chongguo's addresses particularly fascinating for my purposes is Emperor Xuan's responses, which reveal him to be impatient with and dubious of the effectiveness of Zhao Chongguo's proposed stratagems.[38] Emperor Xuan raises the very reasonable doubt that if the army is disbanded and an agricultural settlement is developed with only a nominal defensive force to protect it, the Qiang "upon hearing that the armies have all been released, will collect together their able-bodied men to attack and harass the farmers and the agricultural settlement soldiers posted on the roads. They will once again kill and rob our people."[39] Furthermore, the emperor received a report about other Qiang tribes being unnerved by the passivity of the armies of the Central States. Although the Qiang tribes allied with the Central States provided them with the knowledge of the Xianling Qiang's location, the Central States' armies had not yet initiated an attack. Because of this, the other Qiang tribes are reportedly concerned that the Central States are preparing to attack *all* the Qiang tribes and thus are considering switching allegiances and joining with the Xianling Qiang tribe to wage a campaign against the Han. Therefore, the emperor suggests, there is still the need to defeat the Qiang militarily. And indeed, prior to delivering his addresses to the emperor, Zhao Chongguo himself acknowledged in conversation with his son, that the military commanders of the Central States cannot limit their calculations only to the defeat of their primary target.[40]

Zhao Chongguo's response to these concerns is, *pace* Loewe, neither entirely "systematic" nor "forceful."[41] Zhao is confident that the Xianling Qiang—whose numbers are small ("seven or eight thousand") and whose current situation is dire, being "divided and dispersed, hungry and cold" and at odds with the other Qiang tribes, tribes that have taken advantage of the weakness of the Xianling Qiang—will soon capitulate without the armies of the Central States having to advance against them. The other tribes will be held in check both by the possibility of reward from the empire if the Xianling Qiang are defeated and by the corresponding possibility that they themselves will be captured and killed if they collude with the Xianling Qiang.[42] Yet these assertions do not respond adequately, as they should, to the emperor's concerns about the report of the other Qiang tribes being worried about what the delay in the attack by the Central States means for their own future. Zhao Chongguo's great confidence in the strength of the border defenses and the strength of the remaining force of ten thousand soldiers does little to respond to the emperor's concerns: "Although the cavalry will have been disbanded, the Qiang vermin will see that the ten thousand people remaining in the settlement constitute the means to their certain capture. It won't be long before their lands will be destroyed and they will respond to Your virtue."[43] He then repeats his assertion that their strength and resources will be utterly exhausted in short time and that, cowed by the ten thousand soldiers, they will experience divisions in their ranks. Sending out the army will have no benefit and will leave the interior vulnerable to attack by foreign tribes in other geographic regions. His only direct response to the emperor's concerns about the other tribes is an insubstantial one, that the other Qiang tribes probably do not have divided loyalties and even if they did, it is not a reason enough to send out the troops on an open-ended mission.[44]

These detailed elaborations and analyses of the "facts" presented to the emperor are meant to reveal the potential limitations on their intrinsic effectiveness, even in addresses presented by as expert and thoughtful a military commander as Zhao Chongguo, for resolving the emperor's doubts and concerns. As we can see in the above relatively brief analysis of Zhao Chongguo's addresses to Emperor Xuan, the details are neither fully convincing nor are they actually terribly comprehensive or systematic. Though Zhao Chongguo goes to great lengths to appear systematic by methodically enumerating twelve seemingly distinct advantages to his strategy, several are no more than restatements or consequences of previously (or later) stated advantages. At the heart of the entire address, what Zhao Chongguo is stressing and what he conceives to be of most import to communicate to the emperor is really not much more than three of the four commonsense premises I articulated in Chapter Eight:

1. Military concerns require stratagems and proper strategic deploying of resources.
2. War is an uncertain business and can lead to political and financial ruin.
3. Showing compassion toward those who will suffer (in this case, the commoners, who would surely prefer the development and proper defense of an agricultural settlement to an exhausting military campaign) will ultimately result in greater dividends.

These fundamental commonsense propositions are the basic foundation of many of the addresses, even the most "rationalistic," such as Zhao Chongguo's, Chao Cuo's, or Hou Ying's. That these are fundamental to military addresses is not incredible; yet our understanding that these commonsense propositions serve as the basis of all, or nearly all, of the addresses nonetheless assists in our appreciating just what was at issue and that such concerns were what was common. Such concerns clearly were not limited to a particular ideological background or discursive body. Hou Ying, for instance, argues for repairing and maintaining the roads to the border areas and the barriers at the border areas.[45] He initially composes his argument in terms of controlling the Xiongnu, emphasizing in sections D–G their intractability and their sorrow (and resentment) at having to leave their lands. But in sections H–K, he stresses the consequences of ignoring the administration of the borders: local government officials will take advantage of the central government's neglect and steal from the populace; the children of those attendants who accompanied the military convoys to the border areas and the slaves of border officials will have been exhausted by the turmoil and suffering caused by the mismanagement and will flee into the wilderness; and thieves and bandits will be able to evade prosecution by escaping through the frontiers. In other words, without properly administered defenses, the entire area will erupt into chaos and the common people will suffer for it.

Regarding the third of these apparent "rationalists," Chao Cuo explicitly emphasizes several of the commonsense premises listed in Chapter Eight.[46] In section B, toward the very beginning of his address, he avers both that the successful campaign does not depend on the courage of the common people but on the intelligence of the administration and that, because of the hardships they have suffered, the common people have no thought of victory. Their *qi* "is crushed, injured." Much of the rest of the address is a lecture on the various strengths and weaknesses of the Chinese and Xiongnu armies and the demands posed by various terrains, a lecture that is clearly meant to improve the efficiency and intelligence with which the campaign is being conducted, not to argue the merits or demerits of the campaign itself.

One might perhaps be tempted to see, as Di Cosmo does, any moral emphasis as simply cloaking nonmoral considerations in impassioned moralizing language. However, as I have argued previously, any such simplification would be to ignore the definite and pervasive concern given to moral matters in government discussions. My argument finds evidence in the reintroduction of the moral notion of *tianming*, "Heaven's mandate," as well as the respectful manner in which moral considerations were debated in the early Han period. The latter was demonstrated in the analysis of the debate between Wang Hui and Han Anguo. The displays of a moral consciousness revealed in the early Han debates and addresses regarding military matters were not merely for pedantic or aggrandizing purposes. On my interpretation, in most, if not all, of these early Han official discourses, Han officials routinely mention, and place genuine stress on, not only nonmoral strategic considerations but moral ones.

We can intuitively grasp the pragmatism supporting the nonmoral commonsense considerations. The notions that war is a dangerous, uncertain enterprise that should be avoided whenever possible or that military concerns require stratagems and proper strategic deployment of resources are easily comprehensible. To use Geertz's descriptives, they are eminently accessible, easy to comprehend, and practical, easy to justify in view of the common circumstances of life.[47] Yet with moral considerations, one cannot simply reduce them to nonmoral practical needs. Failing to pay attention to the needs of the common people over the long term may be injurious to the stability of one's state, but their needs can, and are often, ignored for the short term or, if the military campaign is a lengthy one, there are ways to offset or mitigate the stress imposed on a group of commoners. Thus, I would argue, there must be another ground on which moral considerations, if they were genuinely deemed moral, must have been justified, whether in terms of personal sentiment or some other cultural basis. The following conversation between Han Xin and Kuai Tong makes quite unambiguous the reason why moral considerations were not, and could not have been, based on personal or sentimental grounds:

> Han Xin said, "The king of Han, Liu Bang, has treated me very generously. How could I, seeing an advantage, turn my back on his kindness?" Kuai Tong said, "Originally, Zhang Er, the king of Changshan, and Chen Yu, the lord of Cheng'an, swore their friendship would last until death ("would have slit their throats for each other"). But upon their dispute over the affair between Zhang Yan and Chen Shi, the king of Changshan, Zhang Er, turning tail like a frightened rat, returned to the King of Han. Taking an army he marched off to the east and did battle with Chen Yu north of the Hao district. Chen Yu perished south of the Chi River. His head and feet were cut off. These two men were friends, the happiest among All-Under-Heaven and yet, in the end, they wished to annihilate each other. Why? This calamity arose from many competing desires and the fact that the hearts of men are difficult to fathom." 信曰:「漢遇我厚,吾豈可見利而背恩乎!」通曰:「始常山王、成安君故相與為刎頸之交,及爭張黶、陳釋之事,常山王奉頭鼠竄,以歸漢王. 借兵東下,戰於鄗北,成安君死於泜水之南,頭足異處。此二人相與,天下之至驩也,而卒相滅亡者,何也?患生於多欲而人心難測也。」[48]

If what Kuai Tong argues has any general applicability for the early Han moral consciousness—and I would argue that it almost certainly does—personal allegiances or sympathies could not have served as any moral foundation. The personal allegiances or sympathies of either individuals or groups (such as the commoners) could not be depended upon as reliable grounds for moral guidance. As with the friendship between Zhang Yan and Chen Shi, individual sympathy was not a basis for an emperor's sense of a moral mandate. Rather, I have argued, the foundation of any moral mandate is in an idealized self-conception, a religiously articulated sense of the emperor's potential quasi-divinity. The emperor's divine status, the mandate that the emperor received from Heaven, was reinforced by his behaving as "a father and mother to his people," behaving in a way that takes their well-being, and the avoidance of their unnecessary suffering, as a cause for concern. The contentment of the general populace was the symptom or outcome of the instantiation of a moral order.

A Diversity of Evidence 171

SUMMARY CONCLUSIONS ON THE DISCRETE FUNCTIONS OF THE CLASSES OF EVIDENCE

Within those addresses informing these analyses, it appears that, while certain popular-knowledge premises were more frequently appealed to or relied upon as commonly accepted evidence for the arguments and conclusions presented in the addresses, there was nothing inherent in the formal rhetorical structure of the addresses that would necessarily have prevented any or all employed premises of popular knowledge from being emphasized within the address. Similarly, to speak to the three gross categories of evidence—statements of principle, historical precedents, and concrete particulars—although the concrete particulars were most frequently elaborated upon in the addresses regarding military affairs, their dominance did not in itself preclude the insertion of other categories of evidence, nor is it certain that, given that their apparent epistemic function was not of an utterly different caliber than that of the other two categories, addresses or persuasions stressing concrete particulars would have been any more successful than those that merely relied on historical precedents or statements of principle. Indeed, as mentioned previously, numerous addresses not included in these analyses that were presented by notable figures such as Jia Yi couched their arguments almost entirely in abstract statements of principle and references to historical precedents, speaking of military affairs only as a part of a broader instruction about the general principles of governance.

Since the histories only very seldom record the emperor's responses to addresses, it is impossible to be sure which popular-knowledge propositions or even what aspects of the argument, of either the evidence presented or the logic of the argument, were most effective in winning the emperor's sympathies. It is entirely possible and quite probable, if the histories attempted to capture the general dispositions of the personalities involved, that certain classes of evidence were more effective than others at winning the sympathies of a particular monarch. Unfortunately, since the number of substantial addresses recorded in the histories is relatively few, to conduct such an analysis would require that it be performed across topics, introducing numerous variables that cannot be accounted for. Furthermore, even if there were a sufficiently large number of addresses presented to a particular monarch available for analysis, we cannot be certain, without the monarch's responses and a thorough understanding of the relationship between the monarch and the minister, to what degree the evidence was "believed" because of the strength of their personal relationship, a complication I discussed previously in the analysis of Zhang Liang's influence on the deliberations of the High Emperor, Liu Bang.[49]

Nevertheless, we can generalize, based on the examined addresses and other more theoretical statements relating to the function of these classes of evidence, that the three categories of evidence did perform discrete epistemic functions. Even though the concrete particulars were not reliably accurate, their epistemic function was naturally to suggest that the problem had to be delimited to the characteristics of the situation or the problem at hand. In the *Annals of Lü Buwei*, a classic Warring States text that repeatedly examines the problems of political address, a number of statements speak to the use and importance of *shi* 實 or *qing* 情, two words that are commonly associated with the concrete "facts" or "truth" about a particular situation.[50] Though their translation varies, their definition relies upon access to stable concrete particulars. The following passage employs both terms:

> The reins of good government are none other than rectification of names and investigation of divisions of responsibility. Scrutinizing the names they use, therefore, with a firm hand on the reality of the situation (*shi*) is the way to seek the truth (*qing*) in what subjects say; being mindful of the proper categories while listening to their advice is the way to prevent subjects from acting recklessly and contrary to all reason. It is because names frequently do not correspond to reality (*shi*) and because what is done frequently does not correspond to what is useful that the ruler must scrutinize names and divisions of responsibility. 正名審分, 是治之轡已。故按其實而審其名, 以求其情; 聽其言而察其類, 無使放悖。夫名多不當其實, 而事多不當其用者, 故人主不可以不審名分也。[51]

This usage lies in close accord with how these normative terms are used in the Han histories, indeed in all of early Chinese classical literature. But in spite of their idealized normative function, in the histories concrete particulars appear to have by themselves no greater persuasive or normative force, no greater epistemic weight, than statements of principle or historical precedents. As is well known, statements of principle and historical precedent themselves are heavily emphasized in pre-Han and Han philosophical literature as also being quite important. Discussions of *dao* in the abstract, as a "principle" or "way," or as a historicized norm, as with *sheng wang zhi dao* 聖王之道, "the ways of the sage kings," are common in the classical Chinese corpus, as much, if not more so, than discussions of "reality." While statements of principle or historical precedent are not treated as correctives to misinformation or outright prevarication, as statements of reality or fact are, they are asserted as norms that are central to and regulative of how affairs of government are to be discussed, relating to both moral and nonmoral concerns. To know how to govern, to be immune to the manipulation of others does not come merely with knowing the facts but also with knowing principles that govern how facts should be read and the historical precedents highlighting which facts are important. They are no less a part of assessing the "truthfulness" of what ministers communicate to the monarch than the statements regarding concrete particulars that are so important for the correction of "names."

The placement of evidence in the structure of the addresses, a formal characteristic that informs the epistemic weight of the evidence, is apparently guided by only a few loose, obvious standards, which I have discussed at some length in Chapter Five.[52] Concrete particulars are not, as we would have expected, needed or even really used to *prove* some point. They are simply a further buttress for the larger point being made, no more and no less epistemically weighty as a class of evidence in support of the arguments of the addresses, it seems, than the statements of principle or historical precedents. Though the manner in which they act as evidence is distinctive, each category of evidence apparently carries no discretely greater burden of proof than the other categories. To refer to the analyses in Chapters Six and Eight, compared to their opponents' arguments, though their own arguments refer more frequently to concrete considerations than their counterparts', neither Wang Hui's nor Zhang Yi's addresses, or persuasions, ultimately rest on these concrete particulars. This, I argue, is shown by how Wang Hui abandons any reliance on concrete particulars to forward his argument in his debate with Han Anguo and how Zhang Yi merely attempts to create an impression of Qin's force rather than offer specific details in his address to the king of Wei. Some addressors, such as Zhao Chongguo, choose to make concrete particulars the focal point; others, such as Zhufu Yan, do not, placing the emphasis rather on statements of principle or historical precedents. It is quite conceivable that an address relying entirely on statements of principle or historical precedents could have been as or more persuasive to various executive audiences than an opposing address that spoke mostly or only to concrete particulars.

Again, the apparent overriding logic of these addresses, that which speaks to the "truth of the matter," is not to *prove* some point but to suggest a moral, a general principle by which the executive should pursue either the particular military campaign, or military affairs (or simply governance) in general. As I have argued in Chapter Six, what appears to be most important for the epistemic aspect of the argument is not rigorous, air-tight justification but the leaving of an impression, or a suggestion, of what is most relevant relating to the truth of the matter.[53] In sum, the addressors are less trying to justify a carefully articulated argument than the "moral" of their story. The rhetorical banter in which debating addressors participate reveals, as it did with the debates between Su Qin and Zhang Yi and between Wang Hui and Han Anguo, that the objections placed are not leveled so much at the concrete as at the abstract framing of the situation. The emperor's doubts, it seems, were not at the level of information as at the level of conception.

So, in conclusion, if the aim of the addresses is not to convince the executive of the veracity or verifiable truth-content of one's statements or arguments but instead to convince the executive of what impinges upon the "truth of the matter," at what then will the doubts of the executive be aimed? As we can see both in the example of Chen Yu and in the example of Emperor Xuan, they were usually leveled at the larger issues, issues of how apt the strategies proposed were at resolving the issue at hand and maintaining the health and security of the state. The apparatus of conviction was not the veracity or accuracy of any representation—whether of concrete particulars, historical precedents, or statements of principle—but the manner in which these reinforced commonly accepted propositions, or dislodged those open to debate. The correctness of the facts, and the accurate citation of the sources, perhaps even the sources themselves, were less the point than the general propositions being forwarded. And in the forwarding of general propositions, what appears most important was working within the established intellectual culture of the time rather than any faithful representation of canonical teachings.

EXTENSIONS

In relation to its potential effect on other areas and problems under discussion, particularly those relevant for the study of classical China, this project can arguably speak to a host of issues. Below is a sample selection:

1. If we can assess the common intellectual norms under which everyday court debates were held, we can then come closer to a possible reevaluation of the fixity, import, and sincere commitment among public intellectuals and politicians to particular intellectual trends, especially those propounded to be representative of a certain intellectual tradition. If references to classical canonical literature were merely used to reinforce, as a rhetorical appeal to authority, an idea already of some level of common acceptability, then it will become clearer that the role of these texts was not to introduce an alien or novel idea or argue for or from a specific intellectual tradition but to use a source as either a literary embellishment or a canonical instantiation of the argument. Ben Wallacker sets out the same problematic specifically in reference to the influence of Han Confucianism: "How did the tradition and teachings of Confucius manifest themselves? In what ways did the tradition make its presence felt? What skills or knowledge in

the Confucian tradition were valued by the men wielding political power?"[54] Indeed, scholars such as Michael Nylan and Anne Cheng have already argued that Confucians were more classical scholars than loyal partisans to the teachings of Confucius. Perhaps, one might say, the reference to a particular teaching or scholarly tradition was arbitrary; the suggested "truth of the matter" was all.

2. Through careful cross-evaluation of other groups of memorials, by topic or otherwise, we can begin to compose a list of basic commonsense norms that governed general intellectual intercourse. By pinpointing what is commonsensical, that is, what is so well accepted that it lies beyond doubt, we can better appreciate the various aspects of early Chinese intellectual culture in the ways it was manifested in everyday court interaction. Such investigations would also indicate the probable configurations of the intellectual interests and political concerns of Han executives. What the ministers chose to discuss was, in all probability, configured to what was an acceptable topic, or a topic of interest, at court.

3. In addition, through such cross-topical comparisons, various literary and logical features will come to light relating to the use of concrete particulars, canonical references, historical details, philosophical ideas, and so forth. On a more general level, we will be better able to define more precisely the logic of political justification in the early Han, as well as the features that distinguish it from potentially apolitical modes of justification, such as those "proofs" regarding claims about natural phenomena and the workings of the natural realm in general. If it happens that the logic of justification regarding sociopolitical versus that regarding natural phenomena turns out to be similar, if not formally identical—however unlikely—such a finding will improve our comprehension of the development of the formal logic involved in investigations in the natural world.

4. In relation to the composition of the histories themselves, we will be better able to evaluate to what extent the recorded course of history is beholden to the demands of rhetoric, how driven it is by the demands and outcomes of court politics, not just as such relates to narrative plot but how the presence of the addresses affects the organization of the entire historical project.

Appendices

A. LI ZUOCHE (李左車) AND CHEN YU'S (陳餘) EXCHANGE *SHIJI* 92.2615[1]

Han Xin and Zhang Er with their army of many tens of thousands of men desired to march east through the Jing Gorge to attack Zhao. The king of Zhao (Zhao Xie 趙歇) and Chen Yu, lord of Cheng'an, heard that the Han forces were about to launch a surprise attack against them and that they had gathered an army at the mouth of the Jing Gorge which was said to have numbered 200,000 men.[2] Lord of Guangwu, Li Zuoche, persuaded Chen Yu, saying, 信與張耳以兵數萬, 欲東下井陘擊趙. 趙王、成安君陳餘聞漢且襲之也, 聚兵井陘口, 號稱二十萬. 廣武君李左車說成安君曰:

A. "I have heard that the Han general Han Xin has forded the Yellow River to the west, taken the king of Wei hostage and captured Xia Yue, and spilled blood anew at Yanyu. Now with the help of Zhang Er he has held council discussions and desires to send his troops against Zhao. The blades of such an army, riding a wave of victory and fighting far from its state, cannot be opposed. 「聞漢將韓信涉西河, 虜魏王, 禽夏說, 新喋血閼與, 今乃輔以張耳, 議欲下趙, 此乘勝而去國遠鬬, 其鋒不可當.

B. "I, Your servant, have heard it said that, when provisions must be transported a thousand leagues, the *shi*-officers have a malnourished look. They gather wood and straw for the fire after which they cook their meals. The troops do not go to sleep with a full stomach. Now, the road through the Jing Gorge is such that two carts cannot drive side by side, nor two horsemen ride in formation. On a march of several hundred leagues in such a disposition their provisions are sure to be in the rear. 「臣聞千里餽糧, 士有飢色, 樵蘇後爨, 師不宿飽. 今井陘之道, 車不得方軌, 騎不得成列, 行數百里, 其勢糧食必在其後.

C. "I beg Your Majesty to lend me a force of 30,000 surprise troops which I can lead by an obscure route to cut off their supply wagons. If Your Majesty deepens his moats, heightens his ramparts, strengthens his camp, and forbids [his generals] to engage in battle, they will be unable either to advance and fight, or to retreat and return home. With my surprise force I will cut off their rear and cause these men from the wilds to have no way to plunder. Before ten days are out, the heads of their two commanders will be brought and laid beneath Your banners."「願足下假臣奇兵三萬人，從閒道絕其輜重；足下深溝高壘，堅營勿與戰. 彼前不得鬪，退不得還，吾奇兵絕其後，使野無所掠，不至十日，而兩將之頭可致於戲下.」

D. "I beg my Lord to give heed to Your servant's plan. If You do not, You will most certainly find Yourself the captive of these two men (i.e., Han Xin and Zhang Er)."「願君留意臣之計. 否，必為二子所禽矣.」

But Chen Yu, the lord of Cheng'an, was a Ru scholar who always called for "righteous campaigns" and had no use for deceptive schemes or surprise strategies. Chen Yu said: 成安君，儒者也，常稱義兵不用詐謀奇計. 曰：

1. "I have heard that by the principles of warfare if [you outnumber the enemy] ten to one, you surround him, but if [you outnumber him] two to one, you engage him in battle.³ Now although Han Xin's forces are reputed to be several tens of thousands, they do not in fact exceed several thousand. Furthermore, he has marched a thousand miles to launch a surprise attack against us, so he must also already be thoroughly exhausted. 「吾聞兵法十則圍之，倍則戰. 今韓信兵號數萬，其實不過數千. 能千里而襲我，亦已罷極.」

2. "Now, in accord with Your suggestion, if we were to flee and not fight, later when there is a larger force, how would we fight them? The many lords would call me coward and think nothing of coming to attack me!"「今如此避而不擊，後有大者，何以加之! 則諸侯謂吾怯，而輕來伐我.」

Thus he refused to listen to the lord of Guangwu's policy-statements, and the policy-statements went unheeded. 不聽廣武君策，廣武君策不用

B. LIU (LOU) JING'S (劉/婁敬) ADDRESS TO THE HIGH EMPEROR (LIU BANG 劉邦) *SHIJI* 99.2719

Liu Jing came from the Xiongnu to court. He thereupon said: 劉敬從匈奴來, 因言

A. "Among the Xiongnu, the King of Baiyang and the King of Loufan in South of the Yellow River are at the nearest point 700 leagues distant from Chang'an. Their light cavalry, riding only over a day and a night, would be able to arrive at the Area-Within-Qin. Though the Area-Within-Qin is newly destroyed, with few commoners, its soil is fat and rich and the area is ripe for growth. 「匈奴河南白羊、樓煩王，去長安近者七百里，輕騎一日一夜可以至秦中. 秦中新破，少民，地肥饒，可益實.」

B. "As for the period of the initial uprising among the feudal lords against Qin, only the members of the Tian of Qi, the Zhao, the Qu, or the Jing households of Chu were able to rise up against Qin. Now, even though Your Majesty has set up His capital at the Area-Within-the-Pass (i.e., the Area-Within-Qin), in actuality there are few people [who could join and organize any military campaigns]. To the north the Xiongnu bandits lie close, to the east there are the clans of the six states [of former times], clans which are strong. If one day there were trouble, Your Majesty would not rest well. 「夫諸侯初起時，非齊諸田、楚昭、屈、景莫能興。今陛下雖都關中，實少人。北近胡寇，東有六國之族，宗彊，一日有變，陛下亦未得高枕而臥也。

C. "I, Your servant, wish that Your Majesty resettle the Tian clans of Qi, the Zhao, Qu, and Jing clans of Chu, the descendants of the states of Yan, Zhao, Han, and Wei, along with famous families of toughs, to the Area-Within-the-Pass. If there is no [domestic] matter about which Your Majesty needs concern himself, then Your Majesty will be able to make defensive preparations against the Xiongnu. If there is trouble among the feudal lords [of the six states to the east], then it will be sufficient to lead [an army using these powerful families] to do battle in the east. This is the technique by which you strengthen the root and weaken the branch."
「臣願陛下徙齊諸田，楚昭、屈、景、燕、趙、韓、魏後，及豪桀名家居關中。無事，可以備胡；諸侯有變，亦足率以東伐。此彊本弱末之術也」。

The emperor said, "Good," then sent Liu Jing to resettle the one hundred thousand or so people to the Area-Within-the-Pass about which he had spoken. 上曰：「善。」迺使劉敬徙所言關中十餘萬口。

C. ZHUFU YAN'S (主父偃) ADDRESS TO EMPEROR WU (LIU CHE 劉徹) *SHIJI* 112.2954–57

Zhufu Yan was a native of Linzi in Qi. He studied the techniques of Benefit and Detriment and the Vertical and Horizontal techniques, and in his later years studied the *Book of Changes*, the *Spring and Autumn Annals*, and the works of many other traditions. He traveled about and visited many educated men in the state of Qi but none were able to generously receive him. Indeed, the many educated gentlemen of Qi all ostracized and rejected him. He was not welcome in Qi. His family was very poor and had no means by which to borrow money, so he traveled north to Yan, Zhao, and Zhongshan, but nowhere would anyone generously receive him. He suffered great hardship in his attempts to find a patron. 主父偃者，齊臨菑人也。學長短縱橫之術，晚乃學易、春秋、百家言。游齊諸生閒，莫能厚遇也。齊諸儒生相與排擯，不容於齊。家貧，假貸無所得，迺北游燕、趙、中山，皆莫能厚遇，為客甚困。

During the first year of the *yuanguang* era (134 BCE) of Emperor Wu, he finally came to believe that none of the many lords of the Central

States deserved an itinerant teacher and journeyed west through the Hangu Pass to the capital, where he obtained an interview with General Wei Qing. 孝武元光元年中, 以為諸侯莫足游者, 乃西入關見衛將軍.

General Wei Qing mentioned him several times to Emperor Wu, but the emperor did not summon him to court. Although his resources were dwindling, he lingered about the capital for a long time, until many of the public officials and their retainers came to be disgusted with him. At last he submitted a document for the emperor at the palace gate. His address was presented to the emperor in the morning, and that same evening he was summoned for an audience. His memorial spoke to nine matters, eight of which were concerned with statutes and ordinances. The final matter was a remonstrance regarding the attacks being made on the Xiongnu. The contents of his address were as follows: 衛將軍數言上, 上不召. 資用乏, 留久, 諸公賓客多厭之, 乃上書闕下. 朝奏, 暮召入見. 所言九事, 其八事為律令, 一事諫伐匈奴. 其辭曰:

A. "I, Your servant, have heard that an enlightened sovereign does not abhor trenchant remonstrances but uses them to broaden his views; and that a loyal subject does not dare to avoid harsh punishment but remonstrates in a straightforward manner. Because of this, among the matters to be resolved there will be no leftover policy-letters and the effects of the achievements of the ruler will flow onward for ten thousand generations. Now I, Your servant, have not dared to conceal my sense of loyalty to avoid death but instead have offered these doltish assessments of mine. I beg Your Majesty to graciously pardon me and briefly examine them. 「臣聞明主不惡切諫以博觀, 忠臣不敢避重誅以直諫, 是故事無遺策而功流萬世. 今臣不敢隱忠避死以效愚計, 願陛下幸赦而少察之」.

B. "The *Principles of the Marshal* state, 'Even if a state is large, if it is too fond of fighting it is certain to perish. Even if All-Under-Heaven is at peace, if All-Under-Heaven forgets warfare altogether, it will certainly be in danger.' All-Under-Heaven has been brought to peace and the Son of Heaven sings the songs of victory and carries out the spring and autumn (ritual) hunts, while the many lords review their troops in the spring and train their soldiers in the fall. In this way, warfare is not forgotten. 「司馬法曰: 『國雖大, 好戰必亡; 天下雖平, 忘戰必危.』天下既平, 天子大凱, 春蒐秋獮, 諸侯春振旅, 秋治兵, 所以不忘戰也」.

C. "Now anger contravenes virtue, weapons are the tools of misfortune, and strife is the least of the ways to manage affairs. In ancient times, if a lord of men became angry, he would certainly cover the ground with corpses and loose a river a blood. Thus a sage king reflects seriously on acting in anger. No one who has devoted himself to success in warfare and spent all his efforts on military endeavors has ever failed to regret it. 「且夫怒者逆德也, 兵者凶器也, 爭者末節也. 古之人君一怒必伏尸流血, 故聖王重行之. 夫務戰勝窮武事者, 未有不悔者也」.

D. "In earlier times the First Emperor of the Qin, relying upon his overwhelming might in battle, nibbled at All-Under-Heaven until he had gobbled up the other warring states, and all areas within the four seas became one. His accomplishments rank with those of the rulers of the Three Dynasties (the Xia, Shang and Zhou). He devoted himself to overcoming his enemies without rest and wanted to go on and attack the Xiongnu. His minister Li Si remonstrated with him, saying, 'This is not permissible. The Xiongnu have no cities or forts and no stores of provisions. They move from place to place like flocks of birds, and thus are difficult to catch and control. If parties of lightly equipped soldiers penetrate deeply into their territory, their food supplies will certainly become exhausted, and if we try to send provisions after them in order that they may continue on, the baggage trains will be too encumbered to make it in time. Even if we were to seize control of the Xiongnu lands, it would not be enough to profit us any, and even if we were to treat their common people properly, we could never subjugate or control them. And if, after we had won victory, we were to decide to massacre them, such would not be in accord with the way of being a father and mother to the common people. To weaken the Central States and lead to their collapse, and thereby bring satisfaction to the Xiongnu is not a long-range policy.' But the First Emperor would not listen to his advice and sent his general Meng Tian with troops to attack the barbarians. He extended the borders of the empire 1,000 leagues, making the Yellow River the frontier, but the land he won over was nothing but swamps and salty flatlands, in which the five grains would not grow. 「昔秦皇帝任戰勝之威, 蠶食天下, 并吞戰國, 海內為一, 功齊三代. 務勝不休, 欲攻匈奴, 李斯諫曰:『不可. 夫匈奴無城郭之居, 委積之守, 遷徙鳥舉, 難得而制也. 輕兵深入, 糧食必絕; 踵糧以行, 重不及事. 得其地不足以為利也, 遇其民不可役而守也. 勝必殺之, 非民父母也. 靡獘中國, 快心匈奴, 非長策也.』秦皇帝不聽, 遂使蒙恬將兵攻胡, 辟地千里, 以河為境. 地固澤鹵, 不生五穀.

E. "After this the First Emperor sent forth the young men of All-Under-Heaven to control the frontier area at the north of the Yellow River. The troops and divisions were exposed to the elements for over ten years, and the number of dead was immeasurable. In the end they were not able to extend the empire north beyond the Yellow River. Surely this was not because there were not enough men, or because their weapons and equipment were insufficient? Rather it was because the circumstances did not allow it. The First Emperor ordered All-Under-Heaven to rush fodder and grain to the soldiers. Shipments were sent from [as far away as] the provinces of Huang, Chui and Langya by way of the seacoast commanderies and were transported to the frontier area at the north of the Yellow River, but no more than one picul out of an original thirty bushels arrived. Though men labored over their fields, there was not enough grain for the army. Though women wove and spun, there were not enough tents and hangings for the army. The commoners were weakened and exhausted. The orphans and widows, the old and the weak could not be fed, so that dead bodies were seen lying all along the roads. This was why All-Under-Heaven began to revolt against the Qin. 「然後發天下丁男以守北河. 暴兵露師十有餘年, 死者不可勝數, 終不能踰河而北. 是豈人眾不足, 兵革不備哉? 其勢不可也. 又使天下蜚芻輓粟, 起於黃、腄、琅邪負海之郡, 轉輸北河, 率三十鍾而致一石. 男子疾耕不足於糧饟, 女子紡績不足於帷幕. 百姓靡敝, 孤寡老弱不能相養, 道路死者相望, 蓋天下始畔秦也.

F. "Later, when the High Emperor, Liu Bang, had pacified All-Under-Heaven and was monitoring lands in the border areas, he heard that the Xiongnu were gathered north of the valley of Dai and desired to attack them. Secretary to the Imperial Counselor Cheng remonstrated with him, saying, 'This is not permissible. It is the nature of the Xiongnu to gather like wild beasts and disperse like flocks of birds. Trying to catch up with them is like grappling with a shadow. Now, I, Your servant, humbly believe it is dangerous for Your Majesty to apply his ample virtue toward an attack on the Xiongnu.' But the High Emperor did not heed his advice. Instead he rode north to the valley of Dai and consequently was surrounded by the enemy at Pingcheng. He regretted deeply what he had done and forthwith dispatched Liu Jing to conclude a peace alliance [with the Xiongnu], and from then on All-Under-Heaven was able to forget matters of war. 「及至高皇帝定天下, 略地於邊, 聞匈奴聚於代谷之外而欲擊之. 御史成進諫曰:『不可. 夫匈奴之性, 獸聚而鳥散, 從之如搏影. 今以陛下盛德攻匈奴, 臣竊危之.』高帝不聽, 遂北至於代谷, 果有平城之圍. 高皇帝蓋悔之甚, 乃使劉敬往結和親之約, 然後天下忘干戈之事.

G. "The *Principles of Warfare* aver that 'He who raises an army of 100,000 divisions must spend 1,000 pieces of gold a day.' The Qin were constantly gathering masses of men and dispatching troops, several hundred thousand of them. But although they won distinction by overpowering armies, slaying generals, and taking the Chanyu prisoner, such victories served only to insure the resentment of the enemy and deepen their desire for revenge. It was insufficient to compensate for the expense to All-Under-Heaven. Leaders who empty the treasury coffers and military arsenals and exhaust the common people just to disport themselves in foreign countries have not thought through the matter completely. 「故兵法曰『興師十萬, 日費千金』. 夫秦常積眾暴兵數十萬人, 雖有覆軍殺將係虜單于之功, 亦適足以結怨深讎, 不足以償天下之費. 夫上虛府庫, 下敝百姓, 甘心於外國, 非完事也.

H. "The problems of subjugating and controlling the Xiongnu are not those of a single generation. Their plundering and pillaging is how they support themselves and certainly is in keeping with their Heaven-sent nature. Since the times of Emperor Shun and the rulers of the Xia,

Shang, and Zhou dynasties, it is certain that no ruler has overseen or supervised them; instead they have herded them like captured beasts who did not belong to the human race. 「夫匈奴難得而制, 非一世也. 行盜侵驅, 所以為業也, 天性固然. 上及虞夏殷周, 固弗程督, 禽獸畜之, 不屬為人.」

I. "Your Majesty does not observe the standards by which Emperor Shun, the Xia, Shang, or the Zhou dynasties ruled, but goes about imitating the mistakes of recent generations. This causes Your servant great consternation and the common people pain and suffering. Now, prolonged warfare leads to upheaval and policies ("matters") that cause suffering lead to a pondering of changes (of rulership). A consequence [of prolonged warfare and policies that cause suffering] will be that the common people in the border regions will be dispirited and miserable and will wish to emigrate from the empire; and the generals and officers will grow suspicious of each other and will negotiate with the enemy. It was circumstances such as these which caused Superintendent Zhao Tuo and Zhang Han to pursue their own advantage.[4] The reason that the Qin government did not continue to function was because of the power that these two men divided between themselves. The points addressed in this address make clear the causes of loss and gain. It is said in the *Book of Zhou*: 'Safety and danger proceed from the orders given by the ruler; preservation and destruction lies with the means that are employed.' 「夫上不觀虞夏殷周之統, 而下循近世之失, 此臣之所大憂, 百姓之所疾苦也. 且夫兵久則變生, 事苦則慮易. 乃使邊境之民獘靡愁苦而有離心, 將吏相疑而外市, 故尉佗、章邯得以成其私也. 夫秦政之所以不行者, 權分乎二子, 此得失之效也. 故周書曰『安危在出令, 存亡在所用』.」

J. "I hope Your Majesty examines all this very closely, gives it a bit of consideration, and thoroughly ponders Your course of action." 「願陛下詳察之, 少加意而熟慮焉.」

D. CHAO CUO'S (晁錯) ADDRESS TO EMPEROR WEN (LIU HENG 劉恆) *HANSHU* 49.2278-83

At this time the Xiongnu were strong, frequently marauding the border areas. The throne sent out armies to control them. Chao Cuo presented a letter to the throne speaking to military affairs, which stated: 是時匈奴彊, 數寇邊, 上發兵以禦之. 錯上[書]言兵事,曰:

A. "I, Your servant, have heard that since the rise of the Han, the Xiongnu vermin frequently have penetrated the border lands, smaller incursions bringing them smaller profits, larger incursions bringing them larger profits. At the time of the High Empress Lü, they invaded the area of the Longxi Commandery (the commandery west of the Dragon Mountain) twice, attacking the walled cities and slaughtering the people in the townships, taking their animals and robbing them of their crops. Later they again invaded Longxi, killing clerks and infantry soldiers. It was an egregious act of banditry. 「臣聞漢興以來, 胡虜數入邊地, 小入則小利, 大入則大利; 高后時再入隴西, 攻城屠邑, 毆略畜產; 其後復入隴西, 殺吏卒, 大寇盜.

B. "I humbly have heard that 'With the fearlessness that comes from victory in battle, the energy of the common people increases a hundredfold. However, the infantry soldiers of a defeated army will never return.' From the time of the High Empress Lü onward, the residents of the Longxi Commandery have often suffered hardship because of the Xiongnu. The common people's spirit is crushed, injured. They have no thoughts of overcoming the Xiongnu. This year, the clerks of Longxi, relying on the spiritual numinosity of the nation, having received Your Majesty's enlightened edicts, becalmed and organized the *shi*-officers and infantry soldiers, refined and tightened administrative regulations, and lifted up the crushed and injured spirits of the common people in order to oppose the continually victorious Xiongnu. They employed small forces to attack the Xiongnu's massive forces and killed all their kings and defeated their massive forces, all of which greatly profited the empire. These achievements did not depend on the distinction of whether or not the common people of the Longxi Commandery were courageous or cowardly but on whether the administrative measures of the generals and clerks were quick-witted or clumsy. The principles of warfare aver, 'The generals commit to victory; the common people do not.' From this one can make the observation that pacifying the border areas and thereby securing one's accomplishments and reputation is the mark of an exemplary general. Such a general cannot *not* be selected to lead. 「竊聞戰勝之威, 民氣百倍; 敗兵之卒, 沒世不復. 自高后以來, 隴西三困於匈奴矣, 民氣破傷, 亡有勝意. 今茲隴西之吏, 賴社稷之神靈, 奉陛下之明詔, 和輯士卒, 底厲其節, 起破傷之民以當乘勝之匈奴, 用少擊眾, 殺一王, 敗其眾而大有利. 非隴西之民有勇怯, 乃將吏之制巧拙異也. 故兵法曰: 有必勝之將, 無必勝之民. 繇此觀之, 安邊境, 立功名, 在於良將, 不可不擇也.

C. "I, Your servant, have also heard that when applying military force, prior to starting a war and locking swords, there are three points of concern: the first is the understanding of the topography of the land; the second is the drilling and training of the infantry; the third is the soundness and sharpness of one's weapons. The principles of warfare aver 「臣又聞用兵, 臨戰合刃之急者三: 一曰得地形, 二曰卒服習, 三曰器用利. 兵法曰:

> Where there are gulleys over one *zhang*-foot and five *chi*-inches (one-and-a-half *zhang*-feet) deep, where there are waters that will swamp chariots, where there are rocky mountains and forests, where there are swift-running rivers and hillocks, where there are grasses and woods—this is territory for foot-soldiers. 丈五之溝, 漸車之水, 山林積石, 經川丘阜, 屮木所在, 此步兵之地也.

On such terrain, a pair of chariots or cavalry riders could not oppose one [foot-soldier]. 車騎二不當一.

> Where there are large hills and mountain ranges that reach across the landscape without interruption, where there are level plains and vast wild fields—this is territory for chariots and cavalry. 土山丘陵, 曼衍相屬, 平原廣野, 此車騎之地.

On such terrain, ten foot-soldiers could not oppose one [chariot or rider]. 步兵十不當一.

> Where there is a combination of level and hilly ground that stretches out into the distance with rivers and valleys interspersed, where one can look up [at the mountains] and down [into the valleys]—this is territory for longbows and crossbows. 平陵相遠, 川谷居間, 仰高臨下, 此弓弩之地也.

On such terrain, a hundred soldiers with short-range weapons could not oppose one [archer]. 短兵百不當一.

> Where the land forces two battalions of soldiers to press together, where the level ground narrows, where soldiers can only go forward or back—this is territory for long halberds. 兩陳相近, 平地淺, 可前可後, 此長戟之地也.

On such terrain, three soldiers armed with swords and shields could not oppose one [soldier with a long halberd]. 劍楯三不當一.

> Where the terrain is covered with reeds, bamboo and sagebrush, where the trees lie close, where branches and leaves are lush and thick, this is terrain for long and short spears. 萑葦竹蕭, 木蒙籠, 支葉茂接, 此矛鋋之地也.

On such terrain, two soldiers armed with long halberds could not oppose one [soldier with a long or short spear]. 長戟二不當一.

> Where torturous roads wind about, where steep mountainous obstructions lie close to each other, this is terrain for swords and shields. 曲道相伏, 險陀相薄, 此劍楯之地也.

On such terrain, three archers could not oppose one [soldier with a sword and shield]. 弓弩三不當一.

> When *shi*-officers are not vetted [properly], when infantry soldiers not drilled and trained [properly], when periods of movement and rest do not nourish the seminal essence, when activity and passivity are not balanced, then propensities and benefits will not coincide. When the troops run from difficulties and do not follow through, when the advance troops attack while the rear troops retreat, [in the confusion,] the simultaneously sounded bell and drum signals (signaling "attack" and "retreat") will both be missed. 士不選練，卒不服習，起居不精，動靜不集，趨利弗及，避難不畢，前擊後解，與金鼓之指相失.

Such are the deficiencies arising from one's not training or supervising the infantry soldiers. A hundred of these [poorly trained] soldiers could not oppose ten [trained soldiers]. 此不習勒卒之過也，百不當十.

> When weapons are not well-made and sharp, it will be the same as fighting with bare hands. When armor is not woven thick and tight, it will be the same as fighting with one's arms and torso exposed. When crossbow arrows cannot fly long distances, it's the same as using hand-held weapons. When volleys of arrows cannot hit their target, it's the same as having no arrows. When the arrows hit their target but cannot penetrate, it's the same as the arrows having no arrowheads. 兵不完利，與空手同；甲不堅密，與袒裼同；弩不可以及遠，與短兵同；射不能中，與亡矢同；中不能入，與亡鏃同.

Such are the calamities arising from a general not inspecting his army's weapons. Five [soldiers without adequate weapons] cannot oppose one [soldier with adequate weapons]. 此將不省兵之禍也，五不當一. [5]

The principles of war aver, 'When military implements are not sharp, then the ruler hands his soldiers over to the enemy. When soldiers cannot be effectively used, then the ruler hands his generals over to the enemy. When the generals do not understand how to wage a military campaign, then they give their ruler over to the enemy. When the lord does not vet properly his generals, he gives his state to the enemy.'[6] These four considerations are most essential when waging a military campaign. 「故兵法曰：器械不利，以其卒予敵也；卒不可用，以其將予敵也；將不知兵，以其主予敵也；君不擇將，以其國予敵也. 四者，兵之至要也.

D. "I, Your servant, have also heard that the small and the great require different configurations, the strong and the weak require different dispositions, the steep and the level require different preparations. Bowing low in service to the strong—this is the configuration of the small state. Uniting the small (e.g., the various foreign tribes) to attack the great (e.g., the Chinese empire)—this is the configuration of the enemy state (i.e., the Xiongnu state). Pitting foreign tribe against foreign tribe is the essential [strategic] constitution of the Central States. Now the configuration of the Xiongnu lands and their military skills and arts are different from those of the Central States. When climbing up and down mountain slopes or when exiting from and entering into mountain streams and rivers, the horses of the Central States cannot compare with the Xiongnu's. When heading down steep paths while simultaneously galloping and firing arrows, the horsemen of the Central States do not compare with those of the Xiongnu. When braving wind and rain, the Xiongnu will not become tired and neither hunger nor thirst causes them any hardship—in these ways the men of the Central States do not compare with the Xiongnu. These are the special skills of the Xiongnu. In the case where there are plains and level terrain, if we use light chariots and swift cavalry, then the masses of the Xiongnu will easily be thrown into confusion. If we use stout crossbows and long halberds that can shoot far or reach great distances, then the Xiongnu longbows will not be able to hit their target. If we use thick armor and sharp blades, if long and short weapons are intermingled, if roving crossbow archers move hither and thither, if battalions of five and ten soldiers advance together, then the Xiongnu armies will not be able to oppose us. If crack archers[7] rapidly shoot their arrows and the paths of the arrows lead to the same target, then the leather armor and wooden shields of the Xiongnu will not be able to withstand them. If the soldiers dismount from their horses and fight on the ground, when the swords and halberds clash and those fleeing and advancing are pressed close together, then the Xiongnu will trip over their own feet (because they lack infantry training). Such are the special skills of the armies of the Central States. From this we can observe that the special skills of the Xiongnu armies number three and the special skills of the Central States armies number five. Your Majesty has called up a mass of several hundred thousand troops to punish several tens of thousands of Xiongnu troops. Your Majesty's calculations of large and small numbers follow the formula of one fighting against ten. In spite of [Your military dominance], military arms are the instruments of misfortune; warfare is a dangerous matter. What is large can become small and what is strong can become weak with a nod of the head. Achieving victory in battle through the deaths of men who, once fallen, will not rise again, will lead to unending regrets. The way of thearchs and kings arises out of making all things whole. Now the defeated members of the Xiongnu, Yiqu and Manyi tribes have arrived at court to return to the council discussions. Their members number several thousand and their domestic habits and special skills are the same as those of the [belligerent] Xiongnu. If we are permitted to give them thick armor and padded jackets, stout bows and sharp arrows, they'd complement the elite cavalry of the border commanderies. If Your Majesty were to command the enlightened generals that they must know how to adapt to the customs of the Xiongnu so that they can become of one mind, then on the basis of Your Majesty's enlightened covenant they will be able to lead them. Now, there are steep [mountainous] obstructions that we can use to oppose [the incursions of the Xiongnu]. On level terrain and easily traveled roads, we can use light chariots and crack troops to manage them. The two forces (i.e., those of the allied barbarian tribes and those of the Central States) complement each other, with each utilizing its own special skills. Balancing their combined force against that of the masses of the Xiongnu is the technique with which one makes the ten-thousand things whole.「臣又聞小大異形，彊弱異勢，險易異備。夫卑身以事彊，小國之形也；合小以攻大，敵國之形也；以蠻夷攻蠻夷，中國之形也。今匈奴地形技藝與中國異。上下山阪，出入溪澗，中國之馬弗與也；險道傾仄，且馳且射，中國之騎弗與也；風雨罷勞，飢渴不困，中國之人弗與也：此匈奴之長技也。若夫平原易地，輕車突騎，則匈奴之眾易撓亂也；勁弩長戟，射疏及遠，則匈奴之弓弗能格也；堅甲利刃，長短相雜，遊弩往來，什伍俱前，則匈奴之兵弗能當也；材官騶發，矢道同的，則匈奴之革笥木薦弗能支也；下馬地鬥，劍戟相接，去就相薄，則匈奴之足弗能給也：此中國之長技也。以此觀之，匈奴之長技三，中國之長技五。陛下又興數十萬之眾，以誅數萬之匈奴，眾寡之計，以一擊十之術也。雖然，兵，凶器；戰，危事也。以大為小，以彊為弱，在俛卬之閒耳。夫以人之死爭勝，跌而不振，則悔之亡及也。帝王之道，出於萬全。今降胡義渠蠻夷之屬來歸誼者，其眾數千，飲食長技與匈奴同，可賜之堅甲絮衣，勁弓利矢，益以邊郡之良騎。令明將能知其習俗而輯其心者，以陛下之明約將之。即有險阻，以此當之；平地通道，則以輕車材官制之。兩軍相為表裏，各用其長技，衡加之以眾，此萬全之術也。」

    E. "The *Commentary* states, 'The lunatic speaks and the enlightened ruler vets his words.' I, Your servant, Chao Cuo, benighted and lowly, risk death to present to the throne the statements of a lunatic. It will be for Your Majesty to pick and choose which You should give Your attention to."「傳曰 狂夫之言，而明主擇焉。臣錯愚陋，昧死上狂言，唯陛下財擇。」

E. ZOU YANG'S (鄒陽) ADDRESS TO THE KING OF WU (LIU PI 劉濞) *HANSHU* 51.2338-43

Zou Yang was a man of Qi. When the Han dynasty arose, the many feudal lords and kings were themselves governing the commoners and hiring worthies. King Liu Pi of Wu recruited *shi*-officials from the four corners of the empire. Zou Yang, Wu Yanji, Mei Sheng and many others together served as *shi*-officials for King Liu Pi of Wu and all made illustrious reputations as eloquent debaters. A while thereafter, the King of Wu was dismayed because of an affair involving the imperial heir apparent, Liu Qi.[8] Complaining of illness, the King of Wu did not come to court and hatched in secret a nefarious plot.[9] Zou Yang presented a letter containing a remonstrance. Because the king's plot ("affair", *shi*) was still concealed how could he pose a direct critique? Thus he first raised the example of

Qin as a cautionary example and upon the basis of this example, elaborated on the difficulties in the Xiongnu, Yue, Qi, Zhao, and Huainan lands.[10] He then expressed his own attitude. The text of his remonstrance is as follows: 鄒陽, 齊人也. 漢興, 諸侯王皆自治民聘賢. 吳王濞招致四方游士, 陽與吳嚴忌、枚乘等俱仕吳, 皆以文辯著名. 久之, 吳王以太子事怨望, 稱疾不朝, 陰有邪謀, 陽奏書諫. 為其事尚隱, 惡指斥言, 故先引秦為諭, 因道胡、越、齊、趙、淮南之難, 然後乃致其意. 其辭曰:

A. "I, Your servant, have heard that the First Emperor of Qin, relying on the power of the Qutai Temple, placed All-Under-Heaven in the balance, delineated the boundaries [of law] and thus people did not commit crimes.[11] He applied military force to the Xiongnu and Yue. In the Qin dynasty's final days, Zhang Er and Chen Sheng, with the support of the united Vertical Armies, knocked at the gates of the Hangu Pass, and Xianyang (i.e., the Qin capital) was soon in danger of being conquered. What is the reason for this? The various commanderies had no allegiance to each other and the ten thousand households did not come to each other'said.[12] 「臣聞秦倚曲臺之宮, 懸衡天下, 畫地而不犯, 兵加胡越; 至其晚節末路, 張耳、陳勝連從兵之據, 以叩函谷, 咸陽遂危. 何則? 列郡不相親, 萬室不相救也.

B. "Nowadays, the Xiongnu move about with great speed outside the area north of the Yellow River. [They are so many that the dust they kick up] rises to envelop flying birds and below one cannot see the tiger lying in wait.[13] They fight against the cities without cease. Rescue forces have not arrived. The dead lay one next to the other and the pull-carts carrying off the dead go off in succession. Continuous shipments of millet are being sent along the riverways for thousands of leagues. What is the reason for all this turmoil? Powerful Zhao was deprived of the Hejian area,[14] the six Qi monarchs resented Emperor Hui and Empress Lü,[15] the king of Chengyang, Liu Xi, stewed over the Lu and Bo districts in Jibei,[16] and the heart-minds of the three sons of King Li of Huainan pondered his grave mound.[17] 「今胡數涉北河之外, 上覆飛鳥, 下不見伏菟, 鬬城不休, 救兵不止, 死者相隨, 轝車相屬, 轉粟流輸, 千里不絕. 何則? 彊趙責於河間, 六齊望於惠后, 城陽顧於盧博, 三淮南之心思墳墓.

C. "You, Great King, are not worried. But I, Your servant, fear that rescue armies will not join together [to help save the empire].[18] The Xiongnu cavalry will then ride toward and scout out Handan.[19] Yue will travel on water to attack the state of Changsha, after which they will turn about to sail to Qingyang in Wu.[20] If You bring the Liang[21] and the Huaiyang[22] forces together to travel eastward down the Huai River and cross through the Guangling commandery to block the transportation of the Yue men's supplies, Han will also cut off the western portion of the Yellow River and travel down it, protecting to the north the Zhang Waterway, thereby assisting the great state.[23] The Xiongnu will also continue to advance, the Yue will also continue deeper into our territory. This is what I am concerned about on Your behalf, Great King.「大王不憂, 臣恐救兵之不專, 胡馬遂進窺於邯鄲, 越水長沙, 還舟青陽. 雖使梁并淮陽之兵, 下淮東, 越廣陵, 以遏越人之糧, 漢亦折西河而下, 北守漳水, 以輔大國, 胡亦益進, 越亦益深. 此臣之所為大王患也.」

D. "I, Your servant, have heard that flood dragons toss their heads[24] and beat their wings and thus the floating clouds stream out, the mists and rains all gather. The sage kings refine the standards and cultivate virtue, thus the traveling discoursing *shi*-officials will adhere to the norms of social propriety and pine for renown. Now, I, Your servant, exhaust my wisdom and hold council discussions, alter my refined sensibilities in order to perfect my designs, so that no state cannot be imposed upon to assist. If one displays a determined yet humble heart-mind, then what kingly threshold cannot be crossed by the front of one's garment?[25] This being the case, I, Your servant, have with such a disposition visited numerous kingly courts, personally traveled to places a thousand leagues removed from the Huai River, not to antagonize the vassal states (i.e., Wu) but instead to bring contentment to the commoners of Wu.[26] I humbly from my lowly position have attempted to ennoble Your conduct with the emperor,[27] to make especially pleasing the Great King's actions. Thus I hope that the Great King is not hasty and carefully pays attention to others' visions.[28]「臣聞交龍襄首奮翼, 則浮雲出流, 霧雨咸集. 聖王底節修德, 則游談之士歸義思名. 今臣盡智畢議, 易精極慮, 則無國不可奸; 飾固陋之心, 則何王之門不可曳長裾乎? 然臣所以歷數王之朝, 背淮千里而自致者, 非惡臣國而樂吳民也, 竊高下風之行, 尤說大王之義. 故願大王之無忽, 察聽其志.」

E. "I, Your servant, have heard that a hundred gathered birds of prey are no match for one osprey.[29] During the time when Zhao was unified,[30] those military officers who dressed in black[31] and stood at the foot of the Cong Pavilion,[32] whose task was to carry the bronze *ding*-vessels, one day filled the marketplace but could not assuage the 'deep misgivings'[33] of King You of Zhao. When King Li of Huainan gathered swordsmen in the Area-East-of-the-Mountain,[34] the dead *shi*-officials filled the court. They were not able to return King Li of Huainan to the west.[35] Given this, it follows that if one does not thoroughly plan and deliberate, even Zhuanzhu and Mengben[36] will not be able to secure the monarch's position. This is clear. So I hope that the Great King investigates and makes plans, that's all.」「臣聞鷙鳥絫百, 不如一鶚. 夫全趙之時, 武力鼎士袘服叢臺之下者一旦成市, 而不能止幽王之湛患. 淮南連山東之俠, 死士盈朝, 不能還厲王之西也. 然而計議不得, 雖諸、賁不能安其位, 亦明矣. 故願大王審畫而已.」

F. "Previously, Emperor Wen the Filial took possession of the Hangu Pass,[37] entered the capital area and established himself as emperor. With a cold heart-mind and penetrating vision, even before it was light, He put on his clothes. He established himself as the successor to the Son of Heaven and sent the marquises of Dongmou[38] and Zhuxu[39] eastward to become kings⁴⁰ so as to aggrandize these descendants of Yifu (i.e., Liu Fei).⁴¹ Emperor Wen even marked off a great large piece of land for Liu Fei's young child and made him king. He cut up territory for his sons and made them kings of Liang⁴² and Dai.⁴³ He augmented the kingdom of Liang with territories from Huaiyang. He finally toppled the king of Jibei,⁴⁴ incarcerating his followers at Yong.⁴⁵ [If I did not help negotiate with the emperor,] how would I not be considered like Xinyuan Ping and others!⁴⁶ 「始孝文皇帝據關入立，寒心銷志，不明求衣．自立天子之後，使東牟朱虛東襄義父之後，深割嬰兒王之．壤子王梁、代，益以淮陽．卒仆濟北，囚弟於雍者，豈非象新垣平等哉！」

G. "Nowadays the Son of Heaven (i.e., Emperor Jing) newly takes over the unfinished work of the former emperors. To the left He regulates Shandong, to the right He administers Guanzhong, transforming balances and changing dispositions.⁴⁷ The powerful ministers at the imperial court have difficulty understanding what He is doing. 「今天子新據先帝之遺業，左規山東，右制關中，變權易勢，大臣難知．

H. "If the Great King does not examine the situation, I, Your servant, am afraid that the Zhou *ding*-vessels will again surface in Han. Because Xinyuan Ping propounded erroneous plans at court, our state of Wu lacks successors and cannot expect to survive another generation. 「大王弗察，臣恐周鼎復起於漢，新垣過計於朝，則我吳遺嗣，不可期於世矣．

I. "The High August Thearch (Liu Bang) burned the wooden roads erected along the cliffs and flooded Zhang Han's city.⁴⁸ The High August Thearch's armies did not stop their march [eastward]. They took advantage of the exhaustion of the defeated commoners, racing eastward to the Hangu Pass, and Western Chu (i.e., Xiang Yu) was overwhelmingly defeated. When the High August Thearch attacked on water, Zhang Han lost his city. When the High August Thearch attacked on land, King Jing of Chu (i.e., Xiang Yu) lost his lands. All of this is something Your country would not long for. I wish the Great King would carefully examine my proposal."「高皇帝燒棧道，水章邯，兵不留行，收弊民之倦，東馳函谷，西楚大破．水攻則章邯以亡其城，陸擊則荊王以失其地，此皆國家之不幾者也．願大王孰察之．」

The king of Wu did not accept his statement. 吳王不內其言．

F. LIU AN'S (劉安) ADDRESS TO EMPEROR WU (LIU CHE 劉徹) *HANSHU* 64A.2777–85

A. "Your Majesty oversees All-Under-Heaven, exhibiting virtue, extending kindness, relaxing punishments, lowering taxes, grieving for widowers and widows, pitying orphans and the solitary, fostering the aged, and succoring the impoverished and needy. Your abundant virtue rises upward, Your harmonious bounty wets all below, those close by are attached to You as to a parent, those far away embrace Your virtue. All-Under-Heaven is joined together. People feel safe. Until the end of their days, they see neither weapons nor shields. Now I have heard that a *Si*-official is raising an army and is about to punish the Yue tribe. Your servant, An, humbly feels a deep concern for Your Majesty about this. 「陛下臨天下, 布德施惠, 緩刑罰, 薄賦斂, 哀鰥寡, 恤孤獨, 養耆老, 振匱乏, 盛德上隆, 和澤下洽, 近者親附, 遠者懷德, 天下攝然, 人安其生, 自以沒身不見兵革. 今聞有司舉兵將以誅越, 臣安竊為陛下重之.

B. "The territories of the Yue lie beyond the four corners and their common people clip off their hair and tattoo their bodies. One cannot put it in order with the laws and regulations of a civilized nation. Since the time when the three dynasties (i.e., the Xia, Shang, and Zhou dynasties) flourished, the Xiongnu and Yue tribes did not participate in accepting the first (calendar) day of the year. It is not the case that they are so strong they will not submit, not that they are so fierce they cannot be managed. The Yue was considered [by the emperors of the three dynasties] to be an uninhabitable territory with a people who could not be governed and which was not powerful enough to cause trouble for the Central States. In ancient times, the area within the boundary of land reserved for the ruler was the royal zone, outside the boundary was the lords' zone (i.e., the "surveillance" zone), outside the lords' zone was the defensive zone, outside the defensive zone was the zone for negotiating with foreign (*manyi*) tribes, and outside the zone for negotiating with foreign tribes was the zone of wastelands occupied by barbarian (*rongyi*) tribes. The strategic dispositions of far and near are distinct. Since the Han was first established, for seventy-two years the people of Wu and Yue have been attacking each other countless times. Yet the Son of Heaven has not yet raised an army and entered their territory. 「越, 方外之地, 劗髮文身之民也. 不可以冠帶之國法度理也. 自三代之盛, 胡越不與受正朔, 非彊弗能服, 威弗能制也, 以為不居之地, 不牧之民, 不足以煩中國也. 故古者封內甸服, 封外侯服, 侯衛賓服, 蠻夷要服, 戎狄荒服, 遠近勢異也. 自漢初定已來七十二年, 吳越人相攻擊者不可勝數, 然天子未嘗舉兵而入其地也.

C. "I, Your servant, have heard that the Yue lands have neither defensive walls nor townships nor hamlets. They live in ravines and gullies and in bamboo groves. They are practiced in water combat and adept with boats. Their land lies in deep gloom and has many water hazards. If the men of the Central States are not aware of the Yue people's lands' dispositions and obstructions and yet enter them, even a hundred of our soldiers will not be able to oppose one of theirs. Even if we obtain their lands, it will not be possible to organize them into commanderies and districts. If we attack them, they will not be swiftly conquered. When one investigates on a map the mountains, rivers, and strategic defensive positions, their distance on the map from each other is only a couple of inches, but the physical space between them is hundreds or thousands of leagues. The obstructing cliffs and the woods and bush cannot be adequately displayed on a map. To survey this on a map seems quite simple, but to traverse it is extremely arduous. All-Under-Heaven rely on the spirits of the ruler's ancestral temples and within the four corners there is great tranquility. The fact that hoary-headed elders have never seen troops, the common people have achieved a state in which husbands and wives defend each other, fathers and sons protect each other is because of Your Majesty's virtue. The name given to the Yue people was 'Border Servants' yet they ship no harvest or sacrificial tribute to the Great Interior, nor is one solider offered up for service. If they were to fight among themselves and Your Majesty were to send out troops to save them, this, contrary [to what You would wish], is to have the Central States exhaust themselves in the southern tribal (*manyi*) territories. Furthermore, the Yue people are stupid and bull-headed, simple and vapid, and fickle in upholding covenants. It wouldn't even be the length of one day before they stopped applying the laws and measures of the Son of Heaven. If they once do not accept an imperial edict and You wage a military campaign to punish them, I, Your servant, fear that afterwards there will be no cessation in warfare.

「臣聞越非有城郭邑里也，處谿谷之間，篁竹之中，習於水鬥，便於用舟，地深昧而多水險，中國之人不知其勢阻而入其地，雖百不當其一. 得其地，不可郡縣也；攻之，不可暴取也. 以地圖察其山川要塞，相去不過寸數，而間獨數百千里，阻險林叢弗能盡著. 視之若易，行之甚難. 天下賴宗廟之靈，方內大寧，戴白之老不見兵革，民得夫婦相守，父子相保，陛下之德也. 越人名為藩臣，貢酎之奉，不輸大內，一卒之用不給上事. 自相攻擊而 陛下發兵救之，是反以中國而勞蠻夷也. 且越人愚戇輕薄，負約反覆，其不用天子之法度，非一日之積也. 壹不奉詔，舉兵誅之，臣恐後兵革無時得息也

D. "Recently, for several years the harvest has consecutively not come in and thus the common people have depended on selling aristocratic titles and indenturing their children for clothes and food. They are depending on Your Majesty's virtue and bounty to rescue them, so that they will be able to not roll dead into a watery ditch. In the fourth year the crops did not come in, in the fifth year again there were locusts, and the livelihood of the common people has yet to be recovered. Now You are sending troops over several thousand miles, provided with clothes and provisions, to invade the Yue lands, carrying light chariots across the mountain cliffs and dragging boats up along the rivers for hundreds or thousands of leagues. They will be hemmed in by thick forests and groves of bamboo. All along the waterways their boats will smash against rocks. In the forests there will be many poisonous snakes and wild beasts. In the hot summer months, consumptive and deranging ailments will spread among the soldiers, so that in the end, without a single blade having been raised, many will be mortally wounded. Previously when the King of Nanhai rebelled, Your Majesty's former servant, King Li of Huainan, sent

General Jianji to lead troops to attack him. Once his troops surrendered, the King of Nanhai was made to reside at Shanggan. Afterwards, he rebelled again. Just at that time the weather was hot and there was much rain. Soldiers on board the storied warships lived on the water and pulled the oars. Without having ever done battle, over half died of illness. Their family elders wept and cried, their orphaned children wailed, their households were destroyed, their enterprises were dissolved, and their families had to retrieve their corpses from over a thousand miles away, wrap up the remains and return home. The atmosphere of melancholy and woe did not dissipate for many years. Mature adults and the elderly take these circumstances as a warning,[49] even to this day. So without having invaded their territory, the disaster already reaches to this extent. 「間者，數年歲比不登，民待賣爵贅子以接衣食，賴陛下德澤振救之，得毋轉死溝壑．四年不登，五年復蝗，民生未復．今發兵行數千里，資衣糧，入越地，輿轎而隃領，拕舟而入水，行數百千里，夾以深林叢竹，水道上下擊石，林中多蝮蛇猛獸，夏月暑時，歐泄霍亂之病相隨屬也 ，曾未施兵接刃，死傷者必眾矣．前時南海王反，陛下先臣使將軍閒忌將兵擊之，以其軍降，處之上淦．後復反，會天暑多雨，樓船卒水居擊櫂，未戰而疾死者過半．親老涕泣，孤子䪨號，破家散業，迎尸千里之外，裹骸骨而歸．悲哀之氣數年不息，長老至今以為記．曾未入其地而禍 已至此矣．」

E. "I, Your servant, have heard that in the wake of armies and battalions, there will certainly be years of misfortune (i.e., years of poor harvest), by which it is meant that because of each commoner's vaporous emanation of worry and suffering, pressure is put on the harmonizing of *yin* and *yang*, the seminal essence of heaven and earth is stimulated, and thus vaporous emanations of calamity are generated. Your Majesty's virtue joins with Heaven and Earth, Your enlightenment as radiant as the sun and moon, Your charity extended even to the birds and beasts, Your bounty proffered even the grasses and trees. If a single person were to die before reaching the end of his natural life due to cold and hunger (as could happen on a long campaign), Your Majesty would grieve. Now within the four borders no dogs are barking in alarm and yet Your Majesty's armed conscripts are being sent to their deaths. They are exposed to the elements in the Central Plains, their blood stains the mountains and valleys. Because of this, the commoners of the border regions shut their city's gates early and open them late [for fear that] morning will not last until night. I, Your servant, Liu An, humbly feel a deep concern for Your Majesty about this. 「臣聞軍旅之後必有凶年，言民之各以其愁苦之氣薄陰陽之和，感天地之精，而災氣為之生也．陛下德配天地，明象日月，恩至禽獸，澤及草木，一人有飢寒不終其天年而死者，為之悽愴於心．今方內無狗吠之警，而使陛下甲卒死亡，暴露中原，霑漬山谷，邊境之民為之早閉晏開，朝不及夕，臣安竊為陛下重之．」

F. "Of those who are not familiar with the terrain of the southern border region, many consider Yue to have numerous people and a powerful military that could pose problems for the border cities. At the time when Huainan was a whole country, many people of that kingdom acted as clerks in the border region.[50] I, Your servant, have humbly heard that their lands are different from the Central States' lands. Being blocked by tall mountains—where the traces of men disappear and carriage roads do not pass through—this is the means by which outside and inside are separated in the natural world. Were they to enter into the Central States, they would necessarily have to go down tributary mountain rivers. The mountains of the tributary rivers are precipitous and high, and rocks carried by the rivers smash into boats, so it is impossible for large ships to carry provisions down them. If the Yue people want to bring about upheaval, they would first have to work the fields at Yugan on the border,[51] store up provisions and then enter into our lands to fell timber and construct ships. The defending watchmen of the border cities are honest and cautious. Were people from Yue to enter to fell timber, the watchmen would capture and bind them and set fire to their stored provisions. Even if all the many Yue tribes [together were to attempt to invade], what could they do against a border city? For the present, the Yue people are as weak as cotton fibers and thin on ability. They cannot conduct a ground war and also do not employ chariots or archers. In such a situation they are not able to invade the Central States. The lands they protect are treacherous and the men of the Central States cannot manage[52] traversing their waters and lands. 「不習南方地形者, 多以越為人衆兵彊, 能難邊城. 淮南全國之時, 多為邊吏, 臣竊聞之, 與中國異. 限以高山, 人跡所絕, 車道不通, 天地所以隔外內也. 其入中國必下領水, 領水之山峭峻, 漂石破舟, 不可以大船載食糧下也. 越人欲為變, 必先田餘干界中, 積食糧, 乃入伐材治船. 邊城守候誠謹, 越人有入伐材者, 輒收捕, 焚其積聚, 雖百越, 奈邊城何! 且越人縣力薄材, 不能陸戰, 又無車騎弓弩之用, 然而不可入者, 以保地險, 而中國之人不能其水土也.」

G. "I, Your servant, have heard that the Yue armored infantry are no less than several hundred thousand. To invade them, we will need five times their number. Those who pull carts with provisions are not included in that number. The southern border regions are hot and humid. At the onset of summer it becomes extremely[53] hot there. Living on the water, exposed to the elements, with pit vipers and stinging insects,[54] beset frequently by illness and plague—two to three soldiers of every squad of ten will fall to illness before they've shed a drop of blood. Even if You were to conquer and enslave the entire Yue state, it would not compensate such losses. 「臣聞越甲卒不下數十萬, 所以入之, 五倍乃足, 輓車奉饟者, 不在其中. 南方暑溼, 近夏癉熱, 暴露水居, 蝮蛇蠚生, 疾癘多作, 兵未血刃而病死者什二三, 雖舉越國而虜之, 不足以償所亡.」

H. "I, Your servant, have heard rumors that say that the Min-Yue king's younger brother, X,[55] committed regicide and killed him. If because of this X were to be executed, his common people would have no state to attach themselves to. Were Your Majesty to desire to have him come and reside in the Central States, then dispatch important officials to interview him. By displaying virtue and bestowing rewards, You can then draw him to You. In this situation, he will assuredly succor the young and support the old among his people and respond to Your sagely virtue. If Your Majesty has no use for him, then preserve their severed lineage (by installing another from his family on the Yue throne), restore their fallen state, install their king and lords, and thereby show support for the Yue people. In this situation, the Yue will certainly pledge to be boundary servants, and for generations they will provide tribute and service. Your Majesty, by means of an inch-square seal with its twelve-foot cord would pacify and console the areas beyond the borders. Without the labors of one infantry soldier, without the dulling of one spear, might and virtue will both emanate forth. Now if You were to militarily invade their lands, this will unquestionably shock and alarm them. They will believe that the *Si*-officers wish to slaughter and annihilate them, and will assuredly flee like pheasants and rabbits and hide in the mountains and forests, in areas that are treacherous and difficult to travel through. If You turn Your back on them and expel them, then they will band together again someplace else. If You let them remain where they are and guard them, then with the passage of years the officers and soldiers of the Central States will become exhausted and their provisions will run out. The men of the Central States will not be able to plant and sow, the women will not be able to weave and spin. The able-bodied men will follow the army and the old and weak will transport provisions to the armies. Those at home will have nothing to eat and those who travel off with the army will have no provisions to take with them. The common people are suffering because of this military enterprise. Those who desert will certainly be numerous. If You were to strive to pursue and execute them, You would not be able to track them all down. Thieving and robbing will surely become more frequent occurrences. 「臣聞道路言,閩越王弟甲弒而殺之,甲以誅死,其民未有所屬.陛下若欲來內,處之中國,使重臣臨存,施德垂賞以招致之,此必攜幼扶老以歸聖德.若陛下無所用之,則繼其絕世,存其亡國,建其王侯,以為畜越,此必委質為藩臣,世共貢職.陛下以方寸之印,丈二之組,填撫方外,不勞一卒,不頓一戟,而威德並行.今以兵入其地,此必震恐,以有司為欲屠滅之也,必雉兔逃入山林險阻.背而去之,則復相群聚;留而守之,歷歲經年,則士卒罷勌,食糧乏絕,男子不得耕稼樹種,婦人不得紡績織紝,丁壯從軍,老弱轉餉,居者無食,行者無糧.民苦兵事,亡逃者必眾,隨而誅之,不可勝盡,盜賊必起.

I. "I, Your servant, have heard mature and elderly adults say that in Qin times the emperor previously dispatched Superintendent Tusui to attack Yue. He also dispatched Inspector Lu to dig a canal to connect the waterways. The Yue people fled deep into the mountains and forest groves and could not be attacked. The stationed troops settled and defended unoccupied land. As the time spent drew out ever longer, the *shi*-officials and infantry soldiers were worked to exhaustion. The Yue men then came out to attack them. The Qin armies were badly routed and exiled convicts were sent to join the army as reinforcements. During all this, the areas beyond and within the borders were in upheaval. The commoners ran away and hid. Travelers did not return home. Those who departed never came back. No one was able to support himself. There was a constant stream of people fleeing. Gangs of commoners began to thieve and rob and thereupon the difficulties in the region east of the Mountains (i.e., the central Yellow River plain, near Chang'an, the Han capital) began to arise. This is the situation which the *Laozi* describes: 'Where troops have encamped, there will brambles and thistles grow.' Military campaigns are inauspicious enterprises. If on one border there is an emergency, all four sides of the four border regions will be incited [to rescue it].[56] I, Your servant, am afraid that the emergence of upheaval and the creation of criminal behavior begins with this state of affairs. The *Zhouyi* states, 'The High Ancestor did battle with the Ghostly Border Region. After three years, he overcame them.' The Ghostly Border Region denotes the lesser Manyi tribes (i.e., southern tribes, like the Yue). The High Ancestor is the magnificent Son of Heaven of the Shang. The statement about the magnificent Son of Heaven doing battle with the lesser Manyi tribes and defeating them after three years says that the use of the military cannot *not* be given weight. 「臣聞長老言, 秦之時嘗使尉屠睢擊越, 又使監祿鑿渠通道. 越人逃入深山林叢, 不可得攻. 留軍屯守空地, 曠日引久, 士卒勞倦, 越出擊之. 秦兵大破, 乃發適戍以備之. 當此之時, 外內騷動, 百姓靡敝, 行者不還, 往者莫反, 皆不聊生, 亡逃相從, 群為盜賊, 於是山東之難始興. 此老子所謂『師 之所處, 荊棘生之』者也. 兵者凶事, 一方有急, 四面皆從. 臣恐變故之生, 姦邪之作, 由此始也. 周易曰:『高宗伐鬼方, 三年而克之.』鬼方, 小 蠻夷; 高宗, 殷之盛天子也. 以盛天子伐小蠻夷, 三年而後克, 言用兵之不可不重也.

J. "I, Your servant, have heard that the Son of Heaven's (i.e., Your) armies are out on campaign and yet have not done battle, which means that none have dared to resist them. If the Yue people are caused to brave [death] and hope for good fortune in resisting the menial laborers on the frontline, if even one of the foot soldiers responsible for general tasks and driving the carts returns home having sustained injury[57]—even though the King of Yue's head is obtained—Your servant would still humbly be embarrassed on behalf of the great Han nation. Your Majesty takes the four seas as Your borders, the nine provinces as Your household, the eight marshes as Your playground, and the rivers and lakes as Your pools. All those born as commoners are Your male and female servants. Your throng of followers is sufficient to supply the thousand[58] offices; the collection of taxes is sufficient to supply You with manned chariots. With an inquisitive heart-mind and transcendent perspicacity, You uphold and support the sagely way. Behind You is the folding screen with a black and white ax decoration. You lean on the jade table, facing south and listening to judgments, issuing orders and commands to All-Under-Heaven. Within the four seas, none will not sound a response. Your Majesty rains down virtue and kindness to nurture them. You cause the multitudes of common people to feel safe and enjoy their enterprises and thus Your bounty blankets all generations, passed down from son to grandson, extending [Your bounty] to them without cease. The peace of All-Under-Heaven is similar to the peace that emanates from Taishan that extends out to the four directions. How can the land of the foreign tribes be worth a single day of intervention by the Han army and the trouble of bringing horses to a lather? The *Book of Odes* says, 'The King's way has been faithfully effected. The people from the regions of Xu (i.e., the Yi tribe that resided in the Huai River Valley area)[59] have already come [to submit].' This means that the way of the king is very great, so much that distant regions embrace it. I, Your servant, have heard that the farmer labors and the lord nourishes himself on the farmer's labors, the benighted man speaks and the wise man vets his statements. I, Your servant, Liu An, have been fortunate to act as Your Majesty's guard vassal. Using one's body to block and shield—this is the task of a servant. When the borders and boundaries are in a state of alarm, one who holds dear his body and does not exert his benighted mind, such a one is not a loyal servant. I, Your servant, Liu An, humbly fear that the generals' and officials' employment of one hundred thousand troops to wage a military campaign is actually a job for one emissary." 「臣聞天子之兵有征而無戰，言莫敢校也．如使越人蒙徼幸以逆執事之顏行，廝輿之卒有一不備而歸者，雖得越王之首，臣猶竊為大漢羞之．陛下以四海為境，九州為家，八藪為囿，江海為池，生民之屬皆為臣妾．人徒之眾足以奉千官之共，租稅之收足以給乘輿之御．玩心神明，秉執聖道，負黼依，馮玉几，南面而聽斷，號令天下，四海之內莫不嚮應．陛下垂德惠以覆露之，使元元之民安生樂業，則澤被萬世，傳之子孫，施之無窮．天下之安猶泰山而四維之也，夷狄之地何足以為一日之閒，而煩汗馬之勞乎！詩云『王猶允塞，徐方既來』，言王道甚大，而遠方懷之也．臣聞　之，農夫勞而君子養焉，愚者言而智者擇焉．臣安幸得為陛下守藩，以身為鄣蔽，人臣之任也．邊境有警，愛身之死而不畢其愚，非忠臣也．臣安竊恐將吏之以十萬之師為一使之任也．．」

G. ZHAO CHONGGUO'S (趙充國) EXCHANGE WITH EMPEROR XUAN (LIU BINGYI 劉病已) *HANSHU* 69.2984-90

That autumn, Chongguo became ill. The monarch sent a letter which said, 其秋，充國病，上賜書曰：

"An issued edict to the General of the Rear Zhao Chongguo stated: I have heard that you have pain in your thigh and calf, and have stomach trouble. You, the general, are old and becoming increasingly infirm;[60] the transformations of the morning cannot be evaded (i.e., you will probably die soon). I am very worried about this. Now my edict states that the Defeating-the-Qiang General must present himself at the settlement and become the General of the Rear's assistant. It is imperative to take advantage of the great profit[61] in the present course of the heavens and the pronounced energy of the clerks and officers and in the twelfth month attack the Xianling Qiang. Given that your illness is serious, stay at the settlement and do not embark on the campaign. You need only send the Smashing-the-Qiang and Strong-Crossbow generals." 「制詔後將軍：聞苦腳脛、寒泄，將軍年老加疾，一朝之變不可諱，朕甚憂之．今詔破羌將軍詣屯所，為將軍副，急因天時大利，吏士銳氣，以十二月擊先零羌．即疾劇，留屯毋行，獨遣破羌、彊弩將軍．」

Around this time, the number of Qiang who surrendered numbered in the tens of thousands. Chongguo estimated that they would inevitably be defeated and wanted to disband the cavalry and infantry assigned to the agricultural colony and await the Qiang's destruction. His composed hortatory address had not yet been submitted to the throne when he happened to receive a sealed missive from the emperor telling him to advance. Leader of Court Gentlemen Zhao Ang (Zhao Chongguo's son) became afraid and sent a retainer to remonstrate with Chongguo, saying, 時羌降者萬餘人矣．充國度其必壞，欲罷騎兵屯田，以待其敝．作奏未上，會得進兵璽書，中郎將卬懼，使客諫充國曰：

"Even if the emperor insistently orders soldiers to go forth and the Han armies are smashed, the generals killed, and the Han nation thereby is imperiled, it is still permissible for the General (i.e., Zhao Chongguo) to remain and defend the agricultural settlement. Since you have diarrhoea and are ill, what good is there in disputing with the emperor? If one day you are not in accord with the emperor's attitude, he will send a royal scribe to upbraid the General. If the General cannot protect his own person, how then can he secure the nation?" 「誠令兵出，破軍殺將以傾國家，將軍守之可也．即利與病，又何足爭？一旦不合上意，遣繡衣來責將軍，將軍之身不能自保，何國家之安？」

Chongguo sighed and said, 充國歎曰：

"What kind of disloyal statements are these? If originally my statements had been employed, would the situation with the Qiang have reached this point? Previously, when we were to select one who could preemptively move against the Qiang, I selected Xin Wuxian. The Chancellor and the Secretary to the Imperial Counselor replied by announcing that Anguo of Yiqu was to be dispatched. He, in the end, thwarted the Qiang. When the grain from Jincheng and Huangzhong cost eight pieces of copper cash per *hu*, I told Vice Chancellor Geng that if we were to buy up two million *hu* of grain, the men of Qiang would not dare to act (because they would notice the preparations for a long military expedition). Vice Chancellor Geng presented a request to the monarch for the cash to buy up one million *hu* of grain but then only received enough to buy four hundred thousand *hu*. Anguo of Yiqu was sent a second time to fight the Qiang and wasted half of the grain. Because these two stratagems have failed, the men of Qiang will venture to counterattack. "To fall short by a tiny distance is to miss by a thousand leagues"[62]—this is what has happened. Now, if the infantry does not make decisive action for some time, the four Yi tribes in the end will become restless, and offering support to each other will rise up together.[63] Since even a wise man could not make the consequences right [once all of the Yi tribes are involved], how can our worries be limited to the Qiang? I would certainly defend the settlement with my life. Any enlightened ruler would take my remarks as loyal statements." 「是何言之不忠也! 本用吾言, 羌虜得至是邪? 往者舉可先行羌者, 吾舉辛武賢, 丞相御史復白遣義渠安國, 竟沮敗羌. 金城、湟中穀斛八錢, 吾謂耿中丞, 糴二百萬斛穀, 羌人不敢動矣. 耿中丞請糴百萬 斛, 乃得四十萬斛耳. 義渠再使, 且費其半. 失此二冊, 羌人故敢為逆. 失之毫釐, 差以千里, 是既然矣. 今兵久不決, 四夷卒有動搖, 相因而起, 雖有知者不能善其後, 羌獨足憂邪! 吾固以死守之, 明主可為忠言.」

Thereupon, Chongguo submitted a hortatory address to the throne about the agricultural colonies in the border areas, saying, 遂上屯田奏曰:

A. "Your servant has heard that warfare is that by which one brings to light one's virtue and expels harm. Thus if military success are obtained on the periphery (i.e., on the frontier), then good fortune will be created in the interior lands. One cannot *not* be cautious about such. For Your servant to feed the generals, the clerks, the *shi*-officials, horses, and oxen, Your servant each month will need 199,630 *hu* of rice and millet, 1,693 *hu* of salt, and 250,286 *shi* of hay. The difficulties with the Qiang have long not been resolved and the corvée laborers do not rest. I also worry that there will suddenly be unexpected upheaval among the other Yi tribes who will rely upon each other and rise up together. This should be worrisome for the enlightened ruler, for it truly does not accord with the stratagems previously settled upon in the outer court for overcoming the Qiang. The Qiang vermin will easily be smashed using my plan. It will be difficult to break them with the army. So, in Your servant's benighted opinion, I consider that attacking them is not expedient. 「臣聞兵者, 所以明德除害也, 故舉得於外, 則福生於內, 不可不慎. 臣所將吏士馬牛食, 月用糧穀十九萬九千六百三十斛, 鹽千六百九十三斛, 茭藁二十五萬二百八十六石. 難久不解, 繇役不息. 又恐它夷卒有不虞之變, 相因並起, 為明主憂, 誠非素定廟勝之冊. 且羌虜易以計破, 難用兵碎也, 故臣愚以為擊之不便.

B. "My plan for the agricultural settlement takes into account the territory from the Lin Qiang district eastward to Haomen, the Qiang vermin's farm fields of old together with the common farm fields, where the commoners have yet to till the soil, which possibly all told total above 2,000 *qing*. Within this territory many postal relay stations have fallen into ruin. I, Your servant, formerly led divisional *shi*-officials into the mountains to cut down large and small trees, over 60,000 *mei* of wood, all of it which we placed in water (to keep it preserved). I wish to disband the cavalry and to retain the amnestied convicts, volunteers, and also the foot soldiers from Huaiyang and Runan, together with private attendants of the clerks and *shi*-officials, amounting in all to 10,281 men. Each month they will require 27,363 *hu* of grain and 308 *hu* of salt, to be distributed to the strategically significant places in the settlements. When the ice melts we will ship the wood down the river, fix up the districts and neighborhoods, deepen the water channels, repair the seventy bridges on the western road leading from Huangxia, and make the roads extend as far as the area around the Xian River. When planting begins, we will dispense to the people (as a source of income) twenty *mei* of land. In the fourth month when the grain sprouts, we will dispatch a thousand each of the commandery cavalry, cavalry from the dependent Xiongnu states, and the Strongmen staff[64] along with 200 pack horses and send them off to the fields to act as rangers for the farmers. By stocking the Jincheng Commandery with grain, increasing the reserves, minimizing large expenditures, and using[65] the grain sent from the Chamberlain for the Imperial Treasury, we should have enough to distribute to ten thousand people for one year.[66] Your servant respectfully submits an inventory of farm fields and military and agricultural implements needing to be dispensed. It is for Your Majesty to decide how to proceed." 「計度臨羌東至浩亹, 羌虜故田及公田, 民所未墾, 可二千頃以上, 其間郵亭多壞敗者. 臣前部士入山, 伐材木大小六萬餘枚, 皆在水次. 願罷騎兵, 留弛刑應募, 及淮陽、汝南步兵與吏士私從者, 合凡萬二百八十一人, 用穀月二萬七千三百六十三斛, 鹽三百八斛, 分屯要害處. 冰解漕下, 繕鄉亭, 浚溝渠, 治湟陿以西道橋七十所, 令可至鮮水左右. 田事出, 賦人二十晦. 至四月草生, 發郡騎及屬國胡騎伉健各千, 倅馬什二, 就草, 為田者遊兵. 以充入金城郡, 益積畜, 省大費. 今大司農所轉穀至者, 足支萬人一歲食. 謹上田處及器用簿, 唯陛下裁許.」

His Highness responded 上報曰:

"The August Thearch questions the General of the Rear Zhao Chongguo about his remarks regarding his hope to disband the cavalry of ten-thousand men and retain the farmlands. Even if we act according to the General's plans, when will the Qiang vermin submit to punishment (i.e., military defeat)? When will the army achieve decisive action? After you consider carefully the expediency of your plan, present another address." 「皇帝問後將軍, 言欲罷騎兵萬人留田, 即如將軍之計, 虜當何時伏誅, 兵當何時得決? 孰計其便, 復奏.」

Chongguo sent a memorandum to His Highness, which stated, 充國上狀曰:

C. "I, Your servant, have heard that the armies of the five thearchs and the kings of the Xia, Shang and Zhou dynasties achieved victory through completed preparations. In view of this, we should privilege strategy and disparage battle. To do battle and overcome one hundred times is not the most superior way. Better to first act as that which cannot be overcome and await the appearance of that which can be overcome in the enemy. Although the customs of the foreign barbarians are different from those of a nation like ours with rites and propriety, they, like us, avoid harm and are drawn toward profit, cherish their relatives, and fear death. Now the Qiang vermin have lost their resplendent lands and pastures and fret over whether to entrust themselves to distant regions. Among their meat and bones (i.e., close relatives), heart-minds are divided and some of their people have mutinous visions. The enlightened ruler will withdraw his troops and discontinue the campaign. Ten thousand people (i.e., military personnel) will remain to protect the farm fields. If we are in accord with the course of the heavens, rely on the advantages of the terrain, and wait for the Qiang vermin to become vulnerable, though they have not yet acknowledged their crimes [and submitted to military defeat], we can look forward to the decisive military action within the coming year. The armies of the Qiang vermin will fall apart. Altogether over 10,700 Qiang people will surrender and those who hear of our plans and depart (i.e., flee) will, roughly estimated, be over seventy times that many. This will be the means to disperse the Qiang. 「臣聞帝王之兵, 以全取勝, 是以貴謀而賤戰. 戰而百勝, 非善之善者也, 故先為不可勝以待敵之可勝. 蠻夷習俗雖殊於禮義之國, 然其欲避害就利, 愛親戚, 畏死亡, 一也. 今虜亡其美地薦草, 愁於寄託遠遯, 骨肉離心, 人有畔志, 而明主般師罷兵, 萬人留田, 順天時, 因地利, 以待可勝之虜, 雖未即伏辜, 兵決可期月而望. 羌虜瓦解, 前後降者萬七百餘人, 及受言去者凡七十輩, 此坐支解羌虜之具也.

D. "Your servant respectfully lays out twelve aspects ('matters') in which it is expeditious and advantageous not to go out on campaign and to leave [a defensive force to protect] the agricultural fields. 「臣謹條不出兵留田便宜十二事.

"There will be nine barracks of foot soldiers, and ten thousand clerks and *shi*-officials remaining in the settlements to compose a defensive army. Because of their support, the grain can be brought in from the fields. Because of their contribution, Your Majesty's might and virtue are simultaneously promoted. This is the first aspect. 「步兵九校, 吏士萬人, 留屯以為武備, 因田致穀, 威德並行, 一也.

"By expelling and separating off the Qiang vermin and commanding that they not be allowed to return to their fecund lands, we will impoverish and break their multitudes and thereby gradually bring about discord among the Qiang. This is the second aspect. 「又因排折羌虜, 令不得歸肥饒之墜, 貧破其眾, 以成羌虜相畔之漸, 二也.

"The resident commoners will be able to work both [their own and the settlement's][67] fields, and thus they will not suffer loss in their agricultural endeavors.[68] This is the third aspect. 「居民得並田作, 不失農業, 三也.

"The foodstuffs needed to feed the troops and horses for a month I estimate can be apportioned over a year to the *shi*-officers defending the farm fields. By disbanding the infantry and cavalry, we will minimize large expenditures of grain. This is the fourth aspect. 「軍馬一月之食, 度支田士一歲, 罷騎兵以省大費, 四也.」

"In the spring, with a force of lightly armored *shi*-officers and infantry soldiers, we will float grain down the Hehuang river to Linqiang, using this as a means to make a show to the Qiang vermin, increase their perception of our force and martiality and cause them to wish to withdraw for generations. This is the fifth aspect. 「至春省甲士卒, 循河湟漕穀至臨羌, 以際羌虜, 揚威武, 傳世折衝之具, 五也.」

"Using the wood cut during fallow times, we will repair the postal stations and fill up Jincheng with provisions. This is the sixth aspect. 「以閒暇時下所伐材, 繕治郵亭, 充入金城, 六也.」

"To go on a military campaign is to tread on dangerous ground and have unreasonable hopes. If we do not go out on a military campaign, we will force the rebellious vermin to scurry away in cold and windy lands. Once they have suffered epidemics and frostbite brought on by the frost and dew, we will be on the way to certain victory. This is this seventh aspect. 「兵出, 乘危徼幸, 不出, 令反畔之虜竄於風寒之地, 離霜露疾疫瘃墯之患, 坐得必勝之道, 七也.」

"[Not going on a military campaign will mean we will not have] to suffer traversing over difficult landscapes, pursuing them over great distances, or sustaining injuries and death. This is the eighth aspect. 「亡經阻遠追死傷之害, 八也.」

"On the domestic front, we will not lessen the grandeur of our fearlessness and martiality; on the international front, we will not cause the vermin to obtain the position of having advantageous opportunities (i.e., giving the other tribes reason to join the Xianling Qiang). This is the ninth aspect. 「內不損威武之重, 外不令虜得乘間之勢, 九也.」

"[By not going on a campaign we will] have no worries about alarming the Dakai and Xiaokai Qiang from the south of the Yellow River and giving rise to additional upheaval. This is the tenth aspect. 「又亡驚動河南大开, 小开使生它變之憂, 十也.」

"If we maintain the roads and bridges in Huangxia and extend these networks of roads as far as the Xian River, we can administer to the Western Territories, and our trustworthiness and might will be felt for over one thousand leagues. You can send out troops while on Your pillows and mats. This is the eleventh aspect. 「治湟陿中道橋, 令可至鮮水, 以制西域, 信威千里, 從枕席上過師, 十一也.」

"As great expenditures are thus spared and corvée labor rested and ready, we can be on guard against the unexpected. This is the twelfth aspect. 「大費既省, 繇役豫息, 以戒不虞, 十二也.」

"Remaining within the agricultural settlement has twelve benefits, sending out troops loses twelve advantages.「留屯田得十二便, 出兵失十二利.

E. "Your servant Chongguo's talents are limited. The teeth of this domestic animal are falling out. I do not comprehend lengthy stratagems (i.e., stratagems for a drawn-out war). Now for [consideration when composing] Your enlightened edict thoroughly scrutinize the proposal and with the assistance of the honorable Chamberlain and council advisors select and vet a strategy."「臣充國材下, 犬馬齒衰, 不識長冊, 唯明詔博詳公卿議臣採擇.」

His Highness again responded 上復賜報曰:

"The August Thearch made an inquiry of the General of the Rear Zhao Chongguo, who spoke of twelve benefits, to which we have listened. Even though the Qiang vermin have yet to submit to punishment, you say that we can look forward to decisive military action in the coming year. Does this mean by this coming winter? When exactly? The general has simply not considered the circumstance in which the vermin, upon hearing that the armies have all been released, will collect together their able-bodied men to attack and harass the farmers and the agricultural settlement soldiers posted on the roads. They will once again kill and rob our people. How will this be stopped? Also, the Qiang of Dakai and Xiaokai have said previously, 'We reported to the Han troops where the Xianling Qiang were and yet the army has not come to fight. The Han troops have remained at the settlement for a long time now. Will it be of no consequence for the Han government, within the next five years, to not distinguish us from the Xianling Qiang and attack us [together with them]?' Their (i.e., the Qiang of Dakai and Xiaokai's) attitude is one that constantly worries me. Now if the army is not sent out on campaign, would this not give rise to upheaval among the Qiang, resulting in their joining together with the Xianling? The General should carefully consider this and present another address."「皇帝問後將軍, 言十二便, 聞之. 虜雖未伏誅, 兵決可期月而望, 期月而望者, 謂今冬邪, 謂何時也? 將軍獨不計虜聞兵頗罷, 且丁壯相聚, 攻擾田者及道上屯兵, 復殺略人民, 將何以止之? 又大开, 小开前言曰:『我告漢軍先零所在, 兵不往擊, 久留, 得亡效五年時不分別人而并擊我?』其意常恐. 今兵不出, 得亡變生, 與先零為一? 將軍孰計復奏.」

Chongguo presented an address, which stated 充國奏曰:

F. "Your servant has heard that with regard to military campaigns, one should take careful planning as a basis. Those who calculate more will overcome those who calculate less. The crack troops of the Xianling Qiang now do not exceed seven or eight thousand men. They have lost their lands and are taking harbor in distant lands, they are divided and dispersed, hungry and cold. The Qiang of Han, Kai, Moxu all have violently robbed the weak and frail of the Xianling Qiang of their property and livestock. There is no end to the number of Xianling Qiang who abandon the others and return to their old lands, and yet they all (i.e., all those Xianling Qiang tribespeople who are attempting to return) understand the Son of Heaven's illuminated command to give out rewards to those who assist in capturing and killing them. In Your servant's benighted opinion, I believe that we can await the vermin's destruction in the coming days and months, at the latest, by the coming spring. Thus I stated that decisive military action can be anticipated in the coming months.「臣聞兵以計為本, 故多算勝少算. 先零羌精兵今餘不過七八千人, 失地遠客, 分散飢凍. 罕, 开, 莫須又頗暴略其羸弱畜產, 畔還者不絕, 皆聞天子明令相捕斬之賞. 臣愚以為虜破壞可日月冀, 遠在來春, 故曰兵決可期月而望.

G. "I, humbly have seen the northern border stretching from Dunhuang to Liaodong eastwards over eleven thousand five hundred miles. The clerks and infantry soldiers manning the barriers and fanned out over the roads number several thousand men. Though the Qiang vermin attacked them several times with great masses of soldiers, they could not do our soldiers any harm. Now the foot soldiers left to tend to the agricultural settlements are ten thousand strong and the terrain of the agricultural settlement is flat, with the benefit of many surrounding high mountains from which one can look afar. The divisions and regiments protect each another and have built deep moats, high fences, and defensive thatch towers.[69] The interwoven fences are continuous and are good for crossbows and setting up combat weapons. If the signal fires can transmit messages, our disposition will be as if our strength were joined with others and we can then release our reserve labor. This would be to our military advantage.「竊見北邊自敦煌至遼東萬一千五百餘里, 乘塞列隧有吏卒數千人, 虜數大衆攻之而不能害. 今留步士萬人屯田, 地勢平易, 多高山遠望之便, 部曲相保, 為塹壘木樵, 校聯不絕, 便兵弩, 飭鬭具. 烽火幸通, 勢及并力, 以逸待勞, 兵之利者也.

H. "In Your servant's benighted opinion, the settlement, domestically speaking, has the advantage of no expenditures. For external concerns, it can serve as a defensive base. Although the cavalry will have been disbanded, the Qiang vermin will see that the ten thousand people remaining in the settlement constitute the means to their certain capture. It won't be long before their lands will be destroyed and they will respond to Your virtue. Three months from now, the Qiang vermin's horses will be feeble and emaciated. The Qiang men will certainly not dare to force their wives and children to flee to live among other tribes. They will travel far, crossing rivers and mountains, and will come into our lands as bandits. When they see that the *shi*-officers and crack troops in the agricultural settlement number over ten thousand men, they will ultimately not venture to once again take their burdens (wives and children) back to their old lands. This is Your servant's benighted plan, because of which I estimate that the vermin will wreck their communities through infighting.

This is a policy that will result in their self-destruction without our ever having to do battle. As for the Qiang vermin becoming petty robbers and thieves, killing our people from time to time, the causes of this will not be swiftly brought under control. 「臣愚以為屯田內有亡費之利，外有守禦之備．騎兵雖罷，虜見萬人留田為必禽之具，其土崩歸德，宜不久矣．從今盡三月，虜馬羸瘦，必不敢捐其妻子於他種中，遠涉河山而來為寇．又見屯田之士精兵萬人，終不敢復將其累重還歸故地．是臣之愚計，所以度虜且必瓦解其處，不戰而自破之冊也．至於虜小寇盜，時殺人民，其原未可卒禁．

I. "I, Your servant, have heard that as battle does not inevitably end in victory, one should not yearn to cross swords; as fighting does not inevitably end in vanquishing one's enemy, one should not yearn to put the populace to the yoke. If You truly must command the army to go out on campaign, even though You cannot wipe out the Xianling Qiang, if You truly are able to cause the Qiang vermin to never again be petty robbers, then going out on campaign is permissible. As this is the case today (i.e., that the Qiang are returning as robbers) and You are eager to be on the road to victory, Your being in a dangerous position, moving towards the endpoint without seeing any advantage, emptying the interior of soldiers and leading to its being defeated and worn out, dismissive of what is important (i.e., the interior) and leading to its harming itself, such is not the way to display our strength to the foreign tribes. Once the main army is sent out on campaign, when they return they cannot be resettled. Huangzhong also cannot be emptied of soldiers. Since the situation is like this, [if You must pursue the Xianling Qiang, I advise You to] send out the corvée laborers again. Regarding the Xiongnu tribe, one cannot not be prepared; about the Wuhuan tribe, one cannot not be concerned. For a long time now we have suffered turns of fortune and been frustrated by expenses. To upend ourselves with unpredictable employments in order to pacify a corner of the empire, I, Your servant, benightedly believe such not to be expeditious. Commandant Linzhong[70] has been fortunate to benefit from Your might and virtue, been generously granted numerous gifts, has mollified the Qiang hoard, and has, with Your illustrious edicts, made clear to them that it is meet that they all depend on You. Although the other Qiang tribes previously discussed whether 'it is of no consequence for the Han government, within the next five years . . . ', they should not become disloyal. Even if they did, this is not enough reason to send out the troops. 「臣聞戰不必勝，不苟接刃；攻不必取，不苟勞眾．誠令兵出，雖不能滅先零，亶能令虜絕不為小寇，則出兵可也．即同是而釋坐勝之道，從乘危之勢，往終不見利，空內自罷敝，貶重而自損，非所以視蠻夷也．又大兵一出，還不可復留，湟中亦未可空，如是，繇役復發也．且匈奴不可不備，烏桓不可不憂．今久轉運煩費，傾我不虞之用以澹一隅，臣愚以為不便．校尉臨眾幸得承威德，奉厚幣，拊循眾羌，諭以明詔，宜皆鄉風．雖其前辭嘗曰「得亡效五年」，宜亡它心，不足以故出兵．

J. "Your servant has himself humbly deliberated on this. To receive an edict to go out past the barriers, discharge troops to fight afar, exhaust the Son of Heaven's crack troops, disperse cavalry and infantry over the mountains and wilds, even though there will be not an inch's worth of progress, being content with merely being able to avoid suspicion and having no later regrets or excessive debts—this is to the advantage of status-bearing subjects who are not loyal to the emperor. Such is not to the good fortune of the enlightened ruler of the nation. 「臣竊自惟念, 奉詔出塞, 引軍遠擊, 窮天子之精兵, 散車甲於山野, 雖亡尺寸之功, 媮得避嫌之便, 而亡後咎餘責, 此人臣不忠之利, 非明主社稷之福也.

K. "I, Your servant, have been fortunate to have battle-ready crack troops. If in dealing with the unrighteous, I have delayed for too long to mete out Heaven's punishment, my crime deserves ten-thousand deaths. Your Majesty is generous and benevolent, has not tolerated the dispensing of punishment on me, and has commanded Your servant to give these issues careful consideration. Your benighted servant has repeatedly given them the most careful consideration. I do not dare to avoid the axe, and brave death to present my benighted suggestions. They are for Your Majesty to thoroughly scrutinize." 「臣幸得奮精兵, 討不義, 久留天誅, 罪當萬死. 陛下寬仁, 未忍加誅, (今)[令]臣數得執計. 愚臣伏計孰甚, 不敢避斧鉞之誅, 昧死陳愚, 唯陛下省察.」

H. WEI XIANG'S (魏相) ADDRESS TO EMPEROR XUAN (LIU BINGYI 劉病已) *HANSHU* 74.3136

During the Yuan Kang era (65–62 BCE), the Xiongnu sent armies to attack the Han garrison and agricultural settlements in the western state of Cheshi but the Han could not be made to submit. The emperor and the General of the Rear Zhao Chongguo, among others, held a council discussion. The emperor desired to take advantage of the weakness of the Xiongnu and send out armies to attack their right (i.e., western) territories, to cause them not to dare to again disturb the western regions of the Han empire. Wei Xiang submitted a remonstrance to the emperor, which stated, 元康中, 匈奴遣兵擊漢屯田車師者, 不能下. 上與後將軍趙充國等議, 欲因匈奴衰弱, 出兵擊其右地, 使不敢復擾西域. 相上書諫曰:

A. "I, Your servant, have heard that those campaigns that are meant to rescue the nation from chaos and punish violence are called righteous campaigns. When one's campaigns are righteous, one is acting as a true king. If one's enemies exert military force against oneself and there is no other choice but to rise up against them, this is called a 'responding campaign.' Campaigns that are 'responding' will succeed. In those situations where a dispute arises with another[71] over a trifling matter and the leader cannot contain his anger, such campaigns are called 'campaigns of rage.'

Campaigns of rage will fail. In those situations where the campaign is taking advantage of people's lands and treasures, such a campaign is called an 'avaricious campaign.' Avaricious campaigns will be crushed. In those situations where the campaign relies on the great size of the nation, and is boastful about the multitude of their commoners and people, wishing to appear fearsome to the enemy, such campaigns are called 'arrogant campaigns'. Arrogant campaigns will be destroyed. These five categories are not simply abstracted from the affairs of men, they are also abstracted from the ways of Heaven. From time to time, the Xiongnu have had a beneficent attitude and have returned the Han commoners that they had taken hostage and have not invaded the border regions. Even though they have had disputes[72] with the garrison and the agricultural settlements in the state of Cheshi, such is not sufficient to take it as[73] representing their essential attitude toward us. 「臣聞之，救亂誅暴，謂之義兵，兵義者王；敵加於己，不得已而起者，謂之應兵，兵應者勝；爭恨小故，不忍憤怒者，謂之忿兵，兵忿者敗；利人土地貨寶者，謂之貪兵，兵貪者破；恃國家之大，矜民人之眾，欲見威於敵者，謂之驕兵，兵驕者滅：此五者，非但人事，乃天道也．間者匈奴嘗有善意，所得漢民輒奉歸之，未有犯於邊境，雖爭屯田車師，不足致意中．

B. "Now, I have heard that there are many generals who desire to initiate campaigns to penetrate the Xiongnu's lands. I, Your benighted servant, do not know what name to give to this type of campaign. Now the border commanderies are beset by hardship and deprivation. Fathers and sons share the pelts of dogs and goats, consume the seeds of wild grasses and grains, and constantly worry about not being able to keep themselves alive. In this scenario it would be difficult to begin a campaign. 'Inauspicious times succeed the actions of armies,'[74] which states that the common people, because of their fretful and suffering state (qi), will injure the harmony between *yin* and *yang*. If You go out on campaign, even if You overcome the enemy, there will still be worries thereafter, and I am afraid that the unusual transformations of natural disasters will arise because of these worries. 「今聞諸將軍欲興兵入其地，臣愚不知此兵何名者也．今邊郡困乏，父子共犬羊之裘，食草萊之實，常恐不能自存，難於動兵．『軍旅之後，必有凶年』，言民以其愁苦之氣，傷陰陽之和也．出兵雖勝，猶有後憂，恐災害之變因此以生．

C. "Now, the governors and prime ministers of the various states and commanderies are frequently not thoroughly vetted, popular customs and conventions are extraordinarily shallow, and rainy and dry seasons are not timely. According to the statistics for this year, there have been two hundred and twenty cases among the people of sons and younger brothers murdering, respectively, their fathers and elder brothers and wives murdering their husbands.[75] I, Your benighted servant, take this to be no small transformation! 「今郡國守相多不實選，風俗尤薄，水旱不時．案今年計，子弟殺父兄、妻殺夫者，凡二百二十二人，臣愚以為此非小變也．

D. "Now, those advisors to Your left and right do not worry about this but desire to dispatch armies to communicate their petty rage to the distant barbarians. This situation is probably what Confucius was referring to when he said 'I fear that the real worry for Ji Sun does not lie with Zhuanyu, but within the screen of reverence at the Lu court.'[76] 「今左右不憂此, 乃欲發兵報纖介之忿於遠夷, 殆孔子所謂『吾恐季孫之憂不在顓臾而在蕭牆之內』也.

E. "I hope that Your Majesty will carefully consult with the Marquis of Pingchang (Wang Wugu 王無故), the Marquis of Lechang (Wang Wu 王武), the Marquis of Ping'en (Xu Guanghan 許廣漢) and other knowledgeable persons before approving a course of action."[77] 「願陛下與平昌侯、樂昌侯、平恩侯及有識者詳議乃可.」

The emperor heeded Wei Xiang's advice and abandoned the plans for the expedition. 上從相言而止.

I. HOU YING'S (侯應) ADDRESS TO EMPEROR YUAN (LIU SHI 劉奭) *HANSHU* 94B.3803–4

Gentleman of the Interior Hou Ying was trained in border affairs and considered that [the previously discussed request by Huhanxie Chanyu 呼韓邪單于 that he protect the borders from Shanggu 上谷 westwards to Dunhuang, that his commission be extended to his descendants without end, and that the Han border clerks and infantry be released from duty] was not permissible. Emperor Yuan asked for his estimation of the situation. Ying averred, 郎中侯應習邊事, 以為不可許. 上問狀, 應曰:

A. "From the time of the Zhou and Qin to the present, the Xiongnu have been violent and fierce, raiding and invading the border frontiers. After the rise of the Han, the empire was all the more overwhelmed by their ravaging. 「周秦以來, 匈奴暴桀, 寇侵邊境, 漢興, 尤被其害.

B. "I, Your servant, have heard that the northern frontier barriers reach all the way to Liaodong. On the on other side of the barrier lies Mount Yin. From east to west, the distance between the frontier barrier and Mount Yin is over a thousand leagues. [In this area between the frontier barrier and Mount Yin,] the grasses and trees grow luxuriantly and there are many wild beasts.[78] Originally, Maodun Chanyu depended on the protection of its recesses, overseeing the crafting of bows and arrows and coming out to raid our lands. It acted as his wildlife preserve. 「臣聞北邊塞至遼東, 外有陰山, 東西千餘里, 草木茂盛, 多禽獸, 本冒頓單于依阻其中, 治作弓矢, 來出為寇, 是其苑囿也.

C. "When it came to the time of Emperor Wu the Filial, we had been sending out troops on campaigns against the Xiongnu, to expel them and take back the territory [between Mount Yin and the frontier barriers], forcing the Xiongnu to the northern reaches of the desert beyond Mount

Yin. Emperor Wu established barriers and frontiers, created wayhouses and roads, built outer defensive walls, and founded military garrisons in order to defend the area. Thereafter, the border regions were usable and there was less need for peacekeeping. 「至孝武世, 出師征伐, 斥奪此地, 攘之於幕北. 建塞徼, 起亭隧, 築外城, 設屯戍, 以守之, 然後邊境得用少安.

D. "At the northern reaches of the desert, the terrain is flat, with little grass or trees and much coarse sand. When the Xiongnu come to raid, there are few places for them to hide themselves. As they follow along the border defenses going south, the paths take them deep into mountain valleys. Expeditions in and out of this area are beset with difficulties. The adults and elders of the border areas say that after the Xiongnu lost [control of the area south of] Mount Yin, [when the Xiongnu] passed by [Mount Yin], [there were none] who did not weep. If You release the garrison soldiers who man the defenses and barriers, this will suggest an opportunity that will be to the overwhelming advantage of the barbarian tribes. Such is not permissible. This is my first point. 「幕北地平, 少草木, 多大沙, 匈奴來寇, 少所蔽隱, 從塞以南, 徑深山谷, 往來差難. 邊長老言匈奴失陰山之後, 過之未嘗不哭也. 如罷備塞戍卒, 示夷狄之大利, 不可, 一也.

E. "Now Your sageliness and virtue blanket vast areas, Heaven lays the Xiongnu low, and the Xiongnu receive Your life-preserving charity, bowing their heads and coming to court as Your servants. As for the psychological disposition of the barbarians, when they meet with trouble then they are lowly and submissive, when they are strong, then they are arrogant and rebellious. This is their Heaven-sent nature. Earlier, You dismantled the outer defensive walls and cut down on the number of wayhouses and roads [under construction], and now You cut back the number of troops such that they are sufficient only to watch over [the outlying areas] and communicate [changes] via signal fires. In the past, even when the empire was at peace, the rulers did not forget about possible dangers. It is not permissible to release more soldiers. This is my second point. 「今聖德廣被, 天覆匈奴, 匈奴得蒙全活之恩, 稽首來臣. 夫夷狄之情, 困則卑順, 彊則驕逆, 天性然也. 前以罷外城, 省亭隧, 今裁足以候望通烽火而已. 古者安不忘危, 不可復罷, 二也.

F. "Though the Central States government has the teachings of the rites and of social propriety and the strictures of corporeal punishment and fines, the benighted common people still act contrary to government prohibitions. With respect to the Chanyu, how could we be certain that his masses would not break the covenant between us? This is my third point.「中國有禮義之教, 刑罰之誅, 愚民猶尚犯禁, 又況單于, 能必其眾不犯約哉! 三也.

G. "The passes and bridges that the Central States continue to erect to control the many lords are the means by which the Central States quashes the hopes and desires of its subjects (e.g., the Xiongnu). Erecting barriers and frontiers and setting up military garrisons are not only to protect against the Xiongnu, they are also erected for the governance of the subservient common people of the many subsidiary states who originally in the past were Xiongnu people. I, Your servant am afraid they would pine for their former comrades and flee [to join them, and their armies].[79] This is my fourth point. 「自中國尚建關梁以制諸侯, 所以絕臣下之覬欲也. 設塞徼, 置屯戍, 非獨為匈奴而已, 亦為諸屬國降民, 本故匈奴之人, 恐其思舊逃亡, 四也.

H. "Recently, the Western Qiang people have been guarding the barriers and fraternizing with the people of the Han. The Han clerks and commoners were greedy for advantage, invaded the Western Qiang settlements and stole their livestock, their harvested produce, and their women and children (to use as their servants). Because of this, the Qiang hated them, rose up and rebelled. For generations this [conflict] will not end. Now if You dismantle the manned barriers You will see signs of deceptiveness, divisiveness and quarreling. This is my fifth point. 「近西羌保塞, 與漢人交通, 吏民貪利, 侵盜其畜產妻子, 以此怨恨, 起而背畔, 世世不絕. 今罷乘塞, 則生嫚易分爭之漸, 五也.

I. "In the past, of those who accompanied the troops, many disappeared and did not return. Their sons and grandsons suffered destitution and hardship. One morning, they fled out [into the wilderness], following their families. This is my sixth point. 「往者從軍多沒不還者, 子孫貧困, 一旦亡出, 從其親戚, 六也.

J. "In addition, the slaves of the border people have fretted about the turmoil caused by the Xiongnu. Many have wanted to flee. They have said, 'We hear the music of the Xiongnu. There is no way to scout out the danger!' Under these circumstances at one point a group of seven went out through the barriers. This is my seventh point. 「又邊人奴婢愁苦, 欲亡者多, 曰『聞匈奴中樂, 無奈候望急何!』然時有七出塞者, 七也.

K. "Thieves and bandits are ferocious and crafty. If a gang of men broke the law, and was in a tight spot, the men could flee out past through northern frontier (to become bandits) and then could not be controlled. This is my eighth point. 「盜賊桀黠, 群輩犯法, 如其窘急, 亡走北出, 則不可制, 八也.

L. "It has been over a hundred years since the barriers began to be erected (by Emperor Wu). Not all are earthen walls. In some places they use massive mountain rocks, in others they use logs and sticks that have fallen or are broken off of trees, and in others they use valley sluices. They are maintained over time, the infantry soldiers and their assistants rebuilding and attending to them. The effort required many years and cannot be overestimated. I, Your servant, fear that the members of the council will not thoroughly consider the entirety of what has been involved in this endeavor. They want to reduce, for expediency, the number of corvée laborers assigned to the frontier. After ten years, within one hundred years, when the infantry have other troubles to attend to, the defensive barriers broken down and dilapidated, the wayhouses and roads ravaged and abandoned will all demand the deployment of another border garrison to repair and maintain them. Their construction, requiring generations, cannot be quickly redone. This is my ninth point. 「起塞以來百有餘年,非皆以土垣也,或因山巖石,木柴僵落,谿谷水門,稍稍平之,卒徒築治,功費久遠,不可勝計。臣恐議者不深慮其終始,欲以壹切省繇戍,十年之外,百歲之內,卒有它變,障塞破壞,亭隧滅絕,當更發屯繕治,累世之功不可卒復,九也.」

M. "If You release the border guards and reduce the number of scouts and watchmen, the Chanyu will himself take over guarding the frontiers and defending the defenses, which will require that he have a deeply entrenched sense of virtuous duty toward the Han. Even so, his requests and petitions will never end. If we err even in the slightest in attending to his wishes, then the consequences will be unfathomable. Exploiting the divisions between the foreign tribes is the basis to their continued dependence on the Central States. This is my tenth point. 「如罷戍卒,省候望,單于自以保塞守御,必深德漢,請求無已. 小失其意,則不可測. 開夷狄之隙,虧中國之固,十也.」

N. "Even if this is not the means by which we can forever maintain perfect tranquility, it is a long-term policy by which we can cow and administer to the many foreign tribes." 「非所以永持至安,威制百蠻之長策也.」

J. YAN YOU'S (嚴尤) ADDRESS TO WANG MANG (王莽) *HANSHU* 94B.3824-25

Wang Mang's general, Yan (a.k.a. Zhuang 莊) You, remonstrated, saying, 莽將嚴尤諫,曰:

A. "I, Your servant, have heard that the Xiongnu are a menace and that the origins of the problem are old. I have not yet heard of the earliest generations being forced to wage campaigns against them. In later generations, the three houses of Zhou, Qin, and Han waged campaigns against them but none had superior policies. The Zhou conceived of a middle-rank policy, the Han conceived of a low-rank policy, and the Qin did not have any policy at all. 「臣聞匈奴為害,所從來久矣,未聞上世有必征之者也. 後世三家周、秦、漢征之,然皆未有得上策者也. 周得中策,漢得下策,秦無策焉.」

B. "During the time of King Xuan of Zhou, the Xianyun invaded the interior, pushing all the way to Jingyang. King Xuan commanded the generals to wage a campaign against them and they ran them off to the borders and then returned. King Xuan viewed the barbarian incursions as the sting of mosquitoes and *meng*-insects. All one had to do was swat them away. All-Under-Heaven proclaimed [King Xuan] brilliant. It was a middle-rank policy. 「當周宣王時,獫允內侵,至于涇陽,命將征之,盡境而還. 其視戎狄之侵,譬猶蚊蝱之螫,敺之而已. 故天下稱明,是為中策.」

C. "Emperor Wu of Han selected generals to train the army, reduced cargo and lightened supplies, and sent soldiers to penetrate deeply and defend the distant border areas. Even though the Han armies were successful at winning battles and taking prisoners, the Xiongnu immediately repaid them in kind and the army suffered continual misfortune for over 30 years. The Central States were defeated and destitute and the Xiongnu were also chastened by Emperor Wu's attacks and All-Under-Heaven proclaimed Him 'the Martial One.' This policy was a lower-ranked policy." 「漢武帝選將練兵, 約齎輕糧, 深入遠戍, 雖有克獲之功, 胡輒報之, 兵連禍結三十餘年, 中國罷耗, 匈奴亦創艾, 而天下稱武, 是為下策。」

D. "The First Emperor of Qin did not tolerate petty insult and discounted the strength of the common people. He erected the foundational sections of the Long Wall and extended it for 10,000 leagues. He began a [water channel] transportation system in the coastal states. After the erection of the borders and frontiers was completed, the inner regions of the Central States were exhausted and because of this the nation was lost. This policy was no policy at all. 「秦始皇不忍小恥而輕民力, 築長城之固, 延袤萬里, 轉輸之行, 起於負海, 疆境既完, 中國內竭, 以喪社稷, 是為無策。」

E. "Nowadays All-Under-Heaven is encountering the dangers of Yang Nine (i.e., a poor harvest). For a succession of years there has been famine, with the northwest border area being particularly afflicted. If You were to send off a force of 300,000 supplied with 300 days of provisions, from the east You will need to draw upon produce from the regions of the Eastern Sea and Dai Commanderies. From the south You will need to take produce from the regions around the Yangzi and Huai Rivers. This being done, the armies will be provided for. 「今天下遭陽九之阨, 比年饑饉, 西北邊尤甚。發三十萬眾, 具三百日糧, 東援海代, 南取江淮, 然後乃備。」

F. "If one were to calculate the distance, [one can conclude that all the troops] after a year still will not have amassed there. The armies that arrive first will have to settle together in the exposed outdoors. Furthermore, the troops are old and their weapons are broken, so their potential cannot be implemented. This is the first problem. 「計其道里, 一年尚未集合, 兵先至者聚居暴露, 師老械弊, 勢不可用, 此一難也。」

G. "The borders are completely vacant and thus cannot supply troops with provisions. As for sending out troops from the interior commanderies and states, they are not joined in allegiance with us (and thus they won't quickly provide supplies or men for this expedition). This is the second problem. 「邊既空虛, 不能奉軍糧, 內調郡國, 不相及屬, 此二難也。」

H. "Using the calculation that each person needs 300 days of provisions, the dry rations that will be used will be 18 *hu*. Without the power of oxen, You will not be able to overcome [the difficulties of transporting these provisions]. The oxen must also be fed, which will require an additional 20 *hu*. Such will be a heavy load. The Xiongnu lands are sandy and salty and largely devoid of fresh water and grains. If one were to make an estimate based on previous enterprises, the troops won't last 100 days out there and the oxen will certainly die, every last one of them. If there are many more supplemental provisions, the men will not be able to carry them. This is the third problem. 「計一人三百日食, 用糒十八斛, 非牛力不能勝; 牛又當自齎食, 加二十斛, 重矣. 胡地沙鹵, 多乏水草, 以往事揆之, 軍出未滿百日, 牛必物故且盡, 餘糧尚多, 人不能負, 此三難也.

I. "The Xiongnu lands in autumn and winter are terribly cold and in the spring and summer there are great windstorms. With the amount of firewood and charcoal needed for the many cauldrons, the burden will be too heavy to bear. Eating dry provisions, drinking water throughout the entire year, with the troops worrying about plague and infections—for these reasons when previous generations fought the Xiongnu, the campaigns didn't last more than 100 days. Such wasn't because they didn't want them to last longer or that their potential strength was not up to the task. This is the fourth problem. 「胡地秋冬甚寒, 春夏甚風, 多齎鬴鍑薪炭, 重不可勝, 食糒飲水, 以歷四時, 師有疾疫之憂, 是故前世伐胡, 不過百日, 非不欲久, 勢力不能, 此四難也.

J. "Carts laden with provisions follow one after another and rapid-strike forces are few. The army is not able to move quickly. Although the Xiongnu vermin are on a slow retreat, our disposition does not allow us to catch up with them. Even if the army was fortunate enough to engage with the vermin, there are the mounds of provisions [that will prevent quick movement]. Such a situation is akin to being on a steep mountain face, with the horses in single-file and the vermin about to block us both ahead and behind. The danger, I'm afraid, is incalculable. This is the fifth problem. 「輜重自隨, 則輕銳者少, 不得疾行, 虜徐遁逃, 勢不能及, 幸而逢虜, 又累輜重, 如遇險阻, 銜尾相隨, 虜要遮前後, 危殆不測, 此五難也.

K. "If You rely too much on the strength of the commoners, success cannot be firmly established. I, Your servant, humbly worry about this. Now that the soldiers have already been sent off on campaign, with some probably having arrived, You should command Your servant Yan You and the others to enter deep into their territory and strike swift as lightning, thereby chastening the Xiongnu vermin." 「大用民力, 功不可必立, 臣伏憂之. 今既發兵, 宜縱先至者, 令臣尤等深入霆擊, 且以創艾胡虜.」

Wang Mang did not listen to You's statement and sent the army shipments of grain as had been done in the past. All-Under-Heaven was in tumult. 莽不聽尤言, 轉兵穀如故, 天下騷動.

Notes

CHAPTER ONE. INTRODUCTION

1. With *Zuozhuan*, for example, the author(s) speak "to the reader through various characters in the narratives, explaining the causes and significance of events." See Ronald Egan, "Narratives in Tso Chuan," *Harvard Journal of Asiatic Studies* 37, no. 2 (1977): 325.

2. *HS* 78.3286; Pan Ku, *Courtier and Commoner in Ancient China: Selections from the History of the Former Han*, trans. Burton Watson (New York: Columbia University Press, 1974), 218.

3. 府然若渠匽檃栝之於己也, 曲得所謂焉, 然而不折傷。See *Xunzi jijie* 荀子集解, vol. 1 (Beijing: Zhonghua shuju, 1988), 85. See also David Schaberg, *A Patterned Past: Form and Thought in Early Chinese Historiography* (Cambridge, MA: Harvard University Asia Center, 2001), 53.

4. For a recent extended study of indirect court speech, see Schaberg, "Playing at Critique: Indirect Remonstrance and the Formation of *Shi* Identity," in *Text and Ritual in Early China*, ed. Martin Kern (Seattle: University of Washington Press, 2005), 194–225.

5. In fact, Schaberg's and Pines's studies are of addresses, or more specifically remonstrances, composed in the pre-Qin period, when the rhetorical norms of composition and address were more likely in flux, tied to the various traditions of the states in which they were composed. Such remonstrances, while their rhetoric was certainly very carefully crafted, were unhampered by the unifying protocols that later came to be part of the imperial system. See Yuri Pines, "Intellectual Change in the Chunqiu Period: The Reliability of the Speeches in the *Zuo Zhuan* as Sources of Chunqiu Intellectual History," *Early China* 22 (1997): 77–132; and Schaberg, "Remonstrance in Eastern Zhou Historiography," *Early China* 22 (1997): 133–79. A recent, and very important, study of the rhetorical protocols of the early imperial period is Enno Giele, *Imperial Decision-Making and Communication in Early China: A Study of Cai Yong's Duduan* (Wiesbaden: Otto Harrassowitz, 2006).

6. Some, however, are submitted in response to the monarch's queries.

7. David Schaberg also suggests the possible importance of addresses interjected in the histories for the composition of the narrative, specifically in *Zuozhuan*. He argues that its anecdotes are connected not only by a chronological arrangement but also by "less tangible" principles "expressed in the speeches attributed to characters but never directly in the voice of the narrators themselves." While Schaberg is emphasizing the insertion of prescriptions about the need for a ritually embedded order, prescriptions that are expressed in the oral pronouncements of certain of the actors involved in the anecdotes of *Zuozhuan*, I merely wish to emphasize that the speeches or addresses of the classical histories, whether moralizing or not, have a central and decisive effect on the perception of the direction of the narrative. An analysis of their content gives us a sense of what sorts of considerations were involved in the determination of what course of action the executive should take. See Schaberg, "Truth and Ritual Judgment: On Narrative Sense in China's Earliest Historiography," *Historically Speaking* (2004): 33–34.

8. Hereafter referred to as *"Intrigues of the Warring States,"* or simply, *"Intrigues."* The stories in the *Intrigues* were reputedly collected and edited in the Later Han by Liu Xiang but involve events and personalities from the pre-Han period of circa 300 to 221 BCE. There are, however, alternate theses that posit that the *Intrigues* were composed close to, or even during, the Han. Wai-Yee Li in an article mentions that Fang Pao and Wu Ju-lun explain that the episodes in the *Intrigues* are taken from the *Records*: "Although commonly assumed to have been written during the late Warring States period, it might also have included later materials. Cf. Chin Te-chien's theory that the *Intrigues* was written after the Ch'in decree of burning books in 213 B.C., and that the *Intrigues* is actually the same book as 'Eighty-one Arguments' by K'uei T'ung (active during the Ch'in-Han transition)." Wai-yee Li, "The Idea of Authority in the *Shih Chi* (*Records of the Historian*)," *Harvard Journal of Asiatic Studies* 4, no. 2 (1994): 372, n.51. Jin Dejian's argument, unfortunately, rests on the assumption that the *Intrigues* was a historical document and, like other pre-Qin historical documents from states other than Qin, were supposedly burned by the First Emperor of Qin. But Crump reports that Henri Maspéro demonstrated the material *Intrigues* has serious chronological inconsistencies, including, most notably, the date by which one could infer the Vertical Alliance was to have been created. Maspéro's doubts as to the chronological accuracy of the *Intrigues* are further buttressed, according to Crump, by the research conducted by the Qing dynasty scholar Ma Guohan. Paul Goldin shares in this assessment, saying that the *Intrigues* "contain too many internal contradictions, both factual and chronological, to be true history." Paul Goldin, *After Confucius: Studies in Early Chinese Philosophy* (Honolulu: University of Hawaii Press, 2005), 78. If the *Intrigues* cannot be regarded as a collection of historical texts, then Jin Dejian's argument becomes problematic. Naturally, it is possible that the *Intrigues* were composed after the Qin. However, their date of composition does not affect the probability of their reflecting rhetorical and argumentative conventions in practice before the Qin. See *Chan-Kuo Ts'e*, trans. James I. Crump, Jr. (New York: Oxford University Press, 1970), 13–14. See also Jin Dejian 金德建, *Sima Qian suo jian shu kao* 司馬遷所見書考 (Shanghai: Shanghai renmin chubanshe, 1963), 328–37, esp. 332–33.

9. See, for instance, A. C. Graham, *Disputers of the Dao* (La Salle, IL: Open Court, 1989), 313–15; Nicola Di Cosmo, *Ancient China and Its Enemies* (New York: Cambridge University Press, 2002), 201–2. In a similar vein, regarding the works of earlier eras, Herrlee Creel dismissively spoke of the mandate of Heaven as being Zhou "propaganda," an unjustified assertion used to legitimize Zhou rule. See in particular Herrlee Creel, *The Origins of Statecraft in China* (Chicago: University of Chicago Press, 1970), 85–87.

10. H. Paul Grice, "Logic and Conversation," in *Studies in the Way of Words* (Cambridge, MA: Harvard University Press, 1989), 27.

11. See Grice, "Retrospective Epilogue," in *Studies in the Way of Words*, 371.

12. As Grote writes, whenever an endoxic proposition "is fortified by a certain body of opinion, Aristotle admits a certain presumption (greater or less) that it is true." To Grote's remark, Edward Madden further adds that *endoxa* "then have a presumptive probability, but the concept is not synonymous with probability." See Edward H. Madden, "Aristotle's Treatment of Probability and Signs," *Philosophy of Science* 24, no. 2 (1957): 169.

13. The stricture against longwinded speech was certainly not limited to the monarchical circumstance. There have been time limitations on speakers in all political fora. The difference between monarchic and, say, democratic, is the possibility of dire consequence in the monarchic forum for those who taxed the patience of the executive. For an excellent analysis of the ancient Greek setting, see Josiah Ober, *Mass and Elite in Democratic Athens* (Princeton, NJ: Princeton University Press, 1989).

14. Grice also asserts a second maxim of quantity: "Do not make your contribution more informative than is required"; Grice, "Logic and Conversation," 26.

15. Ibid., 27.

CHAPTER TWO. THE SUBVERSIVE
POWER OF THE HISTORIAN

1. In her article, "Sima Qian: A True Historian?" Michael Nylan notes that most studies of the *Records* "see the book as a skillful weaving of fact and legend," a distinction that is based upon our current definition of legitimate epistemic bases, "facts," as demanding accuracy and objective verifiability. See *Early China* 23–24 (1998): 203–4, n. 1 and 4. This distinction, as I will argue, is not necessarily absolute for the composition of the historical texts. Indeed, David Schaberg himself questions the applicability of the distinction when he asks if, instead of seeing the proper occupation of historians and scribes to be the dispassionate recorders of events, we see them instead as those whose commitments to broader truths led them to place a moralizing, yet "fictionalized," historical anecdote alongside more concrete particulars. Accuracy was not necessarily as important as "verbal beauty and generic excellence." See Schaberg, "Truth and Ritual Judgment," 36. Nevertheless, there still exists a sizeable contingent, composed of such twentieth-century scholars as Burton Watson, Jian Bozan 翦伯贊, He Cijun 賀次軍, and Grant Hardy, who seem to place faith in the overall factual reliability of the early extant sources. Such a sympathy is captured in Grant Hardy's

encapsulation of the majority of Chinese criticism of Sima Qian's work: "According [to views expressed by such figures as Emperor Ming of the Latter Han and the statesman Wang Yun (137–92 CE)], Sima Qian wrote the *Shiji* in order to take revenge on his enemies at court, especially Emperor Wu, and as a result his history is riddled with slanderous distortions. Most Chinese critics, however, have taken a more moderate approach that acknowledges Sima's concern for accuracy while at the same time allowing for judgments in the arrangement of his material." See Grant Hardy, *Worlds of Bronze and Bamboo: Sima Qian's Conquest of History* (New York: Columbia University Press, 1999), 123. Sheldon Hsiao-peng Lu, in his recent study, *From History to Fictionality*, characterizes official histories as adhering to a "descriptive realism" by incorporating "significant portions of 'unprocessed' primary materials, historical data, and original documents. Readers of such histories are left with an impression of the authenticity of the historical materials and the factuality of the recorded events. Official historiography is made to appear to be a record and transcription of the real." Yet in spite of any assumption of realism, Chinese historiography, as he correctly notes, is actually far from a "natural discourse"; rather it is "nothing less than an ideology, 'a system (with its own logic and rigor) of representations (images, myths, ideas or concepts . . .) endowed with a historical existence and role within a given society.'" Sheldon Hsiao-peng Lu, *From Historicity to Fictionality: The Chinese Poetics of Narrative* (Stanford, CA: Stanford University Press, 1994), 6. Ban Gu's and Liu Xiang's (77–6 BCE) assessments both assert that Sima Qian wrote a "true account" (*shilu*, 實錄). See *HS* 62.2738 and *Sanguozhi* 三國志 13.418. Nylan notes that Ban Gu ascribed such a viewpoint to both Liu Xiang and Yang Xiong.

2. Henri Maspéro, "La composition et la date du Tso tchouan," in *Mélanges chinois et bouddhiques*, 137–215. Brussels: Institut belge des hautes etudes chinoises, 1931, 207.

3. As David Keightley states, "The diviners might formulate the charges and preside over the divinatory rituals, but with few exceptions, only the king . . . had the ability to read the cracks . . . His monopoly of the crucial interpretive act may plausibly be explained in terms of his kin relationship to the ancestors." David Keightley, "The Shang," in *Cambridge History of Ancient China*, ed. Michael Loewe and Edward Shaughnessy (New York: Cambridge University Press, 1999), 247.

4. In the *Mencius*, we see an explicit statement regarding the monarch's editorial command of the historical record: "When the world declined and the Way fell into obscurity, heresies and violence again arose. There were instances of regicides and parricides. Confucius was apprehensive and composed the *Spring and Autumn Annals*. <u>Strictly speaking, this is the Emperor's prerogative.</u> That is why Confucius said, 'Those who understand me will do so through the *Spring and Autumn Annals*; those who condemn me will also do so because of the *Spring and Autumn Annals*.'" 世衰道微, 邪說暴行有作, 臣弒其君者有之, 子弒其父者有之。孔子懼, 作《春秋》。《春秋》、天子之事也; 是故孔子曰:『知我者其惟《春秋》乎! 罪我者其惟《春秋》乎!』 See *Mencius*, trans. D. C. Lau (New York: Penguin Books, 1970), 6.9. Underlining mine. This ritualized sanctification of the power of the royal family overrode any claims to historical accuracy. For instance, Western Zhou records, such as the bronze inscriptions, did not "accommodate well the complexity and diversity of historical detail . . . Reducing historical knowledge to

a normative and ideal account, they create a memory sanctified by its performance in ancestral sacrifices and other rituals, a linguistically constructed parallel reality that with its own authority overrules the 'factual' one." The preeminence of ritual concerns over factual accuracy seemed to have been preserved in later eras. See Martin Kern, "Poetry and Religion: The Representation of 'Truth' in Early Chinese Historiography," in *Historical Truth, Historical Criticism, and Ideology*, ed. Helwig Schmidt-Glintzer et al. (Boston: Brill, 2005), 61–62.

5. See Mark E. Lewis, *Writing and Authority in Early China* (Albany, NY: SUNY Press, 1999), 130. See also Yang Bojun 楊伯峻, ed., *Chunqiu zuozhuan zhu* 春秋左傳注 (Beijing: Zhonghua shuju, 1981), 1099.

6. Nylan, *The Five "Confucian" Classics* (New Haven, CT: Yale University Press, 2001), 265.

7. On the topic of "remonstrance," see, for instance, Schaberg, "Remonstrance." In more modern terms, the right to "directly remonstrate" would probably be put in terms of "free speech."

8. Goldin, "Appeals to History in Early Chinese Philosophy and Rhetoric," *Journal of Chinese Philosophy* 35, no. 1 (2008): 80.

9. Ibid.

10. Ibid.

11. Ibid., 81.

12. Ibid., 81.

13. Any number of studies in other areas of history reinforce my basic suspicion about the possibility of truth in unstable political climates. See for instance, Charles Walton, *Policing Public Opinion in the French Revolution: The Culture of Calumny and the Problem of Free Speech* (New York: Oxford University Press, 2008).

14. Charles Gardner also attributed factual inaccuracies in the historical records in some significant measure to the oppressive demands of the relationship between the addressor, or historian, and the executive: "Deference to the traditional majesty of the imperial ruling house dictates a systematically distorted presentation of relationships between the emperor or his agents and barbarian tribes, foreign powers, or domestic rebels. Conspicuous neglect of these proprieties is lèse-majesté, an offense almost sure to be reported to the throne, rendering the author liable to condign punishment." Verification of facts, he states, "often involved quite serious difficulty, for officials would hesitate to incur enmity by giving unwelcome information concerning each other. Even in important matters the more vigorous and able emperors relied largely on direct observation." Nevertheless, and somewhat in contradiction to the proposed limitations on the composition of the histories and the documents that informed them, the Chinese conception of history, according to Gardner, demanded a strict focus on the registration of concrete events and overt acts, "which should be exact and dispassionate, without any projection across the scene of the personality of the registrar, who must punctiliously refrain from garbling his presentation by his own perhaps imperfect appreciation of the true sequence of causation." See Charles S. Gardner, *Chinese Traditional Historiography* (Cambridge, MA: Harvard University Press, 1938), 66, 68, and 69.

15. Schaberg, *A Patterned Past*, 22.

16. There are several excellent book-length studies, and numerous articles, devoted to such issues. See, for instance, Schaberg, *A Patterned Past*; and Wai-yee Li, *The Readability of the Past in Early Chinese Historiography* (Cambridge, MA: Harvard University Asia Center, 2007).

17. E. G. Pulleyblank, "Chinese Historical Criticism: Liu Chih-chi and Ssu-ma Kuang," in *Historians of China and Japan*, ed. W. G. Beasley and E. G. Pulleyblank (London: School of Oriental and African Studies, 1961), 162. For the original, see Sima Guang 司馬光, "Da Fan Mengde 答范夢得," in *Qinding siku quanshu* 欽定四庫全書 (Taipei: Taiwan shangwu yinshuguan, 1983), 63.18a.

18. Pulleyblank, "Chinese Historical Criticism," 157.

19. Ibid.

20. See Pulleyblank, "Chinese Historical Criticism," 148. See also Liu Zhiji 劉知幾, *Shitong tongshi* 史通通釋 (Taibei, Taiwan: Shijie shuju, 1988), 20.281.

21. In translations of early Chinese texts, *zheng* 徵 is also commonly rendered as "evidence," though its literal meaning is actually closer to "sign." See *Analects of Confucius: A Philosophical Translation*, trans. Roger Ames and Henry Rosemont Jr. (New York: Ballantine Books, 1998), 3.9:84; and *The Analects*, trans. D. C. Lau (New York: Penguin Books, 1979), 68. A. C. Yu also renders it so, when speaking about Ban Gu's citing Confucius as needing "evidence (*zheng* 徵)." See Anthony C. Yu, "History, Fiction, and the Reading of Chinese Narrative," *Chinese Literature: Essays, Articles, Reviews* 10, no. 1/2 (1988): 4.

22. See Chen Shou 陳壽, *Sanguozhi* 三國志 (Beijing: Zhonghua shuju, 1982), 13.418.

23. See *HS* 62.2738.

CHAPTER THREE. POLITICIZED TRUTH AND DOUBT

1. In my analysis, I reject François Jullien's assertion that "[m]anipulation, not persuasion, was the Chinese way," that the persuader is one who succeeds merely by applying psychological coercive pressure. I assert that Jullien unfairly deemphasizes, or does not take into account, the auditor's freedom, however small and inconsistent, to reject the speaker's influence. He explains his position thus: "The logic of manipulation presupposes an ideological view of our relation to others that rests on the postulate of having other peoples' minds at one's sovereign disposal, instead of treating them themselves as an end (the reverse of the Kantian position). This logic also implies the rejection of all efforts at persuasion, for it rests on profound distrust of the power of words, a distrust characteristic of the ancient Chinese world (in contrast to the Greek world). Admittedly, rhetoric can also be regarded as an art of manipulation. However, it involves at least turning toward others, addressing them, and seeking to convince them; which gives them a chance to reply, defend themselves, and argue the opposite case." Certainly, directly confronting the emperor was not the norm in ancient China, but this in itself, or even their supposed exceptional distrust of language, does not disqualify their addresses as persuasions. The emperor certainly could have, and sometimes did, offer critical, contradicting responses. See François Jullien, *The Propensity of Things: Toward a History of Efficacy in China*, trans. Janet Lloyd (New York: Zone Books, 1995), 68–69.

2. In a recent analysis of Plato's treatment of "probable" myths (*eikos muthos*), M. F. Burnyeat reports that, for the cosmologist Timaeus, "the one unchallengeable proposition about the cosmos that we must hold true, on pain of impiety, is that the Maker made it the best possible the materials allow." Such, I would maintain, was a premise Timaeus was offering as indubitable "common sense," one that all within that particular religiously grounded community must allow. See M. F. Burnyeat, "*Eikos Muthos*," *Rhizai: Journal for Ancient Philosophy and Science* 2, no. 2 (2005): 163.

3. Aristotle, "Rhetoric," in *The Complete Works of Aristotle*, ed. Jonathan Barnes (Princeton, NJ: Princeton University Press, 1984), 1358a18–9.

4. 1360b14–18. See also 1363a8: "That which most people seek after, and which is obviously an object of contention, is also a good; for, as has been shown, that is good which is sought after by everybody, and 'most people' seems pretty well to amount to 'everybody.'"

5. 1363b5–7.

6. See pp. 86–89.

7. Clifford Geertz, "Common Sense as a Cultural System," in *Local Knowledge* (New York: Basic Books, 2000), 78.

8. Ibid., 79.

9. Ibid., 85.

10. Ibid., 89.

11. Ibid., 91.

12. Ibid.

13. This quality is difficult to ascertain without the presence of active users of the language. However, I believe it can be presumed if the addresses are attempting to mimic a real address and the propositions require little or no understanding of a technical vocabulary on the part of the reader for their comprehension.

14. See p. 88.

15. Ober, *Mass and Elite in Democratic Athens*, 149.

16. Glenn W. Most, "The Uses of *Endoxa*: Philosophy and Rhetoric in the Rhetoric," in *Aristotle's Rhetoric: Philosophical Essays*, ed. David J. Furley and Alexander Nehemas (Princeton, NJ: Princeton University Press, 1994), 178.

17. , Ibid., 176.

18. See pp. 143–46.

19. Paul Woodruff, "*Eikos* and Bad Faith in the Paired Speeches of Thucydides," in *Proceedings of the Boston Area Colloquium in Ancient Philosophy* (Lanham, MD: University Press of America, 1994), 116.

20. Elizabeth Belfiore, "'Lies Unlike the Truth': Plato on Hesiod, Theogony 27," *Transactions of the American Philological Association* (1974–) 115 (1985): 49.

21. Ibid., 52.

22. M. F. Burnyeat, "*Eikos Muthos*," 156.

23. For my analysis of possible reasons, see pp. 150–53.

24. See pp. 99–100.

25. Nicholas Rescher, *The Coherence Theory of Truth* (New York: Oxford University Press, 1973), 11.

26. Ibid., 39.

27. Ibid., 56.

28. Ibid., 57.

29. Ibid., 58.

30. Ibid., 64.

31. Ruth Morse, *Truth and Convention in the Middle Ages* (New York: Cambridge University Press, 1991), 3.

32. Ibid., 4.

33. Ibid., 5.

34. Morse gives the example of Thucydides, whose "attempt to solve Herodotus' problem of evidence had been to write about his own times, about events which he had witnessed himself, or events about which other living witnesses could be consulted. But if *The Peloponnesian Wars* established the model of how a historical subject should be selected, it did not regulate the practice of succeeding generations." Morse, *Truth and Convention*, 91.

35. "A question such as, 'But did Henry's corpse *really* smell?', might have seemed to him to miss the point of his description. One or more authorities said so. It might have done. He writes with a presumption of truth, for no one would deliberately write what he knew to be false. Or at least, true according to his lights and not false except under certain special circumstances." Morse, *Truth and Convention*, 1.

36. As Ruth Morse states, "Calling a text 'historical' might have a legitimating function. It might defend the embroidering of a narrative based on another narrative (which had been extracted from a text defined as 'historical'), like so many of the expansions created in the course of the twelfth century and after to tell the stories of Thebes or Troy, King Arthur or Charlemagne, or to celebrate a saint, a relic, a religious house. 'Historical', though, might be thought of as an exemplary narrative based upon events which had occurred at some point in the past, told in order to move and persuade its audience to imitate the good and eschew the evil, a 'true tale about the past' which included a vast range of what modern readers would regard as invented material and inappropriate, if implicit, moralizing." Morse, *Truth and Convention*, 6.

37. Paul Veyne, *Did the Greeks Believe in Their Myths?*, trans. Paula Wissig (Chicago: University of Chicago Press, 1988), 5. Interestingly, citing the source did not guarantee that the historian put much faith in its truth-value: Pausanias himself confesses that he "did not believe a word of the innumerable unlikely legends that he had calmly put forth in the preceding six hundred pages. We think of another avowal, no less tardy, coming from Herodotus at the end of the seventh of his nine books." Veyne, *Did the Greeks Believe*, 11.

38. Veyne, *Did the Greeks Believe*, 13.

39. "A world cannot be inherently fictional; it can be fictional only according to whether one believes in it or not. The difference between fiction and reality is not objective and does not pertain to the thing itself; it resides in us, according to whether or not we subjectively see in it a fiction. They object is never unbelievable in itself, and its distance from 'the' reality cannot shock us; for, as truths are always analogical, we do not even see it." Veyne, *Did the Greeks Believe*, 21.

40. Veyne, *Did the Greeks Believe*, 22.

41. Ibid., 34.

42. Morse makes a similar suggestion: "Internal consistency and verisimilitude appeared to count among the highest criteria for subsequent readers and

writers [of medieval and renaissance histories], who only rarely had external validation to turn to." Morse, *Truth and Convention*, 7.

43. *HS* 7.233.

44. *SJ* 53.2015.

45. I am following Yan Shigu's 顏師古 (581–645 CE) interpretation: "*Yi* means 'a manifold of.' A manifold of flags that exceeds the number of men will cause the enemy to suspect that there are many soldiers." 益, 多也. 多張旗幟, 過其人數, 令敵疑有多兵. See *HS* 1A.22.

46. *HS* 8.273.

47. See, for example, *HS* 25A.1228 and 32.1835 and *SJ* 12.467 and 13.505.

48. There are any number of studies on moral realism. See, for instance, John McDowell, *Mind, Value, and Reality* (Cambridge, MA: Harvard University Press, 1998), 131–50.

49. These translations are taken from a variety of sources. The translators of these texts alter their translations to suit the context. Kern translates *zhi* as "what is on the mind." In his translation of a passage from *Mencius*, Lau translates it as the "mind set on high ideals." Riegel and Knoblock translate it alternately as "mind," "inner mind," and "intentions." Crump translates the term in multifarious ways: "ambition," "unity," "hope," and so forth. Ames and Rosemont translate it as "intention," "heart-and-mind," "purposes," what one "would most like to do," "setting one's sights," "resolute," and so forth. See *Analects of Confucius*, 74, 76, 89, 112, 186; *Mencius*, 106; *Chan-Kuo Ts'e*, 102, 128; *Annals of Lü Buwei*, trans. Jeffrey Riegel and John Knoblock (Stanford, CA: Stanford University Press, 2000), 143–44, 162; Sima Qian, *Records of the Grand Historian: Qin Dynasty*, trans. Burton Watson (New York: Columbia University Press, 1993), 38; and Kern, "Poetry and Religion," 68.

50. *Analects* 16.11 and *Confucius Analects*, trans. Edward Slingerland (Indianapolis, IN: Hackett, 2003), 196.

51. While we do not exactly know the provenance of and period in which this remark was created, there is evidence in the *Hanshu* that its sentiment is not an alien one in the Han: "With regard to the concealed concerns and contracted meanings of the *Book of Odes* and *Book of Documents*, one would want to pursue the considerations behind their *zhi*" 夫詩書隱約者, 欲遂其志之思也. See *HS* 62.2720.

52. Steven Van Zoeren, *Poetry and Personality* (Stanford, CA: Stanford University Press, 1991), 56.

53. Ibid., 57.

54. Ibid., 56: "In the *Analects*, *zhi* was adapted to Confucian concerns; it became the moral project or the ambition of a morally committed person. Thus we find the phrase *zhi yu* 'to set oneself upon' completed in the *Analects* by *dao* 'the Way' (7.6) and *ren* 'humaneness' (4.4)." A translation of *zhi yu* that more captures what I am trying to suggest is Roger Ames's translation of it in 7.6 as "setting one's sights on." See *Analects of Confucius*, 112.

55. Relatedly, in her discussion on Warring States notions of knowledge and wisdom, Lisa Raphals offers several interesting suggestions regarding two adjectives, *zhi* 智 and *ming* 明, which are descriptives regarding some form of intelligence, knowledge, or wisdom. In her discussion of *zhi* 智, Raphals argues that

there is a commonality between the *zhi* of exemplary generals and that of exemplary ministers and that this commonality can be summed up by the term *ming*, which she defines as "clearsightedness, or the ability to perceive realities and circumstances impartially and accurately." This notion of *ming*, however, cannot be fully secularized, separated from a sense of what is important for a moral order, for as Maspéro argues, the true meaning of *ming* is not simply intelligence but *sacred* intelligence. See Lisa Raphals, *Knowing Words: Wisdom and Cunning in the Classical Traditions of China and Greece* (Ithaca, NY: Cornell University Press, 1992), 10–17, particularly 11 and 128.

56. Indeed, Van Zoeren himself uses "vision" in his analysis of *Analects* 11.26: The passage moves from the "relatively grandiose ambition [*zhi*] on Zilu's part to a series of (seemingly) ever more modest visions, from Zilu's intention to accomplish the most difficult military, political, and moral tasks to Zeng Xi's modest and apolitical desire." Van Zoeren, *Poetry and Personality*, 62. See also p. 63: "Zeng Xi's aim is culminating not only because of the vision it implies, but because of its authenticity or sincerity: it is what Zeng Xi really wants."

57. A further passage that ties music together with *zhi*, which Knoblock and Riegel translate as "intention," is the following: "As a general rule, tunes are products of the heart and mind of man. When feelings are aroused in the heart, they are expressed in melody. Melody that takes shape without is a transformation of what is within. This explains how one knows the customs of a people from hearing their music. By examining their customs, one knows their intentions. By observing their intentions, one knows their Powers [*de*]. Whether a person is ascending or declining, worthy or unworthy, a gentleman or a petty man is given visible form in music and cannot be hidden. Hence, it is said, 'What is visible in music is profound indeed!'" 凡音者，產乎人心者也。感於心則蕩乎音，音成於外而化乎內，是故聞其聲而知其風，察其風而知其志，觀其志而知其德。盛衰、賢不肖、君子小人皆形於樂，不可隱匿，故曰樂之為觀也深矣。 Here, clearly, *zhi* is being used in a way that is expressive more of attitudes or dispositions than actions. See *Annals of Lü Buwei*, 143–44, 162.

58. 公伯寮愬子路於季孫。子服景伯以告，曰：「夫子固有惑志於公伯寮，吾力猶能肆諸市朝。」

59. Robert Eno, "Casuistry and Character in the Mencius," in *Mencius: Contexts and Interpretations*, ed. Alan K. L. Chan (Honolulu: University of Hawaii Press, 2002), 195.

60. See Nylan, "Sima Qian," 213, n. 34.

61. *SJ* 18.878. Translation mine. *Zhi* here is functioning as a verb and could be translated more neutrally as "sets his sights upon" the ways of the past, but clearly the usage is meant to be elective, and thus of some positive educational function.

62. Immediately after the remark quoted above, Sima Qian goes on to depreciate the thoughtless application of past conventions and standards: "Past thearchs and kings each had distinct rites and diverse duties. If one wishes to become successful and bring order, how can he tangle the past with the present? If one examines the means by which men win position and favour and the means by which they are dismissed and humbled, he will have the requisite stockpile for success and failure in his own time. What need to consult old testimony?" 帝王

者各殊禮而異務, 要以成功為統紀, 豈可縄乎? 觀所以得尊寵及所以廢辱, 亦當世得失之林也, 何必舊聞? For a variant translation, see also Sima Qian, *Records of the Grand Historian: Han Dynasty*, Burton Watson trans., 2 vols. (New York: Columbia University Press, 1993), 1:428–29. When Sima Qian speaks in the remark above of using the "ways of the past" as a mirror to judge the present, he is criticizing as much the applicability of the past to the present as any ethical commitment to the past.

63. *SJ* 1.3.

64. Even the despised First Emperor of Qin is described as "putting his vision into practice." See *SJ* 6.230.

65. Of course, there is a well-known interpretative tradition, proposed by Roger Ames and David Hall, that treats *dao* as a performative notion, one that could be indicated by the parallelism in the quote from *Analects* 16.11 analyzed above. Indeed, their own translation of this passage reflects this sensibility: "They dwelt in seclusion to pursue their ends and acted on their personal sense of importance (*yi*) to extend their *tao*." Under such an interpretative lens, *dao* could serve in a similar fashion to *zhi*. However, the use of *zhi* is not limited, as *dao* often is, to philosophical or ethical concerns. Furthermore, *zhi* inheres a personalized, subjective aspect in a way *dao* ultimately does not, and thus can be distorted in ways *dao* really cannot. See Roger Ames and David Hall, *Thinking through Confucius* (Albany, NY: SUNY Press, 1987), 226–36.

CHAPTER FOUR. INTERACTIVE CONSTRAINTS AT COURT

1. "Hence it is said: The ruler must not reveal his desires; for if he reveals his desires his ministers will put on the mask that pleases him. He must not reveal his will; for if he does so his ministers will show a different face. So it is said: Discard likes and dislikes and the ministers will show their true form; discard wisdom and wile and the ministers will watch their step." 故曰: 君無見其所欲, 君見其所欲, 臣自將雕琢; 君無見其意, 君見其意, 臣將自表異。故曰: 去好去惡, 臣乃見素; 去舊去智, 臣乃自備。. Han Fei Tzu, "Way of the Ruler," in *Basic Writings of Mo Tzu, Hsün Tzu, and Han Fei Tzu* (New York: Columbia University Press, 1964), 16; "Zhudao" 主道, in *Hanfeizi jijie* 韓非子集解 (Beijing: Zhonghua shuju, 1998), 26–7.

2. "Though the ruler himself has not yet divulged his plans, if you in your discussions happen to hit upon his hidden motives, then you will be in danger." 未必其身泄之也, 而語及所匿之事, 如此者身危。. Han Fei Tzu, "The Difficulties of Persuasion," 74; "Shuinan" 說難, in *Hanfeizi jijie*, 87.

3. Numerous examples are found in the bronze inscriptions of the Western Zhou and *Shangshu* 尚書.

4. Recent research by Michael Nylan, among others, has made it abundantly clear that certain, if not most, early Han emperors with some frequency were obliged to acquiesce to ministerial requests. Emperor Wu, in the following instance, is reported as acceding to Tian Fen's 田蚡 recommendations for official promotion: "At the time, whenever the Chancellor Tian Fen entered the palace to address the emperor on some affair, Tian Fen would pass days on end in discussions with Emperor Wu. Whatever Tian Fen asserted was always heard. In

recommending people for office, a household was at times elevated up to the two thousand picul rank. Tian Fen's judgment displaced and overruled the ruler's. Emperor Wu finally said, 'Is my Lord finished at last with appointing officials or not? I also wish to appoint some officials.'" 當是時, 丞相入奏事, 坐語移日, 所言皆聽. 薦人或起家至二千石, 權移主上. 上乃曰:「君除吏已盡未? 吾亦欲除吏.」See *SJ* 107.2844. Michael Loewe also notes that the Han dynasty "witnessed a number of occasions when the personal powers of the emperor were reduced to a point of disappearance, in favour of the control of government by other parties." See Michael Loewe, "The Authority of the Emperors of Ch'in and Han," in *State and Law in East Asia: Festschrift Karl Bünger*, ed. Dieter Eikemeier and Herbert Franke (Wiesbaden: Otto Harrassowitz, 1981), 82. Nevertheless, I believe that we can still label the form of government—at least in its modes of address, if not its executive style—as closer to a monarchic one than an oligarchic or democratic. Though power was shared and the emperor's influence was at times nominal (particularly when the emperor was a child), the structural presumption was that power was meant to be, and would eventually be, held by the monarch. Indeed, shortly after the episode cited above involving Tian Fen, Tian Fen goes too far, asking for imperial artisans to work on his estates. This request angered Emperor Wu, and Tian Fen, aware he could be punished, is reported to have subsequently retired from office. I thank Michael Nylan for bringing this crucial complication to my attention.

5. See "Nanyan" 難言 in *Hanfeizi xinjiaozhu* 韓非子新校注, 52, and *Hanfeizi jijie* 韓非子集解, 22.

6. An explicit remark about the source of the monarch's doubts deriving from the poisonous atmosphere caused by constant slander and the resulting frequent withdrawing of the service of upright officials can be seen in a particularly poignant passage ostensibly composed by Liu Xiang 劉向, recorded in the *History of the Former Han*: "The reason for slander and wickedness appearing simultaneously is caused by the monarch frequently being in doubt. He may have been employing worthy men and forwarding exemplary governance, but if someone slanders them, then these worthy men will withdraw from service and exemplary governance will go with them. The monarch's possessing a doubtful mindset comes from the influence of slanderous, criminal mouths. His possessing an indecisive attitude opens the door to various distortions. When slander and wickedness are present, the many worthies will withdraw. When various distortions are manifold, then the upright *shi* will disappear." 讒邪之所以並進者, 由上多疑心, 既已用賢人而行善政, 如或譖之, 則賢人退而善政還. 夫執狐疑之心者, 來讒賊之口; 持不斷之意者, 開羣枉之門. 讒邪進則眾賢退, 羣枉盛則正士消. See *HS* 36.1943.

7. Li Xueqin 李學勤, ed., *Yili zhushu* 儀禮注疏, 2:119.

8. Ibid.

9. See Li Xueqin 李學勤, ed., *Yili zhushu* 儀禮注疏, 119–20; and *The I-Li or Book of Etiquette and Ceremonial*, John Steele trans. (London: Probsthain, 1917), 1:47.

10. For instance, in Feng Tang's 馮唐 biography, Emperor Wen is startled and shamed by Feng Tang's unusually unrestrained and brusque remark. Though the emperor is angry, he does not punish Feng Tang but merely asks why he couldn't have waited until others were not around. See *SJ* 102.2757; Sima Qian, *Records of the Grand Historian: Han Dynasty*, 1:473.

11. Schaberg, "Playing at Critique," 194–95.

12. Although its reliability as a source of information about documentary submissions to the executive is suspect, *The Literary Mind and the Carving of Dragons* (*Wenxin diaolong* 文心雕龍) also speaks to the breadth of topics discussed in hortatory addresses: "During the Qin and Han, the memorials [i.e., hortatory addresses] of the officials were known as *zou*. Whether the memorial was concerned with political affairs, institutions and rites, a report of an emergency, or an accusation and impeachment, its general name was *zou*." 秦漢之輔,上書稱奏,陳政事,獻典儀,上急變,劾愆謬,總謂之奏。 See Liu Xie 劉勰, *Wenxin diaolong zhu* 文心雕龍註, comp. Fan Wenlan 范文瀾 (Beijing: Renmin wenxue chubanshe, 1958), 421; and Liu Xie, *The Literary Mind and the Carving of Dragons*, trans. Vincent Shih (New York: Columbia University Press, 1959), 130.

13. See the emperor's response to Zhufu Yan's and Yan An's 嚴安 addresses at *SJ* 112.2960, and Sima Qian, *Records of the Grand Historian: Han Dynasty* (New York: Columbia University Press, 1993), 2:203.

14. Numerous examples can be found throughout the *Hanshu*. See, for example, *HS* 3.96, 6.156, 6.167, 8.238, 10.302, 12.360, 21A.978, 22.1074, 25B.1254, 25B.1257, 25B.1266, 45.2177, 47.2215, 63.2761.

15. See *HS* 78.3275.

16. Unless otherwise noted, all official titles are taken from Michael Loewe, *A Biographical Dictionary of the Qin, Former Han and Xin Periods* (Boston: Brill, 2000), 758–68. For those administrative titles for which Loewe gives no translation, I will depend upon Charles Hucker's. (Enno Giele, in his *Imperial Decision-Making*, offers fewer translations that would pertain to the terms in this study than Loewe does. For consistency's sake, I do not combine translations, except when necessary, even when I prefer an alternate translation.) For Hucker's, see Charles O. Hucker, *A Dictionary of Official Titles in Imperial China* (Stanford, CA: Stanford University Press, 1985).

17. In the Han dynasty, ranks were measured in terms of bushels of grain, a stipend that was commonly, but not exclusively, dispensed for income. But these rankings were only relative, as Enno Giele has pointed out. The two-thousand-bushel rank could denote "the most high-ranking central officials beneath the ministerial level, or the provincial governors, or both, according to context." See Giele, *Imperial Decision-Making*, 57, n. 38. See also Hucker, *A Dictionary of Official Titles*, 16.

18. See *HS* 51.2368 and 81.3346. Both merely state that a certain official was to be assigned to the bureau.

19. The most explicit example of officials intervening when an address was not in order can be found in Wei Xiang's biography at *HS* 74.3135. In Huo Guang's 霍光 biography, Huo Shan 霍山 is quoted as saying that he would put aside letters that were critical of Huo Guang "and not allow them to be submitted to the throne, but the senders became more clever, sealing the entire letter and having the chief of palace writers come out of the inner palace so they could put the letter directly into his hands without clearing it with the [Imperial Secretariat]" 其言絕痛, 山屏不奏其書。後上書者益黠, 盡奏封事, 輒 (使) 〔下〕中書令出取之, 不關尚書。 *HS* 68.2954; Pan Ku, *Courtier and Commoner*, 146.

20. According to Enno Giele, in reference to the staffing of the Imperial Secretariat (*shangshu tai* 尚書臺), the predominant office in which communications

with the emperor were purportedly handled, there was a continual internal power struggle between those associated with the bureaucratic center of government, the council (*san gong* 三公), and the imperial house. Thus it is possible that the imperial family delegated the responsibilities of the Secretariat to officials situated in other offices in order to weaken the power of this office, and that of the bureaucracy in general. In his *Tongdian* 通典, Du You 杜佑 (735–812 CE) describes the duties of the Office of the Imperial Secretary in exactly the same way as Ban Gu describes the duties of the Office of the Imperial Counselor (*yushitai* 御史臺), indicative of the merging of the responsibilities of the two offices. See Giele, *Imperial Decision-Making*, 58 and 62. Another indication of the merging of duties between officials in various areas of the government can be seen in the fact that under the leadership of Huo Guang, a supervisory office was created to oversee the governance of the Secretariat. This supervisory office was headed by an official who held a position in a separate office. In addition, under the Latter Han, Giele declares, "not only regents, but primarily imperial tutors (*taifu* 太傅) or chiefs of staff (*taiwei* 太尉) came to concurrently supervise the affairs of the imperial secretariat." Giele, *Imperial Decision-Making*, 64. Clearly, there was no absolute and permanent separation of duties between the various offices. At the very least, the Imperial Secretariat often found its duties and privileges removed or supervised by members of various other offices.

21. HS 74.3135. Giele translates the final two phrases as follows: "If the wording was improper, it was rejected and not memorialized." Giele, *Imperial Decision-Making*, 67. However, *suoyan* refers to the contents and not merely the wording. For example, in the "Annals of Emperor Wen," Song Chang is quoted as replying thus to a request for a private audience: "If what you have to say is of public interest, say it publicly. If what you have to say is of private interest, a [true] king has no private interests." 宋昌曰：「所言公，公言之；所言私，王者無私。」 (*HS* 4.107)

22. Enno Giele argues that this episode is evidence for Wei Xiang's redressing of Huo Guang's preventing those addresses that could somehow compromise his personal agenda from reaching the young emperor, Emperor Xuan (Liu Bingyi 劉病已). Wei Xiang's correction for these abuses in the same year of Huo Guang's death (68 BCE) brought one of the nefarious plots hatched by the Huo family to light. Giele asserts that Wei Xiang's motives were to increase the power of the Imperial Secretariat through the emperor's abolition of the process of duplicating documents submitted to the throne. This anecdote, however, also proves that the process of censorship—and even probably the standards by which the contents of an address were deemed "unfit" or "without merit" (*bu shan* 不善)—was subject to the vagaries of political scheming and the officials who oversaw their censorship and editing. See Giele, *Imperial Decision-Making*, 67–68.

23. *HS* 78.3273. See also Pan Ku, *Courtier and Commoner*, 201.

24. Li Xueqin 李學勤, ed., *Maoshi zhengyi* 毛詩正義, 3 vols., vol. 1, Shisanjing zhushu 十三經注疏 (Beijing: Beijing daxue chubanshe, 1999), 960.

25. That is, a consummate strategy.

26. *HS* 67.2919–20.

27. See *HS* 67.2921–22. In the Han histories, emperors were repeatedly upbraided for not being interested in or attentive to forthright criticism, and for

allowing their subordinates to keep forthright remarks from ever reaching them. See, for instance, *SJ* 6.258, 120.3110, and *HS* 76.3218.

28. See in particular Schaberg, "Remonstrance in Eastern Zhou Historiography," 133–79.

29. Enno Giele attempts to derive the meaning of *zou* from a study of the *Duduan* 獨斷, attributed to Cai Yong 蔡邕 (133–92 CE). Though his distinction between *zou* and *zhang* 章 is interesting (albeit contested), the definition he elicits from the various citations of the text in the *Duduan* is clearly too limited to be applicable to its use in the historical records. He admits that *zou* was at least occasionally used in a very general sense. See Giele, *Imperial Decision-Making*, 118, 121–22, 179, 182–83.

30. Liu Xie, *The Literary Mind*, 108.

31. Ibid., 109. On p. 95, Liu Xie distinguishes philosophical and the works of the Classics, the two classes of literature that he groups together in his discussion on treatises.

32. Shih is not alone in his low estimation of the use of Liu's classificatory distinctions. See also the commentarial remarks in Liu Xie 劉勰, *Wenxin diaolong jinyi* 文心雕龍今譯, Zhou Zhenfu 周振甫 ed. (Beijing: Zhonghua shuju, 1986), 211–12. From my own analyses, the classifications, and the exemplars used to support them (at least those that can be found in the received texts), do not do the work that Liu Xie argues they do.

33. Ruth Morse makes a similar remark on the distinction between the claims made by Roman rhetors whose topic was grounded in concrete circumstances and those that were not: "Excellence in Roman school displays continued to be a route to success up to the time of Augustine and Jerome, if only to the prestige of being famous for those displays. Indeed, the less the declamations were grounded in the possibilities of real action, the more extravagant the speakers became: when the subject was imaginary, with no consequences dependent on its outcome, method and style became all." Morse, *Truth and Convention*, 19.

34. See, for example, A. F. P. Hulsewé, "Notes on the Historiography of the Han Period," in *Historians of China and Japan*, ed. W. G. Beasley and E. G. Pulleyblank (London: School of Oriental and African Studies, 1961), 42–43.

CHAPTER FIVE. SALIENT FORMAL
CHARACTERISTICS OF THE ADDRESSES

1. Nor are they, interestingly, at all peculiar to the Chinese context. See Aristotle, "Rhetoric," 1359b34–1360a5.

2. By "introduction," I mean those particulars directly preceding the address which can logically or narratively be related to the address. In the biographies, there are often breaks in the narrative where the narrator moves to another, not directly related anecdote or topic (save that it involves the main character of the biography). These breaks are usually temporal.

3. 是時匈奴彊,數寇邊,上發兵以禦之.錯上言兵事,曰... See *HS* 49.2278.

4. See *HS* 78.3279. For other examples, see *HS* 64A.2776–77, *HS* 51.2338, *HS* 74.3136, *HS* 64B.3803, *SJ* 92.2615, *SJ* 112.2953. Much lengthier and

narratively more complex introductions can be found at *HS* 69.2984 and *HS* 70.3008–14.

5. *Chan-Kuo Ts'e*, 205; He Jianzhang 何建章, annot., *Zhanguoce zhushi* 戰國策注釋 (Beijing: Zhonghua shuju, 1990), 13.451.

6. See J. I. Crump Jr., *Intrigues: Studies of the Chan-Kuo Ts'e* (Ann Arbor: University of Michigan Press, 1964), 58–75. Paul Goldin, in a chapter of his book, *After Confucius*, criticizes Crump for the comparison between the persuasions of the *Intrigues* and Latin *suasoriae*. Goldin correctly questions its identification as a teaching handbook, stating that there is no evidence that the materials were arranged categorically, by style or by theme, making the collection very difficult to be used as a handbook (though not impossible, of course). See Goldin, *After Confucius*, 76.

7. See *HS* 50.2314.

8. See *HS* 49.2283.

9. See *HS* 43.2127 and 78.3279.

10. See *HS* 69.2991 and 70.3015.

11. See *HS* 94B.3824 and 51.2338.

12. This peculiarity is remarked upon by Crump, who marvels that the speeches (in the *Intrigues*, the addresses are largely represented as extemporaneous speeches) are rarely interrupted by the ruler: "[O]ne must wonder how the men featured in the *Chan-kuo Ts'e* consistently concocted an approach so clever the ruler was overwhelmed—reduced to that submissive 'So be it' in reply?" See *Legends of the Warring States*, J. I. Crump, trans. (Ann Arbor: Center for Chinese Studies, University of Michigan, 1998), 3.

13. Usually only a brief narration of the executive action concludes the address, merely to demonstrate that the persuasion was successful.

14. Instances are numerous. See, for example, He Jianzhang 何建章, annot., *Zhanguoce zhushi* 戰國策注釋 (Beijing: Zhonghua shuju, 1990), 3.111.

15. Ibid., 3.107.

16. Ibid., 15.540.

17. Ibid., 3.107.

18. Ibid., 3.113.

19. Ibid., 3.108.

20. For examples of how these phrases were employed, see in particular Zhao Chongguo's address and Wei Xiang's address in Appendices G and H respectively. There are numerous linguistic studies focusing on these forms of politeness. See, for example, Penelope Brown and Stephen C. Levinson, *Politeness: Some Universals in Language* (New York: Cambridge University Press, 1987), 146–90, especially 187–90. The acknowledgment of transgressions is, they aver, "really a request for . . . acquittal (even if this is not explicitly asked for)." Brown and Levinson, *Politeness*, 189.

21. See *HS* 1B.52, n. 2. See also Giele, *Imperial Decision-Making*, 92.

22. See Appendix D, sections A–B. See also *HS* 51.2338. Italics mine.

23. With his use of the word *zheng*, "dispute," Wei Xiang seems to be suggesting that the current troubles with the Xiongnu in Cheshi are relatively trifling and do not merit a rash, "angry" campaign. Such a campaign would, based on his categorical statements, inevitably fail.

24. Even though there is a compound, *zhi yi*, in this context, because of the presence of "*zhong*" at the end of the sentence, I follow Zhou Shouchang's suggestion that 致 be taken as meaning 置, "to establish, place." See *HSBZ* 74.3a.

25. See Appendix H, sections A–B. Italics mine.

26. See Appendix H.

27. *Chan-Kuo Ts'e*, 386; He Jianzhang 何建章 annot., *Zhanguoce zhushi* 戰國策注釋, 22.819.

28. *HS* 54.2443–44; Pan Ku, *Courtier and Commoner*, 17.

29. Indeed, its usage is not exclusively limited to the presentation of evidence.

30. *HS* 50.2314.

31. Here I follow Ru Chun's 如淳 (fl. 230 CE) interpretation. Wang Xianqian 王先謙 (1842–1917) also notes that this passage as it appears in the *Wenxuan* 文選 has a *ren* ("person") character above *bu fan*, which suggests the sentence is referring to legal matters. See *HSBZ* 51.9a.

32. See Appendix E, section A.

33. See Appendix I, section B.

34. This, again, is paralleled in various passages in the *Intrigues*. See, for instance, He Jianzhang 何建章, annot., *Zhanguoce zhushi* 戰國策注釋, 5.165–70 and 3.88–101.

35. As in earlier comparisons between the Han histories and the *Intrigues*, there are significant similarities regarding what I am labeling as the major categories of the Han addresses and the persuasions of the *Intrigues*. This point, however, does not require repeated emphasis. In general, future references to the *Intrigues* will be limited to footnotes.

36. Note that not all general statements can be equated or identified with propositions of general principle. General statements may also be inductions from observations germane to the specific circumstance being addressed. As induced from a domain of particulars, there is a level of specificity that is not commonly present in what I am calling propositions of general principle. Regarding the attribution of propositions of general principle, while their attribution may be explicitly anonymous or only from hearsay, the source of the passage may indeed be widely known and the addressor may be "concealing" the source only to maintain a plausible deniability that he has ever read or been taught a text or teaching that may be either out of fashion or forbidden, just as the *Intrigues* or, to use a comparative example, Machiavelli's *The Prince* were in later times. Alternatively, this anonymity may also expose the possibility that there was, for some of what was published in well-known treatises, a general fund of sayings or proverbs that had no known source or that could be found in multiple sources, some of which have not survived.

37. See Appendix G, section C.

38. Wang Niansun (1744–1832 CE) states that *hen* 恨 should be read as *hen* 很, which means "quarreling with each other." 王念孫云恨讀為很鬩相爭鬥也。See *HSBZ* 74.3a.

39. See Appendix H, section A.

40. The *Intrigues* provide the following example: "So an enlightened ruler will not insist on the exhaustion of troops, the exposure of cities and great enmity from all"; *Chan-Kuo Ts'e*, 201; He Jianzhang 何建章, annot., *Zhanguoce zhushi* 戰國策注釋, 12.422.

41. Reading *cong* 從 as *song* 聳, as Wang Niansun suggests. See *HSBZ* 64A.7a.
42. See Appendix F, section I.
43. See above on page 54.
44. It is interesting to note, though not necessarily significant for the point I am trying to make here, that there is a similar remark to be found in Sunzi's classic, *The Art of War*: "The side on which the commander is able and the ruler does not interfere will take the victory." 將能而君不禦者勝。 See Roger Ames, *Sun-Tzu: The Art of Warfare* (New York: Ballantine Books, 1993), 113. Whether Feng Tang knowingly is citing a version of the *Sunzi* or another treatise on warfare, something he only heard, or is presenting something he himself had composed is uncertain.
45. This type of principled proposition, that is, the type that focuses on a deemphasized or misperceived aspect of the matter, is also common in the *Intrigues*: "None the less about enemies I have heard it said, 'Branch and root clear both away, neighbour to calamity neither be nor stay; thus, never become catastrophe's prey.'" (且臣聞之曰:'削株掘根, 無與禍鄰, 禍乃不存。') Zhang Yi, the persuader who relates this saying, goes on to explicate it through the use of historical examples. See *Chan-Kuo Ts'e*, 127; He Jianzhang 何建章, annot., *Zhanguoce zhushi* 戰國策注釋, 3.89.
46. See Appendix F, section I.
47. I am grateful to Edward Shaughnessy for suggesting this line of interpretation.
48. Yan Shigu states that the meaning of this passage from the *Book of Odes* is that the way of the monarch has been faithfully effected throughout All-Under-Heaven and thus the Yi from the Huai, in the region of Xu have come to submit. See *HSBZ* 64A.8a. Arthur Waley translates the passage as follows: "The king's plans have been faithfully effected, / All the regions of Xu have submitted." See Burton Watson, ed., *Book of Songs*, trans. Arthur Waley (New York: Grove Press, 1996), 283.
49. See Appendix F, section J. For the *Shijing* quote, see Mao 263 ("*Chang wu*" 常武), Li Xueqin 李學勤, *Maoshi zhengyi* 毛詩正義, 1256.
50. See Appendix F, section J.
51. Though the poem by itself does not seem to support this type of use, Liu An seems to be following an exegetical tradition (in line with Yan Shigu's interpretation mentioned in n. 246), though not of this precise passage, that harkens back to *Zuozhuan*. Nonetheless, the poem itself makes a clear connection between the military successes of King Xuan and the ensuing capitulation of the Xu tribes. I am grateful to Edward Shaughnessy for this comment.
52. In contrast, the *Intrigues* has several instances in its hortatory addresses on military affairs in which an addressor presents a moralizing principle. A prime example is the following: "Furthermore, I have heard one must 'act in fear and trembling, take more care tomorrow than today. Who fears the Way can hold the empire.' How do I know this is so? Of old when King Zhou of Shang was the Son of Heaven he commanded the hosts of his empire. So numerous were they that his left flank drank in the Qi valley and his right drank the Yuan. So vast were they that the Qi dried up and the Yuan flowed no more. With these forces he hoped to distress King Wu of Zhou. King Wu led three thousand troops in the simplest

of armour and in one day of fighting broke Zhou of Shang's state, captured his person, seized his land and won over his people. All the world was shocked." (且臣聞之:'戰戰慄慄, 日慎一日, 苟慎其道, 天下可有也。'何以知其然也? 昔者, 紂為天子, 帥天下將甲百萬, 左飲於淇谷, 右飲於洹水, 洹水竭, 而洹水不流, 以與周武為難。武王將素甲三千, 領戰一日, 破紂之國, 禽其身, 據其地, 而有其民, 天下莫不傷。) See *Chan-Kuo Ts'e*, 130, and He Jianzhang 何建章, annot., *Zhanguoce zhushi* 戰國策注釋, 3.90. Because of his virtue, with only a relatively small army King Wu of Zhou was able to overcome the vastly larger armies of the last king of the Shang dynasty, King Zhou of Shang. Yet it should also be noted that, if we were to translate the final verb, *shang*, as "injured" or "distraught," as it is commonly translated, the meaning of the entire passage would be utterly different, certainly not as affirmative of King Wu's actions as common use of passages relating to early Zhou history are usually expected to be.

53. Some addresses touching on military affairs that are recorded in the Han histories, such as those by Jia Yi or Mei Sheng, are composed almost wholly in abstract, principled terms. Jia Yi, one of the most celebrated among Han Ruist thinkers, wrote extensively on the problem of subduing the Xiongnu. See his lengthy address at *HS* 48.2230–58 and a similar piece entitled "Xiongnu" in the volume of his collected essays, *Xinshu*. See also Mei Sheng's at *HS* 51.2359–61.

54. At one point in Liu An's address, he pleads to Emperor Wu to take pity on the commoners who are suffering from famine, remarking that the monarch has a "charismatic bounty" with which he can save them, if only he ceases the unnecessary attacks on the foreign tribes: "Recently, for several years the harvest has consecutively not come in and thus the common people have depended on selling aristocratic titles and indenturing their children for clothes and food. They are depending on Your Majesty's virtue and bounty to rescue them, so that they will be able to not roll dead into a watery ditch." 間者, 數年歲比不登, 民待賣爵贅子以接衣食, 賴陛下德澤振救之, 得毋轉死溝壑。See Appendix F, section D.

55. See Appendix F, section E.

56. See Appendix F, section E.

57. *Insultatio*: "Derisive, ironical abuse of a person to his face." See Richard A. Lanham, *A Handlist of Rhetorical Terms* (Berkeley: University of California Press, 1991), 91.

58. See Appendix I, section E.

59. *HS* 51.2359.

60. *Antisagoge*: "Assuring a reward to those who possess a virtue, or punishment to those who hold it in contempt." Lanham, *A Handlist of Rhetorical Terms*, 15.

61. See Appendix C, sections C–E.

62. Here my translation follows Yang Shuda's commentary in Yang Shuda 楊樹達, *Hanshu kuiguan* 漢書窺管 (Beijing: Kexue chubanshe, 1955), 383.

63. See Appendix F, section D.

64. They are instances of *cataplexis*, defined as "threatening punishment, misfortune, or disaster." See Lanham, *A Handlist of Rhetorical Terms*, 31.

65. See Appendix G, section A.

66. See Appendix G, section B.

67. Chen Zhi 陳直, *Hanshu xinzheng* 漢書新證 (Tianjin: Tianjin renmin chubanshe, 1959), 371.

68. Many thanks to Michael Loewe for his gentle corrections of my above translations and his detailed criticisms of my analysis (e-mail correspondence, October 16, 2007). Indeed, the difference in status or rank is exactly how Loewe explains the discrepancy in the ratio of rations calculated in the two tallies. But the figures do not exactly correspond with those in the Juyan figures, not without some modification for other ranks or classes not here listed. Regardless of their ultimate accuracy, in the context of how numerical figures are used generally in the histories, their potential rhetorical effect and persuasive value, could not have been lost on someone as experienced and savvy as Zhao Chongguo. For Loewe's extended analysis of Zhao Chongguo's recommendations, see Loewe, *Records of Han Administration* (London: Cambridge University Press, 1967), 1:78–79, 2:68, and 2:70–71, or in his more recent essay, Loewe, "The Western Han Army: Organization, Leadership, and Operation," in *Military Culture in Imperial China*, ed. Nicola Di Cosmo (Cambridge, MA: Harvard University Press, 2009), 74.

69. See Appendix A, sections B–D.

70. "Were Ch'in to attack Ch'i, however, it would not be thus. Ch'in would have left the lands of Han and Wei at her back; she would have crossed the Yangchin road in Lesser Wei and threaded the passes of K'ang-fu where two carriages can scarce go abreast, where two horsemen cannot proceed side by side, and where a hundred defenders may detain a thousand who think to pass. So even though Ch'in might wish to make such a deep penetration, she must always cast looks behind her, like the wary wolf, to where Han and Wei are observing her." 今秦攻則不然, 倍韓, 魏之地, 至闕陽晉之道, 徑亢父之險, 車不得方軌, 馬不得並行, 百人守險, 千人不能過也。秦雖欲深入, 則狼顧, 恐韓, 魏之議其後也。; Crump, *Legends of the Warring States*, 77, and He Jianzhang 何建章, annot., *Zhanguoce zhushi* 戰國策注釋, 8.327. This persuasion is also found at *SJ* 69.2258.

CHAPTER SIX. RHETORIC IN OPPOSITION

1. Mark E. Lewis, "Warring States Political History," in *The Cambridge History of Ancient China: From the Origins of Civilization to 221 B.C.*, ed. Loewe and Edward Shaughnessy (New York: Cambridge University Press, 1999), 634.

2. See *SJ* 15.727 and 15.731.

3. See *SJ* 44.1849.

4. The exact dates of when each state's ruler arrogated the royal title of "king" are uncertain. The *Records* records different dates in different places. For instance, the ruler of Han 韓, in both the "Tables" 表 and the "Hereditary House of Chu" 楚世家, is said to have taken the royal title in the sixth year of King Huai of Chu (323 BCE) but in the "Annals of Qin" is said to have done so in the thirteenth year of Marquis Huiwen of Qin 秦惠文侯 (325 BCE), two years earlier, the same year the Marquis Huiwen himself assumed the royal title. Nonetheless, according to the "Tables," Zhao apparently did not take the royal title until sometime on or after 325 BCE. See *SJ* 5.206, 15.730, and 40.1722. Lewis

apparently accepts the date ascribed in the "Annals of Qin." See Lewis, "Warring States Political History," 603.

5. See *SJ* 15.730–31 and 70.2284–85.

6. In the "Tables," Zhang Yi supposedly only returns to the Qin chancellorship in 317, the year after Qin has been attacked by Wei, Han, Zhao, Chu, and Yan, the same year that Qin attacks Zhao and Han. This contradicts the account in his biography, which has him returning to Qin from Wei to beg for an alliance at the same time Wei is maintaining its alliance with the other states. This would suggest the earlier date of 321 BCE. The king of Wei appears to be using Zhang Yi to buy for time while it prepares with the other states to mount a united attack against Qin. See *SJ* 70.2287 for the account in Zhang Yi's biography.

7. See Chapter Three, 28–31.

8. See Appendix G and Chapter Five, pp. 67–68.

9. See above p. 55 ff.

10. For example, the principle (or generalization) that "a hundred (i.e., a large group of) gathered birds of prey are no match for one osprey" is not an indubitable proposition in itself but its moral, that an especially strong, fierce leader (or one that projects such qualities) can overcome many ambitious or aggressive adversaries, is worthy of serious consideration. I take this example from an address given by Zou Yang. See Appendix E, section E.

11. For an analysis regarding this specific issue, see Scott Cook, "The Use and Abuse of History in Early China from *Xun Zi* to *Lüshi chunqiu*," *Asia Major* (2005): 45–78; or Pines, "Speeches and the Question of Authenticity in Ancient Chinese Historical Records," in *Historical Truth, Historical Criticism and Ideology*, ed. Helwig Schmidt-Glintzer et al., 196–226. Leiden Series in Comparative Historiography, Boston: Brill, 2005.

12. These are frequently marked by self-reference or structural connectives such as "now" (*jin* 今), "in addition" (*qie* 且), "in all cases" or "all" (*fan* 凡), and so forth. These markers are common but not ubiquitous markers of structural breaks in the persuasions and addresses. At times, the breaks suggest themselves in a shift of content or focus.

13. Relating to the value of concrete particulars, it is worth mentioning that J. I. Crump notes that the text here gives Wei "more land than it could have had"; Crump, *Legends of the Warring States*, 74. This is of some interest in relation to the question of the addresses' geographic or toponymic accuracy, which I will be discussing at more length in the following chapter.

14. Cheng Enze 程恩澤 suggests that *yi* denotes a village located to the north of the Huai River. See He Jianzhang 何建章, annot., *Zhanguoce zhushi* 戰國策注釋, 22.820, n. 15.

15. A version of the story of Goujian (or Jujian) is preserved in the *Records of the Grand Historian*. This version, however, does not tally with Su Qin's. See *SJ* 41.1739–45.

16. Though the received text has *qian*, "thousand," several other texts and commentaries, including the *Records of the Grand Historian*, have *shi*, "ten." See He Jianzhang 何建章, annot., *Zhanguoce zhushi* 戰國策注釋, 22.822, n. 45.

17. He Jianzhang 何建章, annot., *Zhanguoce zhushi* 戰國策注釋, 22.819–23.

18. In Zhang Yi's biography recorded in the *Shiji*, "Jinyang" is rendered as "Yangjin." According to He Jianzhang, Yangjin is in the Wei district and lies near Juan, Yan, Yan, and Suanzao. See He Jianzhang 何建章, annot., *Zhanguoce zhushi* 戰國策注釋, 22.826, n. 22.

19. 裴學海,《古書 虛字集釋》卷八: "猶'然'也." See He Jianzhang 何建章, annot., *Zhanguoce zhushi* 戰國策注釋, 22.826, n. 27.

20. 裴學海,《古書 虛字集釋》卷五: "猶'能'也." He Jianzhang 何建章, annot., *Zhanguoce zhushi* 戰國策注釋, 22.826, n. 28.

21. 何建章: "當讀作'乃', 因聲近." He Jianzhang 何建章, annot., *Zhanguoce zhushi* 戰國策注釋, 22.827, n. 31.

22. Grabbing one's wrists was apparently a sign of great excitement or emotional disturbance. See the entry for 搤腕 in the *Hanyu dacidian*.

23. Modified version of J. Crump's translation in his *Chan-Kuo Ts'e*, 400–402.

24. The Chinese original of this address taken from He Jianzhang 何建章, annot., *Zhanguoce zhushi* 戰國策注釋, 22.823–28.

25. See Aristotle, "Rhetoric," 1354b31: "There is no need, therefore, to prove anything except that the facts are what the supporter of a measure maintains they are." According to Aristotle, the addressor thus does not need to discuss matters that are not relevant to the issue at hand or are beyond doubt, "directly self-evident." See 1356b27–29.

26. Nicholas Rescher offers the following examples of basic human needs: food, health, safety, information, sociability, shelter, and clothing. See Rescher, *Common-Sense: A New Look at an Old Philosophical Tradition* (Milwaukee, WI: Marquette University Press, 2005), 39, 41.

27. See Chapter Three, page 23.

28. The Roman numerals in the parentheses refer to the listed propositions on p. 85.

29. Letters refer to propositions listed on pp. 81–82.

30. See pp. 100–103.

31. See p. 81, proposition f.

32. For the previous discussion of Zhao Chongguo's use of concrete particulars, see pp. 67–68.

CHAPTER SEVEN. COMMITMENT TO THE FACTS

1. Though further analysis still needs to be performed, it is possible to see Liu Bang's illness—which, in this ancient context, cannot necessarily be treated as purely physical—in some measure a consequence of his moral corruption, which deepens as the episode proceeds, to the point where he cannot even be "cured" by Zhang Liang's remonstrance. For examinations of the moral aspect of illness and its treatment in the early Chinese context, see Paul Unschuld, *Huang Di Nei Jing Su Wen: Nature, Knowledge, Imagery in an Ancient Chinese Medical Text* (Berkeley: University of California Press, 2003), 201–2. Moral etiology is also evident in numerous other texts from the early imperial period. For investigations of such, see Grégoire Espesset, "Criminalized Abnormality, Moral Etiology, and

Redemptive Suffering in the Secondary Strata of the *Taiping jing*," *Asia Major* 15, no. 2 (2002): 1–50; and Michel Strickmann, "The Seal of the Law: A Ritual Implement and the Origins of Printing," *Asia Major* 6, no. 2 (1993): 1–83. I would like to thank Don Harper for conferring with me on this matter.

2. *SJ* 55.2045; Sima Qian, *Records of the Grand Historian: Han Dynasty*, 1:110.

3. *SJ* 55.2046; *HS* 40.2035.

4. Another illustrative example: In Zhang Liang's biography, Zhang Liang persuades Liu Bang, who resisted the same recommendation from Fan Kuai 樊噲, not to occupy the palace of the First Emperor of Qin. Liu Bang is then reported as returning to camp at Bashang 霸上. See *SJ* 55.2037; Sima Qian, *Records of the Grand Historian: Han Dynasty*, 1:102.

5. For a comparative perspective, Aristotle speaks about the central importance of *eikos*: that which is probable or plausible, relations or generalizations that hold "for the most part" in rhetorical persuasion. See Aristotle, *Rhetoric*, 1402b14–16. Burnyeat has asserted that "the best guide to what the word [*eikos*] means in Greek is [*Rhetoric to Alexander* 7], 1428a25–26": "It is a probability when one's hearers have examples in their own minds of what is being said." See Burnyeat, "Enthymeme: Aristotle on the Logic of Persuasion," in *Aristotle's Rhetoric: Philosophical Essays*, ed. David J. Furley and Alexander Nehemas (Princeton, NJ: Princeton University Press, 1994), 26, n. 66.

6. As the four wise men state to Lü Ze, "Now [Consort] Qi day and night attends the emperor, and her son Ruyi is always with him in his arms. The emperor himself, they say, has sworn that 'no unworthy son shall ever hold a place above this beloved child.' Is this not clear proof that he intends to replace the heir apparent?" See Sima Qian, *Records of the Grand Historian: Han Dynasty*, 1:110; *SJ* 55.2045–46.

7. "Qing Bu, learning of the situation [about the heir apparent leading the older generals], would march fearlessly west to attack us." See Sima Qian, *Records of the Grand Historian: Han Dynasty*, 1:110; *SJ* 55.2046.

8. "The other generals who will go with [the heir apparent] on the expedition are all veteran commanders who fought with the emperor in the past to win possession of the empire. To put the heir apparent in command of a group of men such as this is like sending a lamb to lead a pack of wolves . . . They would never consent to obey his orders." See Sima Qian, *Records of the Grand Historian: Han Dynasty*, 1:110; *SJ* 55.2045–46.

9. This type of doubt is most explicitly displayed in Chen Yu's objection relating to the size of Han Xin's forces. Though his doubt is not in response to any claim by Li Zuoche to the contrary, it is, nevertheless, an important factor in how he assesses Li Zuoche's claims. See their exchange in Appendix A.

10. I am not asserting that the doubts that could have arisen were the strongest or most robust doubts that could have been raised. In many ways, the political superseded the rational, if by rational we mean the means by which we arrive at either a more precise account of a state of affairs or a more accurate calculation of our long-term interests. I am asserting that the doubts could have been there, that they are couched within a particular dynamic that limited them, and that these doubts were epistemic, not interpersonal.

11. I thus disagree with Frank Kierman's polar opposition between those military reports that hew close to the facts on the ground and those that are "fabulous" and "romantic," "freeing the historian from the onerous and unpalatable task of recording the fleeting, disturbing, and technical facts of warfare." The historical relegation of the military enterprise to the sphere of "fantasy," he asserts, "has encouraged the sort of dreamlike armchair strategy which has marked Chinese military thinking so deeply down the centuries, into our day"; Frank A. Kierman Jr., "Phases and Modes of Combat in Early China," in *Chinese Ways in Warfare*, ed. Kierman and John K. Fairbank (Cambridge, MA: Harvard University Press, 1974), 65. I would suggest that, rather than our perceiving the representation as useless, or even worse, distracting and deceptive fantasy that discourages careful planning of strategy and organization of resources, we accept that the point of the historical record was not to represent things in excruciating detail but instead to allow us to see the historian's product, and his self-appointed task, even in areas that, to our minds, would have benefited from a commitment to absolute accuracy, as arising from a commitment to representing the course of action as it proceeded, or was thought to have proceeded, the motivations for its procession, and the larger generalizations that seemed to have, or in more moralizing representations, ought to have driven the course of events.

12. Thus the sometimes protracted difficulties in establishing where a location, based on the internal evidence of the historical texts, was supposed to be. See, for example, Qian Mu's discussion of the location of Qingyang in his Qian Mu 錢穆, *Shiji diming kao* 史記地名考 (Beijing: Shangwu yinshuguan, 2001), 615.

13. Rémi Mathieu enumerates a series of problems that accompany attempts, whether ours or even perhaps the Chinese historians', to be precise in our determinations of location: (1) The same place was given different names by different parties depending on the business being conducted. Military officials would give it one name, political officials another, tradesmen yet another. (2) Identical toponyms could designate two distinct places that were separated by hundreds, if not thousands, of miles. One often discovers names of known places being used to designate regions that are poorly or not known. (3) Locations sometimes moved when its populace did. "Il en résulte une extrême complexité lors de l'identification des lieux, surtout lorsque s'ajoute a ces difficultés variées, des erreurs de copistes, des interversions des fiches de bambous reproduits ensuite pendant des siècles." The problems for us, as well as for the Chinese historian, in determining the exact location of a place are extremely onerous. There are a plethora of others associated with the means by which measurements were taken. See Rémi Mathieu, "Fonctions et Moyens de la Géographie dans la Chine Ancienne," *Études Asiatiques: Revue de la Société Suisse d'Études Asiatiques* 36, no. 2 (1982):145–50.

14. Kierman, "Phases and Modes of Combat," p. 320, n. 44.

15. Ibid.

16. Ibid.

17. See the address presented by Zhu Ji 朱己 (aka Wu Ji 无忌) to the king of Wei in He Jianzhang 何建章, annot., *Zhanguoce zhushi* 戰國策注釋, 24.907 ff., and the *Weishijia* 魏世家 section of the *Shiji*, 44.1857 ff. See also the address presented by Xu Jia 須賈 to the Marquis of Rang 穰侯, He Jianzhang 何建章, annot., *Zhanguoce zhushi* 戰國策注釋, 24.889 ff., *SJ* 72.2325 ff.

18. In most of the persuasions speaking to military matters recorded in the *Intrigues*, there is no moral language with any significant (or believable) moral content that plays any central role in the persuasion. See He Jianzhang 何建章, annot., *Zhanguoce zhushi* 戰國策注釋, 5.151 (Duke of Xue 薛公), 3.87 (Ling Xiang 泠向), 3.88 ff. (Zhang Yi), 11.419 ff. (Su Qin), 13.451 ff. (Lu Lian 魯連), 22.812–13 (Wu Qi 吳起); *Chan-Kuo Ts'e*, §80, 81, 107, 158, 161, 298.

19. *SJ* 99.2716; William Nienhauser, ed., *The Grand Scribe's Records: The Memoirs of Han China, Part I* (Bloomington: Indiana University Press, 2008), 8:282.

20. *SJ* 99.2716; Nienhauser, *The Grand Scribe's Records*, 8:282. Translation modified.

21. Ibid., 8:282–83.

22. In Zhang Liang's biography, this anecdote is repeated, with the distinction that instead of remarking on the brevity of the Qin dynasty, they argued that Luoyang's landscape had natural defenses that adequately protected the capital against attack and thus was suitable for establishing a capital.

23. Zhang Liang's answer to the emperor's doubts is recorded in "The Hereditary House of the Marquis of Liu": "Liu Jing had advised the emperor to make his capital in the area within the Pass, but the emperor still hesitated. Since most of his followers came from east of the mountains, they urged him to establish the capital at Luoyang, pointing out that it was protected by Chenggao on the east and Mt. Yao and the Min Lake on the west, with its back to the Yellow River and the Yi and Luo rivers flowing before it, and could therefore be easily fortified and held. But Zhang Liang objected, saying, 'Although Luoyang has these natural defences, the area within is so small it does not exceed a few hundred *li*. The land is poor and open to attack from four sides, so that from a military point of view it is quite unsuitable. The area within the Pass, on the other [h]and, is protected by Mt. Yao and the Hangu Pass on the left and Long and Shu to the right [since the emperor is facing south], comprising some 1,000 *li* of fertile plain, with the rich fields of Ba and Shu to the south and the advantages of the pasture lands of the barbarians to the north. With three sides protected by natural barriers, one has only to worry about controlling the feudal lords to the east. So long as the feudal lords are at peace, tribute can be transported up the Yellow and Wei Rivers to supply the capital area in the west, and if the lords should revolt one can descend these same rivers and attack them, assured of an adequate supply of provisions. The area within the Pass is in fact one vast fortress of iron, a veritable storehouse created by nature. Therefore Liu Jing's advice is correct.'" 劉敬說高帝曰:「都關中。」上疑之。左右大臣皆山東人,多勸上都雒陽:「雒陽東有成皋,西有殽黽,倍河,向伊雒,其固亦足恃。」留侯曰:「雒陽雖有此固,其中小,不過數百里,田地薄,四面受敵,此非用武之國也。夫關中左殽函,右隴蜀,沃野千里,南有巴蜀之饒,北有胡苑之利,阻三面而守,獨以一面東制諸侯。諸侯安定,河渭漕輓天下,西給京師;諸侯有變,順流而下,足以委輸。此所謂金城千里,天府之國也,劉敬說是也。」 *SJ* 55.2043–44; Sima Qian, *Records of the Grand Historian: Han Dynasty*, 1: 108–9. Michael Loewe pronounces Zhang Liang's arguments "powerful," but it is hard to see what he said that was substantially different from what Liu Jing had said himself. See Loewe, *A Biographical Dictionary of the Qin*, 413.

24. A fascinating illustration of this point can be found in the biography of Li Ling 李陵 in the *History of the Former Han*. Li Ling was a general who failed in his campaign against the Xiongnu but did not take the honorable course and die

in battle but instead surrendered to the Xiongnu. Sima Qian famously defended him to the emperor, portraying him as filial, trustworthy, and committed to the good of his country. Sima Qian's description of the details of the campaign and the reasons for Li Ling's failure was matter-of-fact and to the point, yet the narrative following the excerpted speech explained that the emperor believed Sima Qian's portrayal was meant to indirectly disparage another general, a general who was not mentioned, directly or indirectly, in Sima Qian's speech. The emperor clearly saw Sima Qian's "facts" as loaded with meaning and judgment. See *HS* 54.2455–56; Pan Ku, *Courtier and Commoner*, 30.

25. This is certainly not to say, as I have argued above, that emperors did not regularly take epistemically justifiable factors into consideration. They often did, if the record of their offering queries and responses as to the advice of their ministers is any indication. See, for example, the exchange between Emperor Yuan and his General of the Right Armies Feng Shi 奉世 about how to manage the Qiang, particularly the emperor's response at *HS* 79.3298.

26. See Chapter Eight, pp. 129–36.

27. Loewe, *Faith, Myth, and Reason in Han China* (Indianapolis, IN: Hackett, 2005), 159–60.

CHAPTER EIGHT. MORAL NORMS AS FACTS

1. The absence of extended discussion or debate in Sima Qian's *Records*, or, alternately, its later inclusion in the *History of the Former Han*, is one of the hallmarks distinguishing the latter. Why this is the case, I can only begin to speculate. The most common explanation is that there were sources available to Ban Gu and his family that were not available to Sima Qian. But the discrepancy might also point to a difference in dramatic or historiographical aims. Conspicuous instances of figures whose biographies can be found in the *Records* but that are missing the extended addresses or exchanges recorded in the *History of the Former Han* are Chao Cuo, whose biography in the latter contains numerous submitted addresses, Zou Yang, Mei Sheng, and Liu An. There are others, such as Zhao Chongguo, Zhuang Zhu 莊助, or Xiao Wangzhi, who are mentioned in the *Records* but have no appended biography. Indeed, if we are to accept the thesis, as Wai-Yee Li does, that the *Records* is critical of emperors and was therefore purged of some of its material, it is curious why the *History of the Former Han*, supposedly less pointed and ardent in its criticisms of the dynasty to the point of being accommodating, contains so many more addresses that *are* very critical. See Li, "The Idea of Authority," 394.

2. 「文具新序善謀下篇, 班氏蓋采之彼。」 Yang Shuda 楊樹達, *Hanshu kuiguan* 漢書窺管, 319.

3. Additions to the text will be marked by braces, {}. Those variants that are, to my mind, relatively insignificant but somewhat noteworthy, I include in footnotes.

4. See Chapter Five, p. 47.

5. This is not an uncommon method of framing the debate. As Nicola Di Cosmo asserts, "Expressions of the political interaction between Chou states

and foreigners abound but have been analyzed almost exclusively under a 'moral' rubric according to a bifurcated ideological approach: If the statements stressed 'peace,' an attempt was carried out to educate and mold the foreigner peacefully (the Confucian-Mencian way); if the statements invoked war, then this was because these 'barbarians' could only be tamed *manu militari* (the 'legalist' approach)"; Di Cosmo, *Ancient China and Its Enemies*, 104. Indeed, even Ban Gu characterizes those debating how to handle the Xiongnu, including Wang Hui and Han Anguo, as divided into two camps: the Ruists and the Militarists, with the Ruists consistently advocating for diplomacy and the Militarists advocating for war. See *HS* 94.3830. This is also a distinction that is frequently applied in the depiction of the discussants involved in the *Debates on Salt and Iron*. In the *Debates on Salt and Iron*, which are framed around the discussions concerning placing a tax on the production of salt and iron (which were very lucrative to manufacture), the two represented parties, namely the supporter of the government policies (the "realist") and the critic of government policies (the "idealist"), offer arguments that at some points resemble arguments forwarded by Wang Hui and Han Anguo here. (For a characterization of the *Debates on Salt and Iron* that follows along these lines, see Loewe, *Crisis and Conflict in Han China* [London: George Allen and Unwin, 1974], 91–112. See also Benjamin E. Wallacker, "Han Confucianism and Confucius in Han," in *Ancient China: Studies in Early Civilization*, ed. David T. Roy and Tsuen-hsuin Tsien [Hong Kong: Chinese University Press, 1978], 223.) I take issue, however, with the positions being defined too starkly using these stereotyped labels, labels that, at least in relation to the debate between Wang Hui and Han Anguo, obscure points of overlap in their positions. Attempts to derive support for any categorizations based on ascribed intellectual heritage are dubious and unconvincing. Though Han historians frequently mention the educational pedigree of Han intellectuals and ministers, the relevance, or even reliability, of this information for the analysis of his speech acts is often questionable. Save for the most zealous of Confucians, there often seems to be little relationship between the pedagogy supposedly received and the teachings promoted or the strategies recommended during the course of an address or a debate. Nor does the historian always know (or bother to record) the educational background of a particular learned figure. There are examples of powerful addressors, such as Zou Yang (see his address in Appendix E), whose intellectual heritage are recorded in neither the *Records* nor the *History of the Former Han* (which, incidentally, share little in their accounts of him). Still others, such as Zhufu Yan (whose address is recorded in Appendix C), were recorded as having studied various divergent and sometimes adversarial intellectual traditions. In his case, Zhufu Yan was said to have studied the techniques of the Warring States persuaders (長短縱橫之術) and then later studied several of the traditional Confucian classics, the *Book of Changes* and the *Annals of Spring and Autumn*, along with the teachings of the many ("hundred") traditions.

6. This debate can be found at *HS* 52.2398–2403. See also *HSBZ* 52.16b–19b, 1102–4. For ease of reference, I will number each response alphabetically.

7. My interpretation follows Li Qi's 李奇 commentary to the *Hanshu* in which he states, "In the time of the Six States, the entirety of the lands of Dai became a single country. If even they are able to fight the Xiongnu, why not now the great

Han?" 六國之時全代為一國, 尚能以擊匈奴, 況今加以漢之大乎! See *HS* 52.2399, n. 2. The "Six States" refer to the six major central states of the Warring States period: Wei 魏, Han 韓, Zhao 趙, Chu 楚, Yan 燕, and Qi 齊. During this period, in 475 BCE, Zhao conquered the Dai kingdom, after which point it became a commandery. See *SJ* 43.1793–94.

8. *Xinxu*: "Ignore" 慢.

9. *Xinxu*: "[They] will not worry about being punished" 不痛之患.

10. It may also be an indirect reference to Liu Xi's 劉喜, Liu Bang's elder brother, failure as the king of Dai to defend against the Xiongnu in 200 BCE.

11. According to the "Dili zhi" 地理志 in the *Hanshu*, the city of Pingcheng was in a district in the Yanmen Commandery 鴈門郡, not uncoincidentally the area in which the Xiongnu are currently causing trouble. See *HS* 28B.1621.

12. Sima Qian, *Records of the Grand Historian: Han Dynasty*, 2:138; *SJ* 110.2894.

13. "The Han forces within the encirclement had no way of receiving aid or provisions from their comrades outside, since the Xiongnu cavalry surrounded them on all sides, with white horses on the west side, greenish horses on the east, black horses on the north, and red ones on the south." See Sima Qian, *Records of the Grand Historian: Han Dynasty*, 2:138.

14. Sima Qian, *Records of the Grand Historian: Han Dynasty*, 2:139.

15. This contention is supported by Nicola Di Cosmo. See Di Cosmo, *Ancient China and Its Enemies*, 161.

16. The Xiongnu strategy, I presume, was to create impasses against escape.

17. A song sung by All-Under-Heaven is mentioned in "The Account of the Xiongnu" in the Hanshu: "All-Under-Heaven sang, 'How truly awful it was at Pingcheng! Seven days of not being able to eat or to fire a crossbow (i.e., to attack the Xiongnu)!'" 天下歌之曰:『平城之下亦誠苦! 七日不食, 不能彀弩。』 See *HS* 94A.3755.

18. This is the same advisor, Liu Jing, mentioned above, who advised Liu Bang to move the capital to the old Qin lands.

19. *Xinxu*: "Amassed" 屯.

20. Han Anguo's interpretation of the reason for Liu Bang's establishing peaceful relations with the Xiongnu is contested by Di Cosmo. Di Cosmo asserts that Liu Bang was "forced" to accept peace, though why this was or even why the Xiongnu would not be inclined to push for further military engagement is not made clear. The empire, Di Cosmo states, "was not in a position to continue to fight after the many years of civil war at the end of the Ch'in." Di Cosmo's reading would thus expose Han Anguo's sympathetic explanation for Liu Bang's actions as a sycophantic piece of etiquette that was uncontestable in front of Emperor Wu (because contestation would make Liu Bang, his forebear, appear impotent). It is, of course, also very possible that Han Anguo's assertions were accurate, that Liu Bang could indeed have decided to pursue retributional military action but decided against it, whether out of economic concerns or, as Han Anguo insists, consideration of the good of the empire. See Di Cosmo, *Ancient China and Its Enemies*, 212.

21. Di Cosmo, in his representation of this part of Han Anguo's reply, states that Han Anguo "praised Han Wen-ti for not having conquered a single inch

of Hsiung-nu territory and for having eventually renewed the peace treaty"; Di Cosmo, *Ancient China and Its Enemies*, 212. This representation risks neglecting Han Anguo's praise for the ethical dimension of Emperor Wen's restraint. It also may elide the implicit suggestion that Wen seemed to have had every intention of engaging militarily. See *HS* 94.3831 for Ban Gu's characterization of this episode.

22. *Xinxu*: "Thus he made a covenant establishing peaceful relations [with the Xiongnu], thereby calming the common people of All-Under-Heaven" 故結和親之約者, 所以休天下之民. The variant expresses a similar idea to the preceding phrase, namely that the emperor took the potential suffering of the commoners into consideration when he decided not to pursue military action against the Xiongnu to avenge his disgrace at Pingcheng.

23. In the entire debate, this response shows the most variance between the *Hanshu* and the *Xinxu* versions. In the *Xinxu* version, a more metaphysical line of argument is forwarded, one that has only a tenuous relationship to the rest of the response. It is never taken up again, directly or indirectly, by either Wang Hui or Han Anguo. Thus I consider it, whether it was "original" to the text or not, not entirely germane to the procession of the arguments and thus have omitted it. In the following, the propositions in question are underlined: 大行曰：「不然！夫明於形者, 分則不過於事; 察於動者, 用則不失於利; 審於靜者, 恬則免於患。高帝被堅執銳, 以除天下之害。蒙矢石, 沾風雨, 行幾十年。<u>伏尸滿澤, 積首若山。死者什七, 存者什三。</u>行者垂泣, 而倪於兵。夫以天下未力厭事之民, 而蒙匈奴飽佚, 其勢不便, 故結和親之約者, 所以休天下之民。<u>高皇帝明於形而以分事, 通於動靜之時</u>。蓋五帝不相同樂, 三王不相襲禮者, 非故相反 也, 各因世之宜也。<u>教與時變, 備與敵化</u>。守一而不易, 不足以子民。今匈奴縱意日久矣, 侵盜無已, 係虜人民, 戍卒死傷, 中國道路槥車相望, 此仁人之所哀也。 臣故曰『擊之便』。」

24. "The three dynasties did not share the same way and yet ruled as true kings, the five hegemons did not share the same laws and yet [all] ruled as hegemons" 三代不同道而王; 五霸不同法而霸; "Gengfapian" 更法篇 in *Shangjunshu zhuizhi* 商君書錐指, comp., Jiang Lihong 蔣禮鴻 (Beijing: Zhonghua shuju, 1986), 4. It is also very interesting to note that Liu Bang also quotes this in his edict responding to the invasion of Dai by the Xiongnu, which led him to be militarily compromised by the Xiongnu. See *HS* 6.173.

25. Here I am referring to the following statement: "The reason he did not respond to the episode at Pingcheng with resentment is not because his strength was not sufficient but because [he wished to] put at ease the heart-mind of All-Under-Heaven." Another possible interpretation is that Wang Hui is suggesting a contrast between Liu Bang's military weakness and Emperor Wu's current military strength.

26. In the *Xinxu*, the last two phrases read as follows: "For this reason, when the lords of old laid plans, they were certain to turn to the sages for guidance. When they acted on political matters, they were certain to select out sayings [of merit]" 是以古之人君謀事必就聖, 發政必擇語. This variant gives the passage less of a traditionalist cast than the one above.

27. The *Xinxu* adds the following: "Their arrival cannot be anticipated and when they depart, they cannot be apprehended" 至不及圖, 去不可追.

28. An almost identical saying can be found in the same essay of the *Shangjunshu*, "Gengfapian": "If profit has not increased a hundredfold, do not alter your

regulating principle; if accomplishments have not increased tenfold, do not change the implements you use" 利不百, 不變法, 功不十, 不易器. What follows in this essay is possibly also somewhat informative: "I have heard that if one takes antiquity as the rule, there will be no error, if one adheres to ritual propriety, there will be no iniquity" 臣聞法古無過, 循禮無邪. In other words, constancy of purpose and adherence to principle are what should drive one's pursuit of an enterprise.

29. Analogous descriptions of the Xiongnu are common to the Han histories. One of the most strikingly similar, in both description and advice regarding their management can be found in a speech attributed to Li Si, the infamous Qin minister, quoted within Zhufu Yan's address: "The Xiongnu have no cities or forts and no stores of provisions. They move from place to place like flocks of birds, and thus are difficult to catch and control. If parties of lightly equipped soldiers penetrate deeply into their territory, their food supplies will certainly become exhausted, and if we try to send provisions after them in order that they may continue on, the baggage trains will be too encumbered to make it in time. Even if we were to seize control of the Xiongnu lands, it would not be enough to profit us any, and even if we were to treat their common people properly, we could never subjugate or control them." Later in the same address, Secretary to the Imperial Counselor Cheng 成 presented a similar estimation of the Xiongnu. Zhufu Yan also notes that it seems in their nature to "pillage and plunder," another stereotype. See Appendix C, sections D–H. See also *HS* 64.2801 for another example.

30. The notion of using a "crossbow" to lance an abscess and drain away harmful fluids can be found in early Chinese medical literature. In particular, see the "Bao ming quan xing lun" 寶命全形論 in the *Huangdi neijing*. As needles drain away harmful fluids from the body, so will a few arrows from the powerful crossbow of the Han army neutralize the harmful Xiongnu presence, bringing the other tribes to support the Han Chinese and leading to the returned equilibrium and greater "health" of the entire area. Wang Hui is thus advising that Emperor Wu use a "surgical" strike to attack the Xiongnu. For more on the use of lances to restore health, see Donald J. Harper, *Early Chinese Medical Literature: The Mawangdui Medical Manuscripts* (New York: Kegan Paul, 1998), 213–18, especially 214, n. 1. I'm grateful to Donald Harper for calling my attention to this.

31. There are some difficulties in determining the group or area to which the term *beifa* refers. In *HS* 6.161, there is a note regarding the phrase, *bei fa qu sou* 北發渠搜, which, according to some commentators, is the name of a kingdom. One commentator, Jin Zhuo 晉灼 (fl. 275), mentions the above text in his discussion, taking the term as referring to the name of a country. If so, the phrase, *bei fa yue zhi*, refers to two areas, and thus two groups, the Beifa and the Yuezhi. Qian Mu, in his *Shiji diming kao*, attempts to make sense of the various references to *beifa* and asserts that it is indeed a reference to a foreign tribe. (See Qian Mu 錢穆, *Shiji diming kao* 史記地名考, 11–12.) Though the evidence is still inconclusive, I believe treating it as referring to a separate foreign tribe, rather than descriptive of the *Yuezhi* tribe, makes the most sense of the various appearances of the term in the Han histories. For Di Cosmo's translation and analysis of this passage, see Di Cosmo, *Ancient China and Its Enemies*, 213. In the rendering of the

succeeding phrase, *ke de er chen ye* 可得而臣也, I aver, *pace* Di Cosmo, that it is not the Xiongnu who are the subject of the verb, *chen* ("to act as a subject"), but the Beifa and Yuezhi tribes. This, I believe, is supported by Han Anguo's mentioning, in his following response, "conscripting" enemy states. Building on Wang Hui's scenario, Han Anguo is suggesting that foreign conscripts can do the work of the Han army. Nonetheless, my conclusion ultimately shares much resonance with Di Cosmo's: "It was perfectly clear to Wang Hui that the political basis of the Hsiung-nu was quite unstable, and that it would be possible for the Han to exploit divisions among the nomads."

32. Here the *Xinxu* includes the following phrase: "The numinous water dragon moves about the depths" 夫神蛟濟於淵.

33. *Xinxu*: "piled logs" 積木.

34. Using a foreign tribe to fight on behalf of the Han empire must have been a relatively common practice, for Chao Cuo in an address to Emperor Wen, remarked that it was the "essential (strategic) constitution" (*xing* 形) of the Central States "to use the Manyi to attack the Manyi," "Manyi" being a designation of all foreign tribes. (以蠻夷攻蠻夷, 中國之形也。) See Appendix D, section D.

35. A weapon not reaching its target is a familiar stock metaphor and can be found in the *Intrigues*: "The soundest barbs and the sharpest points, if they do not utilize the impetus of bowstrings or the mechanism of triggers, will not slay at any great distance. This is so not because the weapons themselves are dull, but because the means of implementing them are not there"; Crump, *Intrigues*, 195.

36. *Xinxu*: "[He] regulates government and disseminates virtue" 整治施德.

37. The *Xinxu* here proceeds in the following way: "Exhausted, they then will meet the enemy and will thus be giving them men to capture" 勞以遇敵, 正遺人獲也. This, however, does not make much sense in conjunction with the remaining statements.

38. My interpretation of this quote follows Yan Shigu's 顏師古 (581–645 CE): "The meaning of this is that one hands soldiers over to the enemy and gives the soldiers orders to take them prisoner" 言以軍遺敵人, 令其虜獲也.

39. *Xinxu*: "I will conceal lightly armored infantry and swordsmen who will await them" 吾伏輕卒銳士以待之.

40. Indeed, the Xiongnu continued their assault on the Han border areas. See Li Guang's biography, *HS* 54.2443; Pan Ku, *Courtier and Commoner*, 16.

41. See p. 117.

42. See pp. 86–89.

43. See p. 81.

44. See p. 79.

45. *Mengzi*, 6A:17.

46. "'It is because of Qin's violent and unprincipled ways that you have come this far. Now that you have freed the world of these tyrannical bandits it is proper that you should don the plain white garments of mourning as a pledge of your sympathy for the sufferings of the people. Having just entered the capital of Qin, if you were now to indulge yourself in its pleasures, this would be "helping the tyrant Jie to work his violence." Good advice is hard on the ears, but it profits the conduct just as good medicine, though bitter in the mouth, cures the sickness. I beg you to listen to Fan Kuai's counsel!' The governor of Pei [i.e., Liu Bang]

accordingly returned and camped at Bashang" 良曰：「夫秦為無道，故沛公得至此。夫為天下除殘賊，宜縞素為資。今始入秦，即安其樂，此所謂『助桀為虐』。且『忠言逆耳利於行，毒藥苦口利於病』，願沛公聽樊噲言。」沛公乃還軍霸上. See *SJ* 55.2037; Sima Qian, *Records of the Grand Historian: Han Dynasty*, 1:102.

47. See Pan Ku, *Courtier and Commoner*, 92–93; *HS* 65.2856–57.

48. 蘇厲謂周君曰：「敗韓、魏，殺犀武，攻趙，取藺、離石、祁者，皆白起。是攻用兵，又有天命也。」See He Jianzhang 何建章, annot., *Zhanguoce zhushi* 戰國策注釋, 2.54. For the rendition of this episode in the *Records*, see *SJ* 4.164–5.

49. Michael Loewe also notices that the notion of *tianming* became less salient in the centuries between the Western Zhou and the Former Han. He furthermore notes that in *Zuozhuan*, references to *tianming*, like the above example from the *Intrigues*, involve "the fate or behaviour of individuals only, without the majestic concern with the destiny of royal houses." See Loewe, "The Authority of the Emperors," 85–86.

50. In the stelae fragment from Mount Lang Ye 琅耶臺, persuasively dated to the Qin era, while it does not use the term *tianming* specifically, it does employ much of the moral vocabulary used by Confucian (or "Ru") specialists, terms such as *sheng* 聖, *zhi* 智, *ren* 仁, *yi* 義, and *de* 德. All of the other stelae inscriptions, as transcribed by Kern (originally preserved in post-Song rubbings or drawings), also use at least one of these moral terms. Of course, these stelae inscriptions are not ministerial addresses so the comparison to their use of language is of limited value. Nevertheless, it does show that Confucian moral language was still present and emphasized in a dynasty as reputedly amoral as the Qin. See Martin Kern, *The Stele Inscriptions of Ch'in Shih-huang: Text and Ritual in Early Chinese Imperial Representation* (New Haven, CT: American Oriental Society, 2000).

51. See p. 118.

52. The tacit acknowledgment of the truth of moral concerns of course does not prevent, as is often the case in the *Intrigues*, their cynical employment. Plato makes a similar point in a number of his dialogues.

53. See Appendix G.

54. At the end of the historical incidents recorded in the *Spring and Autumn Annals*, there are sometimes appended judgmental remarks offered by a "gentleman," or lesser noble. This gentleman has traditionally been treated as the figure of Confucius. The incident is recorded in the *Gongyang Commentary*, Duke Xiang, nineteenth year. Shi Gai was praised by the gentleman for his actions. See Li Xueqin 李學勤, ed., *Chunqiu gongyangzhuan zhushu* 春秋公羊傳注疏, vol. 8, Shisanjing zhushu 十三經注疏 (Beijing: Beijing daxue chubanshe, 1999), 446.

55. *HS* 78.3279–80.

56. There are several examples that substantiate this interpretation. In Wei Xiang's address to Emperor Xuan, he defines the campaign of "righteousness" to be one that "rescues [the population] from chaos and punishes violence." See *HS* 74.3136 and Appendix H, section A. In the *Intrigues*, there is a similar use of "righteousness" in reference to a military endeavor. Su Qin requests that Qi rescue Zhao from a Qin invasion, saying that to do so would show Qi to be "highly righteous" (*gao yi* 高義). Here, also, a "righteous" campaign is one that defends against acts of aggression. See He Jianzhang 何建章, annot., *Zhanguoce zhushi* 戰國策注釋, 9.347; *Chan-Kuo Ts'e*, 216. See also He Jianzhang 何建章, annot.,

Zhanguoce zhushi 戰國策注釋, 15.543; *Chan-Kuo Ts'e*, 258, and He Jianzhang 何建章, annot., *Zhanguoce zhushi* 戰國策注釋, 30.1129; *Chan-Kuo Ts'e*, 539.

57. Taking the reputed ruthless amorality of the First Emperor of Qin and his infamous minister, Li Si, as a prime counterexample, Carl Leban contends that the whole moral vocabulary of the Zhou was merely political propaganda to justify ideologically their military invasions and occupations of other lands. This strategy, he maintains, was borrowed by the rulers of the early Han, particularly after the elevation of the Ru in the imperial court. However, as Martin Kern and others have suggested, the Qin was not nearly as amoral in its tactics or self-presentation as the historians of later dynasties attempted to portray it. See Carl Leban, "Managing Heaven's Mandate: Coded Communication in the Accession of Ts'ao Pei, A.D. 220," in *Ancient China: Studies in Early Civilization*, ed. David T. Roy and Tsuen-hsuin Tsien (Hong Kong: Chinese University Press, 1978), 315–21; and Kern, *The Stele Inscriptions*, 155–96.

58. See Appendices F and H for Liu An's and Wei Xiang's addresses.

59. See Appendix J for Yan You's address.

60. For example, Zou Yang states in his address: "I, Your servant, have heard that flood dragons toss their heads and beat their wings and thus the floating clouds stream out, the mists and rains all gather. The sage kings refine the standards and cultivate virtue, thus the traveling discoursing *shi*-officials will adhere to the norms of social propriety and pine for renown" 臣聞交龍襄首奮翼, 則浮雲出流, 霧雨咸集. 聖王底節修德, 則游談之士歸義思名. See Appendix E, section D.

61. For instance, Liu An states in his address: "I, Your servant, have heard that in the wake of armies and battalions, there will certainly be years of misfortune (i.e., years of poor harvest), by which it is meant that because of each commoner's vaporous emanation of worry and suffering, pressure is put on the harmonizing of *yin* and *yang*, the seminal essence of heaven and earth is stimulated, and thus vaporous emanations of calamity are generated" 臣聞軍旅之後必有凶年, 言民之各以其愁苦之氣薄陰陽之和, 感天地之精, 而災氣為之生也. See Appendix F, section E.

62. Zhufu Yan makes explicit the political costs of lengthy campaigns toward the end of his address: "Now, prolonged warfare leads to upheaval and policies ("matters") that cause suffering lead to a pondering of changes (of rulership). A consequence [of prolonged warfare and policies that cause suffering] will be that the common people in the border regions will be dispirited and miserable and will wish to emigrate from the empire; and the generals and officers will grow suspicious of each other and will negotiate with the enemy" 且夫兵久則變生, 事苦則慮易. 乃使邊境之民獘靡愁苦而有離心, 將吏相疑而外市. See Appendix C, section I. Liu An mentions the natural disorder that proceeds from military campaigns, particularly lengthy ones. See n. 61 above.

63. Liu An: "Your Majesty's virtue joins with Heaven and Earth, Your enlightenment as radiant as the sun and moon, Your charity extended even to the birds and beasts, Your bounty proffered even the grasses and trees. If a single person were to die before reaching the end of his natural life due to cold and hunger (as could happen on a long campaign), Your Majesty would grieve" 陛下德配天地, 明象日月, 恩至禽獸, 澤及草木, 一人有飢寒不終其天年而死者, 為之悽愴於心. See Appendix F, section E. Hou Ying: "Now Your sageliness and virtue blanket vast

areas, Heaven lays the Xiongnu low, and the Xiongnu receive Your life-preserving charity, bowing their heads and coming to court as Your servants" 今聖德廣被,天覆匈奴,匈奴得蒙全活之恩, 稽首來臣. See Appendix I, section E.

64. Wei Xiang: "I, Your servant, have heard that those campaigns that are meant to rescue the nation from chaos and punish violence are called righteous campaigns. When one's campaigns are righteous, one is acting as a true king" 臣聞之, 救亂誅暴, 謂之義兵, 兵義者王. See Appendix H, section A. See also the beginning of Zhao Chongguo's address in Appendix G.

65. See, for example, Appendix C, section D, where Zhufu Yan reports of Li Si speaking to the First Emperor of Qin about exhausting his might in endless, unnecessary and unrighteous military campaigns.

66. See Di Cosmo, *Ancient China and Its Enemies*, 112. Di Cosmo's cynicism is certainly not exceptional. H. Creel and C. Leban also express such. See above p. 247, n. 57.

67. Di Cosmo, *Ancient China and Its Enemies*, 115.

68. Ibid., 116.

69. Ibid., 219. A perhaps more startling example of Di Cosmo's cynicism regarding moral concerns occurs in his descriptions of the arguments against appeasement offered by one of the most prominent of the early Han Confucians, Jia Yi. He states that Jia Yi's position "argues strongly for the restoration of a hierarchical world order and the alignment of foreign policy with the idea of universal emperorship, and yields evidence of the 'ideological' pressures against appeasement present within the Han political debate." Those "ideological" pressures involve issues of ritual, which for Di Cosmo, were merely to differentiate the two camps: those with ritual (the Chinese) and those without. See Di Cosmo, *Ancient China and Its Enemies*, 201–12.

70. Di Cosmo, *Ancient China and Its Enemies*, 219.

71. For instance, Wang Hui, when explaining why Liu Bang did not retaliate against the Xiongnu after his ignominious defeat at Pingcheng, states that he realized that he didn't have the resources to pursue another campaign against them and so, in my translation, "put at ease the heart-mind of All-Under-Heaven." For Di Cosmo, it seems, this last phrase was merely decorative, serving no explanatory function. He seems to believe that Liu Bang was only concerned with the lack of strength, not with the possibility that pursuit of an additional campaign would not have endeared him to his supporters, for whatever reason. See Di Cosmo, *Ancient China and Its Enemies*, 212.

72. See p. 118 above for my translation of this passage.

CHAPTER NINE. HOW DID MINISTERS ERR?

1. Liao Boyuan 廖伯源, *Shizhe guanzhi yanbian* 使者官制演變 (Taipei: Wenjin chubanshe, 2006), 105.

2. One measure to prevent the alteration of documents sent to the court was to mark at the end of the document the total number of graphs, to ensure that nothing was either excised or added. Such is a common feature in the provincial statistics from the end of the Former Han dynasty recorded in the administrative

documents found at Yinwan 尹彎, Jiangsu province. See Giele's article: Ji Annuo 紀安諾, "Yinwan xinchutu xingzheng wenshu de xingzhi yu Handai difan xingzheng" 尹彎新出土行政文書的性質與漢代地方行政, *Dalu zazhi* 大陆杂志 95:3 (1997). See also Giele, *Imperial Decision-Making*, 138. Of course, such measures could not prevent absolutely the outright forgery of a new set of documents; thus, the continued concern on the emperor's part that the information received was false or distorted.

3. Nienhauser, ed., *The Grand Scribe's Records: The Memoirs of Pre-Han China* (Bloomington: Indiana University Press, 1994), 7:235. For another translation of this, see Sima Qian, *Records of the Grand Historian: Qin Dynasty*, 134.

4. Two of the eight appearances of the term in the *Shiji* and the *Hanshu* are used within what seems to have been a familiar maxim: "You will attain nothing if you are (continuously) in doubt about how to handle a matter. You will win no reputation if you are (continuously) in doubt about how to act." 疑事無功, 疑行無名. See *SJ* 43.1807 and 68.2229. For another compelling instance, see *SJ* 122.3139. But there are several substantiating references from other sources. See, for instance, *Liji*, "Quli" *shang*: "Do not positively affirm what you have doubts about; and (when you have no doubts), do not let what you say appear (simply) as your own view" 疑事毋質, 直而勿有. Li Xueqin 李學勤, ed., *Li ji zheng yi* 禮記正義, 3 vols., Shisanjing zhushu 十三經注疏 (Beijing: Beijing daxue chubanshe, 1999), 1:9; *Li Chi: Book of Rites*, trans. James Legge (New York: Oxford University Press, 1885), 1:62. See also *Weishu* 魏書 82.1798.

5. 「今坐朝廷, 讌舉有不當者, 則見短於大臣, 非所以示神明於天下也. 且陛下深拱禁中, 與臣及侍中習法者待事, 事來有以撲之. 如此則大臣不敢奏疑事, 天下稱聖主矣.」See *SJ* 87.2558. I contend that my, and Nienhauser's, translation of *yi* 疑, as "troubling" or "dubious," with the nuance of suspiciousness or questionability, is more accurate than the more general "problematic" or "difficult," as Watson proposes in some of his translations. See Sima Qian, *Records of the Grand Historian: Han Dynasty*, 2:387. Doubt, in early China, was very intimately connected with the suspiciousness of the claim, of the unreliability of the source and the general culture of suspicion. See, for instance, *HS* 53.2419.

6. See *SJ* 6.271.

7. The term is hardly used in much of early Chinese literature. It is used in none of the "Confucian" classics, though it does appear in *Lüshi chunqiu* 16.3: 「瞑士未嘗照, 故未嘗見, 瞑者目無由接也。無由接而言見, 詭。」See *Annals of Lü Buwei*, 381.

8. Though the following instance is not a monarchical response to a debate or address, it very clearly reveals Emperor Yuan's interest in knowing exactly what is going on: "In the first year of the *yung-kuang* era (43 B.C.), frost fell in the spring, the summer was cold, and the sun shone gray and lusterless. The emperor once more issued an order berating the chancellor and imperial secretary on a number of counts, saying, 'Palace attendants returning from the east tell me that the people are in such desperate straits that father and son turn their backs on one another. Are the officials under your jurisdiction hiding the truth and failing to report it to you? Or are those who come from the east exaggerating the true state of affairs? Why should there be such discrepancies? I want to know the truth! It is too soon to predict what kind of harvest we will have this year, but if there should be floods or droughts, the damage will be far from slight. You, the

high officials, are supposed to be able to take steps to prevent future disasters and to remedy those which have already occurred, are you not? I want each of you to give a sincere reply, without fear of saying anything that will offend me!'" 「永光元年, 春霜夏寒, 日青亡光, 上復以詔條責曰:「郎有從東方來者, 言民父子相棄. 丞相、御史案事之吏匿不言邪? 將從東方來者加增之也? 何以錯繆至是? 欲知其實. 方今年歲未可預知也, 即有水旱, 其憂不細. 公卿有可以防其未然, 救其已然者不? 各以誠對, 毋有所諱.」See *HS* 71.3044–45. See also Pan Ku, *Courtier and Commoner*, 169.

9. See Appendix G, p. 201. The late Edward Dreyer offers the following version of the passage: "The Emperor has heard that the General of the Rear says he wants to disband his cavalry and retain [only] 10,000 men to till the fields. What sort of general would plan this? When will the enemy be exterminated? When will our troops gain a decision? If you can figure out why this plan is to our advantage, memorialize again!" See Edward L. Dreyer, "Zhao Chongguo: A Professional Soldier of the Former Han Dynasty," *Journal of Military History* 72, no. 3 (2008): 696. I would like to thank his wife, Dr. June Teufel Dreyer, for sending me a copy of his article.

10. Vogelsang argues that Ying Shao's 應劭 (ca. 140–203/4) comment regarding Ban Gu's appraising Sima Qian's *Records* as a *shilu* 實錄 is the reason for subsequent assertions that Sima Qian was an "objective" historian. Ying Shao defines the *shilu* as that which records "*shishi*" (事實), which are, in Vogelsang's translation, the "facts of the matter." In a footnote, Vogelsang insists that translating the term *shishi* as "facts of the matter" is well supported by its appearances in the *Hanshu*, citing *HS* 25B.1251 and 30.1715. The term appears a total of eight times in the *Hanshu* and twice in the *Records*. Though it is clear that it has something to do with truth, as opposed to erroneous, empty or sycophantic speech, it is not at all clear in its appearances whether it really can be translated as "facts" or "facts of the matter." Indeed, in a very illuminating passage, Zuo Qiuming is said to have "given form" in *Zuozhuan* to the *shishi* noted in *Chunqiu*. See *HS* 30.1715, and Kai Vogelsang, "Some Notions of Historical Judgment in China and the West," in *Historical Truth, Historical Criticism, and Ideology*, ed. Helwig Schmidt-Glintzer et al. (Boston: Brill, 2005), 152, n. 41. Various other scholars also agree that "*shishi*" should be translated as "facts of the matter." See also Kern, "Poetry and Religion," 53–54.

11. See above on p. 138.

12. Indeed, we find the employment of *wu* to be more revelatory in any notion of evidentiary error than many other of terms commonly used to denote error, such as *guo* 過 or *guoshi* 過失, which are more accurately translated as "excess," *cuo* 錯, which should be translated as "confused" or "confusion," or *miu* 謬, which denotes an error in judgment, not in perception or fact.

13. *SJ* 80.2430.

14. *SJ* 89.2583. For alternate translations, see Sima Qian, *Records of the Grand Historian: Han Dynasty*, 1:142; and Nienhauser, *The Grand Scribe's Records: The Memoirs of Han China*, 8:20.

15. See *SJ* 53.2016.

16. See *SJ* 92.2624–25.

17. This distinction would certainly be in keeping with the ancient practice of intentionally misrepresenting embarrassing past events. According to Kern, it

was profoundly irrelevant to the creator whether a bronze inscription or oracle bone record was factually correct. Absolute verifiable accuracy in the representation of events was thus never a culturally enforced norm. See Kern, "Poetry and Religion," 57–58 and 60.

18. See *HS* 10.306–7. See also *HS* 97.3979, 75.3181, 82.3370 for references to the same story.

19. See *HS* 85.3476, 85.3479, 86.3496, 72.3091, 45.2184.

20. Enno Giele notes that, starting in 68 BCE, submissions could be presented directly to the emperor, with the introduction of *fengshi*, or memorials of "sealed matters," submissions that were not screened by the secretariat. "The Biography of Huo Guang" in the *Hanshu* "reveals that direct submissions were not merely a prerogative of the high-ranking officials, but were principally also an option for common people." Yet even these direct submissions "were not really directly communicated from subject to emperor, but had to make use of the eunuch institution of palace secretaries (or perhaps also palace receptionists)," and thus were also subject to tampering. Once instituted under Emperor Xuan, Giele notes, the practice of these direct submissions continued through the Han and into later eras. Though direct submissions were not in the majority of submissions, they were an important source of information about the empire, for as Giele, referring to Liao Boyuan's research, mentions, "they served the emperor in multiple ways by providing a source of more, speedier and better information and by forcing the officials to disclose their attitudes and thereby to keep them under control." See Giele, *Imperial Decision-Making*, 69–71.

21. Kern, "Poetry and Religion," 67.

22. *Zhengyue* 正月, Mao 191. See Li Xueqin 李學勤, *Maoshi zhengyi* 毛詩正義, 706–7. In Zheng Xuan's 鄭玄 (127–200 CE) commentary, he notes that the "first month" is meant to refer to the fourth month of summer; thus the poet's concern about the unnatural weather. Zheng Xuan also defines *e* 訛 as "falsehoods" (*wei* 偽), interpreting the phrase as indicating that moral turpitude is so prevalent that people are using falsehoods to trick each other, leading the king to apply extremely harsh punishments, an unnatural state of affairs that has produced the natural world itself to act unnaturally. Thus, Zheng Xuan concludes, the narrator speaks of the falsehoods of the common people as being especially flagrant. (人以偽言相陷, 人使王行酷暴之刑, 致此災異, 故言亦甚大也。) In this instance, I believe Zheng Xuan's interpretation might be incorrect. In many of the appearances of *jiang* 將 in the *Odes*, its meaning relates to dissemination, offering, presentation—moving about. For instance, in the ode, "Full," the female narrator speaks of her wish to leave with a handsome man, saying, "I regret that I did not go with him." 悔予不將兮 (*Feng* 丰, Mao 88, and Li Xueqin 李學勤, *Maoshi zhengyi* 毛詩正義, 309) In *Zhengyue*, I argue, the narrator is actually speaking to the prevalence of the commoners' remarks, not their falseness. If my argument is correct, clearly, by Zheng Xuan's time, peasant chants were perceived by officials in a very negative light, and often dismissed as falsehoods, a possible indication of the concern about the upheaval that might be brought about were commoners given a voice.

23. For instance, in the *Record of Rites* (*Li ji* 禮記), the "Master" remarks: "If the monarch weighs carefully the words of the common people, then His subjects

will [feel as if they are receiving] Heaven's bestowed favors. If the monarch does not weigh carefully the words of the common people, then they will oppose Him. If His subjects do not [feel as if they are receiving] Heaven's bestowed favors, then disorder will ensue. Therefore if the Gentleman supervises the common people in a trustworthy and humble manner, the common people's reciprocity will be impressive. The *Odes* say, 'In ages past the common people have said that [to understand how to govern], one need inquire with the wood-cutter.'" 子云：上酌民言，則下天上施；上不酌民言，則犯也；下不天上施，則亂也。故君子信讓以涖百姓，則民之報禮重。詩云：先民有言，詢於芻蕘。See Li Xueqin 李學勤, *Li ji zheng yi* 禮記正義, 1406–7; and *Li Chi: Book of Rites*, 2:288.

24. *HHS* 57.1846. In note 6, there is a fascinating reference to a passage from the *Liezi* that might offer further support for my claims: "Liezi said, 'Previously Yao managed All-Under-Heaven for fifty years and did not know if it was managed properly or in disorder. Yao thus traveled in disguise about the thoroughfares. [On one] a young boy chanted, 'If [the emperor] pacifies our common people, there will be no limit to the reaches of your [bounty]. [The commoners] do not comprehend, do not understand [governance], [they just] follow the emperor's rules.'" (列子曰：『昔堯理天下五十年，不知天下理亂. 堯乃微服遊於康衢。兒童謠曰：『立我蒸人，莫非爾極，不識不知，順帝之則。』』) The passage is somewhat different and more expansive in the received *Liezi*：「堯治天下五十年，不知天下治歟，不治歟？不知億兆之願戴己歟？不願戴己歟？顧問左右，左右不知。問外朝，外朝不知。問在野，在野不知。堯乃微服游於康衢，聞兒童謠曰：『立我蒸民，莫匪爾極。不識不知，順帝之則。』堯喜問曰：『誰教爾為此言？』童兒曰：『我聞之大夫。』問大夫。大夫曰：『古詩也。』」See *Liezi*, "Zhongni" 《列子·仲尼》in Yang Bojun 楊伯峻, ed., *Liezi jishi* 列子集釋 (Beijing: Zhonghua shuju, 1979), 143–44.

25. In his address, Li Xun urges Wang to make "broad inquiries" (*bo wen* 博問), emphasizing not only the quality but the number of people Wang formerly employed who could have offered divergent perspectives: "The scholar-officials are the great treasures of the nation and lie at the root of its accomplishment and reputation. You, General, had within your gates nine feudal lords and twenty men of the Red-Wheeled Chariot. Since the Han Dynasty arose, your ministers have been well-treated and very numerous . . . until now."「夫士者，國家之大寶，功名之本也。將軍一門九侯，二十朱輪，漢興以來，臣子貴盛，未嘗至此.」See *HS* 75.3180.

26. *HS* 75.3179.

27. Duke Mu of Qin was advised by the "yellow-haired" Jian Shu 蹇叔 not to wage an attack on the state of Zheng. His troops, led by Meng Mingshi 孟明視, Xi Qishu 西乞述, and Bai Yibing 白乙丙 fell prey to a ruse and were routed by Jin troops led by Duke Xiang 襄 of Jin.

28. *HS* 75.3179; *HSBZ* 75.22b.

29. *HS* 75.3180.

30. 「《書》曰『曆象日月星辰』，此言仰視天文，俯查地理，觀日月消息，候星辰行伍，揆山川變動，參人民繇俗，以制法度，考禍福。」*HS* 75.3180.

31. 「舉錯靜逆，咎敗將至，徵兆為之先見.」*HS* 75.3180.

32. *HS* 75.3182.

33. As Kai Vogelsang notes, "*Kaoxin* 考信 is the word used by Sima Qian, not *kaoshi* 考實. Indeed, *xin*, 'trustworthiness, reliability', seems to have been

the most prominent epithet for historiography in Han times." Vogelsang, "Some Notions of Historical Judgment," 155.

34. 伍子胥諫曰:「夫越, 腹心之病, 今信其浮辭詐偽而貪齊.」 *SJ* 66.2179. Because the trust expressed in these arguments is clearly not simply a personal trust, I argue that, in instances relating to the quality of the information or arguments received, a more precise translation should actually be "belief." Indeed, I might suggest that *xin* 信 would regularly be better translated as "belief" or "believe" to accommodate this application, whether as in "believing in" someone or "believing" a statement. For other instances of *xin* being used in terms of a "belief" in a statement, see *SJ* 79.2425 and *SJ* 83.2473.

35. See, for instance, *HS* 35.1907, *HS* 49.2296, *HS* 76.3235, and *HS* 95.3851.

36. See *SJ* 77.2384, where Sima Qian states that the King of Wei, having repeatedly heard slanderous remarks, "could not not believe them" 不能不信.

37. The entire sentence is as follows:「明主之道, 己喜則求其所納, 己怒則察其所搆, 論於已變之後, 以得毀譽公私之徵。」See *Hanfeizi*, "Bajing," in *Hanfeizi xinjiaozhu* 韓非子新校注, 1075.

38. All of these negative developments were obviously being blamed on the emperor's style of governance.

39. See Mao 257, "Sang rou"《桑柔》, Li Xueqin 李學勤, *Maoshi zhengyi* 毛詩正義, 706–7. My translation borrows from Watson, *The Book of Songs*, 268. The last two phrases are not in the received text.

40. See Mao 235, "Wen Wang"《文王》, Li Xueqin 李學勤, *Maoshi zhengyi* 毛詩正義, 706–7.

41. See *HS* 51.2333.

42. Emperor Wen, at one point, vows he will not punish those who are extremely direct with him: "There are many who are able to speak forthrightly and remonstrate extensively. In the future, they can use such criticisms to correct me without [fear of] being arrested."「能直言極諫者, 各有人數, 將以匡朕之不逮。」See *HS* 49.2290.

43. Of course, our consciousness of a broad, and sometime ironic, charge of slander, even by the historians themselves, must force us to reconsider its veracity. In other words, we cannot assume that the statements behind the charges of slander were false . . . nor can we assume they were true. Like the monarch, we must look to the possible motives behind its assertion or denial.

44. See *HS* 49.2290.

45. See Kern, "Poetry and Religion," 54.

46. See *HS* 60.2676. Of course, an additional subtext is that, like Wang Feng, both of these (as with the third figure with which Du Qin makes an analogy, Tian Fen 田蚡), were open to the charge of attempting to claim too much power.

47. See *HS* 68.2936; *HSBZ* 69.4a, 1298. The address was submitted on behalf of the king of Yan, Liu Dan 劉旦, Emperor Zhao's half-brother, who resented Huo Guang's influence.

48. *Hanfeizi*, "Bajing," in *Hanfeizi xinjiaozhu* 韓非子新校注, 1074.

49.「言必有報, 說必責用也。」*Hanfeizi xinjiaozhu* 韓非子新校注, 1075.

CHAPTER TEN. A DIVERSITY OF EVIDENCE

1. See Max Weber, *Essays in Sociology*, trans. and ed. H. H. Gerth and C. W. Mills (New York: Oxford University Press, 1946), 196–244.

2. As evidence for this interpretation heralding the bureaucratically supported commitment to research, adherents to this line of appraisal have Sima Qian's remark that, because of their official position, he and his father, who initiated the project of the historical records completed by Sima Qian, had access to imperial collections of historical documents. See *SJ* 130.3296.

3. Nylan, "Sima Qian," 204.

4. E. A. Kracke Jr., "The Chinese and the Art of Government," in *The Legacy of China*, ed. Raymond Dawson (New York: Oxford University Press, 1964), 319. Italics mine.

5. Loewe, *A Biographical Dictionary*, 28.

6. Ibid., 703.

7. Ibid., 747.

8. Indeed, judging from a more recent essay, this seems clearly to be the case. See Loewe, "The Western Han Army."

9. See page 67 ff.

10. And indeed, as mentioned earlier, Loewe suspects the difference may simply be due to different classes of individual included in each calculation.

11. He Jianzhang 何建章, annot., *Zhanguoce zhushi* 戰國策注釋, 24.907; *Chan-Kuo Ts'e*, 436. The address can also be found, with minor variations, at *SJ* 44.1857–62.

12. Zhao Chongguo provides one of the few more neutral appraisals of the psychology of foreign tribes. See Appendix G, section C.

13. See Appendix I, section E.

14. See Appendix F, section C. Zhao Chongguo also offers a negative appraisal of the Qiang, saying that, as a result of their deprivations, they will fall to fighting among themselves and robbing Chinese commoners. See Appendix G, section H.

15. See Appendix C, section H.

16. See Appendix J, section A.

17. See Appendix C, section D.

18. See Appendix J, sections H and I.

19. See Appendix F, section D.

20. See Appendix H, section B.

21. See Appendix J, sections E and K.

22. See Appendix F, section D.

23. See Appendix C, section G.

24. See Appendix C, section I.

25. See Appendix A.

26. As I argued at the beginning of Chapter Six, each discussion articulates a particular truth of the matter, for assessments of the good of the state vary, as is what is emphasized as being central to its realization. See pp. 73–74.

27. The claims for which there were no objections are listed in Chapter Six, pp. 86–89.

28. See Appendix C, section D.
29. See p. 128.
30. See p. 159.
31. See page 66 ff.
32. See pp. 79–80 for the fourth and fifth sections of Su Qin's address and pp. 83–84 for the fifth and sixth of Zhang Yi's.
33. See Appendix A.
34. See Appendix B, section C.
35. See Appendix I.
36. See Appendix G, section A.
37. See Appendix G, section D.
38. The types of doubts raised by the emperor to some degree substantiate what I had claimed in a previous chapter in regard to Liu Jing's address to the High Emperor, that is, that relevant concrete considerations are not in themselves sufficiently convincing to the emperor. See p. 106 ff.
39. The emperor's comments can be found just prior to Zhao Chongguo's, located at Appendix G, section F.
40. This remark can be found just prior to Zhao Chongguo's address. See Appendix G.
41. Again, see Loewe, *A Biographical Dictionary*, 703, and p. 156 above.
42. See Appendix G, section F.
43. See Appendix G, section H.
44. See Appendix G, section I.
45. See Appendix I.
46. For Chao Cuo's address, see Appendix D.
47. See Chapter Three, p. 24.
48. *HS* 45.2163. Italics mine.
49. See Chapter Seven, pp. 99–105.
50. This follows A. C. Graham's analysis of pre-Han texts, in which *qing* as a noun means "facts," and as an adjective, "genuine" or "essential." In Graham's definition, "[t]he *qing* of X is what X cannot lack if it is to be called 'X'." Hansen, in a critique of Graham, offers the definition of "reality feedback" or "reality input." Hansen elaborates that *qing* "are all reality-induced discrimination [*sic*] or distinction-making reactions in *dao* executors." This explains why *qing* came to mean both "fact" and "passion," because in it "external reality" and "internal response" meet. See A. C. Graham, "The Meaning of Ch'ing 情," in *Studies in Chinese Philosophy and Philosophical Literature* (Albany, NY: SUNY Press, 1986), 59 and 63; Chad Hansen, "Qing (Emotions) in Pre-Buddhist Chinese Thought," in *Emotions in Asian Thought*, ed. Joel Marks and Roger T. Ames (Albany, NY: SUNY Press, 1995), 207, n. 24 and 201; and Martin W. Huang, *Desire and Fictional Narrative in Late Imperial China* (Cambridge, MA: Harvard University Asia Center, 2001), 31–32.
51. *Lüshi chunqiu* 17.1; *Annals of Lü Buwei*, 406–7.
52. See p. 55 ff.
53. See Chapter Six, pp. 74–76.
54. Wallacker, "Han Confucianism," 223.

APPENDICIES

1. All translations presume the explanations in the commentarial notes of the *HS*. Additional commentaries, whether they be in the *HSBZ*, Chen Zhi's, or Yang Shuda's, whenever they play a significant role in my translations and interpretations of these texts, will be specifically noted.

2. Because of the discussion of the number of troops below, I take this statement to be referring to Han Xin and Zhang Er's 張耳 troops, not Chen Yu and Zhao Xie's 趙歇 troops, as Watson presumes in his translation. See Sima Qian, *Records of the Grand Historian: Han Dynasty*, 1:168–69.

3. Compare with the following passage in the *Sunzi: The Art of Warfare*: "Therefore the art of using troops is this: When ten times the enemy strength, surround him; when five times, attack him; when double, engage him; when you and the enemy are equally matched, be able to divide him; when you are inferior in numbers, be able to take the defensive; and when you are no match for the enemy, be able to avoid him. Thus what serves as secure defense against a small army will only be captured by a large one." 故用兵之法. 十則圍之, 五則攻之, 倍則戰之, 敵則能分之, 少則能守之, 不若則能避之。故小敵之堅, 大敵之擒也。; Ames, *Sun-Tzu*, 110–12.

4. Zhao Tuo turned against the Qin and made himself an independent ruler in Southern Yue; the Qin general Zhang Han deserted, joining an army of rebellious nobles.

5. I am unsure about this entire passage being one single citation, or even being a citation rather than a summary of another text, particularly when a very similar passage can be found in the *Guanzi* that does not include judgments of relative military might as the passage above does. I thus have treated the summary judgments as Chao Cuo's interpolations. Here is the entirety of the relevant *Guanzi* section, which distinguishes itself from previous and later sections of the essay by the repeated use of *tong shi*, "is of the same substance as": 得眾而不得其心, 則與獨行者同實; 兵不完利, 與無操者同實; 甲不堅密, 與俴者同實; 弩不可以及遠, 與短兵同實; 射而不能中, 與無矢者同實; 中而不能入, 與無鏃者同實; 將徒人, 與伐(儌)者同實; 短兵待遠矢與坐而待死者同實。 In W. Allyn Rickett's translation: "If one gains control over the masses but does not win their hearts, it is the same as if one were acting alone. If the weapons are not well-made and sharp, it is the same as being empty-handed. If shields are not strong and tightly woven, it is the same as being without armor. If crossbows cannot shoot a long distance, it is the same as merely having a dagger. If the archers are not able to hit the target, it is the same as being without arrows. If they hit the mark but cannot pierce it, it is the same as having arrows without heads. To command untrained men is the same as being without armor. To oppose long-distance arrows with mere daggers is the same as sitting and waiting for death." See "Canhuan" 參患 in Yan Changyao 顏昌嶢, annot., *Guanzi jiaoshi* 管子校釋 (Changsha: Yuelu shushe 嶽麓書社, 1996), 10.28, 244–45; *Guanzi*, trans. W. Allyn Rickett (Boston: Cheng and Tsui, 2001), 396.

6. Again, a very similar passage can be found in the same essay of the *Guanzi* as the previous section. I quote the entirety of the section from the *Guanzi*, which is distinguished by the parallel logic of a series of statements: 故凡兵有大論, 必先論其器、論其士、論其將、論其主。故曰器濫惡不利者, 以其士予人也; 士不可用者,

以其將予人也；將不知兵者，以其主予人也；主不積務於兵者，以其國予人也。In W. Allyn Rickett's translation: "Therefore, whenever there is a major inspection of the armed forces, it is first necessary to inspect their weapons, and then inspect the troops, their generals, and their ruler. Therefore it is said, 'Having weapons that are of very poor quality and not sharp is to give one's troops to others. Having troops that are useless is to give one's generals to the enemy. Having generals who do not understand arms is to give the ruler to the enemy. Failing to stockpile and pay attention to arms is to give the state to others." See "Canhuan" 參患 in Yan Changyao 顏昌嶢 annot., *Guanzi jiaoshi* 管子校釋, 10.28, 245; *Guanzi*, 396–97.

7. Guo Moruo 郭沫若 offers the following remark in his *Zhongguo shigao* 《中國史稿》 about the term *caiguan*:「西漢初年，地方有經常訓練的預備兵。山地或少馬的地方多步兵，叫做'材官。'」See *Hanyu da cidian suoyin ben* 漢語大辭典縮印本 (Shanghai: Hanyu dacidian chubanshe, 1997), 2466, under the entry for *caiguan* 材官.

8. Michael Loewe renders this account: "During Wendi's reign Liu Pi sent his Heir Apparent to visit Chang'an [the capital city], where he was in attendance on Liu Qi 劉啟, the imperial Heir Apparent who was in time to be known as [Emperor Jing]. The two men engaged in drinking and gaming . . . In the course of an incident which was evidently not marked by courtesy, the imperial Heir Apparent struck Liu Pi's son with his gaming board and killed him . . . The dispatch of the dead man's body back to Wu for burial added insult to the injuries that the [King of Wu] had suffered; as a member of the Liu family he felt that his son had a claim to be buried at Chang'an, and he sent the body back there for the purpose." Loewe, *A Biographical Dictionary*, 335.

9. The history of the rebellion, as represented by Loewe, is as follows: Several kingdoms, including Zhao, Chu, and Jiaoxi 胶西, had under Emperor Jing "suffered the loss of territory as a punishment for the crimes that the kings were alleged to have committed; expecting similar treatment, Liu Pi determined to launch a rebellion. He sent Ying Gao 應高, his Counsellor of the Palace (Zhong Dafu 中大夫) to negotiate verbally with Liu Ang 劉卬, king of Jiaoxi 胶西, who was known as a man of military prowess. He urged Liu Ang to take the lead, pointing out that he too stood in danger of being deprived of some of his territory . . . Not content with Liu Ang's verbal agreement, Liu Pi [the king of Wu] journeyed personally to Jiaoxi to seal a compact with the king. There followed the promise of the kings of Qi, Zichuan 淄川, Jiaodong 胶東 and Ji'nan 濟南 to join the cause of the two kings; and with the help of Chu and Zhao, and the somewhat ineffective and short-lived participation of Qi and Jibei 濟北 [all four of which are mentioned in the address], the rebellion was started in 154. Aged sixty-two at the time, Liu Pi sent round attempting to recruit the help of some of the other kings, in the hope of planning their co-ordinated attack on various localities. In one case Nan Yue 南越 was asked to take part; and in accordance with the terms of an agreement with Zhao and Yan, Xiongnu 匈奴 forces would assist in a drive right into the metropolitan area." Loewe, *A Biographical Dictionary*, 336.

10. This address was delivered probably in 155 or 154 BCE, just before Wu's planned rebellion. It is very difficult to interpret because Zou Yang is obliquely referring to the King of Wu's plans to rebel with the pretense that the King of Wu wishes to help the Han emperor defend the Han empire against the incursion of the Xiongnu and Yue foreign tribes into Zhao and Wu. In actuality, the

Xiongnu and Nanyue tribes and the border kingdoms of Qi, Zhao, and Huainan have joined Wu in the plot, the border kingdoms because of the resentments they hold toward the Han imperial household, as Zou Yang will later mention. Commentators often disagree about the exact meaning of Zou Yang's doubletalk and sometimes provide viable alternatives. Thus my translation must here remain somewhat provisional.

11. Here I follow Ru Chun's 如淳 (fl. 230 CE) interpretation. Wang Xianqian 王先謙 also notes that this passage as it appears in the *Wenxuan* 文選 has a *ren* ("person") character above *bu fan*, which suggests the sentence is referring to legal matters. See *HSBZ* 51.9a.

12. Wang Xianqian 王先謙 (1840–1917 CE) remarks that Zou Yang is using the example of Qin to demonstrate that wealth and power are not enough to maintain one's hegemony. He notes the parallel between the ten thousand households not coming to each other's aid and the comment at the beginning of section C in which Zou Yang expresses the worry that the necessary rescue forces will not come in time, or at all, to help Wu. See *HSBZ* 51.9b.

13. Liu Fengshi 劉奉世 comments that Zou Yang already knew that Zhao had made an alliance with the Xiongnu tribes and Wu with the Yue tribes in their plot. But Zou Yang couldn't speak about this openly so he instead used the artifice of speaking about the Xiongnu attacking Zhao and the Yue attacking Wu. Troops loyal to the empire would not be able to "rescue" them, partially because, as he discusses at the end of section B, the leaders of various kingdoms are resentful of the imperial family, as Liu Pi himself is. See *HSBZ* 51.9b.

14. According to Ying Shao 應劭, after King You of Zhao 趙幽王 (Liu You 劉友) was allowed to starve on the order of Empress Lü, Emperor Wen gave Zhao to Liu You's eldest son, Liu Sui 劉遂, excepting the Hejian area, which he gave to Liu Sui's younger brother, Liu Biqiang 劉辟彊. After Liu Biqiang's son produced no heirs, the kingdom of Hejian was abolished by the emperor and Liu Sui pursued reincorporating Hejian back into Zhao. Having suffered other losses of territory, as a result of Chao Cuo's proposals to the throne to reduce the strength of some of the kingdoms, in 154 BCE he joined Liu Pi's rebellion. Though Zou Yang is here merely referring to the resentment Liu Sui harbored toward Emperor Wen for giving Hejian to his younger brother, he is making oblique reference to Liu Pi's own plot. See *HSBZ* 51.9b, and Loewe, *A Biographical Dictionary*, 363.

15. This reference to the six Qi monarchs relates to an intrigue surrounding Liu Fei 劉肥, King Daohui of Qi 齊悼惠王. The following is Loewe's explanation: "In 197 [Liu Fei] attended court to pay homage to Gaodi. On the next occasion when [he] did so (193), to pay homage to his half-brother Huidi, the latter treated him with the courtesy appropriate to the members of a family rather than with that suitable between sovereign and subject. Such laxity angered the Empress Lü, who attempted to have Liu Fei poisoned but at the last moment prevented this from taking effect, for fear that Huidi would be killed at the same time. Realising the dangers of his situations, Liu Fei doubted whether he would be allowed to escape from Chang'an alive. He succeeded in doing so only after mollifying the empress, by making over the lands of Chengyang as an estate for her only other child, her daughter Lu Yuan Gongzhu 魯元公主"; Loewe, *A Biographical Dictionary*, 295. Rendering both Emperor Hui and Empress Lü as the targets

of the resentment of Liu Fei's six sons makes sense in the context of Zou Yang's other historical references, for then Zou Yang's references indicate that there has been deep resentment toward each and every member of the imperial household and that the rebellions against them have, in each case, led to the demise of the plotters. Zou Yang appears to be warning Liu Pi, King of Wu, that he will meet with the same fate. The six sons to whom Zou Yang is referring are as follows: Liu Jianglu 劉將閭, who was king of Qi proper; Liu Zhi 劉志, king of Jibei 濟北; Liu Biguang 劉辟光, king of Jinan 濟南; Liu Xian 劉賢, king of Zichuan 甾川; Liu Ang 劉卬 as king of Jiaoxi 膠西; and Liu Xiongqu 劉熊渠 as king of Jiaodong 膠東. See Loewe, *A Biographical Dictionary*, 341. Loewe erroneously cites them there as sons of Liu Xiang, though he elsewhere cites them correctly as sons of Liu Fei. It should also be noted that Liu Xiang 劉襄, another of Liu Fei's sons, who succeeded his father in 188 as king of Qi, participated in a failed plot to set himself on the throne after the Lü family was ousted from power on the death of Empress Lü. The plot resulted in the accession of his uncle, Liu Heng 劉恆 (aka Emperor Wen), to the throne. See Loewe, *A Biographical Dictionary*, 375–76. See the following footnote for more of the history of Liu Xiang's attempt to take the throne.

16. The king of Chengyang to whom this reputedly refers is Liu Xi 劉喜, the grandson of Liu Fei, King Daohui of Qi, mentioned in the previous footnote. He, his father, Liu Zhang 劉章, and his father's younger brother, Liu Xingju 劉興居, were instrumental in removing the Lü family from power after the death of Empress Lü. Emperor Wen, who succeeded Empress Lü, originally was planning on making Liu Zhang the ruler of Zhao and Liu Xingju the ruler of Liang but instead, according to Meng Kang 孟康 (ca. 180–260), because Liu Zhang and Liu Xingju had previously wished to establish their elder brother, Liu Xiang 劉襄, the then king of Qi, as the Han emperor, Emperor Wen, changed his mind and made Liu Zhang and Liu Xingju rulers of two commanderies. In 178 BCE, Liu Zhang was made king of Chengyang, a part of the state of Qi that "had at one time been detached from and had recently been restored to Qi," and Liu Xingju the king of Jibei 濟北, another part of the kingdom of Qi. Jibei, and thus Liu Xingju, is mentioned below at the end of section F. See Loewe, *A Biographical Dictionary*, 406. Lu and Bo were districts (*xian*) within the kingdom of Jibei. These districts are meant to refer to Liu Xingju's death in the uprising he staged, an uprising, it is suggested, that Liu Xingju pursued because of his resentment toward Emperor Wen regarding the emperor's decision not to give him and his brother, Liu Zhang, rulership over the states of Liang and Zhao, which he must have felt they deserved after helping to neutralize the threat of the Lü family. See Loewe, *A Biographical Dictionary*, 288, and *HSBZ* 51.10a.

17. Yan Shigu (581–645 CE) identifies the three as the kings of Huainan, Hengshan 衡山, and Jibei 濟北. Zhang Yan 張晏 states that it was the three sons of Liu Chang 劉長, King Li 厲 of Huainan, who were musing upon their father's demotion and murder. (See *HS* 51.2339, n. 11.) The three sons of Liu Chang 劉長, King Li of Huainan, to whom this remark is referring are Liu An 劉安, King of Huainan; Liu Si 劉賜, King of Hengshan; and Liu Bo 劉勃, King of Jibei (and former King of Hengshan). Similar to Liu Pi, the King of Wu, Liu Chang planned a rebellion against the throne, occupied by his father, Liu Bang, with the help of the Xiongnu and Yue tribes. Liu Chang was sent into exile in Shu 蜀. He

was transported in a locked van. "Afraid that he might become violent and pass beyond their control, the officials responsible for the journey refused to unlock the van, and when they had reached no further than Yong 雍 their prisoner died of starvation"; Loewe, *A Biographical Dictionary*, 272. Zou Yang's suggestion here is that Liu Chang's three sons were resentful of Emperor Wen.

18. Zou Yang's "official" explicit story line is that he is worried the states just previously mentioned, because of their resentment toward the throne, will not assist Wu in driving back the invading foreign tribes; but, according to Yan Shigu, what Zou Yang is trying to subtly communicate here is that if Wu rebels, the emperor will come to Wu to fight and even if Wu's allies were to wish to come to Wu's aid, they would not dare to, for fear of the Han empire's reprisal. See *HSBZ* 51.10a for Wang Xianqian's concurring elaboration.

19. Yang Shuda comments that by *kui* 窺 ("scout out"), Zou Yang is really saying that the Xiongnu will come to help Zhao. See Yang Shuda 楊樹達, *Hanshu kuiguan* 漢書窺管, 307.

20. Yang Shuda believes that, although there is extended debate about the location of Qingyang and whether it denotes a location on land or a waterway, Qingyang is clearly not located near Changsha, as Su Lin 蘇林 (fl. 220–65) avers, but is instead is located in Wu. This sentence is meant to communicate subtly Zou Yang's knowledge of Yue's alliance with Wu. Qian Mu makes a similar point. See Qian Mu 錢穆, *Shiji diming kao* 史記地名考, 615; and Yang Shuda 楊樹達, *Hanshu kuiguan* 漢書窺管, 306–7.

21. The king of Liang at this time was Liu Wu 劉武, the son of Emperor Wen. He was made king of Huaiyang in 175 BCE; and then in 168 BCE, he was transferred to be king of Liang on the death of Liu Yi 劉揖 in 168. He was, according to Loewe, "unswervingly" loyal to the Han imperial government at the time of Liu Pi's rebellion. See Loewe, *A Biographical Dictionary*, 367.

22. The current king of Huaiyang was Liu Yu 劉餘, the son of Emperor Jing and his lesser consort, Cheng Ji 程姬. He was nominated king of Huaiyang in 155 BCE. See Loewe, *A Biographical Dictionary*, 402. Naturally, neither Liu Wu, king of Liang, nor Liu Yu, king of Huaiyang, would be sending troops to assist Liu Pi in the rebellion.

23. Zou Yang here is revealing the strategy by which Liu Pi's allies can be hamstrung by the Chinese central government through the cutting off of their supplies. He veils his understanding of this possibility, as Su Lin 蘇林 notes, by asserting, as would follow under his "official" line, that the Xiongnu and Yue would respond by penetrating into the empire even more deeply, which would, if Liu Pi were indeed worried about preserving the Han empire, indeed be very worrisome. Wang Xianqian argues that the "great state" to which Zou Yang is referring is either Wu's ally, the state of Zhao, or itself. Were Emperor Jing to cut off the western portion of the Yellow River, this would, in fact, contribute to cutting Zhao off from its allies in Qi and would contribute toward the defeat of the rebellion. Wang Xianqian also argues that when Zou Yang is speaking of the Yue people having their supplies cut off, he means the people of the state of Wu and that, were the "great state" the state of Zhao, "assist" should be taken as "defend against," "block." Because of these measures, neither Zhao nor Wu would have the resources or support to move inland. Finally, Wang Xianqian

points out that Liu Wu, the king of Liang, was formerly the king of Huaiyang. See *HSBZ* 51.10b–11a.

24. Here I follow Yang Shuda, who argues that 襄 should be read as 驤, which the *Shuowen* defines as "[the action of] a horse raising and lowering [its head]." See Yang Shuda 楊樹達, *Hanshu kuiguan* 漢書窺管, 307.

25. Though he offers the pretense of speaking about himself, Zou Yang is obviously advising Liu Pi to be patient and diplomatic, not to resort to violent means to redress his grievances with the Han empire.

26. Though Zou Yang pretends to be searching for assistance for Wu in its fight against the foreign tribes, he is actually saying that he has attempted to speak in favor of Wu at court, to resolve Wu's grievances.

27. I follow here Yan Shigu's 顏師古 (581–645 CE) interpretation. See *HS* 51.2340, n. 5.

28. The "visions" to which Zou Yang is recommending the king of Wu pay attention to, I suspect, are Zou Yang's own vision.

29. The osprey, of course, is the Han central government; the hundred gathered birds of prey, the rebels.

30. According to Wang Xianqian, Zou Yang is actually referring to the kingdom of Dai 代, which had been conquered by Zhao in the late Warring States period. Upon the accession of Liu Bang to the throne, Dai was given to Liu Pi's father, Liu Xi, in 201 BCE and included in its borders three commanderies: Yunzhong 雲中, Yanmen 雁門, and Dai. In 200 BCE, Xiongnu tribesmen attacked Dai. Liu Xi fled and, though he survived, was demoted to the marquisate of Heyang 郃陽侯. See *HSBZ* 51.11a and Loewe, *A Biographical Dictionary*, 370. The troubled kingdom of Dai also figured in the debate between Wang Hui and Han Anguo discussed previously. See Chapter Eight, p. 115.

31. Their being dressed in black (or perhaps, as Wang Xianqian suggests, a very dark yellow) might mean that they are foreign tribesmen, likely Xiongnu. This would make sense in the context of their not being able to save King You of Zhao, Liu You 劉友, from being allowed to starve on the orders of Empress Lü, just as they wouldn't be able to save his son, Liu Sui 劉遂, the current king of Zhao and a participant in Liu Pi's plot. See n. 14 above.

32. The Cong Pavilion was a pavilion in the king of Zhao's palace. It appears that the Xiongnu soldiers were deeply involved in the ceremonies and government of Zhao and thus were trusted allies.

33. According to Yan Shigu, Liu You's "deep misgivings" is meant to refer to his murder by Empress Lü.

34. This is possibly a reference to Liu Chang's discovered plot to launch a revolt against the Han empire with seventy of his followers at Gukou 谷口, an area east of several mountains, lying close to the Han capital.

35. Again, the implication is that Liu Chang's followers, his "allies," could not save him from his untimely death on the road to Shu. See n. 17 above.

36. Both are legendary strongmen of great courage. See *HS* 51.2341, n. 6.

37. Emperor Wen's "taking possession" of the Hangu Pass is merely symbolic of his taking control of the capital area, of becoming emperor.

38. Liu Xingju, Liu Fei's son, was ennobled in 182 BCE as the Marquis of Dongmou by Empress Lü. Emperor Wen made him the king of Jibei in 178

BCE. See n. 16 above. See also Loewe, *A Biographical Dictionary*, 388; and Cang Xiuliang 倉修良, ed., *Hanshu cidian* 漢書辭典 (Shandong: Shandong jiaoyu chubanshe, 1996), 357.

39. Liu Zhang 劉章, another of Liu Fei's sons, was ennobled in 186 as the Marquis of Zhuxu by Empress Lü. Emperor Wen made him the king of Chengyang in 179 BCE. Both he and his brother Liu Zhang were being sent off to Qi as the kings of Chengyang and Jibei to thank them for their contribution to overcoming the Lü family. See Cang Xiuliang 倉修良, *Hanshu cidian* 漢書辭典, 249.

40. I here follow Liu Fengshi's interpretation. See *HSBZ* 51.12a.

41. Based on Liu Fengshi's interpretation, Wang Xianqian suggests that Yifu is the style name (*zi*) of Liu Fei and that Emperor Wen is sending his sons off to be kings in the Qi region in order to aggrandize Liu Fei's sons assistance in helping him to take the throne. See *HSBZ* 51.12a.

42. The king of Liang to whom Zou Yang is referring is Liu Yi 劉揖 who was appointed to Liang in 179 BCE. See Loewe, *A Biographical Dictionary*, 367.

43. The king of Dai to whom Zou Yang is referring is Liu Wu 劉武 who took over Dai in 178 BCE. See Cang Xiuliang 倉修良, *Hanshu cidian* 漢書辭典, 949.

44. This is Liu Xingju, discussed above in n. 16.

45. This, coincidentally or not, is also the place where Liu Chang, King Li of Huainan, was supposed to have died of starvation. See n. 17 above.

46. Xinyuan Ping was an astrologer who was said to have advised Liu Chang, King Li of Huainan, and Liu Xingju, King of Jinan, to rebel against the empire. See Loewe, *A Biographical Dictionary*, 615.

47. Here Zou Yang seems to suggest that, if Liu Pi continues to act against the imperial throne, even if he decides not to rebel, he may, like Liu Sui before him, have his territory reduced.

48. Zhang Han was a Qin general who made a compact with the Chu rebel leader, Xiang Yu, at the end of the Qin dynasty and became king of Yong 雍. In 206 he was defeated by Liu Bang, then the king of Han 漢, and fled to Feiqiu 廢丘. He died when his city was flooded and then overcome by Han forces. See Loewe, *A Biographical Dictionary*, 681–82.

49. Here my translation follows Yang Shuda's commentary in Yang Shuda 楊樹達, *Hanshu kuiguan* 漢書窺管, 383.

50. Huainan bordered the southern areas occupied by the Yue peoples, so it was natural for their clerks to have some knowledge of Yue lands.

51. Wang Xianqian reports Qi Zhaonan 齊召南 (1703–68) as stating that, according to a treatise (presumably on geography), Yugan 餘干 was actually Yuhan 餘汗 and was a part of the Yuzhang 預章 Commandery, which lay within the borders of the kingdom of Huainan. It was actually not an area belonging to the Yue. The Yugan district, where the Yue people went to work the fields for supplies, lay adjacent to the border. In the comment to the next line of the text in the *Hanshu buzhu*, Wang Xianqian 王先謙 also reports Shen Qinhan 沈欽韓 (1775–1832) as stating that the Yue boats could not travel down these mountain tributaries so they would first have to build their boats to the north side (*bie*) of the mountain (須於嶺北別治船). This hypothesis finds some confirmation in the *History of the Jin Dynasty* (*Jinshu* 晉書) in which Xu Daofu 徐道覆 (presumably under the command of Luxun 盧循), before entering into and marauding the area

of the Central States, first cut trees and built boats in the area of the Yuzhang Commandery. See *HSBZ* 64A.5b; *Jinshu* 100.2634–35

52. Wang Xianqian reports that Qian Daxin 錢大昕 (1728–1804 CE) avers that *neng* has the same meaning as *nai* 耐. See *HSBZ* 64A.5b.

53. Wang Xianqian: *Dan* should be taken as *sheng* 盛. See *HSBZ* 64A.6a.

54. Wang Xianqian reports that Song Qi 宋祁 (998–1061 CE) mentions that in the *Zhe* 浙 edition of the *History of the Former Han*, *sheng* is substituted by *chong* 蟲, "insects." See *HSBZ* 64A.6a.

55. Wang Xianqian reports that, as Gu Yanwu 顧炎武 (1613–81 CE) shows, this younger brother is later identified as Yushan 餘善. See *HSBZ* 64A.6a and 8b. The absence of this identification is explained by the possibility that Liu An did not know his name at the time he submitted this address to the throne. If such is the case, it would speak for the possibility that, at least in some cases, these addresses were not created out of whole cloth by the author(s) of the histories, but were instead at times copied from archival documents.

56. Reading *cong* 從 as *song* 聳, as Wang Niansun suggests. See *HSBZ* 64A.7a.

57. Wang Xianqian 王先謙 states that *bu bei* 不備 should be read as meaning "sustaining injury." (不備謂有損傷) See *HSBZ* 64A.7b.

58. Yan Shigu suggests that this should be "hundred," not "thousand." See *HSBZ* 64A.7b.

59. Yan Shigu states that the meaning of this passage from the *Book of Odes* is that the way of the monarch has been faithfully effected throughout All-Under-Heaven and thus the Yi from the Huai, in the region of Xu have come to submit. See *HSBZ* 64A.8a. Arthur Waley translates the passage as follows: "The king's plans have been faithfully effected, / All the regions of Xu have submitted." See Watson, *Book of Songs*, 283.

60. Yang Shuda makes the following remark: "龔勝傳云‥年老被病, 加疾猶言被病." See Yang Shuda 楊樹達, *Hanshu kuiguan* 漢書窺管, 423.

61. I suspect that "大利" should probably be "地利" because of Zhao Chongguo's use of the formulation in his address, "順天時因地利," but calligraphic styles of "*da*" and "*di*" are not similar. Perhaps, "*da*" could have been incorrectly substituted for "*tu*" 土?

62. Though the statement cannot itself be found in the *Yijing*, the *Dadai liji* records almost the exact same statement: 「《易》曰:『正其本, 萬物理。失之毫釐, 差之千里。』」Given the exact rhyme and the appearance of the statement in the *Dadai liji*, it is probable that Zhao Chongguo is quoting from a source. See "Baofu," *Dadai liji* 《大戴禮記,保傅》. Chen Zhi also notes that in Sima Qian's biography, there is a similar quote attributed to the *Yi*. Yan Shigu remarks that the quote cannot be found either in the *Yi* or the "ten wings" commentaries that he has seen. Thus it must, he concludes, be from a noncanonical version of the *Yi*. See Chen Zhi 陳直, *Hanshu xinzheng* 漢書新證, 371–72.

63. This statement actually reads 「相因而起」 but I am reading it as 「相因並起」, which is the formulation Zhao Chongguo uses toward the beginning of his memorial. See *HS* 69.2985.

64. Chen Zhi argues that *kangjian* is an official military title. See Chen Zhi 陳直, *Hanshu xinzheng* 漢書新證, 373.

65. I follow Wang Niansun's 王念孫 reading of *jin* 今 as *ling* 令. *HSBZ* 69.11a.

66. Presumedly after a year the settlement would become self-sustaining.

67. This is Zhou Shouchang's 周壽昌 (1814–84 CE) interpretation. See *HSBZ* 69.12a.

68. Because they will be able to work their own fields, not just in the fields needed to support the troops.

69. Yang Shuda remarks that *qiao* 樔, in its original form, according to the *Shuowen* means "storage buildings for grains set among the marshes" 澤中守艸樓. Yang Shuda 楊樹達, *Hanshu kuiguan* 漢書窺管, 424.

70. Yang Shuda mentions that this is the younger brother of Xin Wuxian, who was the Smashing-the-Qiang General Emperor Xuan had mentioned at the beginning of this translated episode. See Yang Shuda 楊樹達, *Hanshu kuiguan* 漢書窺管, 424. Xin Wuxian, coincidentally, was implicated in treasonous discussions with Zhao Chongguo's son, Zhao Ang (who counseled Zhao Chongguo against arguing with the emperor in this episode), and "took his revenge by giving information that Zhao Ang had been disclosing matters that were confidential, thereby driving him to suicide." Loewe, *A Biographical Dictionary*, 614.

71. Wang Niansun states that *hen* 恨 should be read as *hen* 很, which means "quarreling with each other." 王念孫云恨讀為很謂相爭鬭也。See *HSBZ* 74.3a.

72. With his use of the word *zheng*, "dispute," Wei Xiang seems to be suggesting that the current troubles with the Xiongnu in Cheshi are relatively trifling and do not merit a rash, "angry" campaign. Such a campaign would, based on his categorical statements, inevitably fail.

73. Even though there is a compound, *zhi yi*, in this context, because of the presence of "*zhong*" at the end of the sentence, I follow Zhou Shouchang's suggestion that 致 be taken as meaning 置, "to establish, place." See *HSBZ* 74.3a.

74. A similar passage can also be found in the *Daodejing*, chapter 30: 「大軍之後, 必有凶年。」In D. C. Lau's translation: "In the wake of a mighty army/ bad harvests follow without fail." See *Tao Te Ching*, trans. D. C. Lau (New York: Penguin, 1963), 35.

75. Such, of course, is symbolic of the traditional filial relationships between son and father, younger brother and elder brother, wife and husband being upended.

76. *Analects* 16.1; *Analects of Confucius: A Philosophical Translation*, 196. In a footnote, Ames and Rosemont explain: "This 'screen of reverence' is the screen used in the court of the Lu ruler. Because, on reaching this screen, the Lu subjects demonstrate their reverence for the ruler, it is called the 'screen of reverence.' 'Within the screen of reverence' refers to the Lu ruler. At this time, Ji Sun had taken over the reins of government, and was in a power struggle with the Lu ruler, knowing that the Lu ruler wanted to deal with him in order to recover his political authority. On this account he was afraid that Zhuanyu [a vassal state of the Ji clan] would take advantage of its strategic location to help the Lu court. As a preemptive strike to maintain his strength, he therefore attacked Zhuanyu. in this passage, Confucius is very critical of the intentions of Ji Sun." See *Analects of Confucius*, 264. What Wei Xiang seems to suggesting is that the emperor's advisors are, like Ji Sun, attempting to subvert the power of the emperor by sending his armies on campaigns of their own against foreign peoples who, like the state of Zhuanyu, may be of some assistance to the emperor.

77. In the *Hanshu buzhu*, Wang Xianqian 王先謙 quotes Su Zhe 蘇轍 as stating that these three aristocrats, who were relatives of the emperor, although not superior to the famous general Zhao Chongguo in terms of military acumen, had a share in the concerns of the state. Because they did not need to establish a name for themselves, their advice would be vastly superior to that of Zhao Chongguo. Su Zhe's analysis, or just Wei Xiang's recommendation, of course, is far from indisputable. See *HSBZ* 74.3b.

78. Wang Xianqian remarks about the area around Mount Yin. From his remarks, I assume that the Han frontier is, at the time of Hou Ying's address, south of Mount Yin. Between the border and Mount Yin is an area that is lush and full of wild animals, a place that could easily support the Xiongnu and provide them with many places to hide and prepare for border raids. To the north of Mount Yin, Wang describes an arid desert area, part of the Gobi desert, full of large moraines, rocky ridges, which is in accord with current descriptions of the Gobi desert as being not sandy but covered with bare rock. This also accords with what is stated later in the address. See *HSBZ* 94B.6b.

79. Here, I believe, is a telling demarcation between *min* and *ren*. *Min* clearly are those people who are occupied with agricultural or menial tasks. *Ren* has a certain status to it that points to military responsibilities or involvement. These Xiongnu *min* had once been *ren*, and wish to be again.

Bibliography

CITED ABBREVIATIONS

HS	*Hanshu*
HSBZ	*Hanshu buzhu*
HHS	*Houhanshu*
SJ	*Shiji*

PRIMARY CHINESE SOURCES

Chunqiu gongyangzhuan zhushu 春秋公羊傳注疏, *Shisanjing zhushu* 十三經注疏. Edited by Li Xueqin 李學勤. Beijing: Beijing daxue chubanshe, 1999.
Chunqiu zuozhuan zhu 春秋左傳注. Annotated by Yang Bojun 楊伯峻. Beijing: Zhonghua shuju, 1981.
Guanzi jiaoshi 管子校釋. Annotated by Yan Changyao 顏昌嶢. Changsha: Yuelu shushe 嶽麓書社, 1996.
Hanfeizi jijie 韓非子集解. Beijing: Zhonghua shuju, 1998.
Hanfeizi xinjiaozhu 韓非子新校注. Shanghai: Shanghai guangming shuju, 2000.
Hanshu 漢書. Compiled by Ban Gu 班固. Beijing: Zhonghua shuju, 1962.
Hanshu buzhu 漢書補注. Annotated by Wang Xianqian 王先謙. Beijing: Shumu wenxian chubanshe 書目文獻出版社, 1995.
Houhanshu 後漢書. Compiled by Fan Ye 氾曄. Beijing: Zhonghua shuju, 1965.
Li ji zheng yi 禮記正義. Vol. 3, *Shisanjing zhushu* 十三經注疏. Edited by Li Xueqin 李學勤. Beijing: Beijing daxue chubanshe, 1999.
Liezi jishi 列子集釋. Annotated by Yang Bojun 楊伯峻. Beijing: Zhonghua shuju, 1979.
Liu Xie 劉勰. *Wenxin diaolong jinyi* 文心雕龍今譯. Edited by Zhou Zhenfu 周振甫. Beijing: Zhonghua shuju, 1986.
———. *Wenxin diaolong zhu* 文心雕龍註. Annotated by Fan Wenlan 范文瀾. Beijing: Renmin wenxue chubanshe, 1958.

Liu Zhiji 劉知幾, *Shitong tongshi* 史通通釋 (Taibei, Taiwan: Shijie shuju, 1988).
Maoshi zhengyi 毛詩正義, 3 vols., vol. 1, Shisanjing zhushu 十三經注疏. Edited by Li Xueqin 李學勤. Beijing: Beijing daxue chubanshe, 1999.
Sanguozhi 三國志. Compiled by Chen Shou 陳壽. Beijing: Zhonghua shuju, 1982.
Shangjunshu zhuizhi 商君書錐指. Annotated by Jiang Lihong 蔣禮鴻. Beijing: Zhonghua shuju, 1986.
Sima Guang 司馬光. "Da Fan Mengde 答范夢得." In *Qinding siku quanshu* 欽定四庫全書. Taipei: Taiwan shangwu yinshuguan, 1983.
Sima Qian 司馬遷. *Shiji* 史記. Beijing: Zhonghua shuju, 1959.
Xunzi jijie 荀子集解. Annotated by Wang Xianqian 王先謙. Beijing: Zhonghua shuju, 1988.
Yili zhushu 儀禮注疏. Vol. 2, *Shisanjing zhushu* 十三經注疏. Edited by Li Xueqin 李學勤. Beijing: Beijing daxue chubanshe, 1999.
Zhanguoce zhushi 戰國策注釋. Annotated by He Jianzhang 何建章. Beijing: Zhonghua shuju, 1990.

SECONDARY WORKS

Ames, Roger. *Sun-Tzu: The Art of Warfare*. New York: Ballantine Books, 1993.
Ames, Roger, and David Hall. *Thinking through Confucius*. Albany, NY: SUNY Press, 1987.
The Analects. Translated by D. C. Lau. New York: Penguin Books, 1979.
Analects of Confucius: A Philosophical Translation. Translated by Roger Ames and Henry Rosemont Jr. New York: Ballantine Books, 1998.
Annals of Lü Buwei. Translated by Jeffrey Riegel and John Knoblock. Stanford, CA: Stanford University Press, 2000.
Aristotle. "Rhetoric." In *The Complete Works of Aristotle*, edited by Jonathan Barnes, v. 2, 2152–69.Princeton, NJ: Princeton University Press, 1984.
Belfiore, Elizabeth. "'Lies Unlike the Truth': Plato on Hesiod, *Theogony* 27." *Transactions of the American Philological Association* 115 (1985): 47–57.
Brown, Penelope, and Stephen C. Levinson. *Politeness: Some Universals in Language Usage*. New York: Cambridge University Press, 1987.
Burnyeat, M. F. "*Eikos Muthos*." *Rhizai: Journal for Ancient Philosophy and Science* 2, no. 2 (2005): 143–65.
———. "*Enthymeme*: Aristotle on the Logic of Persuasion." In *Aristotle's Rhetoric: Philosophical Essays*, edited by David J. Furley and Alexander Nehemas, 3–55. Princeton, NJ: Princeton University Press, 1994.
Cang Xiuliang 倉修良, ed., *Hanshu cidian* 漢書辭典. Shandong: Shandong jiaoyu chubanshe, 1996.
Chan-Kuo Ts'e. Translated by James I. Crump Jr. New York: Oxford University Press, 1970.
Chen Zhi 陳直. *Hanshu xinzheng* 漢書新證. Tianjin: Tianjin renmin chubanshe, 1959.
Confucius Analects. Translated by Edward Slingerland. Indianapolis, IN: Hackett, 2003.
Cook, Scott. "The Use and Abuse of History in Early China from *Xun Zi* to *Lüshi chunqiu*." *Asia Major* (2005): 45–78.

Creel, Herrlee. *The Origins of Statecraft in China*. Chicago: University of Chicago Press, 1970.
Crump, James I., Jr. *Intrigues: Studies of the Chan-Kuo Ts'e*. Ann Arbor: University of Michigan Press, 1964.
Di Cosmo, Nicola. *Ancient China and Its Enemies*. New York: Cambridge University Press, 2002.
Dreyer, Edward L. "Zhao Chongguo: A Professional Soldier of the Former Han Dynasty." *Journal of Military History* 72, no. 3 (2008): 665–725.
Egan, Ronald. "Narratives in *Tso Chuan*." *Harvard Journal of Asiatic Studies* 37, no. 2 (1977): 323–52.
Eno, Robert. "Casuistry and Character in the *Mencius*." In *Mencius: Contexts and Interpretations*, edited by Alan K. L. Chan, 189–215. Honolulu: University of Hawaii Press, 2002.
Espesset, Grégoire. "Criminalized Abnormality, Moral Etiology, and Redemptive Suffering in the Secondary Strata of the *Taiping jing*." *Asia Major* 15, no. 2 (2002): 1–50.
Gardner, Charles S. *Chinese Traditional Historiography*. Cambridge, MA: Harvard University Press, 1938.
Geertz, Clifford. "Common Sense as a Cultural System." In *Local Knowledge*, 73–93. New York: Basic Books, 2000.
Giele, Enno. *Imperial Decision-Making and Communication in Early China: A Study of Cai Yong's Duduan*. Wiesbaden: Otto Harrassowitz, 2006.
Goldin, Paul. *After Confucius: Studies in Early Chinese Philosophy*. Honolulu: University of Hawaii Press, 2005.
———. "Appeals to History in Early Chinese Philosophy and Rhetoric." *Journal of Chinese Philosophy* 35, no. 1 (2008): 79–96.
Graham, A. C. *Disputers of the Dao*. La Salle, IL: Open Court, 1989.
———. "The Meaning of Ch'ing 情." In *Studies in Chinese Philosophy and Philosophical Literature*, 59–66. Albany, NY: SUNY Press, 1986.
Grice, H. Paul. "Logic and Conversation." In *Studies in the Way of Words*, 22–40. Cambridge, MA: Harvard University Press, 1989.
———. "Retrospective Epilogue." In *Studies in the Way of Words*, 339–85. Cambridge, MA: Harvard University Press, 1989.
Guanzi. Translated by W. Allyn Rickett. Boston: Cheng and Tsui, 2001.
Han Fei Tzu. "The Difficulties of Persuasion." In *Basic Writings of Mo Tzu, Hsün Tzu, and Han Fei Tzu*, 73–79. New York: Columbia University Press, 1964.
———. "Way of the Ruler." In *Basic Writings of Mo Tzu, Hsün Tzu, and Han Fei Tzu*, 16–20. New York: Columbia University Press, 1964.
Hansen, Chad. "Qing (Emotions) in Pre-Buddhist Chinese Thought." In *Emotions in Asian Thought*, edited by Joel Marks and Roger T. Ames, 181–211. Albany, NY: SUNY Press, 1995.
Hanyu da cidian suoyin ben 漢語大辭典縮印本. Shanghai: Hanyu dacidian chubanshe, 1997.
Hardy, Grant. *Worlds of Bronze and Bamboo: Sima Qian's Conquest of History*. New York: Columbia University Press, 1999.
Harper, Donald J. *Early Chinese Medical Literature: The Mawangdui Medical Manuscripts*. New York: Kegan Paul, 1998.

Huang, Martin W. *Desire and Fictional Narrative in Late Imperial China.* Cambridge, MA: Harvard University Asia Center, 2001.
Hucker, Charles O. *A Dictionary of Official Titles in Imperial China.* Stanford, CA: Stanford University Press, 1985.
Hulsewé, A. F. P. "Notes on the Historiography of the Han Period." In *Historians of China and Japan*, edited by W. G. Beasley and E. G. Pulleyblank, 31–43. London: School of Oriental and African Studies, 1961.
The I-Li or Book of Etiquette and Ceremonial. Translated by John Steele. Vol. 1. London: Probsthain, 1917.
Jin Dejian 金德建. *Sima Qian suo jian shu kao* 司馬遷所見書考. Shanghai: Shanghai renmin chubanshe, 1963.
Jullien, François. *The Propensity of Things: Toward a History of Efficacy in China.* Translated by Janet Lloyd. New York: Zone Books, 1995.
Keightley, David. "The Shang." In *Cambridge History of Ancient China*, edited by Michael Loewe and Edward Shaughnessy, 232–91. New York: Cambridge University Press, 1999.
Kern, Martin. "Poetry and Religion: The Representation of 'Truth' in Early Chinese Historiography." In *Historical Truth, Historical Criticism, and Ideology*, edited by Helwig Schmidt-Glintzer et al., 53–78. Boston: Brill, 2005.
———. *The Stele Inscriptions of Ch'in Shih-huang: Text and Ritual in Early Chinese Imperial Representation.* New Haven, CT: American Oriental Society, 2000.
Kierman, Frank A., Jr. "Phases and Modes of Combat in Early China." In *Chinese Ways in Warfare*, edited by Frank A. Kierman Jr. and John K. Fairbank, 27–66. Cambridge, MA: Harvard University Press, 1974.
Kracke, E. A., Jr. "The Chinese and the Art of Government." In *The Legacy of China*, edited by Raymond Dawson, 309–39. New York: Oxford University Press, 1964.
Lanham, Richard A. *A Handlist of Rhetorical Terms.* Berkeley: University of California Press, 1991.
Leban, Carl. "Managing Heaven's Mandate: Coded Communication in the Accession of Ts'ao Pei, A.D. 220." In *Ancient China: Studies in Early Civilization*, edited by David T. Roy and Tsuen-hsuin Tsien, 315–41. Hong Kong: Chinese University Press, 1978.
Legends of the Warring States. Translated by J. I. Crump. Ann Arbor: Center for Chinese Studies, University of Michigan, 1998.
Lewis, Mark E. "Warring States Political History." In *The Cambridge History of Ancient China: From the Origins of Civilization to 221 B.C.*, edited by Michael Loewe and Edward Shaughnessy, 587–650. New York: Cambridge University Press, 1999.
———. *Writing and Authority in Early China.* Albany, NY: SUNY Press, 1999.
Li Chi: Book of Rites. Translated by James Legge. Vol. 1. New York: Oxford University Press, 1885.
Li Chi: Book of Rites. Translated by James Legge. Vol. 2. New York: Oxford University Press, 1885.
Li Wai-yee. "The Idea of Authority in the *Shih Chi* (*Records of the Historian*)." *Harvard Journal of Asiatic Studies* 4, no. 2 (1994): 345–405.

———. *The Readability of the Past in Early Chinese Historiography*. Cambridge, MA: Harvard University Asia Center, 2007.
Liao Boyuan 廖伯源. *Shizhe guanzhi yanbian* 使者官制演變. Taipei: Wenjin chubanshe, 2006.
Liu Xie. *The Literary Mind and the Carving of Dragons*. Translated by Vincent Shih. New York: Columbia University Press, 1959.
Loewe, Michael. "The Authority of the Emperors of Ch'in and Han." In *State and Law in East Asia: Festschrift Karl Bünger*, edited by Dieter Eikemeier and Herbert Franke, 80–111. Wiesbaden: Otto Harrassowitz, 1981.
———. *A Biographical Dictionary of the Qin, Former Han and Xin Periods*. Boston: Brill, 2000.
———. *Crisis and Conflict in Han China*. London: George Allen and Unwin, 1974.
———. *Faith, Myth, and Reason in Han China*. Indianapolis, IN: Hackett, 2005.
———. *Records of Han Administration*. Vol. 1. London: Cambridge University Press, 1967.
———. *Records of Han Administration*. Vol. 2. London: Cambridge University Press, 1967.
———. "The Western Han Army: Organization, Leadership, and Operation." In *Military Culture in Imperial China*, edited by Nicola Di Cosmo, 65–88. Cambridge, MA: Harvard University Press, 2009.
Lu, Sheldon Hsiao-peng. *From Historicity to Fictionality: The Chinese Poetics of Narrative*. Stanford, CA: Stanford University Press, 1994.
Madden, Edward H. "Aristotle's Treatment of Probability and Signs." *Philosophy of Science* 24, no. 2 (1957): 167–72.
Maspéro, Henri. "La composition et la date du *Tso tchouan*." In *Mélanges chinois et bouddhiques*, 137–215. Brussels: Institut belge des hautes etudes chinoises, 1931.
Mathieu, Rémi. "Fonctions et Moyens de la Géographie dans la Chine Ancienne." *Études Asiatiques: Revue de la Société Suisse d'Études Asiatiques* 36, no. 2 (1982): 125–52.
McDowell, John. *Mind, Value, and Reality*. Cambridge, MA: Harvard University Press, 1998.
Mencius. Translated by D. C. Lau. New York: Penguin Books, 1970.
Morse, Ruth. *Truth and Convention in the Middle Ages*. New York: Cambridge University Press, 1991.
Most, Glenn W. "The Uses of *Endoxa*: Philosophy and Rhetoric in the *Rhetoric*." In *Aristotle's Rhetoric: Philosophical Essays*, edited by David J. Furley and Alexander Nehemas, 167–90. Princeton, NJ: Princeton University Press, 1994.
Nienhauser, William, ed. *The Grand Scribe's Records: The Memoirs of Han China, Part I*, Vol. 8. Bloomington: Indiana University Press, 2008.
———, ed. *The Grand Scribe's Records: The Memoirs of Pre-Han China*. Vol. 7. Bloomington: Indiana University Press, 1994.
Nylan, Michael. *The Five "Confucian" Classics*. New Haven, CT: Yale University Press, 2001.
———. "Sima Qian: A True Historian?" *Early China* 23–24 (1998): 203–46.
Ober, Josiah. *Mass and Elite in Democratic Athens*. Princeton, NJ: Princeton University Press, 1989.

Pan Ku, *Courtier and Commoner in Ancient China: Selections from the History of the Former Han.* Translated by Burton Watson. New York: Columbia University Press, 1974.

Pines, Yuri. "Intellectual Change in the Chunqiu Period: The Reliability of the Speeches in the *Zuo Zhuan* as Sources of Chunqiu Intellectual History." *Early China* 22 (1997): 77–132.

———. "Speeches and the Question of Authenticity in Ancient Chinese Historical Records." In *Historical Truth, Historical Criticism and Ideology*, edited by Helwig Schmidt-Glintzer et al., 196–226. Leiden Series in Comparative Historiography. Boston: Brill, 2005.

Pulleyblank, E. G. "Chinese Historical Criticism: Liu Chih-chi and Ssu-ma Kuang." In *Historians of China and Japan*, edited by W. G. Beasley and E. G. Pulleyblank, 135–66. London: School of Oriental and African Studies, 1961.

Qian Mu 錢穆. *Shiji diming kao* 史記地名考. Beijing: Shangwu yinshuguan, 2001.

Raphals, Lisa. *Knowing Words: Wisdom and Cunning in the Classical Traditions of China and Greece.* Ithaca, NY: Cornell University Press, 1992.

Rescher, Nicholas. *The Coherence Theory of Truth.* New York: Oxford University Press, 1973.

———. *Common-Sense: A New Look at an Old Philosophical Tradition.* Milwaukee, WI: Marquette University Press, 2005.

Schaberg, David. *A Patterned Past: Form and Thought in Early Chinese Historiography.* Cambridge, MA: Harvard University Asia Center, 2001.

———. "Playing at Critique: Indirect Remonstrance and the Formation of *Shi* Identity." In *Text and Ritual in Early China*, edited by Martin Kern, 194–225. Seattle: University of Washington Press, 2005.

———. "Remonstrance in Eastern Zhou Historiography." *Early China* 22 (1997): 133–39.

———. "Truth and Ritual Judgment: On Narrative Sense in China's Earliest Historiography." *Historically Speaking* (2004): 32–36.

Sima Qian. *Records of the Grand Historian: Han Dynasty.* Translated by Burton Watson. 2 vols. Vol. 1. New York: Columbia University Press, 1993.

———. *Records of the Grand Historian: Han Dynasty.* Translated by Burton Watson. 2 vols. Vol. 2. New York: Columbia University Press, 1993.

———. *Records of the Grand Historian: Qin Dynasty.* Translated by Burton Watson. New York: Columbia University Press, 1993.

Strickmann, Michel. "The Seal of the Law: A Ritual Implement and the Origins of Printing." *Asia Major* 6, no. 2 (1993): 1–83.

Tao Te Ching. Translated by D. C. Lau. New York: Penguin, 1963.

Unschuld, Paul. *Huang Di Nei Jing Su Wen: Nature, Knowledge, Imagery in an Ancient Chinese Medical Text.* Berkeley: University of California Press, 2003.

Van Zoeren, Steven. *Poetry and Personality.* Stanford, CA: Stanford University Press, 1991.

Veyne, Paul. *Did the Greeks Believe in Their Myths?* Translated by Paula Wissig. Chicago: University of Chicago Press, 1988.

Vogelsang, Kai. "Some Notions of Historical Judgment in China and the West." In *Historical Truth, Historical Criticism, and Ideology*, edited by Helwig Schmidt-Glintzer et al., 143–69. Boston: Brill, 2005.

Wallacker, Benjamin E. "Han Confucianism and Confucius in Han." In *Ancient China: Studies in Early Civilization*, edited by David T. Roy and Tsuen-hsuin Tsien, 215–28. Hong Kong: Chinese University Press, 1978.

Walton, Charles. *Policing Public Opinion in the French Revolution: The Culture of Calumny and the Problem of Free Speech*. New York: Oxford University Press, 2008.

Watson, Burton, ed. *Book of Songs*. Translated by Arthur Waley. New York: Grove Press, 1996.

Weber, Max. *Essays in Sociology*. Translated and edited by H. H. Gerth and C. W. Mills. New York: Oxford University Press, 1946.

Woodruff, Paul. "*Eikos* and Bad Faith in the Paired Speeches of Thucydides." In *Proceedings of the Boston Area Colloquium in Ancient Philosophy*, edited by John J. Cleary and William Wians, 115–45. Lanham, MD: University Press of America, 1994.

Yang Shuda 楊樹達. *Hanshu kuiguan* 漢書窺管. Beijing: Kexue chubanshe, 1955.

Yu, Anthony C. "History, Fiction, and the Reading of Chinese Narrative." *Chinese Literature: Essays, Articles, Reviews* 10, no. 1/2 (1988): 1–19.

Index

accurate representation of affairs: and "true" stories, 26–27; and "truth" in early Chinese context, 172–73; commitment to in pre-modern Chinese histories, 17–18, 19–20, 104–105; emperor's desire for, 137–40, 152

ancient historian, as journalist, 29–30

Aristotle: on common reports as evidence, 4, 26, 90; and cultural definition of commonsense, 23

Ban Gu 班固 (32–92 CE), and commitment to historiographical objectivity, 18, 19, 46, 155, 217–18 n. 1

Bureau of Memorials, in the Former Han, 42–44

categories of evidence: and distinctions of epistemic weight, 102–03, 173; epistemic function of, 97–98, 171–74; general division of, 55–70

Chao Cuo 晁錯 (200–154 BCE): foundational common sense propositions, 168–69; use of concrete particulars, 156; use of "I have heard that" and "I humbly have heard that," 50

Clifford Geertz, on qualities of common sense knowledge, 24–25, 89, 169

Chen Yu 陳餘 (Lord of Cheng'an 成安君, ?–204 BCE), 69–70, 162–63, 165, 170, 174

coherence, standard for premodern truth, 18, 27–28, 30–31, 45–46

common sense: as culturally bound, 22–23; dependent on human needs, 88–90; epistemic function of, 75, 90–91, 164; Han moral concerns possibly functioning as, 108, 133; propositions, examples of, 86, 102, 125–26, 128, 168–69; vs. popular knowledge, 4, 24–26

concrete particulars: categories of, 155–61; discrete functions of, 171–74; general role of, in political argument, 66–70, 162–65; regarding domestic vs. foreign campaigns, 165–66; and resolution of emperor's epistemic doubts, 106–08, 166–70; use of, by "rationalists": Yan You, 156, 159–60, 164; by Zhao Chongguo, 67–68, 74, 98, 156–57, 168, 173; by Chao Cuo, 156

Confucius (551–479 BCE), 14

Confucian norms, 108–09, 119, 156, 175

Dai 代, lands of, 113–17, 125, 128, 242 n. 7, 243 n. 24

doubt (*yi* 疑): as crucial concern for Sima Qian, 18–19, 155–56; and distinction between common sense and popular knowledge, 4; and epistemic function of evidence, 73, 162; and informational quantity, 7, 22–23; interpersonal vs. epistemic, 31–33, 106–07; and peripherality of concrete "facts," 151–52, 156–57, 166–70;

and probable evidence, 100–03; and slander, 226 n. 6; successful management of, 93–97

eikos muthos ("probable" myth), 26–27

Emperor Wu of Han (Han Wudi, 漢武帝, 156–87 BCE): bowing to ministerial request, 225–26 n. 4; compared to First Emperor of Qin, 161; and need for moral esteem, 126; and Sima Qian's historiographical project, 19

endoxa, 4, 23, 26

epistemic quality: alteration of, 91, 95; basis of, in Empress Lü's address to Liu Bang, 100–101; of commonsense premises in debate between Su Qin and Zhang Yi, 89–91; of concrete particulars, 157–61; definition of, 6, 162; doubts about, relating to evidentiary propositions, 103, 162; and the fixity of moral ideas in the Han, 109; general basis, of categories of evidence, 164; indirection conditioning of, 52

epistemic weight: of concrete particulars, 165, 172; definition of, 6–7; factors involved in, 102–03; of Li Zuoche's address, 163; moral aspect given, by Xiao Wangzhi, 132–33; propositions not carrying, 104; of three general categories of evidence, 173

error: connected to perception of reality, 33, 140–43; historiographical, politics of, 16–20; leading to failure of an address, 95; of the monarch, for receiving honest appraisals, 151

evidence: analyzing its role in argument, 47, 73–76; and argumentational stereotypes, 6; in coherence theory of truth, 28; decorous indirect presentation of, 52–55; early Chinese scholars showing little concern for its accuracy, 14–15; *endoxa* as, 33; "fictions" as, 28–31; and Grice's maxim of truthfulness, 6; moral, examples of, 134; not a crucial early Chinese historiographical concern, 18; not revealing gross ideological leanings of Han historians, 46; presentation of, and actual audience, 8; quality and weight of, in *Intrigues* debate, 89–91; quality and weight of, in persuasion of Liu Bang, 100–103; Sima Guang's evaluation of, 16–18; and successful management of doubt, in *Intrigues* debate, 93–97; and the trustworthiness of its source, 107–08; use of, as diachronic, 5

facts. *See* concrete particulars; moral 'facts'

fiction, and pre-modern historiography, 28–31

forms of address, 44–46

geographic details, accuracy of, 104–105, 235 n. 13

Grice, H. P., 6–7

Han Anguo 韓安國 (?–127 BCE): accentuation of the moral, 113, 118, 128–29, 135, 169; advocacy of strategic calculation, 120, 122–23, 132; argument of: fundamental needs informing, 126; premises, 128–29; rhetorical reframing of, 124–25

Han Xin 韓信 (?–196 BCE): configuration of his forces, 69; epistemic value of the estimate of his forces, 162; error in trusting Liu Bang, 142, 170; Li Zuoche's recommendation on how to defeat, 163, 165

Hanfeizi 韓非子 (280–233 BCE): on the monarch avoiding manipulation, 147–148, 151–52; on speaking to the monarch, 39–40

Hanshu. *See History of the Former Han*

Heaven's Mandate (*tianming* 天命), import for the Han addresses, 127, 169

History of the Former Han (*Hanshu* 漢書): appearance of "Heaven's Mandate" in, 127; authorial voice in, 1; and narrative conventions of *Intrigues*, 48; presence of extended debate in, 240 n. 1; and representation of Wang Hui/Han Anguo debate, 111; terms for "mistake" in, 139

historical precedents (analogues). *See* precedents

Hou Ying 侯應, 61–62, 158, 162, 166, 168

humilifics, 50–51, 91–93

"I have heard" (臣聞) rhetorical introduction of evidence, 50, 53–54

"I have humbly heard" (臣竊聞), rhetorical introduction of judgmental crux, 50
indirect criticism, 50–52
Intrigues of the Warring States. See *Zhanguoce*

Li Zuoche 李左車 (Lord of Guangwu 廣武), 69–70, 162–63, 165
Liu (Lou) Jing 劉(婁)敬, 106–07, 109–10, 118, 165
Liu An 劉安 (179–122 BCE), 59–61, 65–66, 133, 158, 160–61
Liu Bang 劉邦 (Gaozu 高祖, High Emperor, 256–195 BCE): and four wise men, 99–103; and history of Dai, 115–17; and need for moral esteem, 126
Liu Pi 劉濞 (king of Wu 吳, 215–154 BCE), 62
Liu Xiang 劉向 (77–6 BCE), 19, 111, 216 n. 8, 218 n. 1, 226 n. 6
Liu Zhiji 劉知幾 (661–721 CE), on twisting the facts, 18–19

manipulation, of the monarch, 10–11, 15, 146–150, 172–73, 220 n. 1
misinformation: and corrective value of general classes of statements, 172; intentional, 145, 150–51
mistake. *See* error
moral "facts": increased importance of in Han addresses, 108–110, 125–36; not based on personal or sentimental grounds, 170–71; use of, by "rationalists" Yan You, Chao Cuo and Zhao Chongguo, 130, 133
Morse, Ruth, 28–31

natural signs, as information, 143–46

Pausanias, 29, 70
plausibility of historical information, 16–18, 28–31, 100–05, 146–50
popular knowledge: carrying great epistemic weight, 33, 163; epistemic quality of, 164; moral propositions as, 133–34; possible, in *Intrigues* debate, 86–88; vs. common sense, 24–28
precedents (historical analogues): epistemic function of, 102–03, 164, 171–74; importance for Su Qin, 98; prehistoric versus recent historical, 62–65; Wang Hui's employment of, 119
principle: distinct from other general statements, 231 n. 36; epistemic function of, 102–03, 164, 171–74; propositions of, 231 n. 36; types of, 55–62

Records of the Grand Historian (Shiji 史記): absence of extended discussion or debate in, 240 n. 1; and authorial intent, 1; and evaluating evidence, 18–19; and narrative conventions of *Intrigues*, 48; appearance of "Heaven's Mandate" in, 127; its "vision" (*zhi*, 志), 36–37, 224–25 n. 62; objectivity of, 18–19, 155–56, 217–18 n. 1, 250 n. 10; terms for "mistake" in, 139
righteous campaigns, 25–26, 56, 58, 132, 178
rumor (*e*, 訛), 143–46

Shiji. *See Records of the Grand Historian*
Sima Guang 司馬光 (1019–86 CE), on historiographical evidence, 16–18
Sima Qian 司馬遷 (145–? BCE): accuracy of his geographical representations, 105; on chronology for Su Qin and Zhang Yi addresses, 72; commitment to historiographical objectivity, 18–19; and historiographical distortions, 217–18 n. 1; and transmitting doubt, 18–19, 155–56; as true, "objective" historian, 15, 46, 239–40 n. 24, 250 n. 10; and "trustworthiness" of the records, 252–53 n. 33; "vision" (*zhi*, 志) of history, 36–37, 224–25 n. 62
slander, affecting informational transfer, 15, 40, 147–49, 226 n. 6
strategic considerations: importance of, in Han addresses, 106–10, 130, 169; importance of, in Warring States addresses, 85–87, 105–06
Su Qin 蘇秦, 52, 106, 112, 125–26

"trustworthiness" (*ke xin* 可信), of information, 146–50
truth of the matter ("vision," *zhi* 志), 33–38

Veyne, Paul, 29–31

Wang Hui 王恢 (?–133 BCE), 157, 169, 173–74
Wei Xiang 魏相 (?–59 BCE), 42, 51, 133, 160

Xiao Wangzhi 蕭望之 (?–47 BCE), 43, 130–33

Yan You 嚴尤, 133, 156, 159–60, 164
Yang Xiong 楊雄 (53 BCE-18 CE), 19
Yili 儀禮, 40–41

Zhanguoce 戰國策 (*Intrigues of the Warring States*): dramatic introductions in, 48; evidentiary norms in, comparable to Han, 5, 8, 165; as historical record, 71, 216 n. 8; and moral concerns, 108, 127; and nonmoral concerns, 106; responses of monarch in, 49; use of concrete particulars in, 158, 165

Zhao Chongguo 趙充國 (137–52 BCE): address's core evidentiary ground, 104, 168; emphasis of defensive measures with Xiongnu, 166; not overcoming the emperor's doubts, 140, 167; use of concrete particulars, 67–68, 74, 156–57, 173; use of moral considerations, 130, 133

Zhao Gao 趙高 (?–207 BCE), and control of information, 138–39

Zhufu Yan 主父偃 (?–126 BCE), emphasis on statements of principle and historical precedent, 63–65, 173

zou 奏 ("to present," "to memorialize"), 44–45, 227 n. 12, 229 n. 29

Zuozhuan 左傳: contact between minister and monarch in, 49; historical tensions in, 1; informative folk songs in, 144; and logic of historical narrative, 15–16, 250 n. 10; moralizing in, 13, 109

www.ingramcontent.com/pod-product-compliance
Lightning Source LLC
Chambersburg PA
CBHW020641230426
43665CB00008B/266